The Illustrated History of the Third Reich

Germany's victories and defeat 1939–1945

Chris Bishop & David Jordan

This book was previously published as two volumes, *The Rise of Hitler's Third Reich* and *The Fall of Hitler's Third Reich*.

Published in 2005 by Silverdale Books
an imprint of Bookmart Ltd
Registered Number 2372865
Trading as Bookmart Ltd
Blaby Road
Wigston
Leicester LE18 4SE

ISBN 1-84509-247-3

Editorial and design by
Amber Books Ltd
Bradley's Close
74–77 White Lion Street
London N1 9PF
www.amberbooks.co.uk

Project Editor: Michael Spilling
Design: Graham Curd

Printed in Singapore

CONTENTS

Introduction

In 1933 Adolf Hitler inherited a small, but highly professional army. He oversaw its rapid expansion and became an early convert to the cause of mechanization. He had an elephantine memory for technical detail and a fascination with technology that helped the advocates of armoured forces overcome conservative elements within the army. By the late 1930s Germany had an armoured striking force second to none and an air force equipped with the best warplanes in the world.

'It must be understood that the lost land will never be won back by solemn appeals to the gods, nor by hopes in any League of Nations, but only by force of arms.'

Adolf Hitler, speaking of territory lost in the post-World War I settlement, 1936

From the invasion of Poland in September 1939 to late 1941, the German *Wehrmacht* enjoyed an unbroken run of victories. Norway was occupied despite British naval superiority: a bold stroke demanded by the *Führer* regardless of his generals' anxieties. The army high command planned to invade France exactly as Count von Schlieffen had laid down at the beginning of the century – the plan that had failed in 1914. The main effort would have been made through Belgium, a decision that was anticipated by the French and British. But an audacious stroke planned by General von Manstein was seized upon by Hitler, and forced on a reluctant high command.

In May 1940, Germany's armoured forces poured through the supposedly impenetrable Ardennes forest in eastern Belgium and Luxembourg, bursting through the French Ninth Army to cross the River Meuse and fatally rupture the Allied frontline. The former corporal had overruled his generals and won the most stunning military victory German arms had ever achieved. This was followed by the lightning conquest of the Balkans, before Hitler turned on the Soviet Union. The first few months seemed to conform to the pattern: the *Wehrmacht* carved its way through western Russia to Smolensk and on to the Moscow road. There, in November 1941, the invasion faltered. Zhukov's counterattack in December drove the Germans back and the recriminations began. After the war, several German officers blamed Hitler for changing objectives in Russia: first Moscow was the target, then the Ukraine, then Moscow again.

In 1942 Hitler gambled again, ordering his army to attack across the good tank country of southern Russia in Operation 'Blue'. His stated objective was the Caucasus oil fields, but the attack failed for the same reasons as the previous year's. The distances

were too great, supply problems insurmountable, and operational objectives were switched, leaving the Sixth Army to make a frontal attack on the strategically important city of Stalingrad. The German army found itself locked in a battle of attrition on the frontier of Asia, exposed to a devastating and highly effective counter-offensive.

The failure of Hitler's strategy in 1942 led to the catastrophe at Stalingrad, replicated on a similar scale in North Africa a few months later. From early 1943 the weaknesses in the German war machine became increasingly significant – although they were not always apparent to the Allies. Hitler's armies fought on to the end with diabolical efficiency. Yet their tremendous skill and undoubted bravery was indeed misdirected. Hitler cut himself off from his people, appearing only twice in public after the defeat at Stalingrad.

Isolated in his sunless concrete bunker deep in the East Prussian forest, Hitler directed his armies through the hapless 'yes men' Jodl and Keitel. His attempts to micro-manage the war tied the hands of his front line commanders, who were forbidden to move even their smallest units without permission. His insistence on clinging to indefensible positions cost Germany many thousands of men in futile, short-term defensive actions.

Hitler's strategy played into his enemies' hands in 1944, sending German reserves to the wrong sector of the Eastern Front. When the Allies launched their long-awaited invasion of France in June 1944, German reaction to D-Day was sluggish, with local commanders having to wait for the *Führer*'s permission to counter-attack. To crown a disastrous year for Germany, in December Hitler repeated the failed German strategy of 1918 by launching an all-or-nothing assault in the west. The Ardennes offensive squandered Germany's last reserves, hastening the final collapse of the Third Reich.

Above: Accompanied by members of the Wehrmacht *general staff, Adolf Hitler salutes German infantry as they march towards Poland in September 1939.*

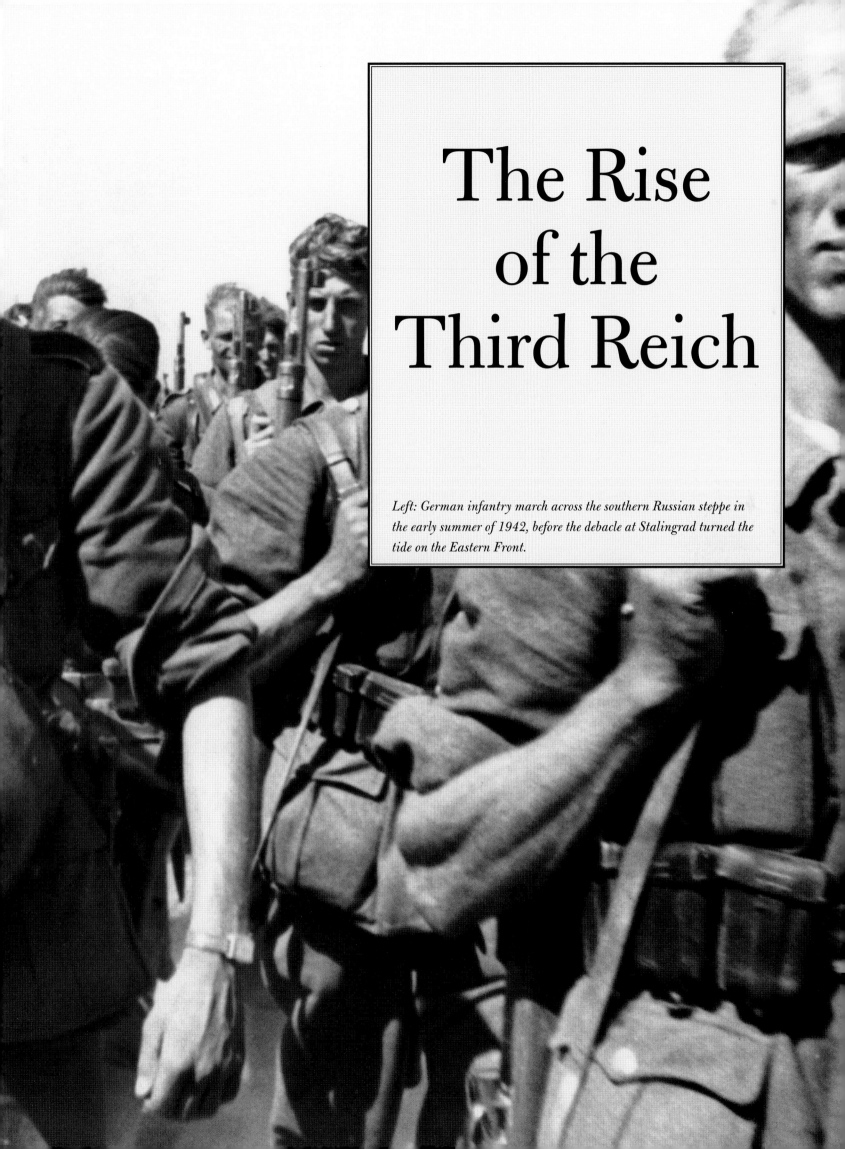

The Rise
of the
Third Reich

Left: German infantry march across the southern Russian steppe in the early summer of 1942, before the debacle at Stalingrad turned the tide on the Eastern Front.

The Road to War

Adolf Hitler never made the slightest attempt to conceal his determination to achieve mastery first of Europe and then of the world, and to do so by force of arms. In the process, he would avenge Germany's defeat in the Great War.

The Treaty of Versailles that ended World War I sowed the seeds of another conflict by handing large parts of eastern Germany to Poland. Demands for vengeance amongst the German citizenry were given added stimulus by economic depression and, to many Germans, Adolf Hitler and the Nazi party offered the only real leadership.

The Origins of a Dictator

Confused and bitter, Hitler had returned to Munich after the end of the Great War, searching for reasons to explain Germany's defeat. Along with many returning soldiers, he felt that they, the front-line troops, had been 'stabbed in the back' by traitors, social democrats, communists and Jews at home in Germany. Pacifists and liberals came in for their share of the blame, but to Hitler and those who shared his opinions, the real villains were the Bolsheviks and the Jews. They were seen as one and the same, since Jewish agitators led many of the soviets set up in the German army and navy late in 1918. In his earliest political speeches, Hitler often referred to Jews as 'November criminals', alluding to the date of the Bolshevik takeover in Russia.

After the war, the army employed Hitler as a spy. His job was to report on right-wing nationalist groups in Munich. One small group was known as the *Politische Arbeiterzirkel* (Political Worker's Circle). Renamed the *Deutsche Arbeiterpartei* (German Worker's Party), it held its first meeting in January 1919. Hitler joined later that year. In an astonishing transformation, given his unpromising early career, Hitler proved to be a politician of demonic gifts and mesmerizing character. He quickly took control of what had been little more than a debating society, and turned it into the *Nationalsozialistiche deutsche Arbeiterpartei* (NSDAP) – National Socialist German Worker's Party. He spent the next decade using the party to build a power base, which was eventually to make him the absolute ruler of Germany.

Opposite: From the moment Adolf Hitler came to power in 1933, a general European conflict was inevitable. The pomp and pageantry of the Parteitage at Nuremberg would soon be followed by war, and the SS would trade in their black uniforms and banners for camouflage gear and Mauser rifles.

11

After a period in obscurity following the failed Munich putsch of 1923, the Nazi Party began to rise again in the mid-1920s. In 1930, the Party gained more than 100 seats in the Reichstag, winning strong support among the middle classes and in the Protestant north, which had been hit hard by the depression. The two bitterly fought elections of 1932 made the Nazis the largest party in the Reichstag, but without an overall majority. A coalition of right-wing interests invited the Nazis into government, but Hitler would accept only if he were made Chancellor. Believing they could control the Nazi leader, the politicians accepted, and on 30 January 1933, Hitler became Chancellor of Germany.

In February 1933, three days after taking office as Chancellor of the German Reich, Hitler addressed a huge gathering of Nazi Party officials and senior officers of the German armed services upon the necessity of 'unqualified Germanization' in the east as far at least as the Urals. On 27 February, an arson attack on the Reichstag (which the Nazis blamed on communist revolutionaries) gave Hitler the excuse to suspend all civil liberties in Germany. By the end of March, the so-called Enabling Act had given him dictatorial powers.

THE *FREIKORPS*

The *Freikorps* were private armies of ex-soldiers formed in Germany in the chaotic years after the end of World War I. Usually raised by their former regular officers and given tacit support by right-wing authorities, they used their battle-proven tactics to defeat communist attempts to foment revolution in Germany. The communists in Bavaria and the Spartacists in Berlin were crushed by the *Freikorps*, and workers in the Ruhr who attempted to organize on socialist lines were also repressed. The tiny *Reichswehr* allowed to Germany by the Treaty of Versailles also made use of the *Freikorps* as auxiliary troops. Captain von Schleicher, a staff officer in the political department of the German Army HQ, secretly paid and equipped *Freikorps* units fighting on the eastern borders against the Poles and Lithuanians. Von Schleicher would later become a general and Chancellor of Germany.

In 1921, the *Freikorps* were officially disbanded. Many *Freikorps* members drifted south to Munich, where they formed much of the initial strength of the Nazi *Sturmabteilung*, or SA.

The *Wehrmacht* (armed forces) was the one institution that could have stopped Hitler coming to power. Indeed, the knowledge that the army could make or break a government had haunted the Weimar republic throughout its short life. Even after 1933, the army could have removed Hitler before he began the war and, once the war was obviously lost, a military coup could have beheaded the highly centralized Nazi regime in an afternoon. Since, according to so many of their post-war accounts, it was only Hitler's idiocy that prevented them winning the war, or at least making peace with the West, why didn't the generals kill Hitler? The truth was that Hitler and the Nazis, no matter how distasteful they were to the Prussian officer class, were providing what they wanted.

Had Hitler attempted to seize power by another putsch, as he was urged to do by the *Sturmabteilung* (SA) – 'Storm Detachment', the thuggish private army of the NSDAP – throughout 1932, there is little doubt that the army would have shot down the brownshirts and probably their leader too. But Hitler was handed power constitutionally. The army high command regarded Hitler, the former corporal, with disdain and was profoundly hostile to the SA, but most generals objected to the methods – street violence – rather than the declared aims of the movement. When Hitler addressed the generals in February 1933, it was, he later claimed, 'the hardest speech of my life'. They heard him

in silence, deaf to his impassioned oratory. Even so, they were hearing what they wanted to hear. Hitler's foreign policy boiled down to revenge for 1918. His domestic plans emphasized public order and a massive rearmament programme. There were no objections from the generals, who felt that they had chafed under the restrictions of Versailles for long enough.

Undoing the Versailles Treaty

The Versailles Treaty had been signed on 28 June 1919. It was designed by the Allies to emasculate post-war Germany. War reparations insisted on by France were crippling. The treaty so limited German power that her armed forces could not guarantee the integrity of her borders.

As Germany was not allowed to participate in the negotiations, the treaty was rejected at home as a 'dictated peace'. The onerous terms ensured a foothold for anti-democratic forces, among which was the small right-wing group that would become the NSDAP.

For a proud nation with a strong military tradition, the treaty was felt to be insulting. Germany was to be limited to a 100,000-man army. The navy was allowed to retain a few obsolete warships, which it could man with no more than 15,000 sailors. The air force and naval air force were disbanded. The production and acquisition of heavy weapons such as tanks and aeroplanes was prohibited.

From the outset, the Weimar government attempted to lessen the harshest terms. This revisionist policy had some little success, although an attempt to reduce the reparations in 1923 led to a brutal French occupation of the Ruhr, Germany's industrial heartland.

Above: In the chaotic state which Germany fell in to at the end of the Great War, political rivalries between left and right spilled out onto the streets. The right-wing Freikorps, established to defend Germany's eastern borders, were also used in street battles with socialists and communists.

Europe in 1920

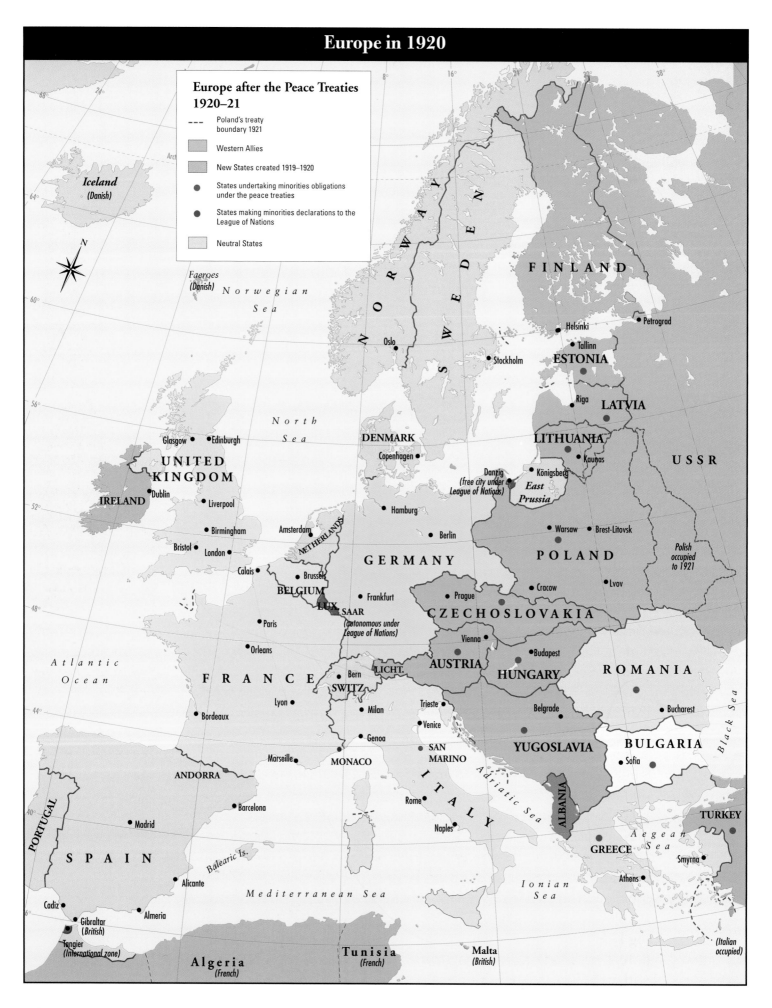

Europe after the Peace Treaties 1920–21

- – – – Poland's treaty boundary 1921
- Western Allies
- New States created 1919–1920
- States undertaking minorities obligations under the peace treaties
- States making minorities declarations to the League of Nations
- Neutral States

Iceland
(Danish)

Faeroes
(Danish)

Norwegian Sea

FINLAND

• Helsinki   • Petrograd

• Oslo

North Sea

• Stockholm

ESTONIA

• Tallinn

• Riga   LATVIA

DENMARK

LITHUANIA

• Glasgow   • Edinburgh

• Copenhagen

Danzig
(free city under League of Nations)

• Königsberg   *East Prussia*

USSR

UNITED KINGDOM

• Kaunas

IRELAND   • Dublin

• Liverpool

• Hamburg

• Berlin

• Warsaw   • Brest-Litovsk

POLAND

Polish occupied to 1921

• Birmingham

Amsterdam

NETHERLANDS

• Bristol   London •

• Calais

GERMANY

• Lvov

• Cracow

• Brussels

BELGIUM

LUX   • Frankfurt

• Prague

CZECHOSLOVAKIA

• Paris

SAAR
(autonomous under League of Nations)

• Vienna

• Orleans

Atlantic Ocean

F R A N C E

• Bern   LICHT.

AUSTRIA   HUNGARY   • Budapest

R O M A N I A

SWITZ.

• Milan

Trieste •

AUSTRIA

• Lyon

• Venice

• Belgrade

• Bucharest

Black Sea

• Bordeaux

• Genoa

SAN MARINO

YUGOSLAVIA

BULGARIA

ANDORRA

• Marseille

MONACO

• Sofia

• Barcelona

I T A L Y

• Rome

Adriatic Sea

ALBANIA

TURKEY

• Madrid

Aegean Sea

S P A I N

• Naples

GREECE

• Smyrna

• Alicante

Ionian Sea

• Athens

• Cadiz

Gibraltar
(British)

• Almeria

Mediterranean Sea

(Italian occupied)

Tangier
(International zone)

Algeria
(French)

Tunisia
(French)

Malta
(British)

Although avowedly socialist, the Weimar government embarked upon a policy of secretly expanding its forces. Even limited to 100,000 men, the post-war *Reichswehr* was a significant military weapon. All of its men were superbly trained career professionals, and they would form the nucleus of a later field army. The *Reichswehr* was composed of former members of the imperial army and navy; as such, it was highly anti-republican in nature. Hitler openly courted this significant power base. Within three days of achieving the chancellorship, he announced plans to the *Reichswehr* generals for the rearming of Germany – plans he would not reveal to the rest of the world for another two years. But first, he had to do something abut the tension between the stormtroopers of the SA, who had brought the Nazis to power, and the army, which was the instrument that would enable him to dominate Europe. Hitler was a pragmatist, and he knew which was more important to his future plans.

In June 1934, Hitler decided to deal with Ernst Röhm, head of the SA and Hitler's major rival in the Nazi leadership. Röhm's desire to disband the army and absorb it into the SA offended the generals. Additionally, the SA had upset two other groups that Hitler needed: its violent radicalism offended the *Führer's* conservative supporters, and Röhm's increasing power on the streets worried Nazi rivals like Göring, Goebbels and Himmler.

Night of the Long Knives

On the night of 30 June 1934, Hitler unleashed the Gestapo and the SS, who had been provided with weapons and logistics support by the army. SS squads arrested or

Above: Stormtroopers of the SA parade through Berlin's streets in 1929. Leading the parade is the prominent young Nazi Horst Wessel. Killed in a brawl, Wessel had a song written about him that became a Nazi anthem – 'Horst-Wessel Leid'.

Opposite: Central Europe changed drastically in the years following World War I. The Austro-Hungarian empire disappeared, replaced by several new states, and large parts of Eastern Germany had been absorbed by Poland.

ORIGINS OF THE SS

In the violent politics of the Weimar Republic, most political leaders employed bodyguards for close protection. Adolf Hitler formed his first bodyguard in 1923. Calling themselves the *Stabswache*, its members were a handful of party fighters who swore to protect Hitler from all enemies within and without the party. This evolved into the *Stosstrupp-Hitler*, an assault squad headed by Julius Schreck and Joseph Berchtold, which was used in the Munich putsch. These units formed the kernel of the protection squads known as *Schutzstaffel*, or SS, from 1925. Hitler's personal bodyguard became known as the *Leibstandarte*, and under the command of Josef 'Sepp' Dietrich was to grow into a powerful military unit. Although nominally part of the stormtroopers of the SA, the SS always considered itself an elite.

murdered SA leaders all over Germany, starting with Röhm, who was arrested by Hitler himself at the head of a unit of his SS bodyguard. A number of private scores were settled at the same time. Estimates on the number killed reach as high as 1000, with 70 or 80 senior SA commanders being executed or 'shot while resisting arrest'.

Hitler proclaimed himself Chancellor and *Führer* of the German Reich in August 1934, upon the death of President von Hindenburg. He ordered the creation of a German air force (forbidden to Germany under the terms of the Versailles Treaty) and the rapid expansion of the German army and navy – the tools with which he intended to achieve his ends. In October 1933, Germany left the League of Nations and the Disarmament Conference. Early in 1934, the army was instructed to treble its strength to 300,000, but in secret.

In March 1935, Hitler came out into the open. He had Göring announce the repudiation of the Treaty of Versailles and the reintroduction of conscription. The peacetime German army would consist of 36 divisions organized into 12 Corps: a strength of around half a million men. Armaments for this vastly expanded army would be provided by concerns like Krupp, which had been carrying out clandestine research and development programmes since the 1920s, and which had been preparing modern armour and artillery designs since 1933.

Development of modern aircraft types had proceeded in parallel with the growth of the army. The result was that at the outbreak of war, the *Luftwaffe* enjoyed technical, if not numerical superiority over potential opponents. It also enjoyed tactical superiority, thanks to a cadre of pilots with real combat experience gained in the Spanish Civil War. Only the *Kriegsmarine* lagged behind: its rearmament plans needed much longer to come to fruition. Britain, France and the League of Nations protested, but did little else. Britain was appeased by an offer from the *Führer* to limit naval expansion.

Under the terms of an Anglo-German naval agreement of June 1935, the *Kriegsmarine* would be limited to 35 per cent of the total British naval tonnage. More importantly, the British would allow Germany to match the Royal Navy's submarine tonnage – a curious agreement from a country that had been on the receiving end of unrestricted U-boat warfare in 1917 and 1918. However, the Germans never intended to be bound by such an agreement: they were already building two 26,000-tonne (25,584-ton) battlecruisers

'My motto is, "Destroy by all and any means. National Socialism will reshape the world".'

Adolf Hitler
Mein Kampf

in contravention of the agreement, and plans were being made to build a fleet of the world's largest battleships by the early 1940s.

Training and Equipping

Hitler benefited from rearmament, but he did not start it. Because of the ban on offensive weapons like tanks, poison gas, aeroplanes and U-Boats, the *Reichswehr* had to keep training with such weapons hidden from the outside world. Thanks to a secret deal with the Soviets, German officers had trained with the Red Army throughout the 1920s.

The Allied Control Commission, which monitored compliance with the terms of the Treaty of Versailles, left Germany at the beginning of 1927. Almost immediately, the Weimar government stepped up design and testing of new weapons and the training of troops in Germany itself. Training troops and expanding the armed forces was all very well, but Hitler knew that his fleets and divisions and squadrons would need weapons. These would have to come from the industrial heartlands of the Saar and the Rhineland – the areas until recently occupied by troops of the Allied powers of 1918, still 'demilitarized' and still denied by treaty to German control.

The Saar region he regained in January 1935 by the simple expedient of holding a plebiscite, which naturally he won, enabling him to present the resumption of German control as a fait accompli to a generally uninterested and as yet unsuspicious world. Next, in March 1936, he sent his troops into the Rhineland – with some trepidation – and watched while Britain and France rationalized both his aggression and their own inaction with such evasions of responsibility as 'He is, after all, only walking into his own back yard.' If Hitler's ambition was the main cause of the world conflict that followed, the pusillanimity and short-sightedness of other European leaders were major contributory factors.

Two months after the reoccupation of the Rhineland, the Spanish Civil War broke out.

Below: Adolf Hitler addresses the party faithful at Nuremberg. He is wearing the brown shirt of the Sturmabteilung, *or SA. He needed the Brownshirts on his road to power, but they became an embarrassment when he was elected Chancellor.*

17

Right: The effects of the great depression were felt all over the world, but nowhere more than in Germany. Hyper-inflation and massive unemployment left the Weimar Republic ripe for an authoritarian takeover by a party promising to provide work – Hitler and his National Socialists.

The Great Depression

The Depression in Europe

	Percentage of industrial workers unemployed
31.7	
28	
23	
18	
13	
No data	

★ Strike waves

☆ Sit-down strikes

✦ Riot, demonstration or single strike

Fascist States in Europe

Democratic countries

Repressive or conservative countries

Fascist countries

Communist dictatorship

● Right-wing activity

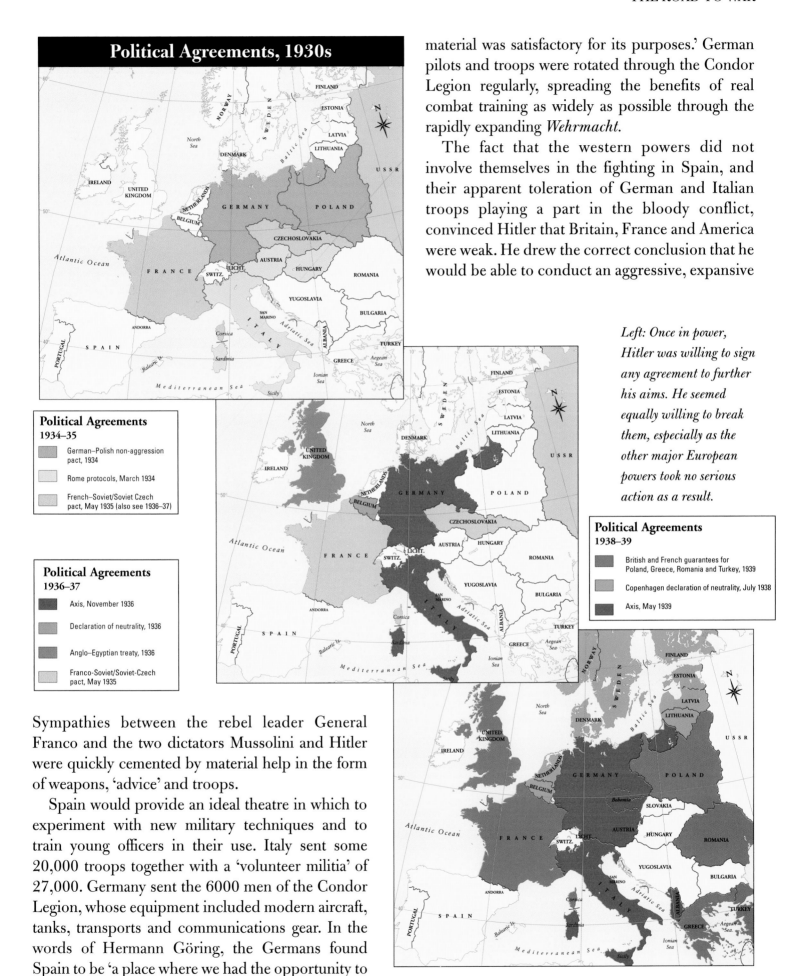

Political Agreements, 1930s

Political Agreements 1934–35

- German–Polish non-aggression pact, 1934
- Rome protocols, March 1934
- French–Soviet/Soviet Czech pact, May 1935 (also see 1936–37)

Political Agreements 1936–37

- Axis, November 1936
- Declaration of neutrality, 1936
- Anglo–Egyptian treaty, 1936
- Franco-Soviet/Soviet-Czech pact, May 1935

Political Agreements 1938–39

- British and French guarantees for Poland, Greece, Romania and Turkey, 1939
- Copenhagen declaration of neutrality, July 1938
- Axis, May 1939

material was satisfactory for its purposes.' German pilots and troops were rotated through the Condor Legion regularly, spreading the benefits of real combat training as widely as possible through the rapidly expanding *Wehrmacht*.

The fact that the western powers did not involve themselves in the fighting in Spain, and their apparent toleration of German and Italian troops playing a part in the bloody conflict, convinced Hitler that Britain, France and America were weak. He drew the correct conclusion that he would be able to conduct an aggressive, expansive

Left: Once in power, Hitler was willing to sign any agreement to further his aims. He seemed equally willing to break them, especially as the other major European powers took no serious action as a result.

Sympathies between the rebel leader General Franco and the two dictators Mussolini and Hitler were quickly cemented by material help in the form of weapons, 'advice' and troops.

Spain would provide an ideal theatre in which to experiment with new military techniques and to train young officers in their use. Italy sent some 20,000 troops together with a 'volunteer militia' of 27,000. Germany sent the 6000 men of the Condor Legion, whose equipment included modern aircraft, tanks, transports and communications gear. In the words of Hermann Göring, the Germans found Spain to be 'a place where we had the opportunity to test with live ammunition whether our military

'In spite of the hardness and ruthlessness I saw in Herr Hitler's face, I got the impression that here was a man who could be relied upon when he had given his word.'

Neville Chamberlain, Munich 1938

foreign policy without risking more than disapproval and complaint from the other European powers. However, Germany's rearmament and Hitler's aggressive speeches eventually began to get through to the governments in London and Paris.

Annexations

During 1937, France and Britain began reluctantly to stir themselves into action. An extension of France's main defences against possible German aggression – the Maginot Line – was agreed and construction actually began. Britain passed an Air Raid Precaution Bill through Parliament, though any further or more rigorous preparation for war by the British was nullified by the succession to the office of Prime Minister of Neville Chamberlain. He was an individual whose whole character and ambition were devoted to entering the history books as the man who saved Europe from war.

On 12 March 1938, Hitler sent his troops across the Austrian border and into Vienna to a rapturous welcome. The following day, he himself travelled to Vienna to declare the *Anschluss* – the indissoluble reunion of Austria and Germany into the Greater German Reich. The German General Staff used the operation as an exercise in moving large numbers of troops by road. All did not go smoothly, but valuable logistic lessons were learnt in the bloodless takeover, lessons that would be put into practice in combat some 18 months later.

Next, Hitler's eyes turned towards the Czechs. The Sudetenland, Czechoslovakia's western and northern border areas facing Germany and Austria, had a German-speaking population of three million. The area of Bohemia had been awarded to Czechoslovakia by the Treaty of Saint-Germain en Laye between Austria and the Allies. The area had rich mineral resources, and it also housed major munitions factories at Pilsen. The indigenous Nazi movement, the *Sudeten deutsche Partei* (SdP) created by Konrad Henlein, kept up pressure for the

Sudetenland to be united with Germany. In 1933, the 9500-strong SdP was banned by the Czech Government, but this seemed only to encourage it. In 1934, Henlein held his first mass meeting and gathered 20,000 people, and by 1938 membership had grown to 1.3 million.

Disregarding any vague promises he may have made to the British the previous November, the *Führer* announced in a secret directive on 30 May 1938 his irrevocable decision to destroy Czechoslovakia, and mobilized what had now become 'his' *Wehrmacht*. Hitler had assumed supreme military command of all Germany's forces in February.

'Peace in Our Time'

Throughout the summer, Hitler could watch with detachment the diplomatic traffic racing to and fro between London, Paris and Prague. His patience was rewarded. On 15 September, Chamberlain flew to Germany to try personally to persuade Hitler not to

Right: Between 1936 and 1939, Hitler nearly doubled the size of the Third Reich. With little opposition, his troops were allowed to march into the Saar, the Rhineland, Austria, the Sudetenland and Czechoslovakia. It was not until the invasion of Poland in September 1939 that Britain and France declared war.

Hitler's Annexations
1936–39

- Germany after 1919
- Troops into demilitarized Rhineland March 1936
- Anschluss (union with Austria), March 1938
- Occupation of Sudetenland October 1938
- Original Czechoslovakian border
- Formerly Czechoslovakia occupied March 1939
- Moravian territory to Poland October 1938
- Memel territory to Germany March 1939
- Protectorate of Slovakia territory to Hungary Nov. 1938
- Czechosovakian territory to Hungary March 1939

Hitler's Annexations

carry out his threats against the only true democracy in mid-Europe. On 22 September, Chamberlain was back with Hitler at Bad Godesberg for a further talk upon the European predicament, and on 30 September in Munich Chamberlain, Daladier, Mussolini and Hitler agreed that the German-speaking Sudetenland should after all be transferred to the Reich as the final stage of Hitler's territorial aggrandizement. Chamberlain then returned to England, waving the signed agreement and declaring, 'I believe it is peace for our time!'

Yet by mid-March of 1939, the British Prime Minister was facing a bitter reality. German troops had moved forward from the Sudetenland, first to Prague and then on into the whole of Bohemia and Moravia. Before leaving Berlin to make another triumphant entry, this time into Prague, Hitler announced that 'Czechoslovakia has ceased to exist' – and Chamberlain was sadly complaining that the *Führer* had broken his word. It was obvious that Hitler now intended for Poland to be his next victim.

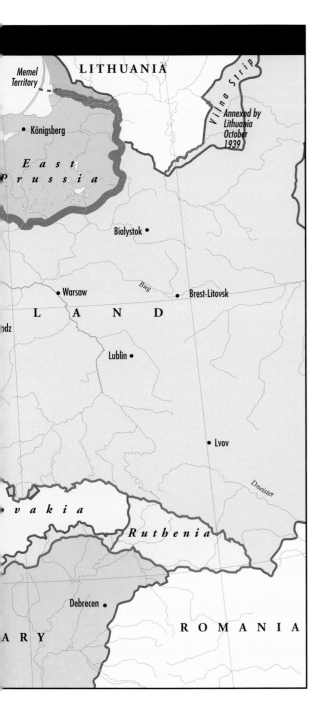

'This is a sad day for all of us, and to none is it sadder than to me.... I trust I may live to see the day when Hitlerism has been destroyed and a liberated Europe has been re-established.'

Neville Chamberlain, BBC broadcast, 3 September 1939

Throughout May, the diplomatic charade continued.

The 'Pact of Steel' was triumphantly announced between Germany and Italy. In August, at the prompting of Winston Churchill, a mission went to Moscow to explore the possibility of a military alliance with the only other country likely to field an army large enough to oppose Hitler's. The mission was still there when the existence of a new non-aggression pact between Russia and Germany was revealed to an astonished world. It was a pact with secret clauses, which were to become all too obvious only too soon. In response, Chamberlain announced Britain's guarantee of Poland's independence.

On 31 August, Hitler ordered the invasion of Poland. At 4.45 on the morning of 1 September 1939, bombers and fighters of the German *Luftwaffe* crossed the Polish frontier. They began the systematic destruction of Polish airfields and aircraft, of road and rail centres, of concentrations of troop reserves, and of anything which intelligence or observation had indicated as likely to house command headquarters of any status. The first *Blitzkrieg* had begun.

The following day, Britain and France demanded the instant withdrawal of all German forces from Polish soil. An ultimatum was sent – and duly ignored. At 11 a.m. on Sunday, 3 September 1939, Chamberlain broadcast the news that Britain was now at war with Germany.

Blitzkrieg and the Phoney War

At 4.45 on the morning of 1 September 1939, without Germany formally declaring war, aircraft of the *Luftwaffe* – Germany's air force – crossed the Polish frontier. The mission of almost 1400 fighters, bombers and dive-bombers was simple: the systematic destruction of Poland.

German Messerschmitts rapidly established air superiority, ruthlessly knocking Polish fighters from the skies while German bombers pounded Polish military and civil targets. Working under the protective fighter cover, German land forces were unleashed against the Polish army. From the start, the outcome was never in doubt. In little more than a month, all resistance had been crushed and the Polish state ceased to exist. Poland had succumbed to a new form of warfare, which would conquer most of western Europe in the next eight months. The Nazis called it *Blitzkrieg* – Lightning War.

The Invasion of Poland
The attack on Poland was a natural development of Hitler's hunger for conquest. He had already absorbed Austria and Czechoslovakia: Poland was his next target. Rivalry between the two countries had already soured relations, and armies on both sides of the German-Polish border were preparing for war.

Planning for the invasion of Poland had begun in April 1939, and Hitler ordered the German General Staff to launch the operation, known as *Fall Weiss* ('Case White') five months later. In many ways, Poland was an ideal theatre for the new kind of combined arms operations being developed by the *Wehrmacht*. It was fairly flat, and therefore suitable for mechanized operations, while its long borders meant that the Polish army was over-stretched.

One hour after the initial *Luftwaffe* strikes, it was the turn of German ground forces to swing into action. Over 40 German combat divisions were committed to the Polish campaign. Providing the spearhead of the German invasion force were six Panzer divisions and eight motorized infantry divisions. These were supported by 27 foot-slogging infantry divisions.

Opposite: The tank force with which Germany launched its Blitzkrieg *in 1939 was not the mighty juggernaut it was to become. Speed and mobility was the key to the* Wehrmacht's *success, and the bulk of its armoured strength in Poland was provided by light tanks armed with machine-guns, like this Panzer I.*

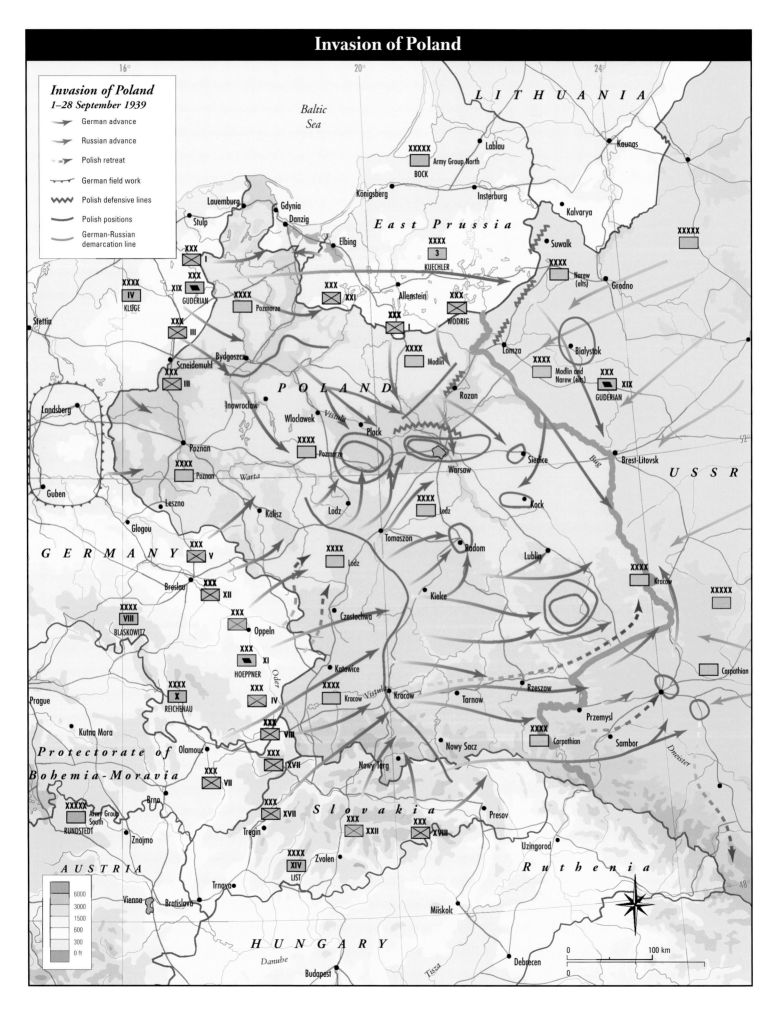

Invasion of Poland

Invasion of Poland
1–28 September 1939

→ German advance

→ Russian advance

⇢ Polish retreat

⌇ German field work

〰 Polish defensive lines

⌒ Polish positions

— German-Russian demarcation line

'CANNED GOODS'

Canned Goods was the codename for a series of fake attacks on German border posts, fabricated in August 1939 to justify the German attack on Poland. Conceived by Himmler, Heydrich and Heinrich Müller, and initiated with Hitler's approval, the operation used about a dozen condemned German criminals and camp inmates, who were dressed in Polish uniforms, given lethal injections and then torn apart by small-arms fire. The international press were then invited to view the bodies, which had been positioned to look as if they had been killed in a cross-border raid. The most important 'target' for these attacks was the radio station at Gleiwitz, where disguised SS troops under command of Alfred Helmut Naujocks added to the effect by storming the radio station, beating up the staff and making crude anti-German broadcasts.

'Poland's existence is intolerable, incompatible with the essential conditions of Germany's life. Poland must go and will go…'

General von Seeckt, speaking in 1922

The main role of the infantry was to engage the bulk of the Polish army while the German mobile forces raced around the flanks, cutting through supply lines and striking at command-and-control centres to the rear.

The role of the *Luftwaffe* was to provide close air support for the German ground forces. However, German aircraft also played a more strategic role, striking at Polish airfields and aircraft, road and rail centres, concentrations of troop reserves, and military headquarters. A number of Polish aircraft survived the initial attacks and put up stiff – if limited – resistance over the following week. But it was too little, too late.

The world was stunned by the pace of the attack. While German Panzers crossed the River Warta, Britain and France demanded the instant withdrawal of all German forces. In the face of the contemptuous silence with which this was greeted in Berlin, the Allies consulted on how best to implement their promises to Poland.

A final ultimatum was sent to Berlin – and ignored. At 11 a.m. on Sunday, 3 September, British Prime Minister Neville Chamberlain broadcast the news that Britain was now at war with Germany. The world would realize, he felt sure, what a bitter personal disappointment this was. After all, Hitler had given his word he would not attack.

The Land Campaign

The campaign was planned as a massive double pincer movement. The inner pincer was designed to close on the Vistula river, surrounding the bulk of the Polish field army, while the outer, faster-moving forces were targeted on the Bug, cutting off any possibility of escape.

The operation was conducted by two German Army Groups – North and South. Von Rundstedt's Army Group South comprised three armies. The Eighth Army on the left flank drove for Lodz, while Fourteenth Army on the right aimed for Krakow. In the centre, von Reichenau's Tenth Army had the bulk of the group's armour. Its mission was to pierce the gap between the Polish Lodz and Krakow armies, link with Eighth Army mobile units and push on to Warsaw. Attacking simultaneously was von Bock's Army Group North. Kuechler's Third Army drove south from East Prussia while von Kluge's

Opposite: The German campaign in Poland was not a true Blitzkrieg – *it was a classical double envelopment. Two great pincers cut off and isolated the main Polish field armies, with the outer pincer being spearheaded by the new panzer corps under Guderian and Hoeppner.*

Fourth Army struck from the west, across the Polish Corridor. This attack was spearheaded by the Panzers of Guderian's XIX Corps.

The plan worked brilliantly. Never before had so much territory been gained in such a short space of time. After just three days of fighting, leading elements of the German army had pushed 80km (50 miles) into Poland. Whole Polish armies were in danger of being isolated. By the end of the first week, the Polish Government had fled from Warsaw. In spite of some successful counterattacks early in the campaign, the Polish air force had been all but wiped out. With the elimination of any aerial threat, German Stuka dive-bombers were free to probe ahead of advancing Panzer columns.

The momentum of the German advance continued virtually unchecked. By 8 September, the German 4th Panzer Division had advanced nearly 241km (150 miles), an average of more than 29km (18 miles) per day. In the same period, the Poles began to prepare Warsaw's defences. The next day, initial German attempts to storm Warsaw were rebuffed. This was followed by a spirited Polish counterattack in the Bzura region, marking the start of the biggest battle of the campaign.

Encirclement

By now, the entire Polish army was becoming trapped inside an ever-decreasing circle of German forces. On 10 September, the *Luftwaffe* began to launch heavy raids on Warsaw, and the Polish Government ordered a general military withdrawal to the southeast. On 15 September, the Germans issued an ultimatum to Warsaw – surrender or be destroyed. The garrison, supported by as many as 100,000 civilians, chose to fight on.

Army Groups North and South met at Wlodawa on 17 September, completing the outer ring of the German double pincer. From this double encirclement, only a small fraction of the Polish army could hope to escape, and on the same day even this hope was dashed. Surrounded and besieged, the Poles received yet another crushing blow with the news that Soviet forces had entered the war on the German side.

Signed the previous month, the secret Russo-German Pact called for the division of Poland. While the Germans crushed any remaining Polish resistance in the east, the Red Army advanced on two fronts north and south of the impassable Pripet marshes, meeting negligible opposition. The Polish Government, which had already changed its location five times, fled into Romania. On 19 September, the Polish

---

ATROCITIES IN POLAND

It was in Poland that the Nazi state showed its true colours. Following on the heels of the German Army as it smashed the Polish military came 15 *Einsatzkommandos*, or Special Units, staffed mainly by members of the SS and the SD (the *Sicherheitsdienst*, or SS security service). The *Einsatzgruppen* were originally established to eliminate political opposition in Austria following the *Anschluss* in 1938.

The task of the SD officers in Poland was to 'combat hostile elements', which in practice meant that the *Einsatzkommandos* conducted terror operations against Jews, the Polish army and the Polish intelligentsia.

In the two months when they were active, the *Einsatzkommandos* in Poland murdered some 15,000 people – a foretaste of even more horrific massacres that were to come after the invasion of the Soviet Union in 1941.

The Soviet NKVD was carrying out similar activities on their side of the line. In March 1940, Stalin signed an order to execute over 25,000 Poles, the most notorious massacre being of 4000 captured Polish officers in the Katyn Forest.

army in the Bzura pocket was finally defeated: more than 100,000 men were taken prisoner. Two days later, the Germans launched a massive bombardment of Warsaw. The next day, the Soviets occupied Lvov, and mounted a joint victory parade with the Germans in Brest-Litovsk. A further ultimatum was issued on 25 September to the citizens and defenders of Warsaw, emphasized by attacks by more than 400 bombers. Polish resistance began to weaken, and on 26 September the *Wehrmacht* launched an infantry assault on the city. Within a day, the Germans had taken control of the outer

Left: Poland's armies could do little to stop the Germans, and it soon became clear to the inhabitants of Warsaw that they would come under attack in a very short time. The population turned out en masse to help dig defences – these school girls are preparing trenches to provide protection from air attack.

Above: Legend has it that the gallant but doomed Polish cavalry charged German panzers with lances. The truth is more prosaic. A Polish cavalry unit was cut off by panzers and to escape had no choice but to try to ride through the enemy armour. Not surprisingly, casualties among men and horses were heavy.

suburbs, and the Polish commander, recognizing a lost cause, offered to surrender. A ceasefire came into effect the next day, 28 September.

The First Triumph

To the victors went the spoils of war. The Soviet-German partition of Poland came into force immediately with the signing of a 'treaty of frontier regulation and friendship' on the 29th. Poland as a nation ceased to exist.

To seal his triumph, Hitler flew into Warsaw on 5 October and took the salute at a victory parade. Organized Polish resistance ceased the next day with the surrender of 8000 troops southeast of Warsaw. For the Poles, defeat was now complete. Despite the desperate gallantry of its soldiers, the Polish army had been outclassed by a vastly more efficient military machine. The fatal weakness in Poland's defences lay in her lack of armour and mobile forces. At the start of the war, 30 Polish infantry divisions had been supported by 13 cavalry brigades, just two of which were motorized: the remaining 11 still used horses.

The whirlwind German campaign introduced a new type of warfare, making use of classic principles of fire and manoeuvre allied to the utilization of the latest weapons in both the air and on the ground. Speed was a major contribution to the *Wehrmacht's* success, as was good intelligence. German troops unerringly found the weak spots in the Polish defences, which were exploited by fast-moving armour and mechanized infantry, driving towards their objectives while all but ignoring flank security. They relied on their speed of penetration to disrupt any potential Polish counterattacks, leaving consolidation to the slower moving infantry following on foot.

The *Wehrmacht's* triumph was recorded by scores of Joseph Goebbels' Propaganda Company cameramen, whose work was soon being shown in cinemas all over the world. This contributed greatly to the myth of *Blitzkrieg*, which would soon be terrifying Germany's enemies. Curiously, many western military professionals did not give the new tactics much attention, wrongly assuming the magnitude of the *Wehrmacht's* victory to be due to the incompetence of the Poles.

For Hitler, the Polish campaign had been a gamble that he'd taken. . . and won. The *Wehrmacht* had committed most of its forces to operations in Poland. No more than a token covering force in the west was left to face an overwhelming French army of 70 divisions and a small British Expeditionary Force. Although dangerously overexposed, Hitler had calculated correctly that the Allies would do nothing if he invaded Poland. Once the subjugation of Poland was completed in early October, Hitler was free to turn his attention to further campaigns in the west. However, fighting in Eastern Europe was

Below: The Luftwaffe's *Ju 87 Stuka dive-bombers gained an awesome reputation in Poland. The crank-winged machines with their screaming sirens and ability to make precision attacks ranged ahead of the advancing* Wehrmacht. *Acting as flying artillery, they destroyed a variety of Polish targets, including bridges, railways, road junctions, field fortifications and strongpoints.*

far from over, and while there was no direct German involvement, the Winter War of 1939–1940 was a direct result of the success of the *Wehrmacht* in Poland.

The Winter War

The Russo–Finnish war began when Finland, formerly a Russian province, refused Soviet demands for border adjustments. The Soviets, fearful of Hitler's future plans, wanted to consolidate their grip on the Baltic states to provide a position of strength on the northern flank of the expanding Third Reich.

First to fall were the Baltic states of Latvia, Lithuania and Estonia, which had been independent since the fall of the Tsarist empire. After the partition of Poland, Stalin bullied the small republics into accepting mutual 'defence' pacts with the USSR. Once the treaties were signed, the Red Army moved large forces into the three countries. Ostensibly these were to provide for their protection, but they were occupying forces in all but name. The citizens of the three Baltic republics could do little in the face of overwhelming force, but their resentment remained, which explained why many greeted the Germans as liberators when they invaded two years later.

Finland had also been part of the Tsarist empire, and the Soviets demanded a similar accommodation with the Finns. Stalin demanded that the Helsinki government must cede southern Karelia to the USSR, as well as allowing the Red Army to base troops on numerous islands in the Baltic as well as on the Finnish mainland. The Finns rejected the Soviet demands outright, and began mobilizing forces along the frontier. Commanding the Finnish defences was Marshal Carl von Mannerheim, a veteran of the Russo-Japanese War of 1905 and a cavalry general in the Imperial Russian army during World War I.

Mannerheim had first planned a line of defences across the Karelian Isthmus after World War I, and over the next 20 years a series of some 200 concrete defensive positions were constructed. Stretching from the Gulf of Finland through Summa to the Vuoksi river at Taipale, these became known as the Mannerheim line. On 30 November 1939,

Right: The bodies of Red Army soldiers lie frozen in the Karelian forest, victims of a poorly planned and executed Soviet invasion of Finland. The Winter War was to cost the Soviets more than a quarter of a million men.

the Red Air Force launched a surprise attack on Helsinki, followed by a full-scale invasion. Almost a million Soviet troops smashed into Finland from the east, the southeast, and from across the Gulf of Finland. Facing them were around 300,000 Finnish troops, 80 percent of whom were reservists.

Stalin reckoned that with such overwhelming force the Red Army would have occupied Finland in less than a month, but he was rudely disillusioned. The Finns proved to be ferocious fighters, and familiarity with the terrain and weather meant that they put up incredible resistance to the Soviet attack. A Russian column attacking at Petsamo in the north made brief progress before being stopped in their tracks, while the amphibious assaults in the south were all beaten back. The main Russian thrust through the Karelian isthmus was beaten back with heavy losses at the Mannerheim line. Other Soviet columns attempting to move through the seemingly endless forests and lakes of central Finland were run ragged by small Finnish ski units fighting a guerrilla-style war to which the Red Army had no answer.

The initial Soviet attack ended with a fierce battle around the village of Suomussalmi, lasting through December and into the first week of January. Harassing Finnish attacks cut the Soviet supply routes, trapping two Russian divisions in and around the village. In a series of slashing assaults, the Finns cut the Soviet troops to pieces. Total Soviet losses exceeded 27,000 killed or frozen to death, while the Finns lost less than 1000.

Above: Finnish irregular ski troops on patrol. Vastly outnumbered by the Red Army, the Finns used their winter warfare ability and familiarity with the terrain to hold the Soviets back for more than three months.

Right: Operations in the Winter war stretched from the Gulf of Finland to the Arctic Ocean. The main thrust was in the south, where the Soviets eventually broke through the Mannerheim Line by using brute force and by ignoring horrendous casualties.

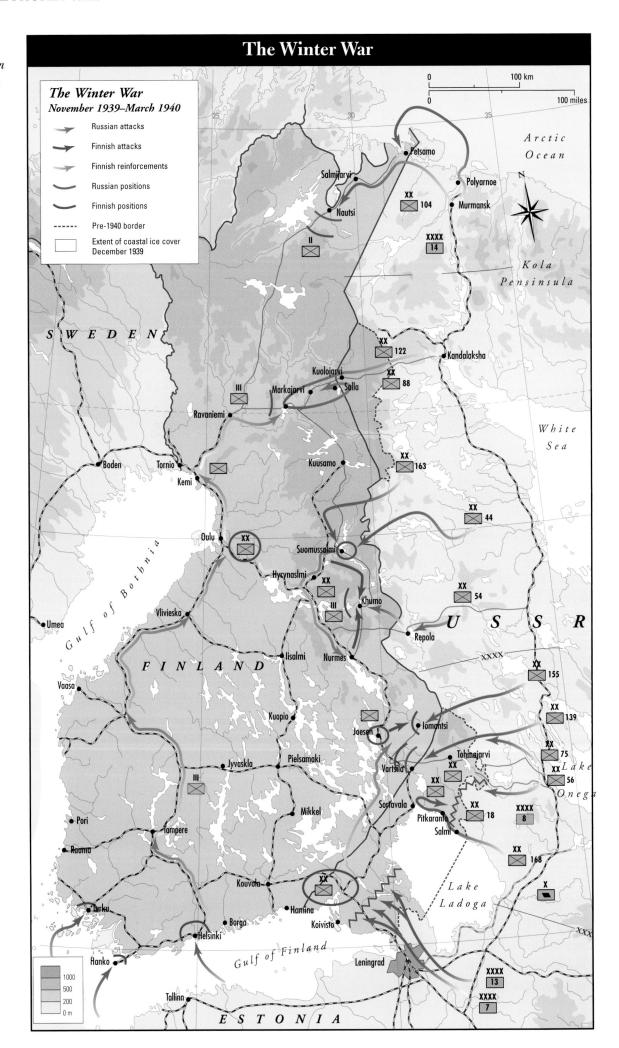

The Winter War

The Winter War
November 1939–March 1940

→ Russian attacks
→ Finnish attacks
→ Finnish reinforcements
⌒ Russian positions
⌒ Finnish positions
- - - Pre-1940 border
☐ Extent of coastal ice cover December 1939

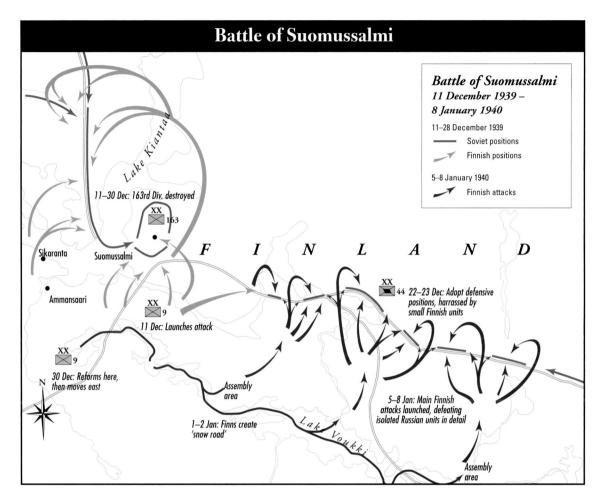

Battle of Suomussalmi

Battle of Suomussalmi
11 December 1939 –
8 January 1940

11–28 December 1939

——— Soviet positions

↗ Finnish positions

5–8 January 1940

↗ Finnish attacks

Lake Kiantaa

11–30 Dec: 163rd Div. destroyed

XX 163

F I N L A N D

Sikaranta

Suomussalmi

Ammansaari

XX 9

11 Dec: Launches attack

XX 9

30 Dec: Reforms here, then moves east

N

XX 44 22–23 Dec: Adopt defensive positions, harrassed by small Finnish units

Assembly area

1–2 Jan: Finns create 'snow road'

Lake Voukki

5–8 Jan: Main Finnish attacks launched, defeating isolated Russian units in detail

Assembly area

Left: The Battle of Suomussalmi saw the Finns using guerrilla tactics to harass and blunt the main Soviet probe into central Finland.

The humiliating defeat forced the Red Army to regroup, and a further half million men were committed to the battlefront under the command of Marshal Timoshenko. The Soviets planned a massive battle of attrition in the Karelian isthmus, aiming to smash through the Mannerheim line by brute force. On 1 February, two Soviet armies, totalling 54 divisions, began battering at the Finnish defences, mounting four or five attacks each day. The Finns inflicted horrific slaughter on the wave after wave of Soviet infantrymen pushing through the snow, but the Soviet high command was willing to accept any losses to achieve its aim. Eventually, on 13 February, the Russians broke through at Summa, and began to roll up the Finnish defences. Over the next month the Finns were forced back, and on 12 March they sued for peace.

The Finns signed an armistice after losing some 25,000 men. Soviet losses were at least 10 times higher, many soldiers freezing to death in the Arctic cold, which on occasion fell to –50°C (–58°F). Stalin did not impose any demands beyond those asked for before the fighting started, knowing that too much repression would probably force the stubborn Finns into a guerrilla war – and nobody on the Soviet side wanted to face that.

The original Soviet invasion had been incompetently planned, led and executed, with little regard to the terrain or the weather. Success came only because the Red Army was willing to accept huge casualties to achieve its aims. The Soviet failure to dominate Finland convinced many Germans – Adolf Hitler and the German high command included – that the Soviet Union was a paper giant, and that an invasion of the USSR was possible.

Above: Over the winter of 1939/1940, the Western Allies believed that the war would never come to anything serious. To many British people, the comfort of the troops was a more important concern. Here, a consignment of new dartboards is about to be shipped to the British Expeditionary Force in France.

The 'Phoney War'

Although the Russo-Finnish War excited great interest among the British and French, in practice it did not affect them a great deal, for their main enemy – Germany – was not involved. Thus once the subjugation of Poland was completed in early October, it almost seemed to the peoples of Western Europe that military operations had ceased. There had been some idea of helping the Finns, but neutral Norway and Sweden had refused permission for Anglo-French supplies or troops to cross their territories, and nothing came of it. Naval operations aside, the 'fighting war' was apparently over and what United States Senator Boragh dubbed the 'Phoney War' began. British Prime Minister Neville Chamberlain called it the 'Twilight War', the Germans called it the *'Sitzkrieg'* ('seated war'), and one perspicacious observer called it the 'Winter of Illusion'.

This it certainly was for the British people and their leaders, for there grew in Britain (and in the United States, though to a lesser degree in France) a dangerous feeling that perhaps it would be possible to get through this war without too much unpleasantness, such as actual battle. True, there had been losses at sea – the aircraft-carrier *Courageous* had been torpedoed and sunk in September and the *Royal Oak* inside Scapa Flow in October – but the defeat of the *Graf Spee* levelled these losses out to some extent. In Britain, there was a growing impression that, ever since the torpedoing of the passenger liner *Athenia* a few hours after the declaration of war, the whole conflict was a sad mistake.

Chamberlain would, of course, allow no suggestion that any sort of deal could be done with Hitler, but once the German people 'had realized that they can't possibly win this war' – a condition he visualized developing by spring 1940 – they would undoubtedly rid themselves of their *Führer*, and probably an agreement could then be arrived at with some other German statesman – Marshal Göring, for instance.

In the meantime, 18,000,000 printed leaflets informing the Germans of the wickedness of their *Führer* would be dropped over Germany by the RAF, who would doubtless continue to suffer their resultant losses with knightly forbearance, at the same time ensuring that no damage whatsoever occurred to German citizens' private property, in case it upset them.

As winter approached, the British Expeditionary Force, some 400,000 strong, had crossed the Channel, and proceeded smoothly to their positions along the Franco-Belgian border around Arras and Lille, where they built pill-boxes and dug trenches. When Major-General Montgomery visited his division in December, Chamberlain queried, 'I don't think the Germans have any intention of attacking us, do you?' The general's reply is not recorded, but the Prime Minister's feelings reflected those of the British population as a whole, and was echoed in France, especially at the top of the French command.

There, the French generals believed they were arguing from a position of strength. Following the end of World War I, France had spent billions of francs on the construction of border fortifications known as the Maginot Line. Stretching from the Swiss border to the Belgian border, the Maginot Line consisted of a series of immense concrete fortresses. They were designed to be impregnable to conventional attack. Manned by more than 400,000 troops, they also sucked up a large proportion of France's available manpower. However, for political reasons, the Line did not extend along the Belgian border. There, the defences consisted mainly of a series of unconnected fortifications, many dating back to before World War I.

Manning the Defences

Both Britain and France still believed that all-out war with Hitler could be avoided. Certainly, there had been no attempt to take pressure off the Poles during their ordeal by military action across the Rhine – much to the relief and astonishment of some of the senior *Wehrmacht* officers, who revealed after the war that a powerful thrust into the Saar during the first month of the war would have been almost uncontested and could quite possibly have precipitated that popular revolt against the Nazi Party and the *Führer* of which Chamberlain so ardently dreamed.

But nothing happened, and once the Poles had been beaten, the combat-tested and battle-proven German divisions moved swiftly back across their country to Germany's western defence, the West Wall (known as the Siegfried Line to the British). Here they settled down to do little for the moment but glower at their opposite numbers and exchange insults with them daily through loudspeakers – but neither side did much to disturb the other's physical comfort. However, remaining on the defensive formed no part of the *Führer's* plans, and behind the fortifications German troop numbers rose dramatically as the *Wehrmacht* began to prepare for the next, even more deadly phase in the fighting.

The Allies expected the Germans to follow their standard plan for the invasion of France. First drawn up by General Count Alfred von Schlieffen in the first years of the 20th century, the Schlieffen Plan envisaged drawing the main French field forces into a battle in Alsace, after which the bulk of the German armies would smash through the

'The French army, the strongest in the world, faced no more than twenty-six German divisions. It sat still, sheltering behind steel and concrete while a valiant ally was being exterminated.'

J. F. C. Fuller,
On the 'Phoney War'

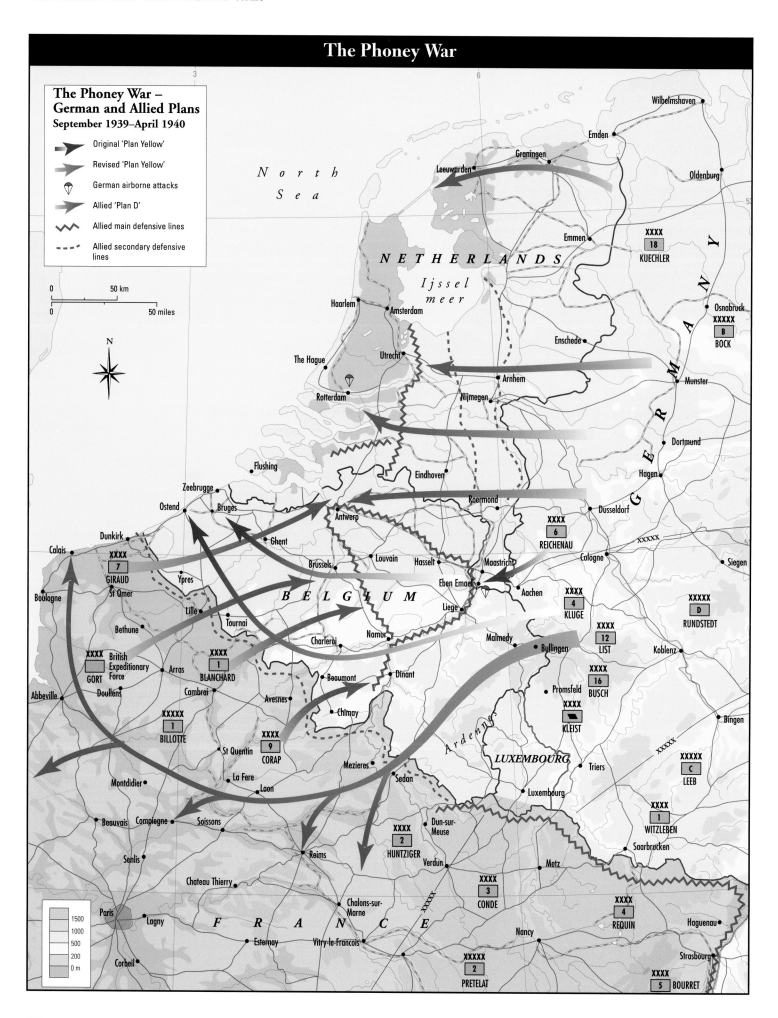

The Phoney War

**The Phoney War –
German and Allied Plans**
September 1939–April 1940

➤ Original 'Plan Yellow'

➤ Revised 'Plan Yellow'

⛱ German airborne attacks

➤ Allied 'Plan D'

〰 Allied main defensive lines

╌╌ Allied secondary defensive lines

0 ___ 50 km
0 ___ 50 miles

N

*North
Sea*

NETHERLANDS

*Ijssel
meer*

Wilhelmshaven

Emden

Oldenburg

Graningen

Leeuwarden

Emmen

XXXX
18
KUECHLER

Osnabruck

XXXXX
B
BOCK

Haarlem

Amsterdam

The Hague

Utrecht

Enschede

Arnhem

Munster

Rotterdam

Nijmegen

Dortmund

G E R M A N Y

Flushing

Eindhoven

Hagen

Zeebrugge

Ostend

Bruges

Ghent

Antwerp

Roermond

Dusseldorf

XXXX
6
REICHENAU

Cologne

Siegen

Dunkirk

Calais

XXXX
7
GIRAUD

St Omer

Ypres

Brussels

Louvain

Hasselt

Maastricht

Eben Emael

XXXX
4
KLUGE

Aachen

XXXXX
D
RUNDSTEDT

Boulogne

Lille

Tournai

Liege

Bethune

Charleroi

Namur

Malmedy

Bullingen

XXXX
12
LIST

Koblenz

B E L G I U M

XXXX
British
Expeditionary
Force
GORT

XXXX
1
BLANCHARD

Arras

Cambrai

Beaumont

Dinant

Promsfeld

XXXX
16
BUSCH

XXXX
KLEIST

Abbeville

Doullens

Avesnes

Chimay

Bingen

XXXXX
1
BILLOTTE

St Quentin

XXXX
9
CORAP

La Fere

Mezieres

Sedan

Ardennes

LUXEMBOURG

Triers

XXXXX
C
LEEB

Montdidier

Laon

Beauvais

Compiegne

Soissons

Reims

Dun-sur-
Meuse

XXXX
2
HUNTZIGER

Luxembourg

XXXX
1
WITZLEBEN

Senlis

Verdun

Saarbrucken

Chateau Thierry

Chalons-sur-
Marne

Metz

XXXX
3
CONDE

XXXX
4
REQUIN

F R A N C E

Paris

Lagny

Esternay

Vitry-le-Francois

Nancy

Haguenau

1500
1000
500
200
0 m

Corbeil

XXXXX
2
PRETELAT

Strasbourg

XXXX
5
BOURRET

38

Low Countries in a massive sickle manoeuvre, taking the French armies in the flank and rear and leaving the road to Paris wide open.

It was partly to counter this that the Allies planned to advance into Belgium and Holland, setting up defences along the Dyle Line, using the many waterways of the area as natural obstacles to a German advance. But both Belgium and Holland were maintaining a strictly neutral posture, which meant that their military commanders did not dare make contact with French and British military planners to coordinate defensive plans. Similarly, the Anglo-French forces could not set up fortifications on the locations where they planned to fight. As the Allies sat and built their defences, the Germans were preparing an invasion force behind the Siegfried Line border. From northern Holland to Switzerland, the *Wehrmacht* amassed more than two million men, deployed in 104 infantry divisions, nine motorized divisions and 10 Panzer or armoured divisions.

A Pause in War

While the two armies faced each other across the Franco-German frontier, the war was having little effect on the life of ordinary Germans. German rearmament had been carried out as a short, sharp process, and no plans had been made to place the German economy on a true war footing. Military production had not risen above pre-war levels, the production of civilian goods was hardly reduced, working hours were not extended, and in spite of severe labour shortages caused by so many men in uniform, no attempt was made to make use of Germany's women, the majority of whom did not work. To farmers and city dwellers alike, the war was something they read about or saw in newsreels, not something they were experiencing.

The British were much more realistic. The lives of British civilians were disturbed by the torrent of bureaucratic regulations that descended upon them from every old and several new departments of government, and their homes were either emptied of their own children if they lived in important cities or filled with other people's children if they lived in the country. A lot of them suffered disability or even death as a result of accidents in the black-out, and life, commented one observer afterwards, 'seemed to have become a continual exhortation, as posters sprouted everywhere enjoining every civic virtue from thrift to celibacy'.

As winter passed and the first signs of spring began to appear in 1940, boredom with the war and all its petty nuisances was a general feeling. But things were about to change.

Opposite: The Allied High Command expected that any German attack would be a repeat of the Schlieffen Plan of World War I – an attack through the Low Countries. Allied forward deployments were based on that assessment – so British, French and Belgian troops were totally unprepared when the Panzers burst through the Ardennes and raced for the coast.

THE WEST WALL

Germany's western defence, the West Wall, had been built in the 18 months before the outbreak of war. Heavily featured in propaganda films of the time, it consisted of more than 14,000 bunkers, gun positions and dugouts, stretching more than 600km (373 miles) from the Swiss border through the Upper Rhine, the Palatinate and the Saar as far as Aachen. Its building consumed more than 7.3 million tonnes (8 million tons) of concrete, 1.8 million tonnes (2 million tons) of steel, and over 18 million tonnes (20 million tons) of rubble and other filler material.

War in the West

The last time German soldiers had poured into France, in 1914, their initial drive had taken them close to Paris. But they were driven back, and had to endure four bloody years of trench warfare. This time, *Blitzkrieg* tactics would ensure a different outcome.

This time, they would break the back of enemy resistance in a single week. After a little more than a fortnight, the British would be evacuating their soldiers, and France would be at Hitler's mercy. The humiliation of 1918 would be avenged – and it would be the *Führer's* master strategy that did it, not the General Staff's. But before Hitler's *Wehrmacht* could achieve its triumph against the enemies of the Great War, Germany's soldiers would have to secure their flanks, in Scandinavia and the Low Countries.

In September 1939, when Hitler unleashed his forces against Poland, the *Wehrmacht* left no more than a covering force in the west to face a French army of 70 divisions, which was supported by 3000 tanks and had complete air supremacy – but only if the *Armée de l'air* had been ordered to fight. Hitler had a feeling that the French would do nothing, and his intuition paid off. The huge French army sat still, while a small British Expeditionary Force (BEF) was shipped to northern France.

The 'Phoney War' lasted through the winter and into the spring, until German forces invaded Denmark and Norway, forestalling an Allied landing by a matter of days. It was not until 10 May, eight months after the outbreak of war, that Hitler sent his armies west.

Exercise Weser

The Scandinavian attack had not been intended to happen, though planning had started at the beginning of the year, just in case it was necessary. It became necessary in April 1940. On 8 April, the First Lord of the Admiralty, Winston Churchill, announced that the Royal Navy was laying mines in Norwegian waters in order to stop the iron ore traffic between Narvik and Germany. This flagrant violation of Norway's neutrality was justified on the curious ground that Germany's reaction was likely to be even more flagrant. As Norway was a distinctly friendly neutral, this struck many British people as odd. But not so odd as the news next morning.

Opposite: When combat erupted on the Western Front, it was not in the Low Countries, as had been expected by the Allies. German troops went into action in Scandinavia, primarily to secure Germany's supplies of Swedish iron ore.

It had been the Winter War between Russia and Finland, and the possibility that British and French reinforcements and supplies might cross from Narvik to Lulea in Sweden and thus interrupt Germany's supplies of iron ore, which first brought Hitler's attention to Norway. Before that, his focus on the west had been concentrated on the Low Countries, but once he had seen the dangers that Allied exploitation of Norway might hold for Germany, and the advantages which would accrue to his *Kriegsmarine* by possession of Norwegian ports and control of her coastline, he ordered planning for what became known as *Weserubung,* or Exercise Weser.

Following the *Altmark* incident on 16 February (see feature box, page 44), Hitler ordered a speeding-up and consolidation of the planning for *Weserubung.* Two days later, General von Falkenhorst and his staff were given control of the operation, and it was one of the ironies of fate that, at the end of March, Hitler decreed that it would be launched at dawn on 9 April – one day after Churchill's announcement.

The result was that, to the watching world, Germany's reaction to the Royal Navy's mining of the Norwegian waters, flagrant violation or not, appeared unbelievably rapid. OKW, the high command of the German armed forces, released a message to the world's press as operations against Denmark and Norway were launched: 'In order to counter British preparations to take away the neutrality of Denmark and Norway, the *Wehrmacht* is taking over the armed defence of both nations.'

Denmark and Norway

The first step was to occupy Denmark, which would provide a springboard into Norway. As of April 1940, the Danish army had fewer than 14,000 men under arms, including 8000 men conscripted in February and March. The men were poorly trained and equipped with little or no armour.

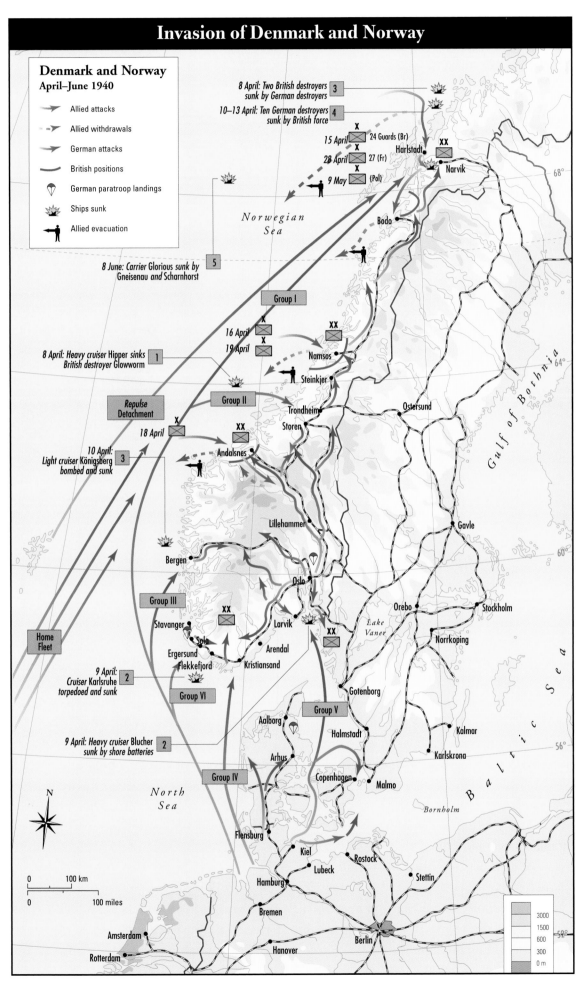

Invasion of Denmark and Norway

Denmark and Norway
April–June 1940

→ Allied attacks

- -→ Allied withdrawals

→ German attacks

⌒ British positions

⚲ German paratroop landings

✹ Ships sunk

👤 Allied evacuation

8 April: Two British destroyers sunk by German destroyers `3`

10–13 April: Ten German destroyers sunk by British force `4`

15 April X 24 Guards (Br)

28 April X 27 (Fr)

9 May X (Pol)

Harlstadt

XX Narvik

Norwegian Sea

Bodo

8 June: Carrier Glorious sunk by Gneisenau and Scharnhorst `5`

Group I

16 April X

19 April X

XX

Namsos

8 April: Heavy cruiser Hipper sinks British destroyer Glowworm `1`

Steinkjer

Group II

Repulse Detachment

Trondheim

Ostersund

18 April X

XX

Storen

10 April: Light cruiser Königsberg bombed and sunk `3`

Andalsnes

Lillehammer

Gavle

Bergen

Oslo

Group III

Orebo

Stockholm

Stavanger

Sola

XX

Larvik

Lake Vaner

XX

Home Fleet

Ergersund

Flekkefjord

Arendal

Kristiansand

Norrkoping

9 April: Cruiser Karlsruhe torpedoed and sunk `2`

Group VI

Gotenborg

Group V

Kalmar

Aalborg

Halmstadt

Karlskrona

9 April: Heavy cruiser Blucher sunk by shore batteries `2`

Arhus

Copenhagen

Malmo

Group IV

North Sea

Bornholm

Baltic Sea

Flensburg

Kiel

Rostock

0   100 km

0   100 miles

Lubeck

Stettin

Hamburg

Bremen

3000
1500
600
300
0 m

Amsterdam

Berlin

Rotterdam

Hanover

Left: After the rapid takeover of Denmark, Norway was invaded in a series of widely separated but coordinated attacks stretching from Kristiansand in the south to Narvik, far to the north of the Arctic Circle.

'We have concluded a non-aggression pact with Denmark. Germany never had any conflict with the Northern States and has none today.'

Adolf Hitler, before the attack on Scandinavia

At 5 a.m. on 9 April, German *Fallschirmjäger* paratroopers were dropped at the unused fortress of Madneso and then at Aalborg airport. At 6 a.m., a battalion of infantry that had been hidden in a merchant ship in Copenhagen harbour, emerged to seize the Danish King and his government. Two divisions of the German XXI Infantry Corps crossed the border and moved into Jutland. Totally outmatched, the Danish army put up little resistance except in North Schleswig, and there was a brief firefight for possession of the Royal Palace in Copenhagen.

At 9.20 a.m., after Germany threatened to use the *Luftwaffe* to bombard Copenhagen, the Danish Government ordered a cease-fire. By the end of the day, Germany controlled all of Denmark. In addition to providing a platform for operations in Norway, occupation of Denmark provided the *Kriegsmarine* with bases for operations in the North Sea and Atlantic. It also provided flank security for the vital supplies of Swedish steel coming to Germany across the Baltic.

At dawn on the same day, German troops were swarming ashore at Oslo, Bergen, Trondheim and even – to the astonishment of a world steeped in the tradition of British supremacy at sea – at Narvik, over a thousand miles from the German homeland. German paratroops seized Sola airport near Stavanger and dropped later on to Fornebu airport near Oslo, while the *Kriegsmarine* ferried the army formations across the Skagerrak and Kattegat, though not without loss. Both the heavy cruiser *Blücher* and the light cruiser *Karlsruhe* were sunk, the first by Norwegian coastal guns and the second by the British submarine *Truant*. The heavy cruiser Admiral Hipper had 37m (120ft) torn out of her starboard bow when she was rammed by the British destroyer *Glowworm* in a self-sacrificial attack, an action that won her commander, Lieutenant-Commander G.B. Roope, the first posthumous Victoria Cross of the war.

On land only the Norwegian forces, reacting with admirable determination after the first shock, could offer any resistance, but the Royal Navy could at least help up at Narvik. Five destroyers led by Captain Warburton-Lee created chaos among the German warships in the harbour, sinking two German destroyers but losing two in the process. On 12 April, the old battleship *Warspite*, accompanied by nine destroyers, raced up the Ototfjord and completed the destruction; but to the south the preponderance of German artillery and trained battalions – and the complete domination of the air by the *Luftwaffe* – ensured the *Wehrmacht's* ultimate success.

'Operation Weserübung warrants examination because it was one of the first "joint" operations, with the German army, navy, and air force fighting as a team in spite of inter-service rivalries.'

R. Hooker/
C. Coglianese,
modern US Department of Defense analysis

In eight days, brigades of the German 163rd and 196th Divisions had advanced 290km (180 miles) and now controlled the vital southern region. When hastily landed British reinforcements eventually arrived, they were incorporated piecemeal into the ragged defences, and beaten, as were the Norwegians, by better trained, better armed, and much better coordinated and commanded German troops. The survivors of two British brigades, landed at Andalsnes in the middle of April, were re-embarked and evacuated by 1 May, and central and southern Norway was virtually abandoned to the Germans.

However, in the far north at Narvik, the situation for the German General Dietl and his 2000 mountain troops was not at first so favourable. Their naval transport and supply had been destroyed and they were chased out of Narvik itself by a combined force of British Guardsmen, French *Chasseurs Alpins* and Polish *Chasseurs du Nord*. By 28 May, Narvik was at last firmly in Allied hands. Thus it was somewhat ironic that orders had already been issued for the rapid return home of all Allied forces, as they and their weapons were urgently needed elsewhere.

Perhaps the most illuminating comment upon the Allied conduct of the Norwegian campaign was written years after the war by the man appointed to command the British reinforcements in central Norway. As Major-General Carton de Wiart, VC walked along

Above: German Gebirgsjäger, or mountain troops, paddle up a Norwegian fjord. Under the command of General Dietl, the 3rd Mountain Division captured Narvik. However, it was recaptured by the British in May.

Whitehall to answer an urgent summons to the War Office in early April, 'It dawned on me that it might be Norway, as I had never been there and knew nothing about it!'

But if the Norwegian campaign was a setback for the British Army, it was a disaster for the Prime Minister.

Political Retribution

The House of Commons was packed, the mood of the members frustrated and angry. The anger concentrated on the figure of Neville Chamberlain sitting in his usual place on the front bench, so pale with fury and humiliation that Churchill, despite the bitter arguments of the past few years, was filled with sympathy for his harassed leader.

The First Lord of the Admiralty could hardly remember such bitter attacks being mounted in the House before. These were attacks against the policies of appeasement to which the Government had clung for so many months, against the pathetic optimism exhibited by the Prime Minister both in his dealings with Hitler before the war and in his attitude to Britain's defences since its outbreak, and especially against the contents of a speech Chamberlain had made but a month before, which had included the unfortunate statement that he believed 'Hitler has missed the bus!'

Nor was the attack delivered entirely by members of the Opposition, for it reached its zenith with a speech from one of Chamberlain's oldest friends and political colleagues, Leo Amery. Quoting Cromwell's scathing indictment of the leaders of Hampden's army as 'old decaying service men,' he turned directly on the Prime Minister and quoted Cromwell for the second time: 'You have sat here too long for any good you have been doing,' he proclaimed. 'Depart, I say, and let us have done with you! In the name of God, go!'

It was a devastating shock to the Prime Minister's ego, underlined by howls from the backbenchers chanting 'Go! Go! Go!' as he left the House. Later that day, he admitted to Churchill that he felt that he could not continue to lead a one-party government in the prosecution of the war, and that a national government embracing members of all parties should be formed. However, he doubted if the Labour leaders would serve under his own direction.

So, in fact, it proved during the somewhat involved talks and negotiations of the next 48 hours. By 11 a.m. on 10 May, Chamberlain had accepted that he must give way to another leader, and sent for the two men between whom he felt the choice must be made: Lord Halifax and Winston Churchill.

'I have had many important interviews in my public life,' Churchill later wrote, 'and this was certainly the most important. Usually I talk a great deal, but on this occasion I was silent.' It must have been a remarkable scene: Chamberlain, still icily certain of the rightness of his every action since taking office but prepared to yield in the face of such uncomprehending and

Below: Scandinavia saw the first major parachute operations of the war, when German Fallschirmjäger *were used to capture key Norwegian and Danish airfields, thus allowing safe landing of additional more conventional forces and supplies.*

incomprehensible hostility, now sure that his preference for Lord Halifax was justifiable; Churchill silent, feeling no doubt the weight of history already pressing about him; Halifax uncertain, his sense of duty unsustained by any driving ambition. It was, as Churchill wrote, 'a very long pause.... It certainly seemed longer than the two minutes which one observes in the commemoration of Armistice Day.'

It was broken, at last, by Halifax. It would be, he said, very difficult for him to direct the War Cabinet from outside the House of Commons, where all the major decisions must be debated, and where, as a member of the House of Lords, he was barred from speaking. It should be remembered that these were the days before a peer could disclaim his title. When he had finished, it was evident that Churchill's would be the name recommended to His Majesty, and after a little more desultory talk the three men parted. The call to Churchill came late in the afternoon, and at 6 p.m. he was shown into the

'I would say to the House, as I said to those who have joined this government: I have nothing to offer but blood, toil, tears and sweat.'

Winston Churchill, 13 May 1940

presence of the King, whom he was to serve so devotedly through such crucial years.

'I suppose you don't know why I have sent for you?' asked the King with a smile.

'Sir, I simply couldn't imagine why,' replied Churchill, matching his mood.

'I want to ask you to form a government'.

So began the premiership of one of the most remarkable men in British history and it is hard to believe that, for most of the rest of the world, the appointment itself and the events surrounding it passed for the moment almost unnoticed.

One of the few who might have taken heed of the new appointment was Adolf Hitler, who had been well aware of Churchill's opposition to the Nazis in the 1930s. Via the Nazi Foreign Office official Ernst Bohle (who had been born of German parents in Yorkshire and brought up in South Africa), Hitler had invited Churchill to Germany for talks, but the Englishman refused. At the time, the Germans considered Churchill to be too much of an outsider to be much of a threat, but now the biggest foe of appeasement was in charge in London. However, they thought that Churchill would be only a minor irritant, who would be swept aside as the full might of the *Wehrmacht* was unleashed.

On the morning of Churchill's appointment, the *Wehrmacht* launched a massive offensive into Belgium and Holland, both of which had been neutral up to that time. As army and SS spearheads crossed the border into the Low Countries, the *Luftwaffe* bombarded Rotterdam and German *Fallschirmjäger* were dropped onto key points along a carefully planned attack route. The days of the 'Phoney War' were gone for ever.

Into the Low Countries

The original army plan for the invasion of western Europe was based on Germany's opening attack in World War I, but was actually less ambitious than the Schlieffen Plan of 1914. The generals intended to occupy Belgium and France's northern industrial regions but no further. They had no intention of repeating the ill-fated march on Paris tried in 1914. Indeed, the army high command believed that the ratio of forces and the power of modern defence admitted no other strategy; new objectives would require a further campaign in 1941. The German generals were not alone in thinking that this was how it would be: the French and British generals agreed too, drawing up plans to push their main mobile forces into Belgium the moment that hostilities began.

Had the attack been delivered when first ordered in autumn 1939, the generals would have had the war they planned. But Hitler had other ideas. He had fought in Belgium, among the shattered villages around Ypres, where a million British and German soldiers were killed in 1917. He knew the ground, how artillery bombardments reduced the ground to a quagmire. Countless small rivers and streams offered endless obstruction to an invader. Surely it would be better to attack further south, perhaps through

RESCUE FROM THE *ALTMARK*

On 16 February 1940, British intelligence discovered that the *Altmark*, one of the *Graf Spee*'s supply ships, was steaming down the Norwegian coast. The converted tanker had a large number of British seamen aboard, taken prisoner during the *Graf Spee*'s raiding cruise. When threatened by the British 4th Destroyer Flotilla under Captain Vian, the *Altmark* took refuge in Norwegian territorial waters, putting in to Josenfjord. With typically Churchillian panache, the orders went out from Whitehall to take the *Altmark*. Vian disregarded Norwegian neutrality, entered the fjord, forced the *Altmark* aground and rescued the prisoners, his boarding party making minor popular history with the call 'The Navy's here!'

the forested hills of the Ardennes? The generals looked down their noses at the idea.

By the time the postponed offensive was ready to roll in the spring of 1940, Hitler discovered that at least some officers shared his vision. General Erich von Manstein was chief of staff to General von Rundstedt, commander-in-chief of Army Group A in the west. Manstein had studied the Ardennes region and come to the same conclusion as the *Führer*. He discussed the idea with the Germany's most influential tank expert, General Heinz Guderian. They argued for a radical strategy: to rush German Panzer divisions along the narrow forest tracks and out onto the gently rolling hills of northern France. Bursting into open country, they would punch through the enemy before the defences were ready for them. It would be difficult to bring enough artillery with these fast-moving formations, and other German commanders envisaged a pause while the guns were brought forward; a World War I-style battle would then take place along the river Meuse. Guderian and his tank men were far more sanguine, confident that they could storm the French defences. The *Luftwaffe's* bombers, especially its fearsome Ju-87 'Stuka' dive-bombers, would provide close support in place of artillery.

Hitler adopted the Manstein plan and changed the orders to his commanders in the west. Manstein would receive due credit in time, but the orthodox generals resented having a relatively junior officer's plan thrust upon them, and posted von Manstein to command an infantry corps in the rear. One thing Hitler could not change was the odds. Although Germany enjoyed superiority in the air, with 4000 aircraft against 3000 Allied, the *Wehrmacht* had only 141 divisions with which to attack 144 Allied divisions. The Allies had some 3383 tanks compared to the German total of 2335 – many of these being light tanks of limited fighting capacity.

Above: British troops captured in northern Norway are marched towards the ships in Trondheim harbour which will take them to prisoner of war camps in Germany.

49

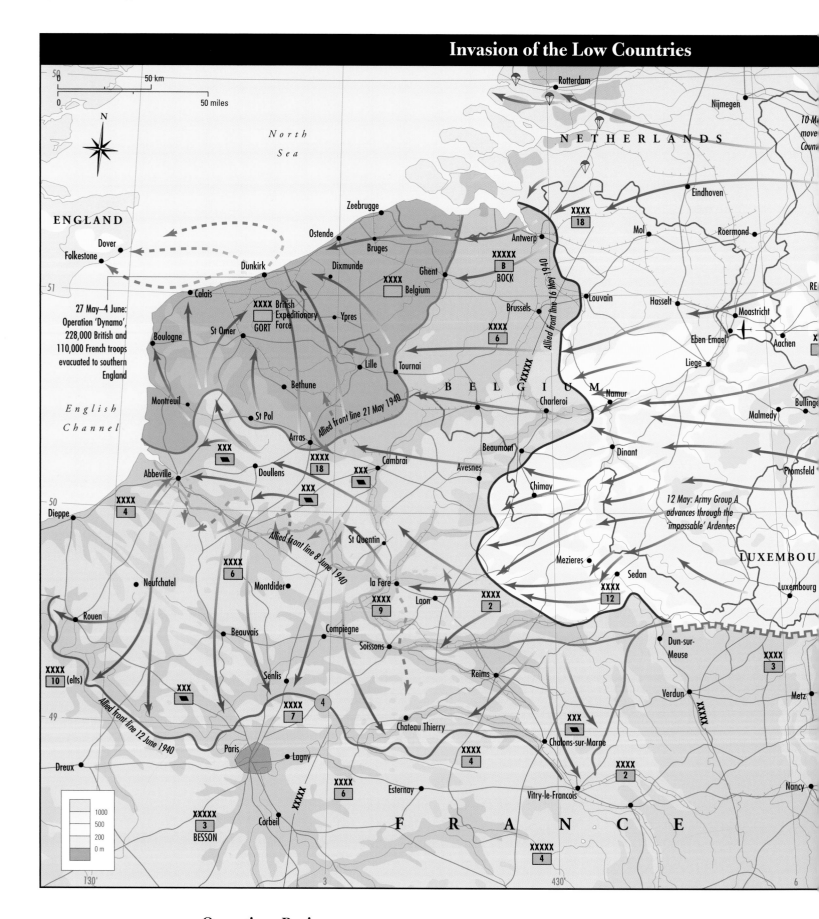

Invasion of the Low Countries

27 May–4 June:
Operation 'Dynamo',
228,000 British and
110,000 French troops
evacuated to southern
England

Allied front line 16 May 1940

Allied front line 21 May 1940

Allied front line 8 June 1940

Allied front line 12 June 1940

12 May: Army Group A
advances through the
'impassable' Ardennes

Operations Begin

Shortly after 2.30 on the morning of 10 May 1940, 64 men of the German army crossed the Dutch frontier; this was the very spearhead of the *Wehrmacht's* advance. Paratroopers were dropped on key bridges near Rotterdam, the Hague, Dordrecht and

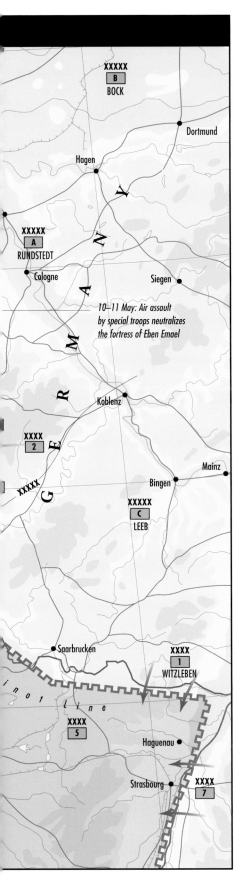

Invasion of the West
May–June 1940

→ German attacks

→ Allied counter-attacks

⇢ Allied retreats

‿ Allied front lines

⊓⊔ Allied defensive lines

⛴ German paratroop drops

✝ German glider assault

10–11 May: Air assault
by special troops neutralizes
the fortress of Eben Emael

Moerdijk, paralyzing any effective Dutch response to the flood coming across the border. More troops crossed the Albert Canal into Flanders. They should have been held back by the huge Belgian fort at Eben Emael, but at 5.30 a.m., glider-borne troops had dropped over the Belgian border to capture and demolish the massive strongpoint.

Five minutes later, the 30 divisions of Army Group B under General Fedor von Bock flooded forward across the frontiers from Maastricht up to the coast at the Ems estuary, while to the south General von Rundstedt's Army Group A of 44 divisions, including the main striking force of seven Panzer divisions under General Kleist, moved forward into the Belgian Ardennes – the wooded country which French military commanders had been describing as impassable for tanks since 1919.

With an almost suicidal alacrity that brought tears of joy to Hitler's eyes, the Allied armies in the north – five divisions of the BEF, eight divisions of the French First Army on their right and seven divisions of the French Seventh Army up on the coast around Dunkirk – left the defensive positions they had spent the bitterly cold winter so arduously preparing, and moved forward to join the Belgian army in accordance with the Dyle Plan, which envisaged a defensive line running along the Dyle and Meuse rivers.

There were obviously some difficulties to be overcome on the way, for the *Luftwaffe* was busy overhead all the time, and it provided the baptism of Allied troops by dive-bombing. It took time for them to become accustomed to the nerve-shaking howl which accompanied it. Moreover, the violence and speed of the German advance and the seemingly continuous *Luftwaffe* attacks had spread panic among the civilian population, and the roads over which the Allied troops were travelling were soon choked by refugees fleeing ahead of Bock's advancing infantry.

Nevertheless, by the evening of 14 May, the Allied line was formed. From the mouth of the Scheldt to just north of Antwerp stood three divisions of the French Seventh Army; the 80km (50 miles) southeast to Louvain were held by 13 divisions of the Belgian army; between Louvain and Wavre, the front was held by the BEF and from Wavre to Namur by six divisions of the French First Army. Many of the battalion and brigade commanders were dismayed by the fragmentary

Left: German operations in the West began as the Allies expected, with an advance into Holland and Belgium. What came as a surprise was the massive armoured assault through the Ardennes.

51

Above: A German MG34 machine gun team in action. The MG34 was the first true general-purpose machine gun, able to lay down sustained fire from a tripod but light enough to be used as a squad support weapon when fitted with a bipod.

nature of the defences they now occupied, and their troops were equally unhappy. They had spent the winter preparing extensive field fortifications along the French border, and now they were expected to hold back the advancing *Wehrmacht* from defensive positions which at best were rudimentary, and many cases were non-existent. At the same time, the divisional and higher commanders were alarmed by news of events further to the south. But, as yet, none of them were aware of the fact that Bock's slowly advancing Army Group was in fact 'the matador's cloak' tempting the mass of the Allied armies forward into the trap that would release Kleist's Panzer Group for the killing thrust.

Allied Collapse

After sucking the Allied mobile forces northwards, Bock was tasked with securing Holland before moving southwards into Belgium and France, providing the anvil to the hammer of the Panzers heading for the French coast. The first task for the Germans was to take key fortifications around which the Dutch and Belgian defences were based. The imposing concrete and steel fortress at Eben Emael had already fallen to a glider assault. Other paratroopers were needed to secure the bridges that made it possible to operate across Holland's vast canal network and drive for the major Dutch cities near the coast.

By 13 May, the German Eighteenth Army under General Georg von Kuechler was pushing into 'Fortress Holland', crossing bridges that had been seized by paratroopers in the previous days. Near Breda they encountered the French Seventh Army under Henri Giraud, which had moved along the coast through Belgium and into Holland. The French were driven back towards Antwerp.

The Dutch destruction of the key bridges across the Ijssel and the flooding of much of the countryside meant that the German push towards Amsterdam, which was spearheaded by the *Leibstandarte* SS, was slowed considerably. Since Hitler did not want his 'show troops' to get bogged down in an infantry slogging match, they were moved south on 13 May to join with the SS-VT regiments and the 9th Panzer Division in the drive on Rotterdam. German *Fallschirmjäger* had already captured the key Moerdijk bridges intact, and the way into the city was open. On the morning of the 14th, the SS men accompanying the Panzers relieved the lightly armed paratroopers holding the Moerdijk bridge, having taken over 4000 prisoners during the advance.

Dutch resistance, though patchy, was holding up the German timetable. The German high command issued an ultimatum, threatening to destroy Rotterdam by artillery and air bombardment unless Dutch resistance ceased. The Dutch, cut off from their British and French allies, had no choice but to comply. However, although the artillery bombardment was cancelled, the orders did not reach the *Luftwaffe*, and Rotterdam was bombed into ruin. Immediately after the bombing, the *Leibstandarte* SS moved into the city. At one point, they saw a number of armed Dutch soldiers and opened fire. Unfortunately for the SS men, the Dutch soldiers had been part of a local surrender, which was being accepted by *Luftwaffe* General Kurt Student. The *Leibstandarte* fire seriously wounded Student, the founder of the German parachute force. He survived to lead the invasion of Crete a year later.

On 13 May, the Queen of the Netherlands and much of the Dutch Government took ship at the Hague, heading for England and exile. General Henri Winkelmen, the commander of the Dutch army, then surrendered. Further south, von Reichenau's Sixth Army poured across the Albert Canal into Belgium. The Belgian army fell back to the line of the River Dyle, where it was joined by elements of the BEF and by General Georges Blanchard's First French Army. By 15 May, some 35 Allied divisions were concentrated between Namur and Antwerp. The German Sixth Army was probing their hastily built defences, while the Eighteenth Army was pushing southwards out of Holland and threatening to take the Anglo/French/Belgian force in the flank.

However, even as they prepared to take on Bock's armies, the Allies were hit by shocking news from the southeast. The French centre had been shattered by new German forces, and all of the Allied troops in Belgium were in danger of being cut off. The campaign in the Low Countries was all but over, and the German plan was, with a few minor exceptions, working as predicted. Bock's advance into Holland had drawn the Allies northwards. Now Rundstedt's armour had been unleashed through the Ardennes, and the Panzers were rampaging through northern France.

'Germany has bombed Rotterdam today, and Utrecht is threatened with destruction. To save the civilian population, I believe to be justified to order the troops under your command to stop fighting.'

General Winkelman, Dutch army commander, 14 May 1940

SS COMBAT UNITS

The armed SS was established after Hitler came to power in 1933. It was designed to provide a politically reliable force to act as a counterbalance to the *Wehrmacht*. Initially it comprised the members of Hitler's bodyguard, the *Leibstandarte*, together with a number of *Politsiche Bereitschaften*, or Political Emergency Squads whose primary function had been to use violent measures against party opponents. These became the SS-*Verfügungstruppe*, or SS-VT.

By the time of the *Anschluss* with Austria, the armed SS had grown dramatically. In addition to the 2600 men of the *Leibstandarte*, there were three SS-VT *Standarten*, or regiments, derived from the *Politische Bereitschaften*. The three regiments were given the names *Deutschland*, *Germania* and *Der Führer* and were trained and equipped as motorized infantry. The three *Standarten* would become the nucleus of the SS-VT division, which saw action in Poland and France. In 1940, the division was renamed *Das Reich*, and it was joined by the *Totenkopf* division, formed around a nucleus of the SS *Totenkopfverbände*, Theodore Eicke's concentration camp guards.

The Battle of France

One of the principal aims of Adolph Hitler's military policy was to see the destruction of France, the enemy that had humiliated Germany after World War I. The invasion of the Low Countries was nothing more than a trap to draw the Allied armies out of position while the *Wehrmacht* prepared its killer blow – a Panzer thrust through the Ardennes.

Once the attack in the West was launched, German forces stormed across Holland and Belgium just as the Allies expected, the imposing concrete and steel fortress at Eben Emael falling to a crack unit of paratroops who landed by glider right on the roof. However, the forces under General von Bock – 30 infantry divisions of Army Group B – were actually a feint. Their intent was designed to convince the Allies that the Germans were following the same old plan which had failed in earlier wars.

The Drive through the Ardennes

The real punch came through the Ardennes, where the 44 divisions of von Runstedt's Army Group A, including seven Panzer divisions under von Kleist, planned to catch the Allies by surprise. The bulk of the French troops were contained in the massive defences of the Maginot line, guarding against an attack across the German border. But the huge works did not cover the Belgian border, French planners having considered that a major attack through the Ardennes was impossible.

The German plan quickly became a reality. Encountering little resistance from Belgian troops in the Ardennes, the Panzer divisions headed down the dirt roads in alarmingly dense columns. Crashing through the 'impassable' forests and hills as though on a peacetime exercise, brushing aside the French light cavalry unit that had been sent out to 'delay' them, the three divisions of General Guderian's Panzer Corps were across the French frontier and had reached the Meuse on each side of Sedan by the afternoon of 12 May.

Military traffic police have seldom had a more decisive impact on a campaign: thousands of vehicles kept to schedule and by the evening of 12 May, German armour controlled the right bank of the Meuse up as far as Dinant. Here, in 1870, the French Emperor Napoleon III had been decisively beaten by the Prussians, going into captivity with his surviving soldiers while revolution broke out in Paris. Seventy years later, the

Opposite: The German invasion of France came after operations in the Low Countries had drawn the main Allied field armies northwards. Bypassing the Maginot Line, the Wehrmacht *was soon rampaging through northern France, spreading havoc and confusion.*

French commander-in-chief, 68-year old General Maurice Gamelin, expected German units to emerge from the Ardennes at some stage in the battle. But since he did not anticipate anything more than a light, probing force, the 9th Army, assigned to protect the area, was stretched more thinly than other French armies.

Once they had got over the shock of the German arrival on the Meuse, the French High Command estimated that the crossing would take at least four days to organize and two to carry out. In fact, the *Wehrmacht* was across the river in strength within 24 hours. On 13 May, Guderian's infantry paddled across the Meuse in rubber dinghies. At the same time, a *Luftwaffe* force of 300 twin-engine bombers and 200 Stukas pulverized the French defences.

The dive-bombers attacked with particular accuracy, knocking out key French gun positions. The foot soldiers were across by 3 p.m. Combat engineers had a ferry

Right: Bursting through the Ardennes, the troops of von Runstedt's Army Group A reached the Meuse at Sedan on 12 May. They were across the river one day later, ahead of combat engineers who would build the bridges needed by the panzers.

operational in an hour, and by 4.30 p.m. a bridge was in place and the tanks could cross to the far bank. French counterattacks came too little and too late. All the first-line troops had been committed to the northern flank. The Allies' strategy unravelled as the Panzer divisions fanned out, racing ahead of their infantry and threatening to cut off the British and French armies in Belgium.

Pushing into France

By the morning of 14 May, Guderian had two bridgeheads consolidating, while up at Dinant the 7th Panzer Division of Colonel-General Hermann Hoth's XV Panzer Corps (commanded by Major-General Erwin Rommel) had formed yet another bridgehead in the face of desperate but sporadic French resistance.

Early on 15 May, the flood burst into France. From each of the bridgeheads, the Panzers roared out, preceded on every front of advance by a cloud of screaming Stukas, covered against attack from British or French fighters by marauding Messerschmitts. Refugees choked the roads. It was bad enough that they were being harried by the *Luftwaffe,* but the helpless civilians were also bullied by frightened and demoralized soldiers and gendarmes of their own side. All too soon, they were being forced into the ditches by strange, ominous, foreign vehicles manned by confident young Germans who waved triumphantly at them as they passed. The *Wehrmacht* troops rarely deliberately harmed fleeing civilians, but in their wake they left an impression of total invincibility.

That evening, German Panzers were reported only 19km (12 miles) from Laon. Daladier, now France's Minister of National Defence, ordered a counterattack, but the French commander-in-chief, General Gamelin, replied that he had no reserves because the bulk of French strength was locked up in the outflanked Maginot Line. At the same time, Gamelin announced that he could no longer take responsibility for the defence of Paris, and he issued orders for a general retreat of all French forces in Belgium. A copy of these orders came, solely by good fortune, to the notice of the British commander-in-chief, Lord Gort, enabling him to ensure that the British Expeditionary Force (BEF) divisions on the Dyle were not left there on their own.

The scale of the catastrophe was now apparent and the French Government prepared to evacuate Paris. With political will equally paralyzed in London – Winston Churchill had only just replaced Neville Chamberlain as prime minister – it was left to Gort to choose between abandoning the French or hazarding most of Britain's tiny regular army in a last attempt to salvage the situation.

In the face of apparently imminent disaster, Churchill flew to Paris on the evening of 16 May. He had been woken by a telephone call from the French premier, Paul Reynaud. In a devastating indication of French morale, Reynaud announced that 'We have been defeated! We are beaten; we have lost the battle!' Churchill's aim was both to put some iron into the French political backbone and to discover for himself the true state of affairs. These became distressingly obvious when in answer to his question 'Ou est la masse de manoeuvre?' ('Where is the strategic reserve?'), Gamelin answered 'Aucune!' ('None!'). But even at this unsettling news, Churchill refused to abandon hope.

There were still considerable French forces to the south of the German breakthrough, he noted, and even larger forces, including the BEF, to the north. Between them, could they not first manoeuvre to channel and then contain the German breakthrough, then counterattack from both north and south and so cut the enemy spearheads off from their main sources of supply and support?

'Well, I don't think you'll get across the river in the first place!'

General Busch's (erroneous) reaction to General Guderian's estimate of being able to operate south of the Meuse within five days of the offensive through the Ardennes.

Attempting a Defence

In the depths of their despondency, the French leaders were reluctant to admit the practicability of such a scheme, pleading lack of air strength unless Churchill were to abandon all thought of retaining RAF fighter squadrons for the defence of Britain and send them all to France instead. Even then, it seemed most likely that the German forces would be either on the Channel coast or in Paris – or both – in a matter of days, in which case the British and French armies to the north most probably faced at least disintegration and, unless a general armistice saved them, possibly total destruction.

Below: The French High Command estimated that it would take the Germans four days to cross the Meuse at Sedan. Guderian's troops, who had seized control of the East bank on both sides of the city, were across in force in less than 24 hours.

Churchill was home by the following morning, but before he left he managed to instil something of his own dogged courage into the French leadership, so that they at least agreed to order some form of counterattack on the German spearheads as he had suggested. Yet the sluggish pace of Allied military planning meant that it would be four days before the counterattack could be attempted, and even then it was bungled. By the evening of 20 May, Guderian's Panzer spearheads had reached Abbeville at the mouth of the Somme, and at this point their line was as attenuated as it ever would be. If the *Wehrmacht* was vulnerable to a determined counterattack, it was here.

On 21 May, four British infantry brigades and a tank brigade were launched southwards from Arras, in theory supported by two French infantry divisions on one flank and one light mechanized division on the other, while equally strong French forces

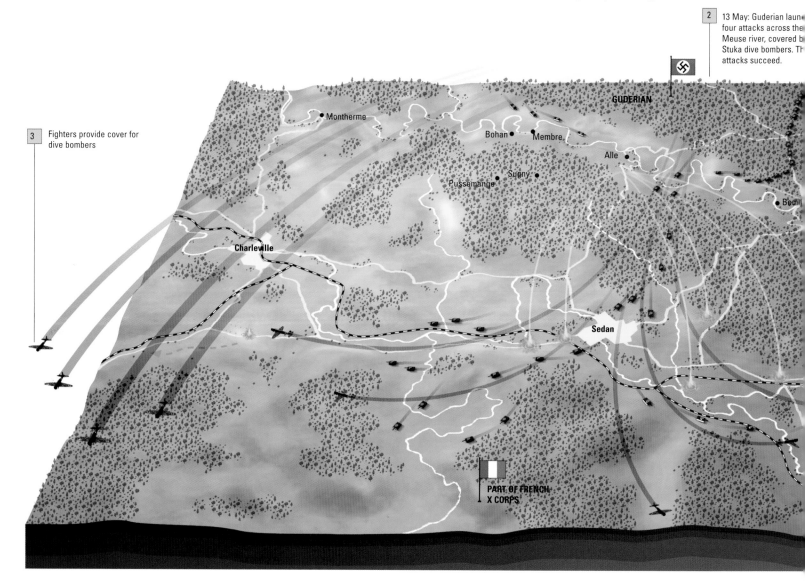

2 | 13 May: Guderian laun[c] four attacks across the Meuse river, covered b[y] Stuka dive bombers. Th[e] attacks succeed.

3 | Fighters provide cover for dive bombers

Montherme

Bohan • Membre •

Alle •

Sugny •

Pussemange •

Beuill

GUDERIAN

Charleville

Sedan

PART OF FRENCH
X CORPS

were assumed to be attacking up from the south to meet them. In the event, only the British forces and the French light mechanized division moved at all. They did manage to inflict a stinging reverse on the SS *Totenkopf* Division, who later took out their frustrations by massacring 100 British prisoners of war at Le Paradis, the first of numerous such atrocities committed by the SS. The British tanks, however, quickly found themselves blocked by Rommel's 7th Panzer Division. Rommel used his 88mm (3.46in) Flak guns to engage the heavily armoured British infantry tanks, which were virtually invulnerable to smaller German anti-tank weapons. After a brisk battle, which at least managed to worry Rommel seriously, the 7th Panzer Division drove the British back to their original positions and threatened them with encirclement.

By the evening of 23 May, Gort was withdrawing the British brigades further north, and two days later it became evident to him that only a rapid retreat to the coast and

Panzer strike through the Ardennes
12–14 May, 1940

Armoured advance

Air support

Artillery support

French retreat

1 12 May: XIX Panzer Corps Commanded by Gen. Guderian advances using country lanes and tracks through the lightly defended Ardennes forest. It quickly brushes aside the French forces.

4 14 May: French forces harassed by armoured and air attacks fall back, unable to reorganize. Efforts by Ravigny's XXI Corps to mount an armoured counterstroke are defeated by the power of Guderian's Corps.

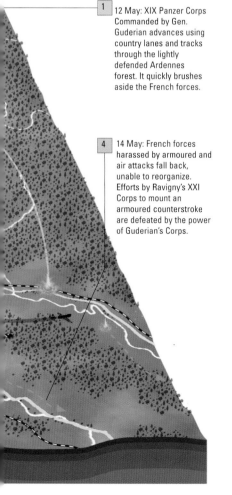

evacuation to England would save even a quarter of his command. On his own responsibility, he issued the necessary orders: the British III Corps withdrew to the beaches on each side of Dunkirk, I Corps fell back to hold the western flank with one French division on their right and the British II Corps on their left, while the Belgian army held the eastern end of the perimeter. However, on 28 May King Leopold of Belgium signed an armistice with the Germans, the Belgian army ceased to exist, and a large gap yawned on the left of the British positions.

The gap was filled during the night by a manoeuvre of extraordinary difficulty carried out with admirable efficiency by the 3rd Infantry Division under command of Major-

Above: Soldiers from the 'Das Reich' division take a break to eat during the rapid German advance through northern France.

General Montgomery. It is not too much to say that this operation saved the British Expeditionary Force. And then fate stepped in. The *Führer* ordered his Panzers to stop, allowing the British a breathing space in which to organize one of the greatest evacuation operations in history.

Operation Dynamo

Operation Dynamo was the attempt to evacuate the British Army, and as many French soldiers as possible, from the trap into which they had been lured. Over a thousand boats took part in this evacuation. They varied in size from a Royal Navy anti-aircraft cruiser down to dinghies, which were sailed across the Channel by their owners from a hundred tiny slips along the south coast or along the reaches of the Thames. At least 250 of these craft were sunk and many of the yacht owners were killed or wounded, but an astonishingly large number of soldiers were saved to fight again, and to form the basis of new armies. The highest hopes before the evacuation began were that perhaps 50,000 men might escape capture or worse; in the event, 338,226 reached the shores of Britain during those miraculous nine days, of which, on Churchill's insistence, over 100,000 were French. He had returned to Paris on 31 May, and there agreed that British troops would share in holding the rear guard, and that French troops in the bridgehead would be evacuated in the same proportion as the British.

As it happened, French formations were fighting furiously to the south of the bridgehead (thus holding back powerful German forces that would otherwise have been free to attack Dunkirk), and these never reached the sea. Many of those which did arrive towards the end of the operation refused the chance to escape, and the last ships to sail were almost empty. As quite a large number of French troops who did get away, quickly decided that they did not care for life in Britain and chose to return to France (where most of them soon found themselves in German prison camps), Churchill's well-meant gesture was to a great extent wasted.

To the British people, however, the escape of the bulk of the BEF at Dunkirk was a miracle. To such an extent did their spirits rise, indeed, that Churchill found it necessary to sound a cautionary note. 'We must be very careful not to assign to this deliverance the attributes of a victory,' he said in his report to Parliament. 'Wars are not won by evacuations.' Yet the miracle of Dunkirk kept Britain in the war.

German Consolidation

In spite of stiffening resistance in places like Normandy, some of Hitler's Panzers turned west, moving with incredible speed to secure the Atlantic coast. Others sped south,

---

HITLER'S 'STOP ORDER'

Why did Hitler order his Panzers to stop their advance against the British around Dunkirk? There have been several suggestions. It may have been a political gesture to allow the British time to come to terms with defeat and sue for peace. Hitler might also have been worried about the terrain, stopping his forces to prevent the Panzers from getting bogged down amid the canals and marshes around Dunkirk. However, the most commonly held belief is that the order was intended to allow Hermann Göring to make good on his boast that the *Luftwaffe* could finish the job. In the event, the Germans met with stiff resistance from the Spitfires and Hurricanes of the RAF, and in spite of some successes were never able seriously to impede the British evacuation from Dunkirk.

Left: Heinz Guderian, the architect of the German panzer force, led the spearhead of the Wehrmacht's advance. As with most German Generals, he led from the front, using a well-equipped communications half-track. Note the Enigma coding machine being used by the operator nearest the camera.

Right: Cut off by the rapid German advance, the bulk of the British Expeditionary Force retreated to the coast at Dunkirk. Most were saved by the Royal Navy in Operation Dynamo. Many were plucked off the beaches by an armada of small craft that had been pressed into service for the purpose.

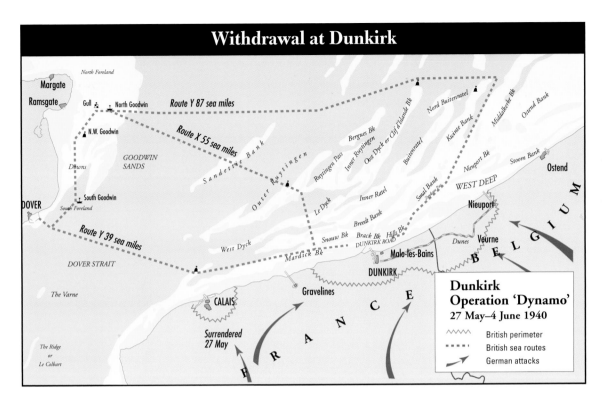

Withdrawal at Dunkirk

Margate
North Foreland
Ramsgate
Gull *North Goodwin*
Route Y 87 sea miles
N.W. Goodwin
Route X 55 sea miles
GOODWIN SANDS
Downs
Sandettie Bank
Outer Ruytingen
Nord Buitenratel
Kuene Bank
Middelkerke Bk
Ostend Bank
Bergues Bk
Inner Ruytingen
Oost Dyck or Clif d'Islande Bk
Buitenratel
Ostend Bank
DOVER
South Goodwin
South Foreland
Ruytingen Pass
Le Dyck
Inner Ratel
Small Bank
Nieuport Bk
Stroom Bank
Ostend
WEST DEEP
Route Y 39 sea miles
West Dyck
Snouw Bk
Breedt Bank
Brack Bk
Hill Bk
Nieuport
DOVER STRAIT
Mardick Bk
DUNKIRK ROAD
Malo-les-Bains
Dunes
Veurne
BELGIUM
The Varne
Gravelines
DUNKIRK
**Dunkirk
Operation 'Dynamo'
27 May–4 June 1940**
The Ridge or Le Colbart
CALAIS
Surrendered 27 May
FRANCE

∿∿∿ British perimeter
∙∙∙∙∙ British sea routes
➤ German attacks

Left: *In the nine days of Operation Dynamo, 338,226 French and British soldiers were taken off the beach by a fleet of over 900 vessels, ranging from cabin cruisers and trawlers to cross-channel ferries and destroyers. More than 50,000 vehicles were abandoned, and the evacuation was made possible only by a valiant rearguard action by 40,000 French troops.*

completely bypassing the Maginot line, leaving more than 400,000 French troops bewildered and demoralized in their suddenly useless fortifications. Once the German army had occupied Dunkirk and the French coast as far west as Abbeville and the mouth of the Somme, there was nothing except Hitler's orders to stop them turning south and driving down into the body of France; as early as 29 May, the *Führer* had intimated to both Rundstedt and Bock that his next plans would be to 'settle the French army's account'. Britain could wait, or better still, come to terms. He was convinced that with Germany and its partners in control of Europe, the British would eventually have to make peace.

As a result, even before the Dunkirk evacuation was over, Bock had deputed his Eighteenth Army to clear up Belgium and press on westwards, and had directed the remainder of his Army Group B down to take position along the line of the Somme, alongside von Rundstedt's triumphant infantry and Panzer divisions closing up to the coast. By 5 June, the 10 Panzer divisions of both army groups had been redeployed into five armoured corps (three under Bock, two under Rundstedt), and that morning at dawn, preceded as usual by clouds of dive-bombers, two of them burst out of bridgeheads west of Amiens and drove for the Seine.

'The second great offensive is starting today with formidable new resources!' announced Hitler, while General Weygand, who had been recalled from the Levant to take command of the French army when it became obvious that Gamelin had lost control, appealed to his troops: 'May the thought of our afflicted country inspire in you an unflinching resolve to stand firm. The fate of your country and the future of our children depend on your firmness.' This was hardly the most inspiring message for troops in a desperate situation.

Nevertheless, French troops hurriedly assembled into 'hedgehogs' around what their commanders considered strategic nodal points and held back the flood for a few hours, destroying the leading Panzer formations as they came within range, and giving the German commanders pause for thought. 'The French are putting up strong opposition,' reported one of them. 'We are seeing a new French way of fighting.'

*Right: The crew of a
massive French Char B
tank surrenders to
German infantry.
French tanks were not
concentrated like those
of the* Wehrmacht: *they
were distributed in
penny packets among
infantry formations.*

But in a very short time the 'hedgehogs' were being bypassed, and by 11 June Hoth's XV Panzer Corps controlled the Seine from Vernon to Le Havre. Two of Bock's Panzer corps, XXXIX and XLI, had passed the Chemins des Dames and were driving down between Rheims and the Aisne, and his Ninth Army was heading straight for Paris. The following day, Rommel's 7th Panzer Division reached St Valery and captured the western flank of the French Tenth Army, including the survivors of the British 51st Highland Division under General Fortune. Two days later, on 14 June, German troops drove into Paris, which was saved from damage by an 'open city' declaration from the French Government as it hastily left for Bordeaux.

It must be said that the spectacular advance of the German army was aided throughout by the dilatoriness and uncertainty of the French High Command. Under Gamelin, this had been a major factor in precipitating disaster, and under Weygand it showed little improvement. Even the 'hedgehog' formations were described by one French general as: 'only a last resort to enable these weak but brave troops to resist with honour before being overwhelmed'. Reynaud, the French premier, when asked on the evening of 7 June if hope was fading, replied, 'No, it can't be! And yet I know that the battle is lost!'

Some French divisions, nevertheless, defended their positions resolutely, especially on the eastern sector, where the 14th Infantry Division under General de Lattre de Tassigny held XLI Panzer Corps (and in one action took 800 prisoners). A little further west at Rethel the 2nd

*Opposite: A young
German soldier poses
for the camera in the
advance towards
Dunkirk. He is armed
with a Kar-98 rifle and
has a grenade tucked into
his belt.*

64

Division for a whole day fought off every attack mounted against it. Instead of continuing to assault these positions, the Panzers found the space between and drove through to Rheims. Even at the lower levels of the French army, there seems to have been no understanding of the impracticability of static defence against strong and mobile armour. At one point, an armoured battle did take place, when a counterattack was put in by a formation of French heavy 'B' tanks – the strongest in the world at that time – which worried Guderian when he saw his anti-tank shells ricocheting 'off the thick plate of the French tanks'. The French armour drove north towards a small village called Perthes, where they rescued an infantry regiment that had been surrounded – only to find that they were surrounded themselves and out of petrol!

Everywhere else, though, the French divisions were overwhelmed or cut off and control from headquarters lost. As the Panzers cut deeper into the heart of France, and the grey-clad columns marching so cheerfully behind them occupied more villages and towns, French morale plummeted and the French army moved closer to disintegration.

The Fall of France

As early as 9 June, Weygand had stated, 'our armies are fighting the last possible defensive battle. If this attempt fails, they are doomed to rapid destruction.' Two days later, he moved his GHQ out of Paris to Briare on the Loire, where that evening the last of the Anglo-French conferences was held. Churchill arrived accompanied by Eden and Generals Ismay and Spears, while General Weygand was supported by Marshal Petain and attended – somewhat guardedly, one suspects – by Brigadier de Gaulle. Weygand opened the meeting with the declaration that 'the last line

CHURCHILL'S ORATORY

During his speech to Parliament following the British evacuation from Dunkirk, Winston Churchill delivered what was to become one of the most famous passages of rhetoric in British history:

'Even though large tracts of Europe and many old and famous States have fallen or may fall into the grip of the Gestapo and all the odious apparatus of Nazi rule, we shall not flag or fail. We shall go on to the end. We shall fight in France, we shall fight on the sea and oceans, we shall fight with growing confidence and growing strength in the air; we shall defend our island, whatever the cost may be. We shall fight on the beaches, we shall fight on the landing-grounds, we shall fight in the fields and in the streets, we shall fight in the hills; we shall never surrender; and even if, which I do not for a moment believe, this island or a large part of it were subjugated and starving, then our Empire beyond the seas, armed and guarded by the British Fleet, would carry on the struggle, until, in God's good time, the New World, with all its power and might, steps forth to the rescue and liberation of the Old.'

of defence has been overrun and all the reserves are used up. We are on a knife-edge, and don't know which way we will fall from one minute to the next.' When eventually the argument and discussions died away, he closed the conference with the warning: 'Once our disposition is upset, and that won't be long now, there is no hope of reforming it, because of our lack of reserves. In this case, I can see no way of preventing an invasion of the whole of France.'

'These three hours of discussions achieved nothing,' wrote de Gaulle later. 'I thought how empty this chatter was, because it was not directed towards the only viable solution; recovery across the sea.' This was indeed a solution that Weygand was to reject with venom. On the evening of the day Paris fell, Reynaud suggested that Weygand should follow the example of the Dutch chief of staff, and surrender to the Germans the army on metropolitan soil, while the Government went to North Africa with the whole of the French navy, whatever formations of the French air force could fly there, and every French soldier who could escape. From there, it could continue the struggle alongside Britain – and America and every other freedom-loving country as soon as they saw fit to join in. 'I rejected the proposal with indignation!' Weygand claimed later. 'I would never

Above: The Wehrmacht *was still largely equipped with light tanks in 1940, but significant numbers of larger and more capable Panzer IIIs and Panzer IVs were now making an appearance. The Panzer IV seen here was armed with a short-barrelled 7.5-cm (3in) cannon.*

Above: The rapid destruction of the French Army left tens of thousands of Poilus – *ordinary French conscripts – without leaders. Some tried to get home: others wandered aimlessly through the ruins of France. Many were rounded up and taken into captivity by the Germans.*

agree to inflicting such shame on our flag! This would have been the ultimate crime, damning and doing irreparable harm to the military honour of our nation....I cannot think of such an ignominious proposal without a shiver of disgust!'

What 'ignominy' Weygand saw in this proposal is difficult to understand, especially as only eight days later he was to order the remaining French army formations in and behind the Maginot Line, some 400,000 troops, to 'ask for a cessation of fighting, with war honours'. Under the French Code of Military Justice, the 'ultimate crime' is 'to surrender without having exhausted every means of defence', so the behaviour of the French C-in-C during June 1940 presents something of an enigma.

On 16 June, Reynaud resigned and Marshal Petain took his place, determined to obtain an armistice from the Germans as quickly as possible and to establish a form of government of which Hitler would approve. By 20 June, German troops were in Lyons and Grenoble in the south, along the Swiss border to the east and controlling the Biscay coast to the west as far south as Royan. Mussolini, who had declared war on both France and Britain 10 days earlier, was endeavouring furiously to prod his soldiers into crossing the Franco-Italian frontier and capturing Nice before the Germans got there.

They were prevented by the events of the following day. At 3.30 p.m. on 21 June, a French delegation headed by General Huntziger was led into the very railway carriage at Compiègne in which the 1918 Armistice had been signed. Hitler had arrived with an entourage including Göring, Keitel, Ribbentrop and Hess. He read the inscription at the museum of Compiègne, which condemned 'the criminal pride of the German Empire'. His face bore a look described as 'combining hatred, scorn, revenge, and triumph'. He did not stay beyond listening to the preamble of the terms, and then joked with his subordinates in a rare display of good humour.

Little negotiation took place, for Hitler knew very well that he had won, and any arguments which Huntziger might have put up had to be referred back to Petain, who tended to agree wholeheartedly with Hitler. Forever the shrewd politician, Hitler knew just how much to give. For appearances' sake, he had to let the French people convince themselves that French national pride had been salvaged even in defeat.

Map, page 66: After the fall of Paris, France's defeat became a rout. German columns raced west, southwest and southeast. Within a week, they had reached the Brittany coast, the Spanish border, the Alpes Maritimes and the border with Switzerland.

Armistice Signed

Article three of the Armistice acknowledged Petain's government as the government of all metropolitan France, as well as of her overseas territories. France was allowed to keep her empire and the illusion of her national sovereignty. The promise was also made that the French battle fleet in Toulon and other Mediterranean ports would remain there under French command. Hitler was very satisfied with this, for one of his main fears had been that the powerful French battleships might join the Royal Navy.

By 7 p.m. on 22 June, the Armistice had been signed, the limits of German occupation agreed. But the terms were a sham. Hitler wanted to punish France. No particular date was given for the release of the two million French soldiers in captivity. The Vichy army was to have no more than 100,000 men, and in a further echo of Versailles, the French people were to pay not only reparations to Germany, but also had to finance the occupation.

Hitler, usually uninterested in visiting the places that he had crushed, made an exception for Paris. The amateur architect visited the French capital during his trip, accompanied by Albert Speer and his favourite sculptor Arno Breker. The city seemed deserted – its population had fallen from three million to 800,000 in the exodus that accompanied the German advance. The *Führer* visited the Eiffel Tower, paid homage at Napoleon's tomb in the Hotel des Invalides, and commented on the ugliness of the Sacre Coeur. 'It would have pained me greatly if I had had to destroy Paris,' he later added. He marvelled at having laid low the arrogant and decadent French whose love of culture, he claimed, had so undermined her martial spirit.

The humiliation of France was complete. She had been betrayed by leaders who did not have the stomach for a fight. In Paris, as the posters and German radio broadcast the terms of the disgrace, the people wept. By contrast, the German public shared Hitler's joy, and the *Führer* enjoyed a Roman-style Triumph on his return to Berlin. The streets were strewn with flowers and lined with adoring crowds. They were celebrating the man that in seven years of struggle had transformed Germany. Little more than a pariah among nations in 1933, the Reich was now the master of Europe.

The German Administration

On 25 June, Marshal Petain announced over French radio, 'Honour is saved! We must now turn our efforts to the future. A new order is beginning!' Seventeen days later, he

'Under the deeply moving impression of the capitulation of France, I congratulate you and the whole German Wehrmacht on the mighty victory granted by God.'

Former Kaiser Wilhelm II, letter to Hitler, July 1940

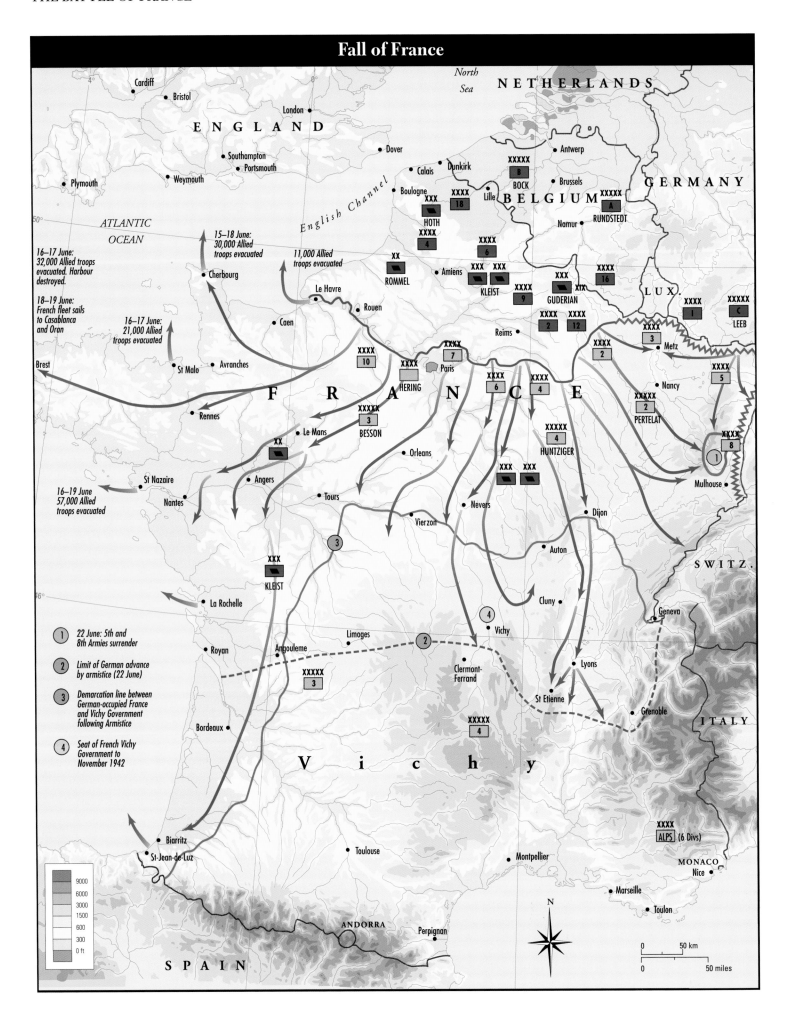

Fall of France

16–17 June:
32,000 Allied troops
evacuated. Harbour
destroyed.

18–19 June:
French fleet sails
to Casablanca
and Oran

16–17 June:
21,000 Allied
troops evacuated

15–18 June:
30,000 Allied
troops evacuated

11,000 Allied
troops evacuated

16–19 June
57,000 Allied
troops evacuated

1 — 22 June: 5th and
8th Armies surrender

2 — Limit of German advance
by armistice (22 June)

3 — Demarcation line between
German-occupied France
and Vichy Government
following Armistice

4 — Seat of French Vichy
Government to
November 1942

NETHERLANDS

North
Sea

GERMANY

BELGIUM

ENGLAND

ATLANTIC
OCEAN

English Channel

Cardiff
Bristol
London
Southampton
Portsmouth
Weymouth
Plymouth
Dover
Calais
Dunkirk
Boulogne
Lille
Antwerp
Brussels
Namur

BOCK
RUNDSTEDT
HOTH
KLEIST
ROMMEL
Amiens
GUDERIAN
LUX.
LEEB
Metz
Nancy
PERTELAT
Mulhouse

Cherbourg
Le Havre
Rouen
Caen
Reims
St Malo
Avranches
Brest
HERING
Paris
BESSON
Rennes
Le Mans
Orleans
HUNTZIGER
Angers
St Nazaire
Nantes
Tours
Vierzon
Nevers
Dijon
Auton
Cluny
SWITZ.
KLEIST
La Rochelle
Limoges
Vichy
Lyons
Royan
Angouleme
Clermont-
Ferrand
St Etienne
Grenoble
Geneva
ITALY
Bordeaux

V i c h y

ALPS (6 Divs)

MONACO
Nice
Biarritz
St-Jean-de-Luz
Toulouse
Montpellier
Marseille
Toulon

ANDORRA
Perpignan

SPAIN

N

0   50 km
0   50 miles

9000
6000
3000
1500
600
300
0 ft

indicated the form of the new order with an announcement of the 'First Bill of the Constitution', which opened: 'We, Philippe Petain Marshal of France, in accordance with the Constitutional Law of the 20th of July, hereby assume the functions of the Head of the French State.' The Republic was abolished; Parliament was dismissed.

Although many attempts were later made to blame her defeat on social causes which had sapped the morale of the rank and file of her army, it should be remembered that one of the aphorisms of France's most famous soldier, Napoleon Bonaparte, had been: 'There are no bad soldiers, only bad officers.'

Hitler had achieved such a complete and unexpectedly rapid victory over France that he could not immediately decide what to do with her. Paralyzed by his success, he lost out on bringing down Britain as well. For the moment, he was content to look at the white cliffs of Dover across the mere 32km (20 miles) of sea that separated them from Nazi Europe. Hitler never did develop any clearly defined long-term strategy for France. In the event, he treated it much as he did other occupied territories, looting the country to fuel the aims of his foreign policy elsewhere.

The Nazis quickly set about dismembering the French state. A small area of south-eastern France was allocated to the Italians, and a total exclusion zone around the Pas-de-Calais was established to protect the Reich from the area nearest England. Both of

Above: General von Briesen, military governor of Paris, takes the salute as the victorious Wehrmacht *parades down the Champs Elysees. The city fell on 14 June: France's new leader, General Petain, was to sue for an armistice a week later.*

Opposite: French North African troops peel potatoes in a German prisoner of war camp. These were some of the lucky ones: colonial troops captured by SS units, especially Africans from south of the Sahara or from West Africa, were considered to be subhuman and were often shot out of hand.

these zones were greatly extended after 1942. The rest of France was split between the 'zone occupée' and the 'zone libre', the latter to be controlled directly by the regime established at Vichy. Ordinary French people soon nicknamed the zones 'Zone O' and 'Zone NoNo'.

Hitler, always a pragmatist, was content to leave some part of France with a semblance of self-government. It suited his needs, as occupied territories were less of a drain on finances if they could govern themselves. Petain could rule in the south until the *Führer* determined otherwise. On the occasions that the two leaders met, Hitler could barely conceal his contempt for a man and a nation once great that had fallen so low.

The French spirit was so cowed by the German victory that in the early months of the occupation Hitler was able to maintain his grip on the country with a mere 30,000 troops – a ratio of just 1 German to every 1000 French citizens.

In Paris, the presence of the occupying power was quickly made evident when a vast Swastika was placed atop the Eiffel tower. The engineers doing the job had to climb the structure, the lifts having been sabotaged in a spirit of futile resistance by the departing French. And the legend *'Deutschland Siegt an allen Fronten'* – Germany Victorious on all Fronts – was placed on the Palais Bourbon in enormous letters 13m (43ft) high.

At the earliest opportunity, the German army staged a victory march down the Champs Élysées, and repeated the exercise every day until the liberation of Paris. The street signs were now in Gothic lettering, and everywhere was the presence of field-grey uniforms.

In just a few weeks, Norway, Denmark, Holland, Belgium and France had capitulated to the mightly *Wehrmacht*. Only Britain remained to oppose Hitler as master of Europe, and it was towards the British Isles that Hitler now turned his attention.

Britain Alone

France's collapse in June 1940 gave Hitler the victory he wanted most, since he blamed the French for the most vindictive terms of the Treaty of Versailles. However, the British, now led by Prime Minister Winston Churchill, adamantly refused to accept defeat.

The German high command knew that it was essential to keep Britain under pressure, initially from the air and then by the threat of a seaborne invasion. On July 16, Hitler issued Directive 16, ordering that plans for *Seelöwe* – Operation Sealion – be prepared, and engineers started converting large river barges into landing craft. There was a problem, however. Any force trying to cross the Channel would be at the mercy of the Royal Navy.

The first step in dealing with superior British sea power would be to win air superiority. The *Luftwaffe* was tasked with neutralizing the RAF. If the RAF could be eliminated, the *Luftwaffe* could, along with the *Kriegsmarine,* hold back the Royal Navy long enough for the German ground forces to be ferried across the Channel.

The *Luftwaffe* was the newest and most glamorous of Germany's combat arms. In 1939, Hermann Göring, creator of Hitler's air force, sent an order of the day to his men. 'I have done my best in the past few years' he said, 'to make our *Luftwaffe* the largest and most powerful in the world.' Within a year, that same *Luftwaffe* – which had not existed five years before – had spearheaded the all-conquering *Wehrmacht* as it rampaged its way to mastery of Europe. Only the stubborn British were holding out, but their defeat could only be a matter of time…

Air Supremacy

At the outbreak of war, the *Luftwaffe* comprised 302 *Staffeln* with 2370 operational crews and 2564 combat aircraft of all types. They were to enjoy considerable success in the first years of the war, and German aircrews were better trained and tactically superior to their opponents. As dawn broke on the morning of 1 September 1939, three Junkers Ju 87s of *Stukageschwader 1* came screaming down out of the sky, dropping bombs from a near vertical dive onto the Dirschau Bridge across the Vistula. Eleven minutes later, German Panzer divisions began pouring across the Polish frontier. Hitler's *Luftwaffe* had fired the opening shots of World War II.

Opposite: The crew of a Junkers Ju 88 prepares for a bombing mission over England. For the first time, the Luftwaffe *was to encounter an air force as determined, as well-equipped and as well organized as itself, and the Battle of Britain was to prove the first setback for Hitler's dreams of conquest.*

Above: A Heinkel He 111 passes over London's docks. The German decision to switch from attacking the Royal Air Force in favour of bombing cities gave the RAF a much needed respite.

The initial task for the 1600 aircraft of *Luftflottes 1* and *4* was to destroy the Polish air force. Air bases were heavily bombed by Heinkels and Dorniers, and obsolete Polish PZL fighters were hacked out of the sky by the *Luftwaffe's* Bf 109 fighters. Aerial opposition was wiped out within two days. The dive-bombers were tasked with attacking enemy troops and key communications targets. The Panzer formations used the Stukas as flying artillery, blasting any military opposition. In the process, the ugly crank-winged bombers spread fear and confusion amongst enemy troops and civilians.

By 9 September, German tanks were approaching Warsaw. Over the next week, while the capital held out, the *Wehrmacht* smashed what remained of Polish armed resistance, and then turned its attention on the city. Heavy artillery bombardment, followed by an aerial attack by the massed *Kampfgruppen*, left Warsaw in ruins, and the Poles capitulated on 27 September.

Although Britain and France had declared war on 3 September, there was little aerial activity over the cold winter of 1939/1940. Before the war, the British, like many others, believed that bombing alone could defeat Germany. However, although the *Luftwaffe* had been designed as an offensive weapon, German planners had not neglected the nation's defences. As a result, the RAF found the task to be far more difficult than expected.

The initial British raids in 1939 dropped only leaflets. Combat operations were limited to attacks on ports and coastal targets. In a daylight raid on Wilhelmshaven in 1939, 24 unescorted Wellington bombers were intercepted by radar-directed Messerschmitt Bf 109s, and 12 were shot down. This and similar experiences forced the RAF to switch to night operations.

In the spring, the *Luftwaffe* was again in action, supporting operations in Scandinavia. Close co-operation between land, sea and air elements saw the *Luftwaffe* transporting large numbers of troops in surprise air-landing assaults in Denmark and Norway, performing its customary close-support mission, and providing an anti-shipping strike force to counter the anticipated intervention by the Royal Navy.

The *Wehrmacht* launched its major assault in the west on 10 May 1940. Three entire Army Groups – 141 divisions – struck into France, Belgium and the Netherlands. *Luftwaffe* strength included 1100 medium bombers and 400 Stukas, escorted by 850 Bf

'Night gangsters! For this crime, I will exact a thousand-fold revenge!'

Adolf Hitler, after the RAF's first night bomber attack on shipyards at Bremen in 1940.

THE ORGANIZATION OF THE *LUFTWAFFE*

In September 1939, the *Luftwaffe* was organized into four *Luftflotten* (air fleets), but as the war progressed three more were added, including *Luftflotte Reich*, which was formed for the defence of Germany. Each *Luftflotte* had a strength of up to 1250 aircraft, grouped in a number of *Fliegerkorps*, or smaller *Fliegerdivisions*.

Both corps and division contained a number of *Geschwader* that equated roughly to an RAF Group or a USAF Wing. Each was divided into three *Gruppen*, in turn composed of three to four *Staffeln* (squadrons) of 12 aircraft. These were designated by type.

Kampfgeschwader operated the *Luftwaffe's* medium bombers. *Stukageschwader* were equipped with the dive-bombers that many Germans believed would be war-winning weapons. Later in the war, the *Stukageschwader* were superseded by *Schlachtgeschwader*, or ground-attack wings. Another new type of which much was expected was the *Zerstörer*, or destroyer. These heavy twin-engine fighters were flown by *Zerstörergeschwader*. *Jagdgeschwaders* flew single-engine fighters, and were tasked primarily with escorting the bombers.

109s and 350 Bf 110 fighters. Five hundred transport aircraft and gliders were available for supply and airborne missions.

The attack followed the pattern set in Poland. The *Kampf-* and *Stukagruppen* struck opposing airfields at first light, and then ranged far into the enemy rear, hitting communications and transport targets. At the same time, small units of *Fallschirmjäger* dropped by parachute and glider to seize key river crossings. Most were successful, though fierce resistance meant that losses in the Junkers Ju 52 force were high.

Kampfgruppen were also deployed against enemy cities: the bombing of Rotterdam on 14 May destroyed the heart of the port, killing 1000 civilians and making more than 70,000 homeless. Air superiority was quickly established over the whole front. The Bf 109 was superior to the French Morane Saulnier MS 406 and the British Hawker Hurricane, and the German advantage in training and tactics was decisive. Even when Allied aircraft did get through the fighter cover, they encountered a storm of anti-aircraft fire from *Luftwaffe* flak units operating with the ground troops. On the afternoon of 14 May, Fairey Battle light bombers attacked the German pontoon bridges across the Meuse: 28 out of 37 aircraft were shot down.

Without fear of enemy attack, the *Luftwaffe's* dive-bombers were free to provide total support to the army. Whenever the Panzers encountered resistance on the ground, Stukas would be on the spot within minutes. The psychological effect of these screaming pinpoint attacks was considerable; by the end of the campaign, British and French troops were running almost as soon as they heard the distinctive sound of a Stuka's sirens. By the end of May, the British Expeditionary Force was pinned to the coast at Dunkirk, and it seemed only a matter of time before it was overwhelmed. Indeed, Hermann Göring claimed that the *Luftwaffe* could win the battle on its own, and Hitler ordered his Panzers to stop.

But for the first time in the war, the *Luftwaffe* could not win air superiority over a battlefield. Over Dunkirk, they encountered the Supermarine Spitfire, which the Royal Air Force had held back during the battle for France. Now the Messerschmitt pilots were engaging an aircraft at least as good as their own. The bombers and dive-bombers could no longer count on getting to their targets unscathed, and although they inflicted heavy damage on the evacuation force, their own losses were substantial. They could not prevent the evacuation: over 300,000 British troops escaped.

It was clear to the men on the front line that the Royal Air Force was going to be a formidable opponent in the weeks and months to come.

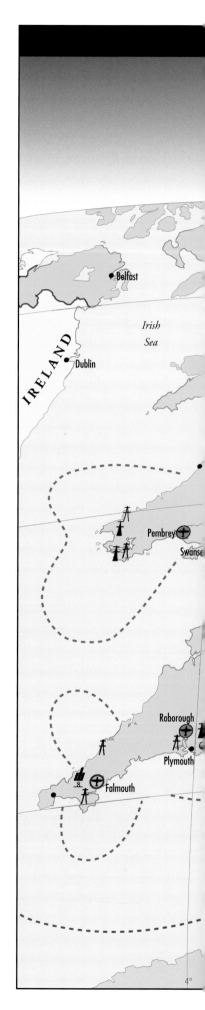

Battle of Britain

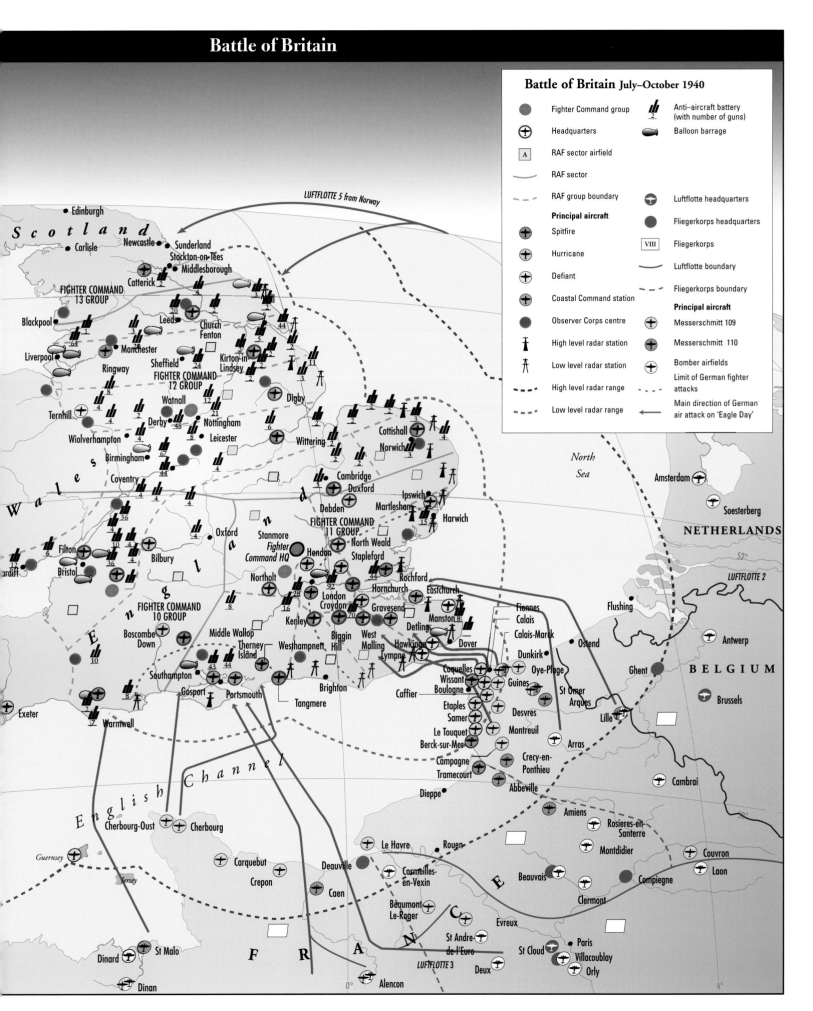

Battle of Britain July–October 1940

⬤ Fighter Command group		🛩 Anti–aircraft battery (with number of guns)	
⊕ Headquarters		Balloon barrage	
A RAF sector airfield			
RAF sector			
RAF group boundary		Luftflotte headquarters	
Principal aircraft		Fliegerkorps headquarters	
⊕ Spitfire		VIII Fliegerkorps	
⊕ Hurricane		Luftflotte boundary	
⊕ Defiant		Fliegerkorps boundary	
⊕ Coastal Command station		**Principal aircraft**	
⬤ Observer Corps centre		⊕ Messerschmitt 109	
High level radar station		⊕ Messerschmitt 110	
Low level radar station		⊕ Bomber airfields	
High level radar range		Limit of German fighter attacks	
Low level radar range		← Main direction of German air attack on 'Eagle Day'	

LUFTFLOTTE 5 from Norway

Edinburgh

Scotland

Carlisle

Newcastle
Sunderland
Stockton-on-Tees
Middlesborough
Catterick 2

FIGHTER COMMAND 13 GROUP

Blackpool
Leeds
Church Fenton
Hull

Liverpool
Manchester
Sheffield
Kirton-in-Lindsey
FIGHTER COMMAND 12 GROUP

Ringway
Ternhill
Watnall
Derby
Nottingham
Leicester
Digby

Wiolverhampton

Birmingham

Coventry

Wittering

Cottishall
Norwich

Wales

Oxford
Cambridge
Duxford
Debden
Martlesham
Ipswich
Harwich

Filton
Bristol
Bilbury

FIGHTER COMMAND 11 GROUP

Stanmore
Fighter Command HQ
Hendon
North Weald
Stapleford
Northolt
London
Croydon
Hornchurch
Rochford
Eastchurch
Manston

Cardiff

FIGHTER COMMAND 10 GROUP

Kenley
Gravesend
Detling

Boscombe Down
Middle Wallop
Biggin Hill
West Malling
Hawkinge
Dover

Therney Island
Westhampnett
Lympne

Southampton
Brighton
Gosport
Portsmouth
Tangmere

Exeter

Warmwell

English Channel

North Sea

Amsterdam

Soesterberg

NETHERLANDS

LUFTFLOTTE 2

Flushing

Antwerp

Ghent

BELGIUM

Brussels

Ostend
Dunkirk
Oye-Plage
Coquelles
Wissant
Calais
Calais-Marck
Fiennes
Boulogne
Guines
St Omer
Arques
Caffier
Etaples
Samer
Desvres
Le Touquet
Montreuil
Berck-sur-Mer
Campagne
Crecy-en-Ponthieu
Tramecourt
Abbeville

Lille

Arras

Cambrai

Dieppe

Amiens

Rosieres-en-Santerre

Montdidier

Couvron

Laon

Guernsey

Jersey

Cherbourg-Oust
Cherbourg

Carquebut
Crepon

Deauville
Corneilles-en-Vexin

Le Havre
Rouen

Beaumont Le-Roger

Beauvais

Compiegne

Clermont

Evreux

Caen

St Andre-de-l'Eure

St Cloud
Paris
Villacoublay
Orly

FRANCE

LUFTFLOTTE 3

Deux

Dinard
St Malo

Dinan

Alencon

79

Right: Pilots of No 92 Squadron scramble for their fighters early in 1941. The squadron took part in the final stages of the Battle of Britain, but by this time they had switched to offensive operations over France.

The Attack on Britain

The main German air assault on the United Kingdom, which Churchill was to call the Battle of Britain, did not begin until 13 August 1940. However, as early as 30 June, Göring had issued 'General Directions for the Operation of the *Luftwaffe* against England'. These defined the *Luftwaffe's* primary targets as the Royal Air Force, its airfields and its supporting industries. On July 11, the *Reichsmarschall* announced that shipping in the Channel was to be attacked. However, as the Germans tried to intercept the British convoys, the RAF attacked the bombers, with the previously all-conquering Stuka proving especially vulnerable. In June and July, the *Luftwaffe* launched small-scale raids on England from airfields in France, Belgium, Holland and Scandinavia. These allowed the RAF to test their defensive measures before the main attack came in August and September. It was soon clear that the *Luftwaffe* had numerical superiority, but the RAF had some decisive advantages as well.

To fight the British, the Germans had amassed a force of 1260 medium bombers, about 320 dive-bombers, 800 single-engine and 280 twin-engine fighters and several hundred reconnaissance aircraft. *Luftwaffe* forces were divided into three air fleets. Field Marshal Albert Kesselring's *Luftflotte 2* was based in eastern France and the Low Countries, while Field Marshal Hugo Sperrle's *Luftflotte 3* operated from western France. Colonel-General Hans-Jurgen Stumpff's *Luftflotte 5* would attack across the North Sea from bases in Scandinavia.

Ranged against the *Luftwaffe* was RAF Fighter Command, led by Air Chief Marshal Sir Hugh Dowding. One Fighter Group was assigned to protect each of the major areas of the country. The southwest was covered by 10 Group; 11 Group under Air Vice Marshal Keith Park was closest to the enemy in the southeast; 12 Group commanded by Air Vice Marshal Trafford Leigh-Mallory was based in East Anglia and

'*Let us therefore brace ourselves to our duties, and so bear ourselves that, if the British Empire and its Commonwealth last for a thousand years, men will say, "this was their finest hour".*'

Winston Churchill, 18 June 1940

the Midlands; and 13 Group operated from the north and Scotland. Fighter Command had 900 fighters in the main operational area, of which Dowding could commit 600 to action.

The RAF were supported by the Chain Home belt of radar stations. Even though it had been invented only five years before, British radar could detect high-flying aircraft deep over northern France. Low-level intruders were picked up only at about 35km (22 miles) – the width of the Straits of Dover. A sophisticated system of ground control allowed the British to make best use of their resources. Primed with radar information,

the sector control stations allowed RAF fighters to be scrambled early and vectored to attack the *Luftwaffe* before it had reached its targets.

Engines of War

In the Messerschmitt Bf 109, the Germans had an excellent single-seat fighter. Very fast, agile, with a good climb and dive performance, its only major drawback was its range, which limited it to escort missions over southeast England. Going as far as London meant that its pilots had only a few minutes of combat time before having to turn for

The Blitz

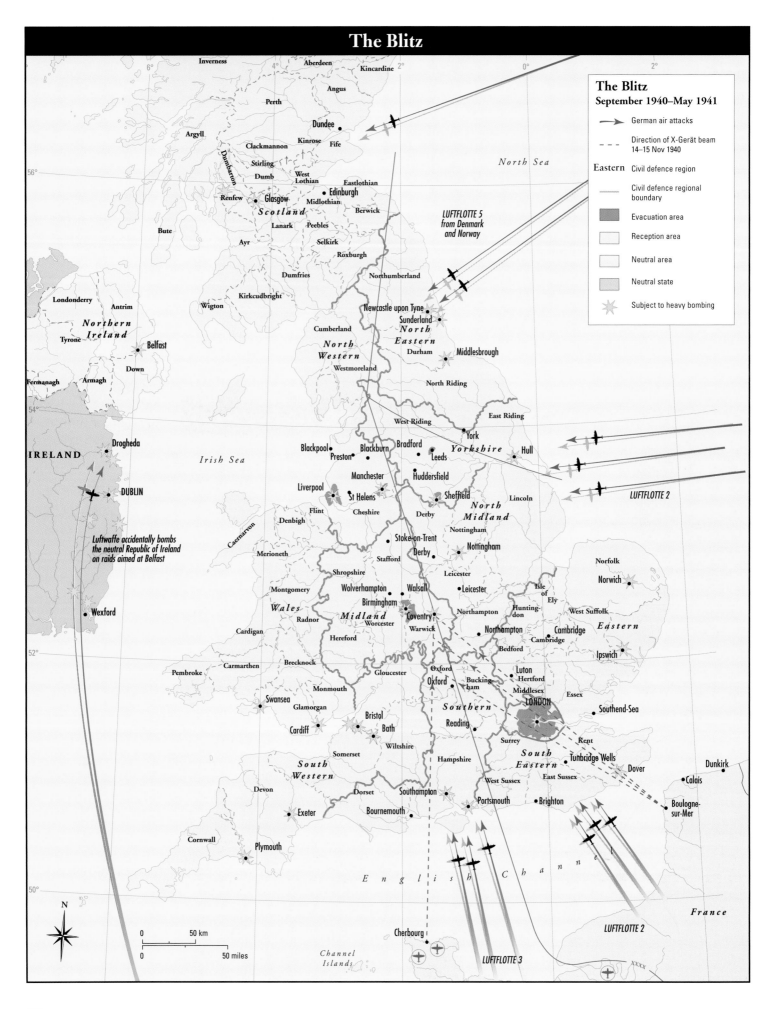

The Blitz
September 1940–May 1941

→ German air attacks

- - - Direction of X-Gerät beam
14–15 Nov 1940

Eastern Civil defence region

Civil defence regional
boundary

Evacuation area

Reception area

Neutral area

Neutral state

✳ Subject to heavy bombing

Inverness

Aberdeen

Kincardine

Angus

Perth

Dundee

Argyll

Kinrose

Clackmannon

Fife

Stirling

Dumb

West Lothian

Dunbarton

Eastlothian

Renfew

Glasgow

Edinburgh

Midlothian

Scotland

Berwick

Bute

Lanark

Peebles

North Sea

Ayr

Selkirk

Roxburgh

Dumfries

Northumberland

*LUFTFLOTTE 5
from Denmark
and Norway*

Londonderry

Antrim

*Northern
Ireland*

Wigton

Kirkcudbright

Tyrone

Newcastle upon Tyne

Belfast

Sunderland

*North
Eastern*

Down

Cumberland

*North
Western*

Durham

Middlesbrough

Fermanagh

Armagh

Westmoreland

North Riding

Drogheda

East Riding

IRELAND

Irish Sea

West Riding

York

DUBLIN

Blackpool

Blackburn

Bradford

Yorkshire

Hull

Preston

Leeds

Manchester

Huddersfield

Liverpool

St Helens

Sheffield

Lincoln

*Luftwaffe accidentally bombs
the neutral Republic of Ireland
on raids aimed at Belfast*

Flint

Cheshire

Derby

*North
Midland*

LUFTFLOTTE 2

Denbigh

Caernarvon

Stoke-on-Trent

Nottingham

Wexford

Merioneth

Derby

Nottingham

Stafford

Leicester

Norfolk

Shropshire

Norwich

Montgomery

Wolverhampton

Walsall

Leicester

*Isle
of
Ely*

Wales

Birmingham

Midland

Coventry

Northampton

**Hunting-
don**

West Suffolk

Eastern

Radnor

Worcester

Warwick

Northampton

Cambridge

Cardigan

Hereford

Cambridge

Ipswich

Bedford

Pembroke

Carmarthen

Brecknock

Gloucester

Oxford

Luton

Essex

Monmouth

Oxford

**Bucking-
ham**

Hertford

Swansea

Middlesex

Glamorgan

Bristol

Southern

LONDON

Southend-Sea

Cardiff

Bath

Reading

Surrey

Kent

Somerset

Wiltshire

*South
Eastern*

Tunbridge Wells

Dover

Dunkirk

Hampshire

Calais

*South
Western*

Dorset

Southampton

West Sussex

East Sussex

Devon

Portsmouth

Brighton

**Boulogne-
sur-Mer**

Exeter

Bournemouth

Cornwall

Plymouth

English Channel

France

N

0   50 km

0   50 miles

Cherbourg

LUFTFLOTTE 2

*Channel
Islands*

LUFTFLOTTE 3

XXXX

home. The Messerschmitt Bf 110 *Zerstörer* was big, fast, and had the long range its smaller sibling lacked. It also had a formidable armament packed in its nose – four machine guns and two 20mm (0.79in) cannon. But it was no match for the faster and more manoeuvrable Hurricanes and Spitfires. The Junkers Ju 87 Stuka had been a battle winner in Spain, Poland and France, earning an awesome reputation. However, in combat against high-performance fighters it proved to be horribly vulnerable. Slow and cumbersome in flight, it was hacked out of the sky in large numbers by the RAF.

Left: Once Adolf Hitler cancelled the planned invasion of the United Kingdom, the British Army could concentrate on re-equipping and training for the day when they returned to Europe. These infantrymen mounted in a Bren-gun carrier are in the middle of a 24-hour gasmask exercise.

Opposite: Defeat in the Battle of Britain meant that the Luftwaffe *was forced to switch to night bombing operations. With less of a fighter threat than by day, bombers were able to mount raids from airfields in France, Holland, Denmark and Norway.*

Germany's bomber fleet was intended to carry the weight of the air war, but for the first time it proved unequal to the task. The *Luftwaffe's Kampfgeschwader* had cut their teeth in tactical operations in which ground forces could capture airfields that had been neutralized by air attack. However, the bomber force was not designed for long-range strategic bombing of industrial centres. The Dornier Do 17 and Heinkel He 111 had been considered very fast before the war, but in the face of determined single-seat fighter opposition they proved vulnerable. The more recently introduced Junkers Ju 88 was a much better combat aircraft, but was still no match for a Spitfire.

On the British side, the mainstay of RAF operations was the Supermarine Spitfire and the Hawker Hurricane. Both were armed with eight 7.7mm (0.303in) Browning machine guns. The Spitfire was the superior aircraft, though there were far more Hurricanes in service – which is reflected in the fact that the Hurricane scored the majority of the RAF's kills in the battle. The faster Spitfires would take on the Bf 109 escorts, while the slower but equally agile Hurricanes attacked the bombers.

Since the RAF was operating over home territory, any RAF pilot who survived being shot down without serious injury could be returned to his squadron and be flying within 24 hours or less. Downed *Luftwaffe* crew went straight to the POW camp. For those pilots who landed in the English Channel, high-speed launches and seaplanes operating from Britain or German-occupied France ran competing rescue missions.

On 19 July, Hitler directed a speech in the Reichstag at Britain. Dubbed 'The Last Appeal to Reason', he said 'If we do pursue the struggle, it will end with the complete destruction of one of the two combatants. Mr Churchill may believe that

Opposite: Prime Minister Winston Churchill visits Britain's coastal defences. Without the heavy equipment and artillery abandoned in France, how they would have stood up to a German Panzer attack is questionable. Fortunately, neither the Luftwaffe *nor the* Kriegsmarine *had the ability to deliver or protect an invasion force from the RAF or the Royal Navy.*

'The gratitude of every home in our Islands goes out to the British airmen... Never in the field of human conflict was so much owed by so many to so few.'

Winston Churchill, 21 August 1940

85

Early Bombing of Europe

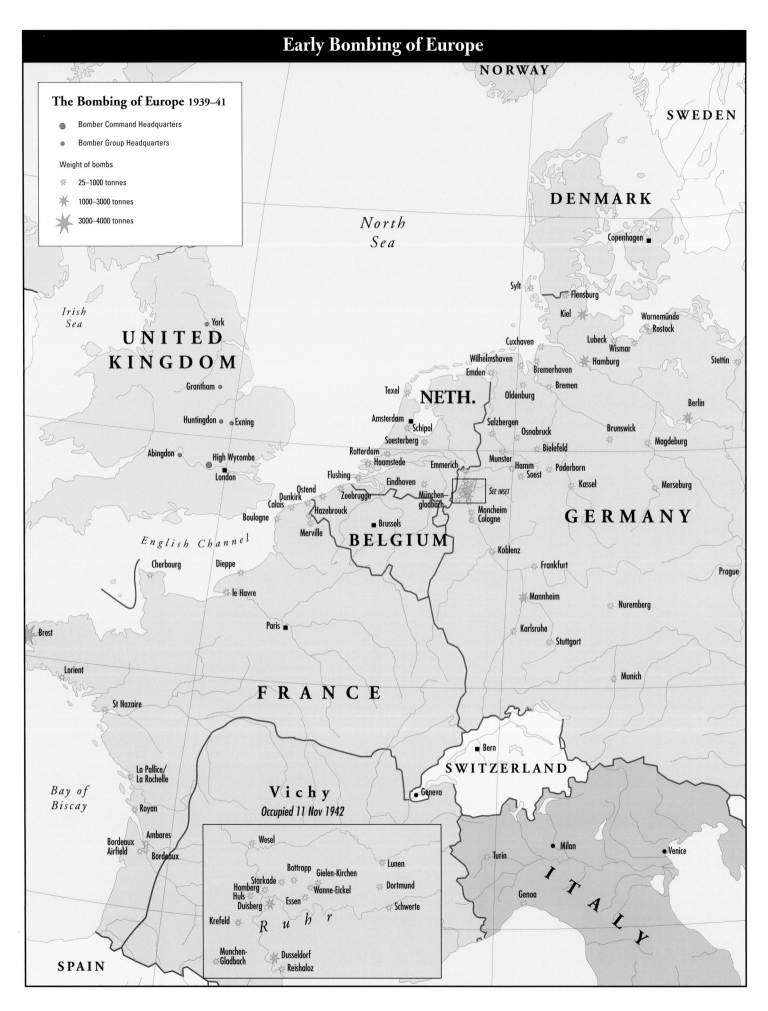

The Bombing of Europe 1939–41

- Bomber Command Headquarters
- Bomber Group Headquarters

Weight of bombs

- ✳ 25–1000 tonnes
- ✳ 1000–3000 tonnes
- ✳ 3000–4000 tonnes

NORWAY

SWEDEN

DENMARK

Copenhagen

North Sea

Sylt

Flensburg

Kiel

Warnemünde
Rostock

Cuxhaven

Lubeck
Wismar

Hamburg

Stettin

Wilhelmshaven

Bremerhaven

Emden

Bremen

Berlin

Irish Sea

York

Texel

NETH.

Oldenburg

Salzbergen

Osnabruck

Brunswick

Magdeburg

UNITED KINGDOM

Grantham

Amsterdam

Schipol

Soesterberg

Bielefeld

Huntingdon

Exning

Rotterdam

Haamstede

Emmerich

Munster

Hamm
Soest

Paderborn

Kassel

Merseburg

Abingdon

High Wycombe

London

Flushing

Ostend

Eindhoven

München–gladbach

See Inset

Moncheim
Cologne

GERMANY

Dunkirk

Zeebrugge

Calais

Hazebrouck

Boulogne

Merville

Brussels

BELGIUM

Koblenz

English Channel

Cherbourg

Dieppe

Frankfurt

Prague

le Havre

Mannheim

Nuremberg

Paris

Karlsruhe

Stuttgart

Brest

Lorient

FRANCE

Munich

St Nazaire

Bay of Biscay

La Pallice/
La Rochelle

Royan

Vichy

Occupied 11 Nov 1942

Bern

SWITZERLAND

Geneva

Milan

Venice

Turin

ITALY

Bordeaux
Airfield

Ambares

Bordeaux

Genoa

Wesel

Bottrapp

Gielen-Kirchen

Lunen

Starkade

Homberg
Huls

Wanne-Eickel

Dortmund

Duisberg

Essen

Ruhr

Schwerte

Krefeld

Munchen-
Gladbach

Dusseldorf

Reishaloz

SPAIN

it will be Germany. I know it will be England'. Since this drew no positive response from the British Government, orders were given to launch a major air assault against the RAF on *Adlertag* – Eagle Day, 12 August.

The Battle Begins

Among the German targets was the important radar station at Ventnor on the Isle of Wight, which was put out of action. On the 13th, the weather was poor and though some squadrons took off, the planned massed assault was called off. It was not until the 15th that the three *Luftflotten* attacked in concert, putting 2000 aircraft over Britain in an afternoon.

Luftflotte 5 launched 169 bombers from Aalborg in Denmark and Stavanger in Norway against Scotland and the northeast of England. Operating beyond the range of single-seat fighters, they were escorted by twin-engine Messerschmitt Bf 110 *Zerstörers*. No match for Spitfires or Hurricanes, the 110s proved unequal to the task, and the bombers suffered badly at the hands of 12 and 13 Groups. Sixteen bombers and seven Bf 110s were shot down. Without adequate fighter protection, *Luftflotte 5* was to play little further part in the battle.

Raids of between 100 and 150 aircraft from *Luftflottes 2* and *3* crossed the Channel all through the afternoon of 15 August. If *Luftwaffe* crews did not know they were in a serious fight, then the events of 'Black Thursday' convinced them. The British lost 34 fighters that day, but 75 German aircraft did not return. During the air operations, both the RAF and the *Luftwaffe* overestimated their victories – understandable in the confusion of a dogfight, when two pilots might both claim the same aircraft as a 'kill'. The huge figures of enemy losses were undoubtedly good for morale, but were not the basis for sound planning.

Similarly, bomb damage to airfields, which could look spectacular in aerial photographs, was often relatively superficial. *Luftwaffe* planners took such intelligence at

Opposite: The Royal Air Force was the only means of striking back at Germany that Britain had. Early daylight raids were savagely mauled: forced to fly by night, the RAF mounted numerous small raids. However, the accuracy of the bombing was abysmal.

Below: No match for British single-seat fighters, the Messerschmitt Bf 110 heavy fighter was used as a fighter bomber in the later stages of the Battle of Britain, but it found its true métier later in the war, as a night fighter.

face value, however, and thought that the RAF was hurting more than in fact it was. The Germans believed that the RAF now had only 300 front-line aircraft, and the *Luftwaffe* commanders decided to go all out to destroy Fighter Command once and for all.

Small groups of bombers flew to Britain as bait to draw up the RAF fighters. As Spitfires, Hurricanes and Bf 109s battled through the summer skies, more bombers slipped through to hit key airfields at Biggin Hill, Hornchurch, North Weald and West Malling. RAF losses started to climb. However, just as they were close to achieving their operational goal, the Germans switched their attacks to British cities.

The Blitz

Why the *Luftwaffe* took the pressure off the RAF is still disputed. The high command may have been convinced that they had broken the back of the RAF. Alternatively, a night raid by the RAF on Berlin on August 25 – timed to coincide with a visit by Soviet Foreign Minister Molotov – might have enraged Hitler and prompted retaliation.

The RAF raid was itself a reaction to a lost *Luftwaffe* bomber, which had jettisoned its payload over the East End of London. However, the Berlin raid was not an isolated incident: the RAF mounted small-scale raids over Germany all through the period. The largest involved 169 twin-engine bombers sent to Berlin on 8 November 1940, during which 21 aircraft were lost. In a military sense, the British raids had little effect. Hitting a target at night was almost impossible with the technology of the time, and the November raid killed only 11 on the ground.

For whatever the reason, German air attacks against British cities began with daylight raids on London on 7 September. Carried out by 300 bombers with 600 escorting fighters, these initially enjoyed considerable success, causing huge fires around the London docks. On 15 September, the *Luftwaffe* abandoned its usual practice of sending diversionary attacks to confuse radar and ground controllers – possibly believing that the RAF was a spent force. But the RAF was waiting.

The respite from direct attacks on its airfields had allowed the RAF to replenish its fighter strength in the south. The raids on London gave 11 Group in particular more time to get fighters aloft. Park was able to get paired squadrons into the air, and Leigh Mallory's 12 Group formed even larger formations in what were known as 'Big Wing' attacks. The *Luftwaffe* was met by massed fighters, and by the close of the day had lost 60 aircraft. Total *Luftwaffe* losses since 7 September totalled 175, all caused by a force that German pilots had been told was beaten. Two days later. Hitler postponed Operation Sealion indefinitely, as he turned his attention towards the Soviet Union.

The *Luftwaffe* switched to night raids. Up to 400 bombers attacked London each night until mid-November, weather permitting. Contrary to pre-war theories about air power, the raids, known to the citizens of the UK as the Blitz, did not cause panic in the civilian population, nor did they break the national will. There was a lull in midwinter, though the raiders returned in the New Year. In a series of raids lasting until May, *Luftwaffe* bombers also attacked Liverpool, Birmingham, Plymouth and Bristol.

Intensification

Between 19 February and 12 May 1941, the *Luftwaffe* intensified attacks against London and the Channel ports. In some raids, they employed 700 bombers, though others involved single fighter-bombers. These would fly fast and low across the Channel, keeping beneath the British radar cover.

Opposite: Victims of German bombers are pulled from the wreckage of their home during the Blitz. Attacks on populated areas were designed to wear down civilian resistance: in fact, they heightened community spirit and made ordinary civilians more determined than ever to do their bit to win the war.

'Then whose bombs are these that we are sheltering from?'

Reputedly said by Soviet Foreign Commissar Molotov during an air raid on Berlin in November 1940, on being informed by German Foreign Minister Ribbentrop that Britain was defeated.

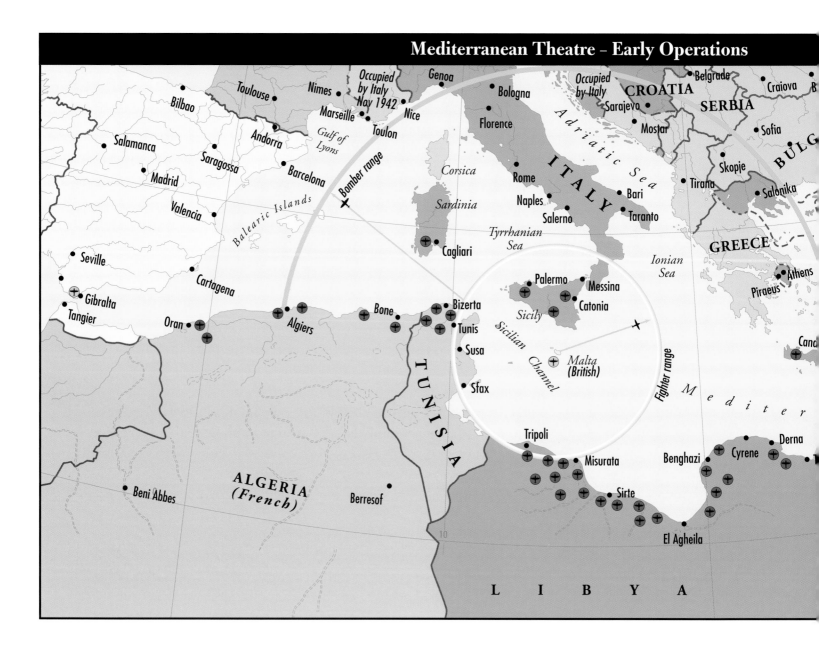

Mediterranean Theatre – Early Operations

Above: The war in the Mediterranean was dominated by lines of communication: Axis troops in North Africa could be supported from Italy only a short distance across the Mediterranean. The British had much longer and more vulnerable supply routes, but these were anchored by key bases at Gibraltar, Malta and Alexandria.

The intensification of the bombing was to some extent a cover for the German military redeployment eastwards: by 21 May, the *Luftwaffe* had shifted 90 per cent of its forces to eastern Germany, occupied Poland and East Prussia, ready for operations against the USSR. During its attacks on Britain in 1940 and 1941, the *Luftwaffe* dropped 49,359 tonnes (54,420 tons) of bombs and incendiaries. Most raids were against area targets, killing 40,000 people and injuring 86,000. Two million homes were destroyed, of which 60 per cent were in London. Exact air losses are still disputed, but the best estimates are that the *Luftwaffe* lost 1294 aircraft between 10 July and 31 October 1940, while the British lost 788. During the night Blitz, the *Luftwaffe* lost a further 600 bombers, though many of these were due to flying accidents in bad weather. However, by 1941 the RAF had become a formidable enemy even at night, with twin-engine radar-equipped night-fighters supplemented by radar-controlled searchlights and anti-aircraft guns on the ground.

Taking the War to Germany

The Battle of Britain was the first major setback for Germany's armed forces. Even though the British were gravely weakened, they remained implacably opposed to Hitler and the Nazis, and would provide one of the springboards by which Germany would

The map legend reads:

The Mediterranean
Late 1942

- Under German or Axis occupation
- Allied to Germany
- Italian territory
- Under Italian occupation
- Allied or under Allied occupation
- French, under Vichy control
- Axis occupied
- Neutral countries
- ⊕ Allied airfield
- ⊕ Axis airfield

ultimately be defeated. In the meantime, however, the only way Britain could strike at Germany was from the air, and the RAF continued its night bombing raids over the German homeland.

Initially targeted against key industrial and communications targets, RAF crews found that accurate navigation and bombing by night was almost impossible – so much so in fact, that bombers were simply instructed to bomb towns and cities. Aircrew returned with reports of large fires burning and immense damage done, but neutral news reports out of Germany were painting a different picture.

To assess the effectiveness of the campaign, D.M. Butt of the War Cabinet Secretariat was asked to examine over 600 operational photos, comparing them with crew claims and Bomber Command assessments. The Butt report, released in August 1941, was devastating. Many bombers were not finding the correct target – some were not even bombing the right towns. Only one bomber in three was getting within 8km (5 miles) of its target and over the vital Ruhr industrial area, which was often covered in haze, only one in ten. On moonless nights, the ratio fell to one in fifteen. These poor results had come at the cost of 700 British bombers destroyed and thousands of aircrew killed or captured.

Clearly something would have to be done. It would not be until the appointment of Air Marshal Arthur Harris as the head of Bomber Command in 1942 that the bomber campaign began to receive added impetus, greatly helped by the introduction into service of powerful new four-engine bombers.

The Mediterranean Theatre

Although the bomber campaign was the only way that Britain could strike directly at the Third Reich, British forces were also very active in the Mediterranean. The main threat to the British there came from the powerful Italian Fleet. Mussolini had declared war on Britain and France on 10 June 1940. On 9 July, the British Mediterranean Fleet was preparing to escort two convoys to Malta, while the Italian Fleet was returning to Italy after covering a supply convoy to Benghazi. The two forces met off Calabria. In a confused action that started at about 3 p.m., the battleship *Warspite* hit the Italian battleship *Giulio Cesare* at a range of 23,764m (26,000 yards), the longest such hit in history. The drawn battle left neither side in control of the local seas.

Two months later, on 13 September 1940, the Italian Army under Marshal Graziani invaded Egypt from Libya. Pushing tentatively forward, the Italians made contact with British troops and settled down in a series of fortified positions around Sidi Barrani, while the British were centred on Mersa Matruh, about 121km (75 miles) further east. The Egyptian army held back from the conflict. Indeed, young nationalist officers, including Gamel Abdel Nasser and Anwar el Sadat, made clandestine contact with the Germans in the hope of ensuring Egyptian independence in the event of a British defeat.

MALTA

In 1941/42, many officers of the German high command made a strong argument for a German assault on Malta, from which the RAF and Royal Navy inflicted unsustainable losses on the Italian convoys on which Rommel's army depended. German and Italian airborne forces were assembled and trained for Operation Hercules, and the island bombed by the *Luftwaffe* and the *Regia Aeronautica*.

Malta was the key to holding the Mediterranean, but the 250,000 Maltese and 20,000 British defenders were dependent on imported food and oil that had to run the gauntlet of Axis bombers. In September 1941, eight of nine merchant ships arrived in Malta, bringing 77,095 tonnes (85,000 tons) of supplies.

However, a February 1942 convoy of three ships from Alexandria could not get through. One month later, three cargo ships and an oiler attempted a resupply mission, a heavy Royal Navy escort managing to keep the Italian navy at bay. But German air attacks resulted in one of the cargo vessels sunk, and the tanker was destroyed within sight of the island. The two survivors reached Malta, but were sunk at their moorings just as unloading got under way. Under constant bombardment, Malta could support no submarines or bomber aircraft. Italian merchant ships enjoyed a welcome respite and Rommel's forces were replenished. Malta existed under a state of virtual siege until May 1943, during which time over 5000 Maltese civilians were either killed or wounded by the bombing.

While the two sides faced each other in North Africa, the British navy was establishing its dominance over the Mediterranean. On 11 November 1940, Admiral Cunningham's Mediterranean Fleet launched a surprise attack against the major Italian naval base at Taranto. Launched from the carrier HMS *Illustrious*, a force of just 21 antique Swordfish biplanes torpedoed and bombed the Italian fleet, sinking or badly damaging three battleships and two cruisers for the loss of just two aircraft. This strike gave the Royal Navy a decisive edge in the Mediterranean – and impressed the Japanese navy so much that it was to use the same technique on a much larger scale at Pearl Harbor just over a year later.

Britain's North African Offensive
In December 1940, the British finally acted against the Italians in Egypt. General Archibald Wavell unleashed the Western Desert Force, commanded by General Richard O'Connor, through a gap in the Italian chain of defences. O'Connor's force, numbering some 31,000 men, was outnumbered more than four to one. However, in a lightning campaign of mobility, the British leapfrogged each Italian position, reaching Bardia at the end of the year. By the beginning of February 1941, the British had reached Beda Fomm. In two months, O'Connor's men had advanced 805km (500 miles), taking 130,000 prisoners and effectively knocking out the Italian presence in Cyrenaica. However, a month later, they were facing a new challenge as the German Afrika Korps, sent to Africa to save Mussolini's forces,

Opposite: A column of Indian troops from Wavell's Western Desert Force move through the town of Berna as part of General O'Connor's campaign to push the Italian army out of Cyrenacia.

mounted its first attacks at El Agheila.

At the same time as the Western Desert Force was ripping through Italian Libya, another British campaign got under way against the Italians in East Africa. In a rapid offensive action, the British, under Generals Platt and Cunningham, mounted a two-pronged invasion of Somaliland and Eritrea, and by 4 April had captured Addis Ababa. On 18 May, the Italian forces under the Duke of Aosta surrendered.

Success on land in Africa was matched by further success at sea, though a new threat had emerged with the arrival of German fighters, dive-bombers and bombers on Sicily in February 1941. These aircraft quickly made the narrow seas between Italy and Africa an extremely dangerous place for British shipping, and Malta came under intense bombardment.

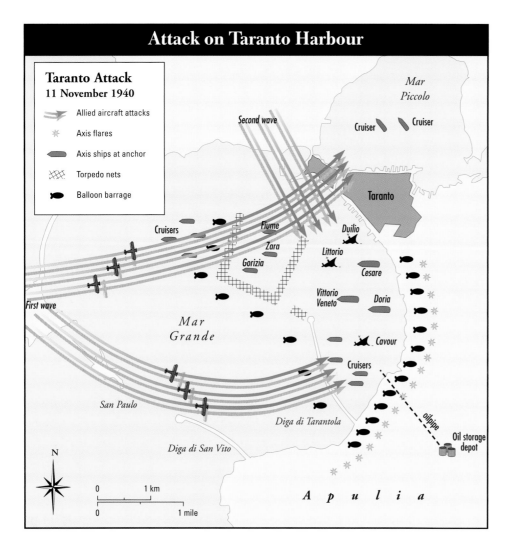

Attack on Taranto Harbour

Taranto Attack
11 November 1940

⬿ Allied aircraft attacks

✳ Axis flares

⬭ Axis ships at anchor

▨ Torpedo nets

🎈 Balloon barrage

Mar Piccolo

Second wave

Cruiser   Cruiser

Taranto

Cruisers

Fiume

Zara

Gorizia

Duilio

Littorio

Cesare

Vittorio Veneto

Doria

First wave

Mar Grande

Cavour

Cruisers

San Paulo

Diga di Tarantola

oilpipe

Oil storage depot

Diga di San Vito

N

0   1 km

0   1 mile

A p u l i a

Rising tensions in the Balkans led the British to send troops to Greece in March. In an attempt to intercept these movements, Admiral Angelo Iachino sortied with an Italian fleet of three battleships, eight cruisers and supporting elements. Harassed by the cruisers and aircraft carriers of Admiral Cunningham's Mediterranean fleet off Cape Matapan, the southernmost tip of mainland Greece, the powerful battleship *Vittorio Veneto* was damaged, as was the heavy cruiser *Pola*. The *Pola* had to be left behind, protected by the heavy cruisers *Zara*, *Fiume* and four destroyers.

At about 10 p.m. on 28 March, Admiral Cunningham with the battleships *Warspite*, *Valiant* and *Barham* closed with the three heavy cruisers and their escorts. Opening fire with radar guidance at near point-blank range, the British sank five Italian vessels in a matter of minutes,

Above: On the night of 10 November 1940, a force of 21 obsolete Fairey Swordfish biplanes launched from HMS Illustrious *ripped the heart out of the Italian fleet anchored at Taranto. The surprise attack gave the Royal Navy a moral advantage over the Italians, which was never to be challenged for the rest of the war.*

Right: A flight of RAF Fairy Swordfish biplanes armed with torpedoes prepare to attack Italian shipping near Malta.

including all three cruisers. The *Vittorio Veneto* and the rest of the Italian fleet did not offer battle, escaping into the darkness.

Kriegsmarine to the Rescue

In September 1941, with German supplies to Rommel's forces in North Africa being ravaged by British submarines and aircraft, the *Kriegsmarine* decided to send 25 U-Boats to bolster Mussolini's navy. Over the next two years, a total of 62 boats managed to run the gauntlet of the British-controlled straits of Gibraltar. Nine more were sunk while attempting the passage, while 10 had to abort their missions due to damage. Those that got into the Mediterranean quickly had an effect. On 13 November 1941, *U-81* under *Kapitanleutnant* Guggenberger torpedoed the aircraft carrier *Ark Royal* not far from Gibraltar. Initial damage did not seem serious, but progressive flooding eventually sank the ship, for the loss of only one life.

The veteran battleship HMS *Barham* was not so lucky. She was torpedoed by *Oberleutnant* Freiherr von Tiesenhausen's *U-331* on 25 November while hunting for an Italian supply convoy off the Egyptian/Libyan coast. Hit three times, the old vessel rolled over and exploded, taking 862 of her crew with her.

The German U-boats in the Mediterranean sank 95 Allied merchantmen totalling 407,429 tonnes (449,206 tons), as well 24 major Royal Navy warships, including the carrier HMS *Eagle*, four cruisers and 12 destroyers. However, none was to return to Germany: all 62 U-Boats were sunk in action or scuttled by their crews after their Italian bases were overrun.

Below: British superiority in the Mediterranean was sealed on 28 March 1941, when Admiral Cunningham's Mediterranean Fleet smashed an Italian heavy cruiser force off the southern tip of Greece, and forced the battleship Vittorio Veneto *to run for home.*

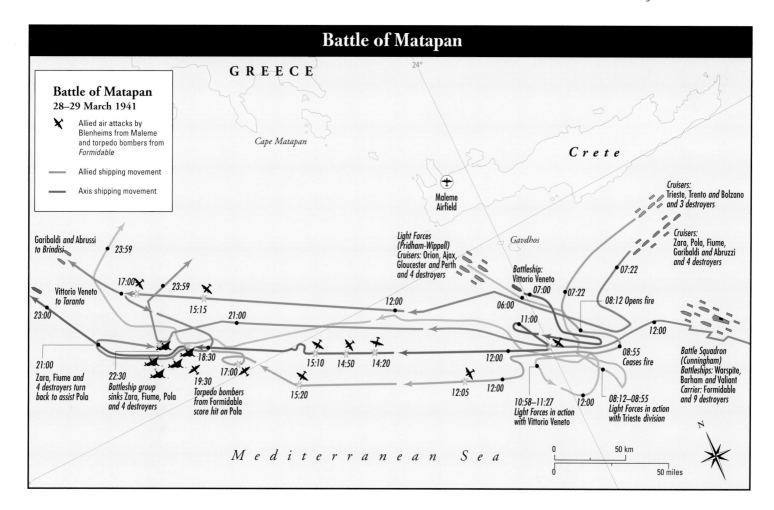

War at Sea, 1939–43

Ranging far out into the Atlantic and preying on sea-borne British trade, the *Kriegsmarine's* U-boat fleet was the biggest threat to Britain's survival during World War II. In 1939, half the food eaten in the United Kingdom came from overseas. Two-thirds of the raw materials required by Britain's war industries were imported too. If the German navy could stop this flow of goods by sinking Allied merchant ships, Hitler might win the war. However, like Napoleon before him, Hitler did not understand the importance of sea power.

The *Führer's* attitude to the navy was succinctly expressed in 1936. 'The Navy,' he asked. 'What need have we of that? I cannot conceive of a European war that will hang in the balance because of a few ships.' Nevertheless, as part of Germany's massive rearmaments programme in the 1930s, Hitler sponsored the development of the now famous 'Z plan'. The scheme to build a massive surface and underwater fleet of very modern design was due for completion in 1944.

The Atlantic Lifeline

At the outbreak of war, some 3000 ocean-going merchant ships flew the British flag and another 1000 coasters plied the waters around the UK: a combined total of 17.5 million tonnes (19.3 million tons) of shipping. In home waters and in the North Atlantic, the ships were organized into convoys, typically protected by four to six escorts armed with depth-charges. Heavier units from the Home Fleet were also assigned as distant escorts when intelligence was received of the possible presence of German warships.

The seaborne lifeline was vital. Without it, Britain could not even feed its population, let alone manufacture weapons, and it would be impossible to fight a war if the flow of imports stopped. However, the *Kriegsmarine,* not expecting to fight until the middle of the 1940s, was woefully unprepared to take advantage of Britain's vulnerability. Unable to face the British fleet to fleet, Germany had to resort to a campaign of commerce raiding.

The *'Deutschland'* class heavy cruisers, known as 'pocket battleships' because of their powerful 28cm (11in) guns, were Nazi Germany's first major warships. Purpose-

Opposite: The crew of a Type VII U-boat enjoy a rare meal in the open air. U-boat crews would spend many weeks on operational patrol, in the cramped confines of their submarine.

designed for commerce raiding, their diesel engines gave them excellent endurance. KMS *Admiral Scheer* and KMS *Graf Spee* had been sent out into the Atlantic before the outbreak of war, ready to go into action immediately war was declared. Both achieved some success, snapping up merchantmen sailing unescorted in the central and south Atlantic. *Scheer's* five-month raid sank 16 ships totalling 100,000 tonnes (110,254 tons).

However, operating alone made the pocket battleships vulnerable to concentrations of force made by the much more powerful Royal Navy, and *Graf Spee* was chased down by a cruiser squadron in the South Atlantic and was scuttled in the River Plate in December 1939. The *Kriegsmarine's* newer heavy warships were less suited to raiding operations. The 'Hipper' class heavy cruisers used high-pressure steam propulsion, and their notoriously high fuel consumption limited their range. Even so, the *Admiral Hipper* made a relatively successful cruise in February 1941, intercepting a convoy off West Africa and sinking seven ships totalling 27,210 tonnes (30,000 tons).

Too lightly armed to take on a real battleship, the battlecruisers *Scharnhorst* and *Gneisenau* had an indifferent war after their early success in sinking the carrier HMS *Glorious* during the Norway campaign. They largely failed in their attempts to harry British convoys in the North Atlantic, since the Royal Navy was assigning old 'R' class and 'Queen Elizabeth' class battleships to escort convoys.

The *Bismarck*

The *Kriegsmarine* did have one asset which could make a difference, however, and that was the powerful battleship *Bismarck*.

KMS *Bismarck* was launched by the Iron Chancellor's great grand-daughter on 14 February 1939. From completion to destruction, the huge battleship lasted only nine months, eight of which were spent on training. When she slipped out of the Baltic on 20 May 1941, escorted by the heavy cruiser *Prinz Eugen*, her mission was to disrupt the British supply line in the Atlantic. The Royal Navy was very conscious of the threat, and detailed

Right: In the early stages of the Battle of the Atlantic, German submarine attacks were concentrated on the approaches to the British Isles. Boats were small and few in number, and they had to make the long and perilous voyage around the North of Scotland to reach the Western Approaches.

Battle of the Atlantic I
September 1939–May 1940

——	Border of Pan-American Neutrality Zone (1939)
—	Extent of air escort cover
▢	Major convoy routes
•	Allied merchant ships sunk by U-boats
↙	U-boats sunk
▨	Territory under Allied control
▨	Territory under Axis control
▢	Neutral territory

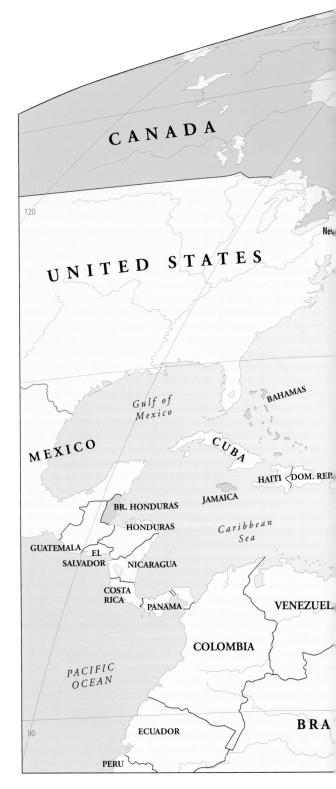

considerable resources to neutralize her. Initially shadowed by the cruisers *Suffolk* and *Norfolk*, the German squadron was intercepted off Iceland by the powerful battlecruiser HMS *Hood* and the new battleship HMS *Prince of Wales*.

The engagement was a disaster for the Royal Navy. The *Hood* was hit by a shell from *Bismarck's* main armament and exploded and sank, taking with her all but three of her

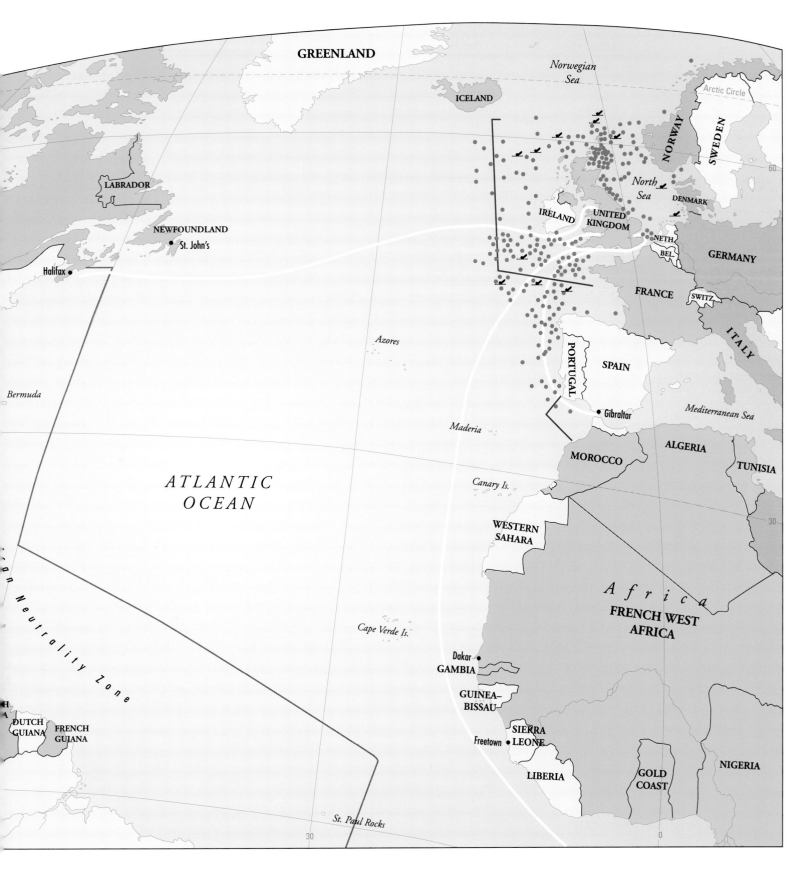

crew, and *Prince of Wales* was damaged and had to withdraw. No more serious blow was made by German warships to the British navy in the whole of World War II.

Bismarck's damage appeared minimal. She had been hit below the waterline, marginally decreasing her speed, and she was losing fuel. Admiral Lütjens, the German commander, ordered *Bismarck* and *Prinz Eugen* to proceed independently to Brest, where they would join the *Scharnhorst* and *Gneisenau*. In retrospect, Lütjens should have returned to Norwegian waters, perhaps polishing off the *Prince of Wales* on the way. He could then have waited until the *Bismarck's* sister ship *Tirpitz* was completed. The two massive battleships could then have tried to break out into the Atlantic again.

Although Lütjens succeeded in shaking off the shadowing British cruisers, the battleship was sighted again by a Catalina flying-boat on the morning of 26 May. By then, she was so far from the British Home Fleet that only a carrier strike could touch her before she reached friendly air cover. Launched from HMS *Ark Royal*, a strike by 15 Swordfish disabled the *Bismarck's* steering gear.

Unable to steer, the *Bismarck* was attacked on the morning of 27 May by the battleships HMS *Rodney* and HMS *King George V*. Within an hour, the German ship had been battered into ruin by 35.5cm (14in) and 40cm (16in) shells. The heavy cruiser *Devonshire* was then called in to administer the *coup de grâce*. After taking three torpedoes, the *Bismarck* sank by the stern, taking Admiral Lütjens and most of her complement of 2192 men to the bottom.

The U-boat War
The *Kriegsmarine* used armed merchant cruisers to much greater effect. These vessels were designed to look like ordinary merchantmen, but their sheep's clothing concealed

Below: To extend the operational range of its U-Boats, the Kriegsmarine *deployed* Milchcows: *large transport boats with extra fuel, supplies and torpedoes, which could be used to replenish U-boats far out in the Atlantic.*

very heavy weaponry. In terms of numbers of vessels sunk, their effect was not large, and they never threatened Allied command of the seas. But their activities did spread alarm, and forced the Royal Navy to devote considerable resources to tracking them down. They achieved most of their successes in distant waters before the end of 1941.

Whilst the activities of the *Kriegsmarine's* surface raiders made good copy for the propaganda machine, the German navy was never able to concentrate its capital ships to make a decisive difference, and the piecemeal operations of those raiders had little more than nuisance value.

In marked contrast to the surface fleet, the *Kriegsmarine's* U-boat force was a much more dangerous threat. The *Kriegsmarine's* submarine supremo, Admiral Karl Dönitz, well understood his priorities. He reckoned that a fleet of around 250 or even 300 submarines would be necessary to do the job. Hitler's pre-war 'Z-plan', the insanely ambitious Nazi naval construction programme, actually planned for such a fleet to be operational by 1943. But at the same time, the *Kriegsmarine* was to have two squadrons of giant battleships, bigger than any other warships in the world.

THE FOCKE-WULF FW 200 CONDOR

The Allied convoys had more to worry about than being shadowed by U-boats. There was what Winston Churchill called 'the Scourge of the Atlantic' – the Focke-Wulf Fw 200 Condor, which was the first demonstration of the value of air power in the Atlantic. The Fw 200s of *Kampfgeschwader 40* flew a giant loop from their base near Bordeaux in France, out over the convoy routes to their northern bases in Norway, doing the same trip in reverse the following day.

The idea was that once the Fw 200s found a convoy, the big aircraft were used as orbiting beacons. By transmitting continuously, they provided course data both to the high command and for the packs of U-boats, which could home in on their transmissions. Condors were fragile and vulnerable to fighters, but the British had been too hard-pressed for many a month to spare carriers or even catapult-launched aircraft to beat off the bombers.

The Condors did more than spot convoys for the U-boats, however. They also bombed stragglers and independently sailing merchantmen. In the first two months of 1941 alone, they sank 46 ships totalling 152,215 tonnes (167,822 tons) – the U-boats had themselves had only sunk 60. Only the continued disagreement and distrust between the *Kriegsmarine* and the *Luftwaffe* prevented a development that could have been catastrophic for the British.

The high command's obsession with battleships delayed the submarine-building programme, and was, in the view of Dönitz, irrelevant. He believed that only submarines offered a realistic prospect of blockading Britain.

Dönitz had learned his trade in U-boats during World War I. The Imperial German Navy was the first to make extensive use of submarines in attacking an enemy's trade, and in spite of the fairly primitive nature of the boats of the time, it achieved considerable success. U-boats wreaked havoc on British trade in the Mediterranean, and the unrestricted submarine warfare of 1917 and 1918 came within a whisker of bringing Britain to its knees. It was a major reason why Germany was denied a submarine force under the terms of the Treaty of Versailles after the war.

In spite of the ban, Germany set up clandestine U-boat design offices in Holland in 1922 and in Berlin in 1927. In 1932, months before Hitler's rise to power, the Weimar government approved a naval building plan that included 16 U-boats. The rise of the Nazis accelerated the navy's plans. In 1935, Hermann Göring announced Germany's intent to rearm, repudiating the Treaty of Versailles. Hitler managed to push through an

Anglo-German naval agreement, which allowed naval construction up to a ceiling of 45 per cent of the Royal Navy. Curiously, since the British had painful experience of what submarines could do, the agreement also allowed Germany to match the Royal Navy's submarine force, ton for ton.

Dönitz was given command of Germany's first post-war submarine flotilla that year and set about training a new U-boat fleet that could succeed where his generation had – by a narrow margin – failed. Once in charge of the German submarine force, he was able to define the types of boat best suited to near and distant operations as well as the number.

One requirement identified was for a coastal submarine, and the Type II went quickly into production. Type II U-boats proved to be handy and manoeuvrable, and could crash-dive in 25 seconds. Their profile and lively handling earned them the nickname of 'canoe'. But their small size and weapons load were handicaps in an open-ocean conflict, and construction ceased in 1941.

The majority of U-boats that fought the Battle of the Atlantic were Type VIIs. Like the Type II, the Type VII was originally designed for Finland and built in 1930. They were built in huge numbers, more than 800 being completed by the end of the war. Although intended for ocean operations, size was limited to allow the maximum number of boats to be built within treaty limits. This had the added advantage of making them agile and quick to dive.

As with most submarines of the period, the Type VII was powered by diesel engines on the surface and used battery-driven electric motors underwater. Under diesel drive, a Type VII could reach around 17.5 knots – more than enough to run rings around a slow-moving convoy. Underwater it could not do much more than 5 knots, and could sustain that speed for only a few hours. The Type VII carried between 11 and 14 torpedoes. Early boats also had a deck gun, but later in the war this was often exchanged for an increasingly heavy anti-aircraft gun fit.

Right: The introduction of larger, longer-ranged boats and of Milchcow *supply submarines in 1940 and 1941 saw U-Boat sinkings extend further out into the Atlantic and south as far as the coast of West Africa.*

Battle of the Atlantic II
June 1940–March 1941

—— Pan-American Neutrality Zone

—— Extent of air escort cover

– – Extent of surface escort cover

☐ Major convoy routes

• Allied merchant ships sunk by U-boats

⚓ U-boats sunk

▨ Territory under Allied control

▨ Territory under Axis control

▨ Territory under Vichy government (unoccupied France)

☐ Neutral territory

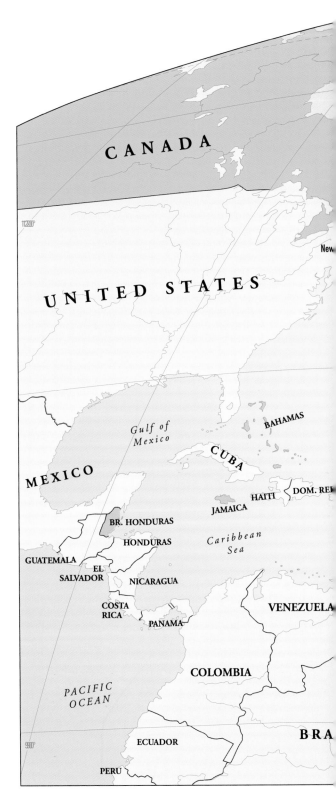

The larger Type IX class was designed for ocean warfare. Early Type IXs had enough range to operate in the southern hemisphere, mounting long patrols into the South Atlantic. Later versions with increased range could reach the Indian Ocean and even the Pacific without refuelling. Habitability was improved for these long-duration operations, and the number of torpedoes carried, at 22, was about 50 per cent more than those of a

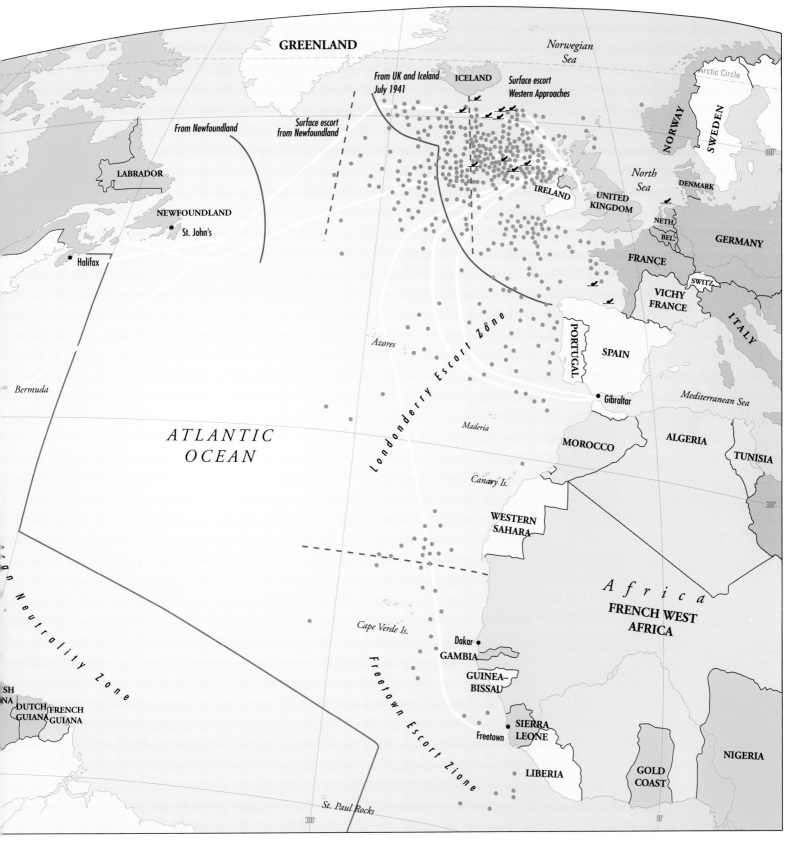

'As far as the
Navy is
concerned,
obviously it is in
no way very
adequately
equipped for the
great struggle
with Great
Britain... the
submarine arm is
still much too
weak to have any
decisive effect on
the war.'

*Grand Admiral Erich
Raeder, Kriegsmarine
C-in-C, 1939*

Type VII. Even so, crews preferred the smaller boats, since they could crash-dive more quickly and were quicker to manoeuvre under water. The big Type IX took up to 40 seconds to submerge in an emergency, leaving it vulnerable to air attack much longer.

Hunting the British

As late as the summer of 1939, Hitler was telling the German navy that there was little danger of war. Dönitz had only 46 operational submarines, of which more than half were the coastal 'ducks' – Type IIs – primarily used for training.

For the first eight months of the war, U-boat activity against Britain's vital supply lines was small – and was almost entirely directed against the few ships that sailed independently rather than in convoy. Indeed, during the Norwegian campaign, all U-boats were withdrawn from the Atlantic for operations in the North Sea.

That was about to change. Between the wars, Dönitz had developed theoretical group attack tactics. Once in control of Hitler's U-boats, he tested the concept of the 'wolf pack': co-ordinated strikes by groups of submarines far out into the ocean. Another technique Dönitz advocated was one he had learned in World War I: the most effective attacks were made by night on the surface. In 1939, he published a book, describing these methods – how the small silhouette of a submarine would be hard to see at night, and how the surfaced submarine of the 1930s enjoyed a considerably higher speed than the average merchant ship. No-one in Britain appears to have noticed.

The declared war zone first extended about 800km (497 miles) west of Ireland. In the first months of the war, pickings were rich amongst merchantmen returning individually to the UK. U-boat commanders had a healthy respect for British destroyers, whose Asdic underwater sound systems could detect the range and bearing of a submerged submarine. But there were never enough of them, and a frantic building programme undertaken to replace them with sloops and corvettes would take years to reach peak production.

The shortage of escorts on the major routes between the UK and Canada saw convoys escorted through only 15° longitude from either end. Empty ships could only be escorted to a line some 500km (311 miles) west of Ireland, where the escort would meet a heavily laden convoy coming home. In the middle of the Atlantic, the convoys were on their own. Thus began what U-boat commanders were to call the first 'Happy Time'.

Crisis in the Convoys

Early qualms about attacking liners were long gone. Merchant ships were escorted, armed and given instructions to ram on opportunity, so the *Kriegsmarine* considered that an unrestricted sinking policy was legally justified. Admiral Dönitz warned that ships of any nation entering the war zone would be subject to attack, whether belligerent or neutral. The crippling loss of Allied shipping in the early years of the war at sea was out of all proportion to the number of submarines causing that loss. There were rarely more than a dozen at sea at any one time.

After the fall of France, a higher proportion of the U-boat force was operational in the mid-Atlantic. They no longer had to make the long passage across the North Sea and around Scotland: the boats were now based in vast reinforced-concrete submarine pens on the Atlantic coast of France. From there, they could reach their patrol waters more quickly, and could stay on station longer. The shorter journey was not without risk. To reach the shipping lanes, they had to cross the Bay of Biscay. Travelling on the surface to get into action as quickly as possible, they ran the gauntlet of British long-range aircraft, often submerging by day to hide

A bigger threat came from Berlin. Building programmes were still skewed to large warships – U-boats, no matter how successful, were a lower priority. As a result, losses of U-boats exceeded commissioning so that, as late as February 1941, only 22 boats were actually operational. In July and August 1940, 27 Italian boats arrived in Bordeaux. But the Italian boats were of unsuitable design and national temperaments clashed. In the first two months, the Italians sank just one ship, while the German boats sank 80.

Allied Airbases in Canada and on the British west coast enabled RAF Coastal Command to maintain anti-submarine patrols at either end of a convoy's journey. But not in the middle. Once a convoy reached the 'Atlantic gap', it was on its own. In an attempt to evade the marauding wolfpacks, British convoys were routed as far north as possible as they crossed the Atlantic. Convoys also followed zig-zag routes, radical changes of course in the night being designed to lose shadowing U-boats.

Operational control of the U-boat fleet was maintained from Wilhelmshaven, though Dönitz also had a forward headquarters at Kerneval, overlooking Lorient on the coast of Brittany. The *Kriegsmarine* kept tight control of its boats, maintaining regular radio contact.

Without the threat of aerial attack during the day, the U-boats could assemble in lines up to 20km (12 miles) apart. Positioned across likely convoy routes, they assembled into

Below: Torpedomen service their weapons in the torpedo compartment of a U-boat. Note the foldaway bunks lining the hull: about a third of the crew of 50 or so sailors was berthed here.

informal groups often named after pirates, famous battles, areas of Germany or characters from Norse mythology. More than one pack could operate at a time; convoy SC 52 out of Nova Scotia was driven back to port by 20 boats from wolfpacks *Mordbrenner*, *Reisswolf* and *Schlagtod*.

Once a convoy was located, Dönitz assigned one or two U-boats as 'shadowers'. These followed the convoy, reporting its course and speed to U-boat HQ. Position reports were sent to operational boats in the Atlantic, and the wolf pack gathered for the kill. The procedure generated a lot of radio traffic, which would eventually contribute to the submarines' defeat, but until the codes were broken and direction-finding equipment perfected, Dönitz's system worked very effectively.

The first attacks were made underwater, but ace skippers quickly learned that night surface attacks were more effective, trusting to their low silhouette to avoid detection and to the U-boat's ability to outpace most escorts. More cautious skippers remained submerged and fired fans of torpedoes at the columns of merchant ships.

In the early days of the war, convoys were only lightly escorted. The first boats to attack, drew off the escorts, leaving later arrivals, often attacking from a wide arc, a free run in on the hapless merchantmen. Curiously, a U-boat became easier to detect when it submerged. These were the days before effective radar had been widely deployed aboard escorts, but they all had ASDIC detection gear, which used sound waves to search for submerged boats.

Convoy SC 7

One of the most destructive attacks occurred when the convoy SC 7 was targeted by a 'wolf pack' including 'aces' Kretschmer, Schepke, Endrass and Frauenheim. Convoy SC 7, consisting of 34 ships, left Nova Scotia on 5 October 1940 with a single sloop in attendance. By the 16th, it was 800km (498 miles) west of Ireland, where it was met by another sloop and one of the new 'Flower' class corvettes. Also in attendance was one lone U-boat,

Right: Through 1941, the most profitable operating area for the U-Boat was in the mid-Atlantic gap: the stretch of the ocean south of Iceland that was beyond the range of air cover where convoys were at their most vulnerable.

Battle of the Atlantic III
April–December 1941

— Limit of US merchant responsibility from April

— Extent of air escort cover

-- Limit of surface escort from April

☐ Major convoy routes

• Allied merchant ships sunk by U-boats

⚓ U-boats sunk

▓ Territory under Allied control

▓ Territory under Axis control

▓ Territory under Vichy government (unoccupied France)

☐ Neutral territory

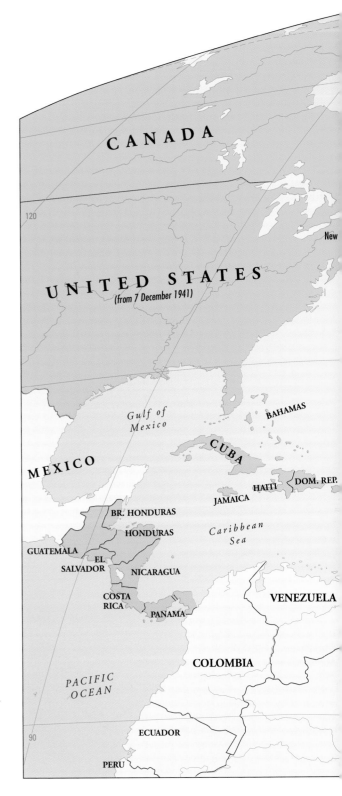

---

which promptly signalled all relevant details to headquarters and then, in bright moonlight, torpedoed two of the transports and slipped away. In their inexperience, the escorts stayed behind to pick up survivors. The convoy steamed on unescorted until the

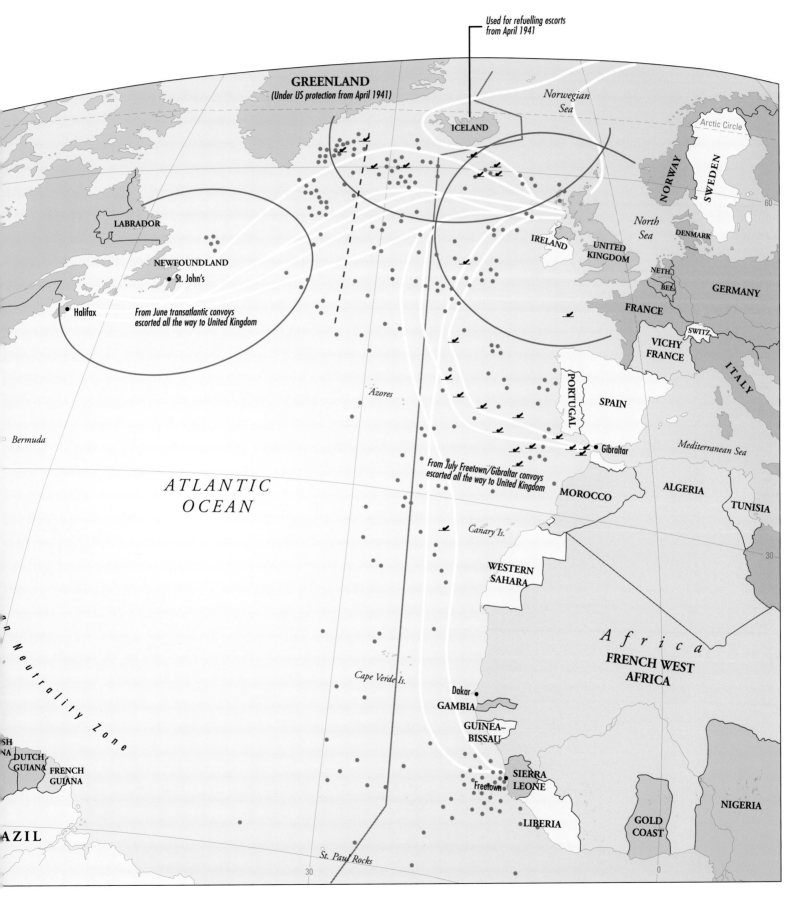

Used for refuelling escorts
from April 1941

GREENLAND
(Under US protection from April 1941)

Norwegian
Sea

Arctic Circle

ICELAND

NORWAY

SWEDEN

60

LABRADOR

North
Sea

DENMARK

NEWFOUNDLAND

St. John's

IRELAND

UNITED
KINGDOM

NETH.

GERMANY

BEL.

From June transatlantic convoys
escorted all the way to United Kingdom

Halifax

FRANCE

VICHY
FRANCE

SWITZ

ITALY

PORTUGAL

SPAIN

Bermuda

Azores

Mediterranean Sea

Gibraltar

ATLANTIC
OCEAN

From July Freetown/Gibraltar convoys
escorted all the way to United Kingdom

MOROCCO

ALGERIA

TUNISIA

30

Canary Is.

WESTERN
SAHARA

Africa
FRENCH WEST
AFRICA

Cape Verde Is.

Dakar

GAMBIA

GUINEA–
BISSAU

Neutrality Zone

SH
NA
DUTCH
GUIANA
FRENCH
GUIANA

SIERRA
LEONE

Freetown

NIGERIA

GOLD
COAST

LIBERIA

AZIL

St. Paul Rocks

30

0

Above: The primary weapon of Allied convoy escorts was the depth charge. Once an enemy submarine was forced to submerge, its speed and endurance was cut drastically, and it became vulnerable to patterns of depth charges laid from the stern of destroyers and corvettes.

following evening, when another U-boat damaged a third transport. By nightfall on 18 October, two sloops and a corvette were shepherding the remaining 31 ships. Just over the horizon was waiting a patrol line of six U-boats, whose commanders knew exactly where and when their quarry would arrive. Two of these commanders were the acknowledged aces, Joachim Schepke of *U-100* and Otto Kretschmer of *U-99*.

They struck just after midnight and a night of chaos and confusion followed. It was filled with death and destruction for the unfortunate convoy – and high excitement and triumph for the U-boat crews. All around, ships were burning, blowing up, sinking. Some settled slowly and wearily, the frigid waters lapping higher and higher until the final lurch; others broke in half, with one section sticking upright out of the water until the imprisoned air leaked out and it went down with a rush and a gulp. The steamship *Sedgepool*, with her bow blown off, knifed down into the sea like a U-boat doing a crash dive, propeller still whirling high in the air.

The escorts could do little but pick up survivors. Their Asdic was useless – the U-boats had attacked on the surface – and radar to replace it had not yet been fitted. By morning, the convoy had disintegrated and of the original 34 ships only 12 reached port – and that was only because word had reached Kretschmer and his comrades that yet another convoy, HX 79, was close behind and ripe for their attention. Of the 49 ships of this convoy, the U-boats sank 12 and damaged two more.

Allied Countermeasures

The U-boat war was not all one-sided. If a U-boat was detected, a deadly game of cat and mouse would follow in which the submarine, with its low underwater speed and limited submerged range, was at a distinct disadvantage. The crew listened as the 'ping' of enemy sonar echoed around them. If full speed on the electric motors and rapid alterations in course failed to shake the pursuer, they could try to escape by stealth, but all too often the U-boat men would hear the awful express train sound of a destroyer passing overhead to drop depth charges. The thunderous detonations of the explosive devices reverberated through the submarine. A near miss could smash dials, crack open valves and plunge the boat into darkness.

Bold skippers would take the boat down through the pre-war safety depth of 50m (164ft), the hull creaking as the pressure increased, down to and even beyond the normal maximum permissible depth of 150m (492ft). To escape from a particularly accurate depth-charging attack in 1939, Otto Kretschmer dived *U-99* beyond 210m (698ft). His gamble paid off because early-war British depth charges had a maximum depth setting of 150m (492ft). If the U-boat men were lucky, the escorts would lose contact or be compelled to abandon the attack and rush to head off an attack on another part of the convoy, at which point and the submarine could slink away.

The effect of such an attack was often to leave the U-boat a long way astern of the convoy. As long as the boat was not too seriously damaged, it would creep up to periscope depth after an hour or two. Catching the convoy again would be impossible while submerged, so captains would bring their boats back to the surface as soon as possible, using the U-boat's superior surface speed to regain contact, ready to renew its attack the following night. Once out of torpedoes, a U-boat commander would often be instructed to continue to shadow the convoy, sending position reports for the benefits of fresher boats arriving on the scene, before receiving the order to return.

Early in the war, boats spent a good proportion of their time on the surface. However, the biggest danger to any U-boat was that of surprise attack from the air, and as the war progressed more and more commanders would submerge by day when in range of Allied air bases. Even so, many were caught by surprise.

A well-trained crew could submerge a Type VII boat in 20 seconds, the bridge lookouts hurling themselves down the ladder. Minor injuries were frequent, and terrible mistakes sometimes occurred. The first watch officer of *U-451*, accidentally left on the bridge when the boat crash-dived to escape a British aircraft, was rescued by a British warship. The submarine and the rest of the crew were never seen again.

U-boat losses exceeded new production throughout 1940, and by January 1941 there were just 22 boats operational: fewer than the number available in September 1939. Even so, from July 1940 until the worsening winter weather – and more numerous escort vessels – began to have effect, the U-boats had a clear run. They sank 520 ships totalling 2.17 million tonnes (2.4 million tons) by December 1940. They could have sunk considerably more, but German torpedoes were not reliable, and would not become so until late 1941.

Changing Fortunes

The Battle of the Atlantic changed dramatically in December 1941, when Hitler declared war on the United States. Dönitz had anticipated his chief's decision, sending five Type IX boats to the US coast 48 hours before the declaration. But Dönitz's men now had a new challenge: they would have to sink merchant ships faster than the world's most powerful economy could build them. For a brief period – the second 'Happy Time' – they did. Slow American reactions to the U-boat threat left merchantmen sailing individually without escort, and until a proper convoy system was established the U-boats wreaked havoc on America's eastern seaboard. Once the US Navy set up a proper convoy system, the

THE ATLANTIC ACES

The U-boat 'aces' were the new heroes of the Nazi pantheon: young, aggressive skippers prepared to attack on the surface and close to point-blank range before firing their torpedoes. The top three, Kretschmer, Luth and Topp, sank 121 ships totalling 623,109 tonnes (687,000 tons) between them. As with fighter pilots, it was the small number of aces who inflicted most of the damage. Ace status required a score of 45,350 tonnes (50,000 tons), later increased to 90,700 tonnes (100,000 tons) and was recognized by the award of the *Ritterkreuz* (Knight's Cross). As triumphant captains returned to port, their crews were awarded medals too, on the dockside by Dönitz in person. He would continue to greet his men as they made port, through the 'happy time' and into the grim months of 1943, when losses soared to unsustainable levels. Dönitz was an inspiration to the U-boat men, his praise desired, his anger dreaded.

'The enemy holds every trump card, covering all areas with long-range air patrols and using location methods against which we still have no warning... The enemy knows all our secrets and we know none of his.'

Grand Admiral Karl Dönitz

Type IXs moved down to the Caribbean and the Gulf of Mexico, where they wreaked havoc among the vital tanker traffic coming out of Texas and Venezuela.

Yet even though the picture looked black for the Allies, the tide was on the turn. In December 1940, convoy losses had reached such proportions that defeat through starvation threatened Britain. Only immediate and drastic measures could avert catastrophe. More escorts were needed, guarding more closely controlled convoys, with better detecting equipment. Fortunately, these measures were taken – just in time.

A year later, with the danger of German invasion past, fast escort destroyers could be released from home waters. Smaller escort vessels were coming off the slips at an increasing rate. Most significant of all, British scientists had made a major breakthrough: a practical and effective airborne radar that would allow surfaced U-boats to be detected, day or night, whatever the weather. The 'Happy Time' was coming to an end.

That was difficult to see at the time. The massacre of Allied merchant shipping in 1941 had been frightening. But 1942 was worse: 1664 ships – nearly 7.26 million tonnes (8 million tons) – were sunk. And U-boat operational strength was rising fast: from 91 boats in January to 212 in December. As Churchill was to write, 'The U-boat campaign of 1942 was our worst evil.'

After the war, Churchill claimed that the only thing that had really worried him was the Battle of the Atlantic. The genuine fears of the Government and the Royal Navy, the universal impact of rationing, and horror stories like the massacre of convoy SC 7 created an enduring impression.

But the picture is misleading. For every convoy decimated like SC 7, many others reached Britain without serious loss. By December 1941, the British had sailed some 900 convoys, and of 12,000 inbound ships, the U-boats had sunk less than 300. Also, by this time the best of the pre-war trained U-boat men were at the bottom of the Atlantic in the shattered hulls of their 'iron coffins'. Few aces enjoyed their glory for long. Prien and Schepke had been killed in March, and Kretschmer had been captured.

Despite some notable setbacks, most convoys still managed to cross with little incident. During 1941, close cover became possible for the whole crossing, not least because of the crucial expansion of the Royal Canadian Navy. A sustained air offensive against transiting U-boats in the Bay of Biscay also produced an excellent return. Having contacted a convoy, submarines were now also likely to find an escort carrier providing local air cover to keep them down, while cruising escort groups quickly reinforced the close escort at the onset of any threat.

The Allied Victory

The climax of the campaign came in March 1943. The Allies lost more than 453,000 tonnes (500,000 tons) of shipping in that month alone, but from then on it was the U-boats which suffered. Between May and August, 98 new boats were commissioned – but 123 were lost. Each represented a trained crew perished or prisoner.

Despite the horrendous loss rate, and in the face of Allied efforts to disrupt the German building programme by bombing, total U-boat strength remained well over 400 until the end of hostilities. But their North Atlantic success rate declined dramatically: 463 ships were sunk in 1943 but only 132 in 1944. The Allied victory in the Battle of the Atlantic was, arguably, the single most important campaign victory of the western war. It was a close-run thing; even though only one in three U-boats actually sank an Allied vessel, their operations cost the Allies some 13 million tonnes (14.3 million tons) of

Left: U-Boat crews were young, dedicated and courageous. They had to be: by 1943, Allied countermeasures were becoming increasingly effective and U-Boat losses were soaring. The 'Happy Times' were far in the past, and the average sailor in submarines stood about one chance in nine of surviving to the end of the war.

shipping. U-boats also accounted for 158 British warships and 27 from the US Navy.

However, whatever the losses the Allies suffered, the U-boats suffered in kind. Being a U-boat crewman was probably the most dangerous occupation of the war. More than 1100 boats were built between 1935 and 1945, of which 863 sailed on operational patrols. A total of 754 boats were lost in action: 27,000 U-boat crewmen died, a casualty rate of 85 per cent. A further 5000 were taken prisoner. People sent to concentration camps had a better chance of survival than these doomed warriors of the Reich.

The Balkans and Crete

The last thing that Adolf Hitler wanted in the spring of 1941 was a war in the Balkans, since his mind was full of the forthcoming invasion of Russia. However, his ally, Italian dictator Mussolini, was in serious trouble, and German troops and aircraft were needed to prevent catastrophe.

Unfortunately for his plans, the *Führer* got more than he bargained for. Yugoslavia's stand against the Nazis was rewarded with invasion, and initially, the *Wehrmacht* seemed to be unstoppable. But the German foray into the Balkans became more extensive as the Greeks doggedly resisted conquest, and before long a ferocious partisan war was diverting resources badly needed elsewhere. This was exacerbated by British attempts to intervene (though these proved unsuccessful) and German paratroopers went on to seize Crete, inflicting another defeat on the British Empire.

The Balkans Flashpoint

Much of the blame for the Balkans war was Mussolini's. The Italian leader had originally been the dominant figure in European fascism. However, as the Nazis consolidated their grip on Germany, he was rapidly being surpassed by his German rival. Jealous of Hitler's military triumphs, which confirmed Germany as the senior partner in the Axis alliance, *Il Duce* resolved to carve out his own place in the sun.

Past military adventures had been restricted to targets unable to resist and with no friends to intervene. Libya, Abyssinia and Albania were incorporated into his latter day Roman Empire. This was achieved at the minor cost of international censure from the toothless League of Nations. Depicted by cartoonists as the opportunist jackal to the Nazi lion, Mussolini waited until the defeat of France was certain before declaring war, but unlike the triumphant *Wehrmacht*, the Italian Army suffered a humiliating setback as the French held the invaders back in the south of the country. Mussolini decided to go for what he believed would be an easier target and launched an invasion of his own, deliberately not informing Hitler until his armies were on the move.

On 28 October 1940, Italy invaded Greece. Unfortunately for Mussolini, the Greek army was a very different prospect from the ill-equipped African tribesmen that his armies had defeated in the 1930s. Not only did the Italian invasion break down that

Opposite: Adolf Hitler and Benito Mussolini were the acknowledged leaders of European Fascism. Il Duce *was one of the few men the* Führer *respected and would continue to respect to the end of his life. This was in spite of the fact that the Italian leader's adventurism drew the* Wehrmacht *into conflicts Germany did not want.*

Opposite: The German campaign in the Balkans proceeded rapidly, in spite of the rugged terrain which characterized the region. Yugoslavia fell quickly, followed by Greece. However, an easy victory was not followed by an easy occupation: the partisan war that followed was as fierce and uncompromising as any in history.

winter, but a Greek counteroffensive in December drove the invaders back into Albania and back another 80km (50 miles) for good measure. Mussolini's invasion of Greece infuriated Hitler. The German dictator was annoyed with the blatant disregard of his stated opinions on the subject, and with its effect upon his own long-term plans. It soon became obvious, however, that Hitler could not leave Mussolini to collapse into defeat. Pulling him out of trouble would necessarily be a military, not a political, matter.

The German Involvement

Hitler had already laid plans for a drive down through Bulgaria to occupy the northeast coast of the Aegean. This was intended to secure the southern flank of his planned onslaught on Soviet Russia. The operation was codenamed *Marita*, and it also made provision for dealing with Greek resistance. If the Government in Athens could not be persuaded to accept German occupation of the north, the operation also included plans for the conquest of the whole of mainland Greece, should that become necessary.

But Hitler had hoped that the bonds between his own dictatorship and that of the Greek ruler, General Metaxas, would be sufficient to avoid actual battle. Hitler wanted a peaceful occupation, similar to those already in place in Romania and Hungary, and intended for Bulgaria. He also hoped for a peaceful solution to the problem posed by Yugoslavia. Even before the war started, Germany had arranged to take Yugoslavia's entire production of copper, plus substantial quantities of lead and zinc, in return for supplies of aircraft and guns. Hitler summoned the Yugoslav foreign minister to Berchtesgaden on 27 November 1940 to suggest that Yugoslavia place herself unreservedly upon the side of the Axis.

The *Wehrmacht* had been funnelling troops into Hungary and Romania – allied to Germany by treaty – since the autumn of 1940. By February 1941, more than 650,000 were in place, primarily to secure the southern flank of the invasion of the USSR, which at that time was planned for May.

When it became necessary to take action against the Greeks, who were putting up a stiff fight against the Italians, Hitler bullied the Bulgarians and Yugoslavs into signing the Tripartite Pact. This allowed Field Marshal List's 12th Army to cross their borders on its way to Greece.

Bulgaria was forced to allow the *Wehrmacht* free passage, and German forces began to assemble opposite the 'Metaxas Line' defences that separated these ancient enemies. But an assault through Bulgaria would restrict the invasion to a relatively narrow front, which the Greeks were well prepared to resist. More Nazi browbeating secured permission from the Yugoslav Government for German forces to cross their territory to attack Greece.

British troops were already landing in Greece. Bolstered by two Commonwealth infantry divisions, an armoured brigade and RAF Hurricanes, the Greeks prepared to meet the threatened invasion. On 19 March, Hitler gave Yugoslavia five days in which to agree to neutrality and the demilitarization of the Adriatic coast. Hitler made it quite obvious that if the Yugoslavs failed to sign, life would become increasingly difficult in the very near future. On 25 March, the Yugoslav foreign minister signed the pact at a ceremony so lacking in the festive spirit that even Hitler likened it to a funeral.

Hitler's plans were disrupted with 48 hours. Hardline Serb officers organized a military coup in the name of the young King Peter, overthrowing his uncle, the Regent Prince Paul. When news of the coup reached Hitler, he thought at first that it was a joke. But amusement soon vanished, replaced by fury. He interrupted a meeting of *Wehrmacht*

Invasion of the Balkans

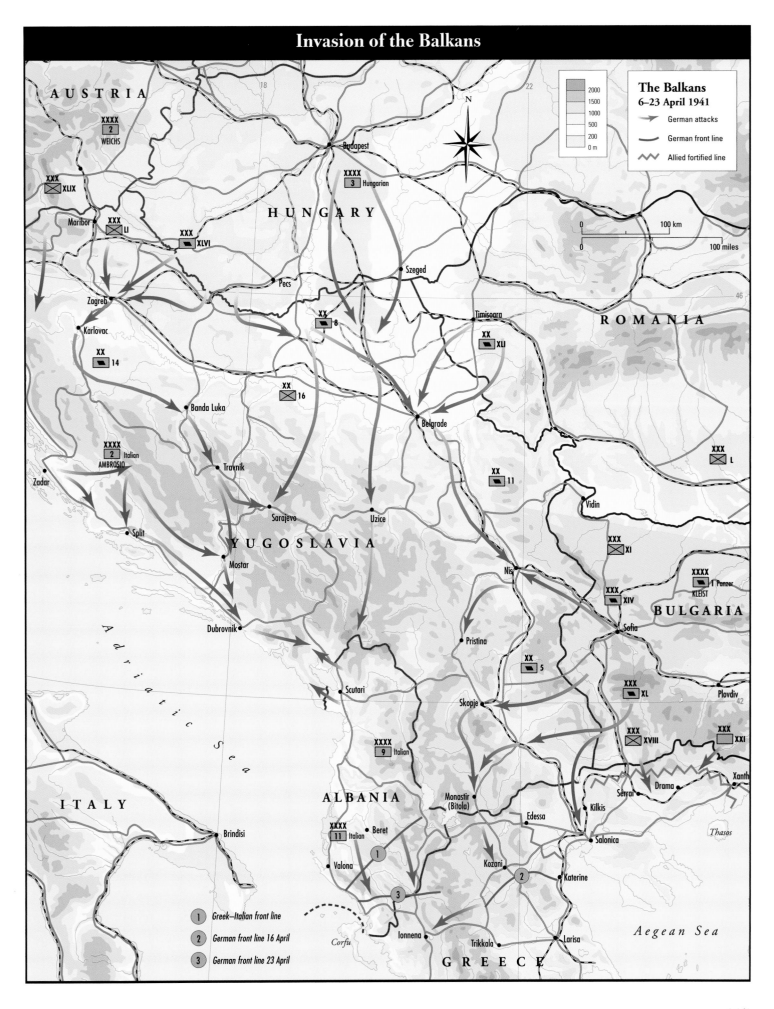

The Balkans
6–23 April 1941

→ German attacks
━ German front line
∿∿ Allied fortified line

2000	
1500	
1000	
500	
200	
0 m	

AUSTRIA

XXXX 2 WEICHS

XXX XLIX

Maribor

XXX LI

XXX XLVI

Zagreb

Karlovac

XX 14

HUNGARY

Budapest

XXXX 3 Hungarian

Szeged

Pecs

XX 8

Timisoara

XX XLI

ROMANIA

Banda Luka

XX 16

XXXX 2 Italian AMBROSIO

Zadar

Travnik

Belgrade

XXX L

Split

Sarajevo

Uzice

XX 11

Vidin

YUGOSLAVIA

Mostar

XXX XI

Dubrovnik

Pristina

XXXX 1 Panzer KLEIST

XXX XIV

Sofia

BULGARIA

Scutari

XX 5

Plovdiv

Skopje

XXX XL

A d r i a t i c   S e a

XXXX 9 Italian

XXX XVIII

XXX XXI

ITALY

Brindisi

ALBANIA

Monastir (Bitola)

Edessa

Kilkis

Drama

Xanth

Serrai

Thasos

XXXX 11 Italian   Beret

①

Valona

③

Kozani

②

Katerine

Salonica

Aegean Sea

Corfu

Ionnena

Trikkala

Larisa

GREECE

① Greek–Italian front line
② German front line 16 April
③ German front line 23 April

115

Above: Hungarian officers look on as members of a reconnaissance unit, part of the elite SS Das Reich *division, pass through Budapest on their way to the Yugoslav border.* Das Reich *had moved from the south of France to take part in the Balkan operation.*

commanders. Within hours, they had received new and unequivocal orders – there was to be no misunderstanding of the form Operation *Strafgericht* (Punishment) was to take. 'The *Führer* is determined...to make all preparations for the destruction of Yugoslavia, militarily and as a national unit....Politically it is especially important that the blow against Yugoslavia is carried out with pitiless harshness....The main task of the *Luftwaffe* is to start as early as possible...and to destroy the capital city, Belgrade, in waves of attack.'

The Assault on Yugoslavia

Spearheaded by *Luftwaffe* bomber and dive-bomber attacks, General Ewald von Kleist's XIV Panzer Corps attacked towards Belgrade. At the same time, the *Leibstandarte* 'Adolf Hitler', an elite brigade of the SS, and the 9th Panzer Division drove through Macedonia towards Skopje: the aim was to block any possible union of the Yugoslav and the Greek armies. The German onslaught began on Palm Sunday, 6 April 1941, with spectacular strikes by the *Luftwaffe*. The citizens of Belgrade were awakened by the noise of aircraft circling above them at 5.30 a.m. and within half an hour bombs were raining down on the railway station, the Royal Palace and the airfield at Zemun, where much of the Yugoslav air force was caught on the ground. For the whole of that day, the attack continued, until the centre of Belgrade was reduced to rubble. By the following evening, 17,000 people had been killed and fires continued to rage.

About 800km (500 miles) south, the menacing drone of approaching aircraft was heard in the Greek port of Piraeus. Soon afterwards, German bombers dropped mines at the harbour mouth. Then followed sticks of bombs that rained down across the shipping and warehouses along the harbour edge.

One of the victims was the SS *Glen Fraser*, anchored by the main quay. A bomb burst aboard her, and the 276 tonnes (250 tons) of explosives in her holds blew up with a shattering roar that devastated the port, and smashed doors and windows in Athens 12km (7 miles) away.

Back in Yugoslavia, the country splintered along its pre-1914 boundaries. Two Croatian divisions mutinied and a breakaway Croat republic welcomed the Germans into Zagreb while Belgrade burned. The Yugoslav Government requested an armistice on 14 April, and although Yugoslavia now fell under the iron grip of the Nazis, partisan forces would maintain a bloody campaign against the occupiers until the end of the war.

Fighting in Greece

The German attack on Greece was conceived as two main thrusts. A combined SS and armoured drive would turn south along the Albanian border, while List's Twelfth Army would attack though Macedonia, piercing or bypassing the Greek defensive lines. A smaller force was to make a series of landings on the Greek islands along the Turkish coast. The attack began on 6 April with the Twelfth Army advancing from Bulgaria with three corps. XXX and XLVIII Corps drove directly to the Aegean Sea, punching clean through the Greek defences. A British armoured brigade deployed in the north was ordered to fall back along the eastern coast. The German XL Corps included 5th Panzer Division and SS *Leibstandarte* Adolf Hitler. This force overran southern Yugoslavia to cross the Yugoslav-Greek frontier at Monastir on 10 April.

Air power was a decisive factor. The Greeks had no means to oppose the *Luftwaffe* and the British could not spare more than a token force of aircraft. Any attempt to move by day brought Stukas screaming out of the clear Mediterranean sky. Fighters joined in, and even bombers were used to strafe Allied road transport columns. It became so bad that drivers started to abandon their vehicles at the mere sound of aircraft approaching.

When Allied ground troops turned to fight, their positions were subjected to a hail of bombs. Communications broke

Below: The German invasion of Yugoslavia was supported by the Croatian Ustase *movement, which created a breakaway fascist state in Croatia under the leadership of Ante Pavelic. Members of the Croatian Legion were to serve alongside the German Army in Russia.*

down, artillery and anti-tank positions were knocked out, fuel and ammunition failed to arrive, and the wounded had to be left behind. At the same time, the Italian army launched a new offensive to coincide with Hitler's intervention. Their forces in Albania had been re-supplied and re-equipped, whereas the Greek logistic situation had not improved. Outgunned, out-numbered, and with the Germans pouring into northern Greece, the Greek army started to give way.

Hitler's Directive No.27 called for the encirclement of the Allied forces by a breakthrough in the direction of Larissa, the key road junction south of Mount Olympus. All north–south traffic east of the Pindus mountains came through this junction. With 5th Panzer Division charging down the roads and two German mountain divisions outflanking defensive positions in the valleys, the plan nearly succeeded in trapping the British.

By 12 April, the British commander General Wilson knew that the Germans were about to outflank him on the east. He ordered an evacuation southwards. By the 14th, those forces that had successfully disengaged were setting up defences along the line of the Aliakmon River and in the passes around Mount Olympus. They held the flood of German armour and infantry for four days while lorries full of exhausted men, trudging files of troops, and farm carts full of bewildered Greek families and their belongings fled

Opposite: The ancient pre-dreadnought Kilkis, *the former USS* Mississippi, *was bought by the Greek Navy from the USA in 1914. On 23 April 1941, during the German invasion of Greece, Kilkis was sunk at the Salamis naval base by German Junkers Ju 87 dive bombers.*

THE YUGOSLAV PARTISAN WAR

Following the Yugoslav armistice in April 1941, two separate groups of Serbs scattered into their barren mountains: *Chetniks*, loyal to the monarchy, and communist partisans dominated by Josip Broz, the guerrilla leader known as 'Tito'. The stage was set for an internecine war that would continue to the end of the 20th Century.

The German occupation of Yugoslavia opened a can of worms. In general, the Croats supported the Germans. Indeed Croatian *Ustase* nationalists conducted a genocidal campaign against the Serbs in Croatia and Bosnia. Some Serbs, led by local quisling General Nedic, also supported the Germans. Others – mostly pro-royalist fragments of the army and gendarmerie – took to the hills. Led by Draza Mihailovich, they adopted the old Serbian name of *Chetnik*, from *ceta*, or regiment. But the *Chetniks* were also deadly foes of the communist rebels led by Tito. The *Chetniks* offered to come over to the German side to fight the communists, while continuing to fight the Croatian fascists who were being supplied by the Germans. Internal rivalries were often more important than resisting the invaders. Serb fought Croat, *Chetnik* fought Communist, and Muslims, Catholics and Orthodox Christians killed each other with unbridled enthusiasm.

The communists were by far the most effective opposition to the Germans, and by the end of the war they claimed almost 200,000 men and women under arms. Although Tito himself was a Croat, he did more than any other Yugoslav to bring the war home to the Germans and their Croatian allies. Tito's partisan army won the support of the Western allies in preference to the unreliable Serbian *Chetniks*, since by their actions they tied down no less than 35 German divisions.

'As a base for air warfare against Great Britain in the Eastern Mediterranean, we must prepare to occupy the island of Crete; the Operation will be known as "Merkur".'

Adolf Hitler, War Directive 28, 25 April 1941

Above: German mountain infantrymen march through the dusty streets of Lamia, near the ancient battlefield of Thermopylae. The rugged terrain of Greece meant that the fitness of such elite troops was tested to the limit.

south. They were harried mercilessly by Stukas and machine-gunned by fighters. But the Allied positions were again being outflanked: German armour was driving for Ioannina and the Thessaly region to the west.

The British fell back to the ancient battlefield of Thermopylae on 18 April. British intelligence provided General Wilson with a stream of deciphered German signals that helped keep the withdrawal one step ahead of the advancing Germans, no mean trick given the mobility and tactical initiative of German commanders. On 19 April, Commonwealth troops were streaming back past Thermopylae, the rearguards digging in for yet another 'last stand'. Already Royal Navy ships were evacuating base personnel from Piraeus. But 50,000 men could not be lifted from one port, so troops were sent south to keep open the bridge over the Corinth Canal and to guard the open beaches on the Peloponnesian coast, preparing for a Dunkirk-style evacuation.

The Greek commander, General Papagos, advised the King on 21 April that the Greek army could fight no more. To General Wilson he said that the British promise to fight alongside the Greeks had been faithfully kept, but now the time had come for them to go.

The rearguards at Thermopylae held on until 24 April, then slipped away; General Wilson left Athens on the morning of 26 April and crossed the Corinth Bridge, glad to know that he had been preceded by over 40,000 men. An orderly evacuation, however, was imperilled on the same day by a daring *coup de main*. German paratroops dropped nearby to capture the bridge, and German gliders landed in support. The bridge was blown even as the Germans raced over it searching for the charges – dropping them and the bridge neatly into the canal below.

For the next two days, only the *Luftwaffe* could harass the Commonwealth evacuation, and this they did, sinking one transport and two destroyers on the night of 26 April. But the Royal Navy carried on, lifting 21,000 men off five open beaches on the 27th.

Shortly after dawn on 28 April, 5th Panzer Division and the SS *Leibstandarte* crossed the Corinth Canal and drove south. The Panzers headed for Kalamata, where after a vicious fight it became obvious that no ships would be able to get in to rescue the 7000 Imperial troops still there. Many of these had fought in all the rearguards from the Vevi Gap southwards. The British and Commonwealth troops laid down their arms after exhausting their ammunition.

Athens Falls

German troops entered Athens on 27 April. Others embarked in commandeered local vessels to occupy the Ionian islands of Samothrace, Lesbos and Chios. However, in keeping with the strict timetable for Operation Barbarossa (the invasion of the Soviet Union), the bulk of the German invasion force began withdrawing in May, leaving Greece to be held by a mixture of German reserve units and Italians.

Greek losses in the brief campaign were almost 16,000 dead and missing and nearly a quarter of a million taken prisoner. Italy lost over 90,000 dead, wounded or missing. For Germany, the cost was nearly 5000 dead and wounded. The British lost nearly 4000 dead, wounded or missing and 9000 prisoners of war. But more importantly, 50,000 British and Commonwealth soldiers lived to fight another day, plucked from the Greek fishing ports and open beaches by the Royal Navy.

Many of the troops were evacuated to Crete. They assumed that the next stop would be Egypt and a welcome break from the war. What they did not know was that the Germans were planning to make the world's first full-sized airborne assault. The last battle for Greek territory was about to begin.

Airborne Operation

Crete lay to the south of Greece. It was a large island, 275km (171 miles) long and up to 48km (30 miles) wide. It had a good anchorage for warships at Suda Bay, and strategically located airstrips at Maleme, Retimo and Heraklion.

For Hitler and his planners, Crete presented a potential problem. Royal Navy warships based at Suda could control the Aegean and Ionian Seas. Should the RAF base bombers on Crete, they would be within range of the Romanian oil fields at Ploesti. Romanian oil was going to be vital to the success of Operation Barbarossa, the massive attack about to be launched against the Soviet Union. In German hands, those airfields would be invaluable for attacking British positions in Egypt or Libya, and ideal for harassing British shipping in the southern Mediterranean. Crete would have to be neutralized.

Such a task was easier said than done. Though the Axis powers enjoyed local air superiority, they did not command the sea. The Italian fleet had been severely mauled by

'We are determined to face the Axis by whatever means and sacrifices may be necessary. We shall do our duty to the end as devoted and loyal friends, even if we have to count only on our own forces.'

Greek communiqué following the German invasion

the Royal Navy and was in no position to support a major amphibious operation. However, British warships would not be a factor if the attack came from above, and it was decided to mount a major airborne assault. This was not without its risks. German paratroopers – *Fallschirmjäger* – had achieved great success in small-unit actions on the western front in 1940. But an airborne invasion was a whole order of magnitude greater.

Unlike most of the major combatants in World War II, whose airborne forces were part of the army, the elite German parachute and gliderborne troops were part of the *Luftwaffe*. Though this had some operational disadvantages when fighting alongside the *Wehrmacht*, it provided a unique bond between the transport pilots and ground-attack aircraft crews who supported the paratroopers in combat on the ground.

German intelligence about the island and garrison was patchy. They knew that there were about 6000 British and Greek troops stationed on Crete, but did not know that numbers had been swelled with 27,000 men who had been evacuated from Greece – though most had left their arms and equipment on the mainland. Almost all the troops lifted off the Peloponnesian beaches had been taken to Crete, thus releasing the ships for a quick return to pick up more of the hard-pressed British and Anzacs.

There were also some 400,000 Cretans who, though lacking military skills, would prove to be valiant supporters of the Allies. In addition, there were 14,000 Italians on the island, who had been taken prisoner in Albania. They all had to be fed, and now the only source of everything the island needed to exist, let alone to fight off an invader, was Egypt – the only supply route was across the Mediterranean from Alexandria.

Crete is dominated by a steep and narrow mountain range, which falls sharply to the sea along the south coast, but which

Above: Messerschmitt Bf 110s of Zerstörergeschwader (ZG) 26 patrol over the Greek coast. Although vulnerable to modern fighter opposition, the Bf 110 was used extensively over the Mediterranean.

in the north leaves three areas of flatter ground. The westernmost of these is around Canea and Suda Bay, and included the airfield at Maleme; the centre area is around Retimo and the most eastern area is around Heraklion, both with their own airfields.

The German plan of attack was the result of a compromise. Colonel-General Alexander Lohr of *Luftflotte 4* was in overall command of the operation. He favoured landings around Canea and Maleme in the west and a thrust eastward along the island. Commanding the paratroopers was Lieutenant-General Kurt Student, one of the founding fathers of the German airborne forces. He wanted landings at three points – Canea/Maleme, Retimo and Heraklion. The compromise was a two-phase attack, phase one consisting of a drop on Maleme/Canea on the morning of 20 May, with further drops on Retimo and Heraklion in the afternoon. These were the areas in which New

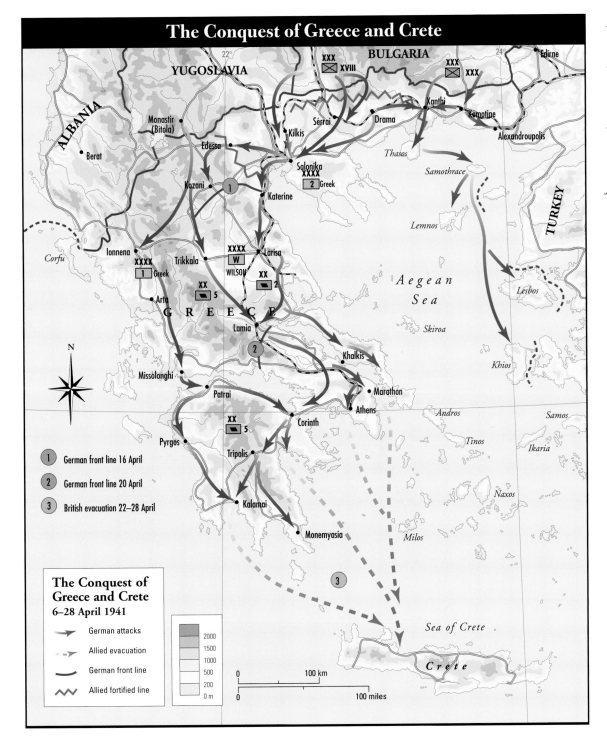

The Conquest of Greece and Crete

The Conquest of Greece and Crete
6–28 April 1941

- German attacks
- Allied evacuation
- German front line
- Allied fortified line

1 German front line 16 April
2 German front line 20 April
3 British evacuation 22–28 April

2000
1500
1000
500
200
0 m

0   100 km
0   100 miles

Left: The speed of the German assault meant that the small Commonwealth force sent to assist the Greeks could do little but fall back. By the last week in April, the Greek government had fallen and the British were evacuating to Crete.

Zealander General Bernard Freyberg had concentrated his defence. There were two brigades around Maleme, supported by three Greek battalions. At Suda Bay, three battalions reinforced the 2000 men of the original garrison force. Three Australian and two Greek battalions were posted at Retimo. At Heraklion, he deployed another five battalions. In all, the defending force numbered around 40,000 troops by 7 May.

General Wavell, commander of British forces in the Middle East, helped as much as circumstances allowed. From his depots, he scraped 22 obsolete light tanks and infantry tanks, with some worn-out artillery in addition. The Allies on Crete trained, they dug defences – and they waited. The Germans were also preparing. The men, aircraft and equipment necessary for the assault were scattered through France, Germany and Greece. There was a lot of message traffic as the force was gathered, and as coded signals

passed back and forth, they were intercepted. For years after the battle for Crete, the Allied cover story for their initial effective reaction to the airborne assault was to say that tactics had been based on a *Luftwaffe* manual captured during fighting in Holland in 1940. In fact, thanks to British success in decoding the German ULTRA signals, Freyberg knew the enemy plans almost as well as the German paratroopers who were about to land.

The main strike component of *Luftflotte 4* was General Student's *Fliegerkorps XI*. This comprised *Fliegerdivision 7* with a fighting strength of around 8000 men. Major-General Conrad commanded the transport element of the corps – nearly 500 Ju 52 trimotor transports and 72 DFS 230 gliders. Air support was provided by *Fliegerkorps VIII*, under the command of Lieutenant-General Freiherr von Richthofen. This comprised 180 fighters, over 200 dive-bombers and a similar number of medium bombers. Although almost exclusively a *Luftwaffe* operation, the invasion relied on the army for follow-up troops. These consisted of the 5th *Gebirgsjäger* division under Lieutenant-General Julius Ringel, whose three mountain rifle regiments and single motorcycle battalion were to be flown into action once the paratroopers had secured an airfield. Two further battalions of mountain troops would come by sea. Their vehicles, anti-aircraft guns, field artillery and support engineers were to be transported in two waves aboard Greek fishing boats, escorted by Italian motor torpedo boats.

The Attack on Crete

On each morning prior to the attack, German aircraft had been arriving overhead, either on reconnaissance or on the nuisance missions Allied troops called 'the morning hate'. However, at dawn on 20 May, the note and emphasis was entirely different. German fighters wove along the northern coastal strip between Maleme and Retimo. They strafed and shot up anything that moved. There were so many of them that to one startled observer there seemed to be a Messerschmitt or a Stuka for every human target.

Then, as men ducked into their trenches, a new note sounded – a prolonged buzz, like that of an approaching swarm of angry bees. As it got louder and louder, the New Zealanders around Maleme saw a huge fleet of transport planes come in towards them across the sea. As they arrived overhead, the sky blossomed with parachutes dangling men and containers. The battle for Crete had begun.

To the British and Commonwealth forces that were on the receiving end, the airborne attack on Crete was unlike anything ever seen before in war. Wearing high-laced rubber-soled boots and carrying sub-machine guns, the German paratroops in their zippered jump smocks could almost have come from another planet. This contrasted with the ordinary British soldier who still wore thick serge uniforms and leather gaiters, and who was armed with a bolt-action rifle dating from the 19th century. The first assault troops to arrive, the spearhead of Group West, were 500 glider troops delivered to the airfield at Maleme, followed by over 1800 paratroopers. The garrison reacted aggressively. Many Germans were killed as they floated down on their parachutes or as they struggled out of their harnesses. Some of the gliders crashed, killing their passengers. The Germans did, however, manage to achieve a foothold to the west of Maleme airfield and around Canea – but they were hard-pressed.

In the afternoon, the second wave of paratroops was dropped at Retimo and Heraklion. The fire coming up to meet them was just as devastating as at Maleme. This time, the paratroopers did not have the element of surprise. The survivors of the Retimo drop were reduced to two groups, besieged in a chapel and an olive oil factory.

At the *Luftwaffe* operational headquarters in Athens, Student decided that reinforcements should be committed to Group West only. A Ju 52 transport flown by Captain Kleye had managed to land at Maleme, albeit under small-arms fire, on the afternoon of the 20th. Reinforcing was risky, but was considered possible.

In the confusion of the battle, two understrength New Zealand battalions covering Maleme and Point 107 – the high ground closest to the airfield – were convinced that they were being outflanked. They pulled back on the night of the 20th. It was a move that would prove critical, since their withdrawal left Point 107 unoccupied. Fire from that high ground, which dominated the airfield, would have prevented its use for reinforcement.

Things were going even worse for the German seaborne attack. During the nights of 21 and 22 May, the Royal Navy intercepted and sank most of the seaborne elements of Ringel's mountain division. Three cruisers and a number of destroyers made short work of the fishing boats, and the glare of the searchlights and flashes of gunfire could be seen by the soldiers in Canea and Maleme less than 30km (19 miles) away.

At dawn on 21 May, German patrols discovered that Point 107 was undefended. With

'The enemy's stubborn defence could have led to our defeat, if he had grasped the situation from the very outset and had made use of all his available forces and resources.'

General Ringel, commander of German ground operations at Canea

Above: The British heavy cruiser HMS York *lies aground in Suda Bay, Crete. Damaged by an Italian explosive motor boat, she was later wrecked after being subject to numerous Luftwaffe attacks.*

Maleme airfield almost secure, the Germans piled on the pressure. Student committed his last reserve. On the 22nd, 1950 troops were landed and by the following day the total reached 3650. With reinforcements arriving, the paratroopers and men of the mountain division started to push eastwards to link up with their comrades at Canea. Under constant air attack, the Commonwealth garrison began to withdraw.

Withdrawal and Evacuation

General Freyberg, with victory snatched from his grasp, realized reluctantly that he would have to order the evacuation of Crete. The only viable port for the Royal Navy to evacuate troops from around Canea and Maleme was the tiny fishing point of Sphakia on the south coast. However, by now the Germans held the village of Galatas straddling the road south. On the 25th, two New Zealand companies were ordered to clear the village. The two companies found their numbers swelled by individuals and groups who were eager for revenge against the Germans. New Zealand, Australian and British troops who only a few days earlier had had the enemy on the run, were determined to prove they could do it again. Yelling a Maori *haka* and supported by two light tanks, the men charged into the village and drove the Germans out, clearing the road south.

On 26 May, General Freyberg ordered a general withdrawal over the mountains to the south coast and asked General Wavell to begin organization of an evacuation from the beaches at the village of Sfakia. On 28 May, the last rearguard action in the plains was fought. The long trudge over the White Mountains in progress, British commandos formed a perimeter across the ridges and ravines above Sfakia, through which the exhausted remnants of Freyberg's command made their painful way. All the time, the Germans were pushing southwards, and Stukas harassed the retreating soldiers.

The Royal Navy, with Narvik, Dunkirk and Greece behind them, were only too accustomed to the part in the drama that now occurred. They began taking troops off the beachhead on 27 May. Altogether, they lifted off over 16,000 men and took them back to Alexandria. *Luftwaffe* attacks wrought havoc during the evacuation. So high were Royal Navy losses – three cruisers and six destroyers sunk and 17 warships damaged – that the evacuation was abandoned on the 30th, leaving 5000 men to be taken prisoner.

At Heraklion, the Royal Navy was able to evacuate the garrison, but at Retimo, which had put up the most effective defence, they were all taken prisoner. Some of the men who had not been evacuated, evaded capture and a few of them managed to find craft to cross the 300km (186 miles) of water to North Africa. Others were evacuated by submarine. British and Commonwealth losses were 4000 killed, missing or wounded, with a further 11,000 captured. The Royal Navy lost 2000 men killed and nearly 200 wounded.

Occupation

When the fighting was over, unfounded rumours circulated that Cretan civilians had murdered German paratroopers. The Cretans suffered a harsh occupation, which began with the execution of 700 men whom the Germans regarded as *francs-tireurs* – civilian snipers. In four months, the occupation forces executed 1135 Cretans and destroyed four villages.

For the German airborne forces, it had been a Pyrrhic victory. Of the 8500 men dropped or landed by glider on Crete, 44 per cent were killed, the majority on the first day. As Churchill was later to put it, the 'very spearhead of the German lance' had been shattered. As for the price in aircraft, nearly half of the German transports had been destroyed. Losses were so high that Hitler came to a very similar conclusion as the British Prime Minister. Some days later, he decorated the more outstanding of the officers who had fought in Crete, then entertained them to lunch. Over coffee, he turned to Student and said: 'Of course, you know, General, that we shall never do another airborne operation. Crete proved that the days of parachute troops are over.'

With these words, the *Führer* ensured that the superbly-trained German *Fallschirmjäger* would no longer be used in airborne assaults, and would be expended as infantry. Hitler was proved wrong – as Allied forces were to show later in the war.

Apart from a few small operations, German paratroopers would never again be used on such a huge scale. They may have captured the island in May 1941, but Crete proved to be 'the grave of the German paratroop arm'.

Below: A wounded British soldier is helped by a comrade, following their capture after the fall of Crete. Over 11,000 British and Commonwealth troops were taken prisoner in the Greek campaign.

The Desert War, 1940–42

The war in North Africa began in earnest on 9 December 1940. Hitler watched, with caustic amusement, as Benito Mussolini tried to expand the Italian empire in North Africa. *Il Duce's* armies crept tentatively from Libya into Egypt. Then the British counterattacked. Italy was threatened with the annihilation of her forces and the total loss of her colonies. Germany would have to come to the rescue.

The Italian disaster threatened Fortress Europe. For his own security, Hitler felt that he had no option but to intervene on behalf of his ally. By the middle of February 1941, the first contingent of German support had reached Tripoli. It was not large – in fact, it consisted of one general and two staff officers – but the general was a man called Rommel.

Enter Rommel

As the commander of the 'Ghost' Division in France, Major-General Erwin Johannes Eugen Rommel had won a reputation as a brilliant commander. His orders were to stabilize the situation in North Africa. Rommel's force initially included only the 5th Light Division. For the moment, he was simply expected to stiffen Italian resistance. Perhaps, in due course, he would be given the resources to do more, but he was to await orders from above before contemplating offensive action.

Yet Rommel would not wait. Within days, he was planning a full-scale counterattack. With that would begin two years of cut-and-thrust battles between the Germans and British and Commonwealth forces. The battlefield was to be the Libyan desert, an area aptly described as a tactician's paradise and a quartermaster's nightmare.

Disobeying orders with a diligence that compels respect, Rommel moved the German 5th Light Division from Tripoli towards Agedabia on 24 March. There, on 3 April, Rommel set up his headquarters. He then cast aside all established principles of warfare by deliberately splitting the already tenuous forces at his disposal into three. He sent a mixed German and Italian force under Graf von Schwerin eastwards in a wide arc. While this passed through Giof el Matar and Tengeder towards Mechili, he directed the bulk of 5th Light to advance through Antelat and Msus. Rommel himself accompanied the armoured cars and light vehicles of the 3rd Reconnaissance Battalion to the north,

Opposite: British cavalrymen pose aboard their Vickers Light Tank on the Egyptian border with Libya. Commonwealth troops in North Africa were lightly equipped, but they were more than a match for the more numerous but poorly led Italian opponents.

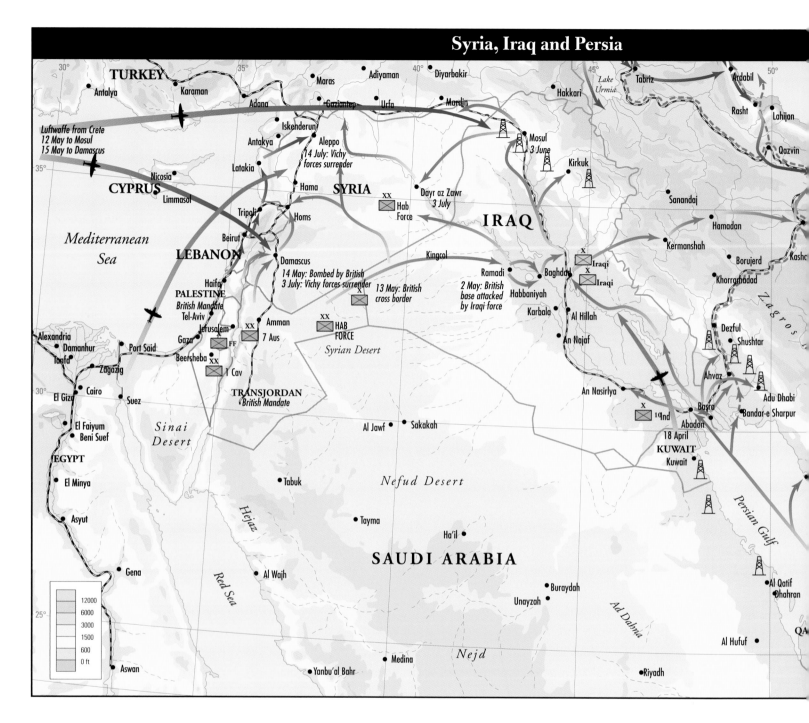

Syria, Iraq and Persia

Luftwaffe from Crete
12 May to Mosul
15 May to Damascus

TURKEY

Antalya · Karaman · Adana · Gaziantep · Urfa · Mardin · Maras · Adiyaman · Diyarbakir · Hakkari · *Lake Urmia* · Tabriz · Ardabil · Rasht · Lahijan · Qazvin

Iskenderun
Antakya · Aleppo
14 July: Vichy
forces surrender

CYPRUS · Nicosia · Limmasol

Latakia · Hama · **SYRIA** · Dayr az Zawr 3 July · Mosul 3 June · Kirkuk · Sanandaj · Hamadan

Mediterranean Sea

Tripoli · Homs · XX Hab Force · **IRAQ** · Kermanshah · Borujerd · Kashe

Beirut · **LEBANON** · Kingcol · Ramadi · Baghdad · X Iraqi · X Iraqi · Khorrahadad · *Zagros*

Damascus
14 May: Bombed by British
3 July: Vichy forces surrender
13 May: British cross border
2 May: British base attacked by Iraqi force

Haifa · Habbaniyah · Karbala · Al Hillah · Dezful · Shushtar

PALESTINE *British Mandate* · Tel-Aviv · Jerusalem · XX FF · Amman · 7 Aus · XX HAB FORCE · An Najaf · Ahvaz

Gaza · *Syrian Desert* · An Nasirlya · Basra · Adu Dhabi · Bandar-e Sharpur

Beersheba · XX 1 Cav · **TRANSJORDAN** *British Mandate*

Alexandria · Damanhur · Tanta · Port Said · Zagazig

El Giza · Cairo · Suez

Sinai Desert · Al Jawf · Sakakah · X Ind · Abadan 18 April · **KUWAIT** · Kuwait

EGYPT · El Faiyum · Beni Suef · El Minya

Asyut · *Nefud Desert* · *Persian Gulf*

Gena · *Hejaz* · Tabuk · Tayma · Ha'il · **SAUDI ARABIA**

Red Sea · Al Wajh · Buraydah · *Ad Dahna* · Al Qatif · Dhahran

Aswan · Yanbu'al Bahr · Medina · *Nejd* · Unayzah · Riyadh · Al Hufuf · QA

12000 / 6000 / 3000 / 1500 / 600 / 0 ft

Iraq, Syria and Persia
April–September 1941

→ Allied forces movements

→ Free French forces movements

→ Russian forces movements

✈ Allied bomber movements

✈ German bomber movements

- - → Allied supply routes

⛟ Oilfield

towards Suluch. Then, having heard rumours that the British were evacuating Benghazi, he ordered them to drive straight for the port. Here his troops were welcomed as conquering heroes. The *Afrika Korps* had come to liberate the Italian Empire in Cyrenaica, and the joy at seeing the advancing Germans appeared genuine. However, the wild enthusiasm exhibited by the inhabitants reminded one American observer of the jubilation with which the Australians had been received only a few months before. The desert taught the lessons of pragmatism.

Now free to manoeuvre in open desert, Rommel pushed his reinforcements forward. With numerical, and, more importantly, psychological advantage, the Germans surged east. The British were now in headlong retreat, being harried all the way by the Axis air forces, which enjoyed total control of the skies.

By 7 April, Rommel had captured Derna and isolated Mechili, and his reconnaissance units were probing eastwards south of Tobruk. Mechili fell to the Germans on the

morning of 8 April and the victorious Panzer troops encountered the all too familiar evidence of a broken enemy. All around was the detritus of a fleeing army – abandoned tanks, troop carriers and trucks, and, of course, the bodies of the fallen.

By the 9th, Rommel's reconnaissance units reached Bardia, with the Egyptian frontier, Halfaya Pass and Sollum just a few miles on. Some surviving British formations were scurrying past them towards the bases from which they had launched their own offensive only four months previously. But many had no opportunity to flee; large numbers were surrounded and others had already surrendered.

Rommel's headlong advance recovered all the territory lost by the Italians. He was soon talking to his staff about Egypt and the Suez Canal. But he would have to take into account the reactions of the Italians.

It is worth noting that the Axis forces in North Africa remained under Italian command until early 1943. At this time, Rommel was only a corps commander. The theatre commander in Africa was Italian, as were the majority of Rommel's troops. In that situation lay a problem. Italian units had dash and elan, but no endurance. Importantly, in the mobile warfare for which Rommel was so suited, their infantry divisions were not mechanized and so could rarely exploit the successes of German armour. All of the *Afrika Korps* units were mobile, and therefore the German infantry could keep pace with the Panzers and exploit the breaches made in the Allied lines.

Under Rommel's leadership, two Italian divisions, the *Ariete* armoured division and the *Trieste* motorized division, fought extremely well. The rest of the forces were of varying levels

Left: In addition to dealing with the primary theatre of operations in North Africa, the British Middle East Command was also responsible for campaigns against the Vichy French in Syria and for securing the vital Iraqi oilfields, threatened by a German-inspired uprising.

IRAQ UPRISING

In May 1941, the Germans added to General Wavell's problems in the Middle East by instigating an uprising in Iraq led by Rashid Ali, the Iraqi Prime Minister. Attacks at Basra and Habbaniyah threatened the supplies of oil vital to Britain's continued prosecution of the war. The Germans provided supplies and munitions, and set up an airbase at Mosul, in the north of the country. The British fought off the attacks, the airfield at Habbaniyah being defended by clerks and ground crew with support from hastily armed RAF trainers and transport aircraft. A small British relief column advanced from Palestine, and more reinforcements were sent from India. Taking the offensive, the British bombed the air base at Mosul and a ground column advanced on Baghdad, taking the city on 30 May.

To further add to the complications, the British also had to deal with the threat from 35,000 German-advised Vichy French troops in Syria. Churchill ordered Wavell to eliminate the threat. The hard-pressed commander managed to scrape together another 20,000 troops, who invaded Syria from Iraq and Palestine on 8 June. The British forces included Free French under General Georges Catroux. Damascus was captured on 21 June, and the Vichy forces surrendered on 12 July. Syria and Lebanon were transferred to Free French control, and most of the Vichy troops volunteered to join Catroux.

of mediocrity and when under pressure could be counted upon to fold like a house of cards. They did, however, prove reasonably effective if 'corsetted' at key points by intermingling with German units.

To consolidate and extend his gains, Rommel would need adequate reinforcement and supply. For this, he had to rely upon the Italian merchant navy. Here was another problem, because the Axis did not control the Mediterranean shipping lanes. The Royal Navy attacked Italian convoys with merciless professionalism. Cruiser and destroyer squadrons sortied from Egypt and submarines from the island of Malta, which lay conveniently astride the convoy routes. By the end of 1942, Italy had hardly a merchant ship left in service; the rest were on the bottom of the Mediterranean.

Facing the Germans

Rommel's forces reached the key port of Tobruk on 10 April 1941, but a hastily organized assault was beaten off by the Australian garrison. Rommel's offensive attracted the interest of the General Staff, which despatched Colonel-General Friederich Paulus to investigate. He was not impressed, describing Rommel as 'headstrong'. Paulus also worried that what had begun as a sideshow could become a major drain on resources just as the invasion of Russia was about to begin.

DESERT CONFLICT

The desert war was unusual in many respects. There were few cities and few obstacles to the rapid movement of mechanized forces. Armies required vast quantities of petrol and water. Supplies of fresh vegetables and fruit were scarce for both sides. Without enough water to drink, there was certainly none to be spared for washing. Occupation of oases was vital to both sides, and any fight over a water source was guaranteed to be hard.

More than in any other theatre, the desert war was fought by logistics. The length of the supply lines dictated the yo-yo nature of the North African campaign. The further from the supply port, the more difficult it was to sustain the advance. Conditions were not helped by the poor state of the roads – deeply rutted dust tracks in the summer and quagmires in winter. Consequently, there were never enough supplies. Rommel insisted on eating the same rations as his men, and his health steadily deteriorated as a result.

Yet the conventions of the desert war harked back to more civilized days. Rommel was a star in the Nazi propaganda machine, yet had no time for the ideology of the *untermensch*. There were no SS units in Africa, no *Einsatzgruppen*, and the civilian population, such as it was, consisted of Arab nomads, often well disposed to the Germans. Allied prisoners could expect reasonable treatment from their captors and did not starve even when the Germans themselves did not have enough.

Above: The smashing success of the Desert Force offensive in December 1941 left the British with a rich haul of captured Italian equipment. Here, a British Morris armoured car tows an Italian tankette.

Arguments about German offensive aims in Africa were rendered academic by a succession of British attacks. In May, General Wavell launched Operation Brevity, which was defeated. In June, the Allies tried again, this time reinforced with nearly 300 new tanks shipped from England. Operation Battleaxe showed Rommel and the *Afrika Korps* at their best. British armoured units tried to seek out and engage Rommel's armour in a tank-versus-tank battle. But the Germans made masterful use of their towed anti-tank guns, firing from well-concealed positions. They inflicted terrible losses before the Panzers wheeled in from the flank to finish the business. The *Luftwaffe's* 88mm (3.46in) anti-aircraft guns were pressed into service in a ground role since the army's standard 37mm (1.46in) weapon could not penetrate the British 'infantry' tanks, Matilda and Valentine. Ironically, the British had a similar weapon available, the equally high-velocity 93mm (3.7in) anti-aircraft gun, but lack of imagination and inter-service squabbling prevented them from using it the way the Germans employed their '88'.

In three days' fighting, known as the battle of Sollum by the Germans, the *Afrika Korps* demonstrated its superior leadership and vastly better staffwork. Wavell was sacked and replaced by General Auchinleck as Commander-in-Chief Middle East Command, who was pressed by London to renew the attack and relieve Tobruk, still besieged by the Axis forces. Both sides sent reinforcements, but Germany had little to spare as the invasion of the USSR was now in full swing. Rommel developed jaundice in August, but soldiered on, his forces now designated *Panzergruppe Afrika*.

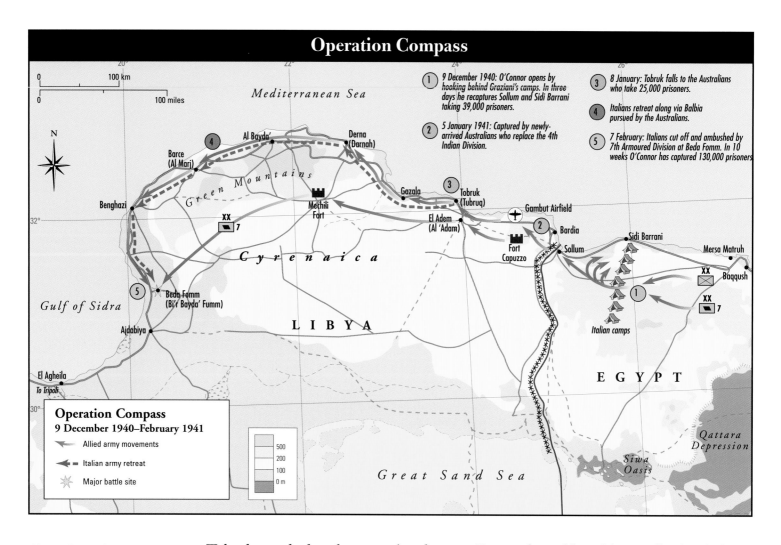

Operation Compass

Mediterranean Sea

1 9 December 1940: O'Connor opens by hooking behind Graziani's camps. In three days he recaptures Sollum and Sidi Barrani taking 39,000 prisoners.

2 5 January 1941: Captured by newly-arrived Australians who replace the 4th Indian Division.

3 8 January: Tobruk falls to the Australians who take 25,000 prisoners.

4 Italians retreat along via Balbia pursued by the Australians.

5 7 February: Italians cut off and ambushed by 7th Armoured Division at Beda Fomm. In 10 weeks O'Connor has captured 130,000 prisoners

Operation Compass
9 December 1940–February 1941

Allied army movements

Italian army retreat

Major battle site

Above: Operation Compass, the British offensive against the Italian army in North Africa, was a smashing success. Under the command of Major General Richard O'Connor, the outnumbered Desert Force advanced as far as Beda Fomm in little more than two months.

Tobruk was the key: by capturing the port, Rommel would get his supplies landed just behind the front, instead of having them driven across the hundreds of kilometres of coast road from Benghazi. Thanks to the ULTRA code-breakers, the British knew all about Rommel's plans for Tobruk. They deliberately staged their own offensive within days of the planned German assault. On 17 November, Rommel's signals staff reported 'complete English radio silence' – a sign of an impending attack. He ignored them, and ignored the first reports of a major British attack.

The British Eighth Army under Lieutenant-General Cunningham advanced to relieve Tobruk, its powerful tank force surging across the desert to find and destroy the German armour. On 19 November, the key airfield at Sidi Rezegh was overrun by British tanks. Rommel was reluctant to abandon his own attack on Tobruk, but when he reacted, he did so with his usual vigour. Fighting raged around Sidi Rezegh until 23 November, the combatants manoeuvring aggressively in the open terrain. There was no real front line. Both sides had headquarters units and supply columns taken by surprise by enemy tanks. Both sides also suffered heavily, but had only a hazy idea of their opponents' losses. In such a battle, psychological strength is a priceless asset. On 24 November, Rommel struck out behind the British, heading for the Egyptian frontier rather than staying to beat back the British assault along the coast road. It was a daring move, but it left the German commander out of touch with his own headquarters for several days. Cunningham, who had narrowly avoided capture in the chaotic battle, was sacked by Auchinleck. The British commander-in-chief placed his own chief of staff, Lieutenant-General Ritchie, in command of the Eighth Army.

Rommel's 'dash to the wire' failed to relieve the small garrisons left in the wake of the British advance. His own staff regarded it as premature, and it was ended on his own initiative by Lieutenant-Colonel Westphal at Rommel's HQ, who ordered the 21st Panzer Division back to Tobruk. Rommel remained out of communication as he raced around the battlefield micro-managing the operation.

Defeat and Victory

Rommel admitted defeat and fell back towards Gazala. But there was no obvious defence line, and he soon announced that the retreat must go on back to the Gulf of Sirte. There, in bad weather and worse tempers, Operation Crusader, or 'The Winter Battle' as the Germans called it, fizzled out in the desolate sands around El Agheila. It had been from there, nine long months before, that Rommel had launched the first spectacular advance of the *Afrika Korps*.

It seemed as though history was repeating itself: the victorious British, scattered and disorganized after a long advance; the Axis pushed back deep into its own territory. But as it would soon prove, the *Afrika Korps* had recoiled like a spring. By January 1942, it was compressed, ready to be unleashed. The 'Benghazi handicap', as some wags had dubbed it, was not over yet.

Rommel had excellent intelligence from reconnaissance and decrypted enemy radio traffic. In January 1942, he knew that he had a window of opportunity to counterattack. The British were preparing their own offensive, but judged the Axis forces too weakened by their recent defeat and withdrawal to be capable of immediate action.

Below: Stretched by two months of hard fighting, the British were in no shape to resist Rommel's newly arrived Afrika Korps. *Even as British troops were being evacuated from Crete, the Commonwealth force in North Africa was forced to give up the ground won during Operation Compass.*

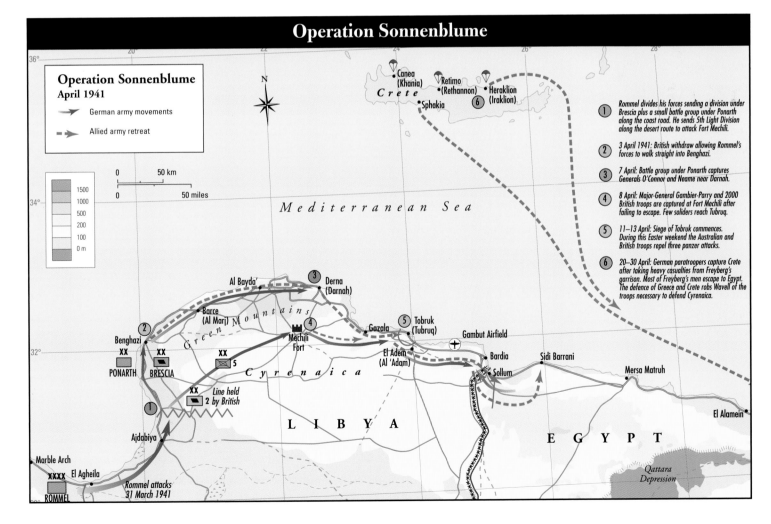

Operation Sonnenblume

Operation Sonnenblume
April 1941

→ German army movements

⇢ Allied army retreat

1. Rommel divides his forces sending a division under Brescia plus a small battle group under Ponarth along the coast road. He sends 5th Light Division along the desert route to attack Fort Mechili.

2. 3 April 1941: British withdraw allowing Rommel's forces to walk straight into Benghazi.

3. 7 April: Battle group under Ponarth captures Generals O'Connor and Neame near Darnah.

4. 8 April: Major-General Gambier-Parry and 2000 British troops are captured at Fort Mechili after failing to escape. Few soliders reach Tubruq.

5. 11–13 April: Siege of Tobruk commences. During this Easter weekend the Australian and British troops repel three panzer attacks.

6. 20–30 April: German paratroopers capture Crete after taking heavy casualties from Freyberg's garrison. Most of Freyberg's men escape to Egypt. The defence of Greece and Crete robs Wavell of the troops necessary to defend Cyrenaica.

In contrast to the divided counsels of the British Eighth Army, Rommel was very much his own man. Theoretically subordinate to Army Command South-West and the Italian high command, he would ignore his German superiors. His Italian superiors learned of his plans only once their own formations were discovered to be on the move.

Both sides knew the Germans had landed over a hundred new tanks in North Africa. This was, as Rommel's chief of staff, Fritz Bayerlein, remarked, 'as good as a victory in battle'. Some of these new tanks were the up-gunned Mark IVs, better than anything the British could field. Rommel was not the man to allow men and material to stay idle if he could see a worthwhile purpose for their employment. On 21 January 1942, the Axis

forces caught the British by surprise, who were soon again in helter-skelter retreat.

By 10 February, weary, weatherworn, thirsty but triumphant, *Panzerarmee Afrika* under its remarkable leader was well back into Marmorica, with Tobruk – for so long their apparently unobtainable objective – again only 56km (35 miles) beyond their grasp.

In the meantime, Rommel's superior, Field Marshal Kesselring, advised against further precipitate action – at least until more men, more Panzers, more ammunition and especially more fuel were to hand. Even Rommel saw the wisdom of this, so for the moment only his reconnaissance units pressed much further forward than Tmimi. There they quickly found that Commonwealth troops had reassembled on a line running south from the Gazala inlet as far as the *Beau Geste*-style fort at Bir Hacheim. In the north and centre, they were in the process of building themselves defensive positions of considerable strength. Deep minefields bridged the gap down to Bir Hacheim. It was clear that *Panzerarmee Afrika* would need all its expertise to break through or to bypass these defences.

Both sides were engaged in a logistical race to assemble as powerful a force as possible for the next battle. However, Axis operations in the Mediterranean could not affect supplies being sent the long route around Africa, and by the spring of 1942 the first American supplies reached Egypt, including numbers of M3 medium tanks, known to the British as 'Lees' and 'Grants'. The M3 featured a 37mm (1.46in) gun in a turret plus a 75mm (2.95in) gun in the hull. The vehicle could not fight 'hull down', but it compared well to the thin-skinned British Cruiser tanks in widespread service and, being American, did not break down with the depressing regularity of so many British-built tanks.

Left: Much of the terrain in North Africa was perfect for armoured warfare – but by the same token, it provided unobstructed fire for anti-tank guns. Here a British 6-pdr crew go into action alongside a burned out Panzer III.

'To every man of us, Tobruk was a symbol of British resistance, and we were now going to finish with it for good.'

*Erwin Rommel,
June 1942*

Objective: Tobruk

By mid-May, Rommel's battlefield reconnaissance teams detected signs that the British offensive was imminent. He was still outnumbered, but persuaded Kesselring to release many of his squadrons from the Malta operation, including dive-bombers and also

Messerschmitt Bf 109Fs, which were superior to any RAF fighters then in North Africa.

The British defences consisted of a succession of fortified camps, or 'boxes', occupied by infantry brigades with supporting artillery. Dug in behind barbed wire, with some 500,000 landmines surrounding them, they were designed to break up and channel the enemy attack. Behind these lines, the British armoured divisions waited, theoretically concentrated and ready to deliver a knock-out blow, but in reality scattered about the desert with confused command arrangements.

Rommel believed the British just did not understand the basic principles of war. In truth, his opponents grasped the theory; it was a failure of execution owing to the 'command by committee' syndrome that prevailed in the Eighth Army.

Rommel had visited Hitler in March and personally obtained permission for a new offensive. His objective was Tobruk. His orders were to go no further and to return the *Luftwaffe* squadrons to Sicily within a month. His own correspondence reveals greater ambition. He planned, even before the battle of Gazala, to break clean through to Egypt and the Suez canal, converting a hoped-for local success into a major strategic victory.

Rommel attacked on 26 May. Neither his plan nor that of the British survived first contact with the enemy. His feint at the centre of the British line failed to draw the British reserves; his predictable wide flanking manoeuvre was not intercepted by British tank divisions, which sat immobile while their commanders bickered.

General Cruewell, commander of the *Afrika Korps* (Rommel was by this time the commander of the entire *Panzerarmee*, of which the *Afrika Korps* was one element), was shot down in his light aircraft and captured. This occurred just as Kesselring was visiting

Below: Operation Crusader forced the Germans to retreat into Libya. In what was to become a characteristic of the Desert War, the back-and-forth nature of the conflict led to some troops giving it the nickname 'The Benghazi Handicap'.

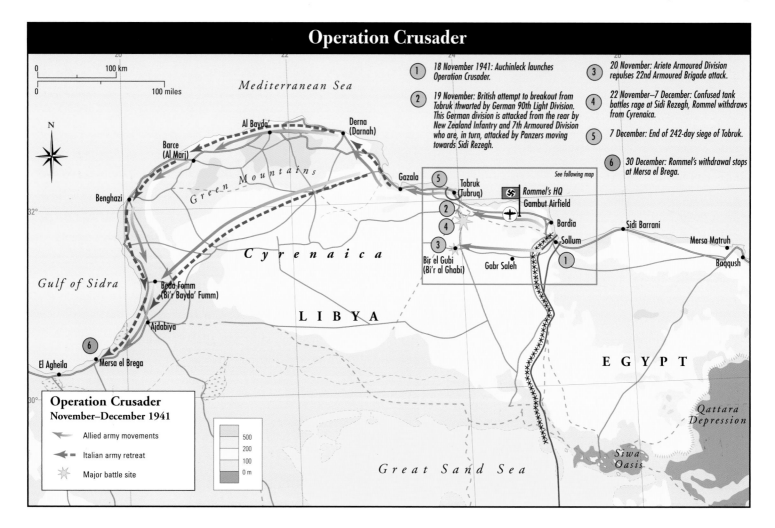

Operation Crusader

1 18 November 1941: Auchinleck launches Operation Crusader.

2 19 November: British attempt to breakout from Tobruk thwarted by German 90th Light Division. This German division is attacked from the rear by New Zealand Infantry and 7th Armoured Division who are, in turn, attacked by Panzers moving towards Sidi Rezegh.

3 20 November: Ariete Armoured Division repulses 22nd Armoured Brigade attack.

4 22 November–7 December: Confused tank battles rage at Sidi Rezegh, Rommel withdraws from Cyrenaica.

5 7 December: End of 242-day siege of Tobruk.

6 30 December: Rommel's withdrawal stops at Mersa el Brega.

Operation Crusader
November–December 1941

→ Allied army movements

◄- - Italian army retreat

✳ Major battle site

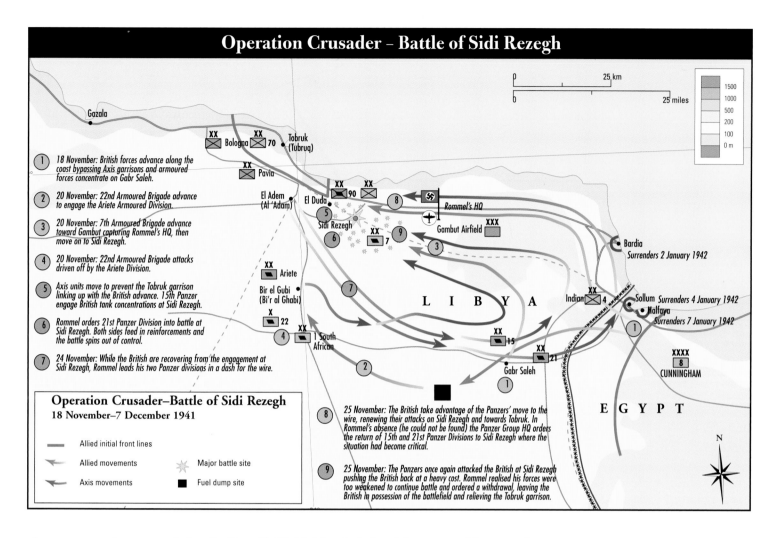

Operation Crusader – Battle of Sidi Rezegh

1. 18 November: British forces advance along the coast bypassing Axis garrisons and armoured forces concentrate on Gabr Saleh.

2. 20 November: 22nd Armoured Brigade advance to engage the Ariete Armoured Division.

3. 20 November: 7th Armoured Brigade advance toward Gambut capturing Rommel's HQ, then move on to Sidi Rezegh.

4. 20 November: 22nd Armoured Brigade attacks driven off by the Ariete Division.

5. Axis units move to prevent the Tobruk garrison linking up with the British advance. 15th Panzer engage British tank concentrations at Sidi Rezegh.

6. Rommel orders 21st Panzer Division into battle at Sidi Rezegh. Both sides feed in reinforcements and the battle spins out of control.

7. 24 November: While the British are recovering from the engagement at Sidi Rezegh, Rommel leads his two Panzer divisions in a dash for the wire.

Operation Crusader–Battle of Sidi Rezegh
18 November–7 December 1941

— Allied initial front lines

← Allied movements

← Axis movements

✷ Major battle site

■ Fuel dump site

8. 25 November: The British take advantage of the Panzers' move to the wire, renewing their attacks on Sidi Rezegh and towards Tobruk. In Rommel's absence (he could not be found) the Panzer Group HQ orders the return of 15th and 21st Panzer Divisions to Sidi Rezegh where the situation had become critical.

9. 25 November: The Panzers once again attacked the British at Sidi Rezegh pushing the British back at a heavy cost. Rommel realised his forces were too weakened to continue battle and ordered a withdrawal, leaving the British in possession of the battlefield and relieving the Tobruk garrison.

Gazala

Bologna · 70 · Tobruk (Tubruq)

Pavia

El Adem (Al 'Adam) · El Duda · 90

Sidi Rezegh · 8 · Rommel's HQ

Gambut Airfield

Ariete

Bir el Gubi (Bi'r al Ghabi) · 22

1 South African

Gabr Saleh

15

21

LIBYA

Indian 4

Bardia · Surrenders 2 January 1942

Sollum · Surrenders 4 January 1942

Halfaya · Surrenders 7 January 1942

CUNNINGHAM

EGYPT

N

the command post and the *Luftwaffe* Field Marshal (and former artilleryman) spent an enjoyable afternoon taking charge, as senior officer present, until Rommel arrived. For a commander often criticized for not paying regard to logistics, Rommel turned the tables on the British by personally organizing a night re-supply for 15th Panzer Division. His tanks had broken through the British lines, but found themselves surrounded. The British commanders believed they had him trapped.

It is one of the classic military maxims that commanders are beaten only when they themselves believe it. Rommel's confidence was supreme, as witnessed by a captured British officer who described him directing this most confused of battles. Hunched over a map in his command vehicle, headphones on, Rommel issued an endless succession of orders with quiet authority, his confidence, his grip on the battle in such dramatic contrast to the confusion on the other side.

There was no real front line. Situation maps showed a hideously complex intermingling of forces. Victory went to the man who believed he would win, defeat to commanders who, deep down, believed themselves and their system inferior. Fighting around the 'Knightsbridge' box, held by the Guards brigade, went in favour of the Germans. The southernmost anchor of the Allied line, the Free French position at Bir Hacheim, was attacked and taken after over a week of epic resistance. The British withdrew, their retreat taking on the appearance of a rout as Rommel threw every last man and every precious litre of petrol into the pursuit. Suddenly, Tobruk was under serious threat. Rommel attacked the southeastern quadrant of Tobruk's defences at 5.20 a.m. on the morning of 20 June. Unfortunately for the British, they were convinced

Above: Known to the Germans as 'The Winter Battle', Operation Crusader stopped Rommel's dash to the wire. Isolated at the end of long, vulnerable lines of communications, the Afrika Korps *had to retreat back as far as the Gulf of Sirte.*

'We have a very daring and skilful opponent against us, and, may I say across the havoc of war, a great general.'

Winston Churchill on Erwin Rommel

that the attack, when it came, would be from the southwest. Most of the artillery and the entire 2nd South African Division were stationed in the western half of the fortress. In addition, most of the mines that had been used at Gazala had been taken from the defences at Tobruk, weakening the southeastern perimeter at the point where Rommel launched his assault. The German attack went like clockwork. Three hours after Kesselring's bombers had opened the offensive, the 15th Panzer Division punched through the British lines and fanned out. The Italian *Ariete* and *Trieste* divisions exploited the gaping breach in the defences. Once the Axis troops were through the perimeter, they were able to roll up the defences in true *Blitzkrieg* fashion.

The next day, to the astonishment and fury of the British and Commonwealth troops still defending doggedly, a huge white flag was hoisted above brigade headquarters. As it flapped open in the first morning breeze, a great moan of disappointment, anguish and misery welled up from all over the western half of the garrison. Defeat is bitter in any circumstances, but now, in the minds of thousands who were experiencing it, it was compounded by disgrace. Over 30,000 Allied prisoners were taken that day. As they moved off in file they passed a triumphant Rommel. Most probably did not recognize him. After all, which of their commanders would have shared the dangers of actual combat? The spoils were immense. Two thousand vehicles, 4535 tonnes (5000 tons) of supplies and 1814 tonnes (2000 tons) of fuel were given up. Rommel now calculated that nothing stood between him and ultimate victory.

The Collapse of the British

The capture of Tobruk brought exultation to the *Panzerarmee* and a field marshal's baton to Rommel. But there was to be no rest for either of them.

Rommel dismissed the news of his promotion with the comment that he would far rather have had another Panzer division. To the congratulations of his staff, he responded with the brusque order, 'All units will assemble and prepare for further advance.' For his eyes were now on the Egyptian frontier and the vast prize of the Nile Delta, the Suez Canal and all the horizons beyond. Rommel answered remonstrances from Kesselring and the Italian commanders by saying that the enemy were in such disarray that they would be able to offer little or no resistance to the swift and powerful drive he was about to launch. He added that, with the stores dumps of Tobruk now at his disposal, no critical shortage would impede his progress. As for previous plans and agreements, such overwhelming victory swept away the need for caution, a conclusion in which he was later supported by both Mussolini and Hitler.

By the evening of 22 June, the 90th Light Division was in Bardia and 21st Panzer was on its way to join it. By the following day, 15th Panzer and the *Ariete* Divisions were closing up to the Egyptian frontier to the south, shepherding the remains of Eighth Army before them. Rommel himself was examining another huge supply dump that 90th Light had seized at Fort Capuzzo, which contained particularly large quantities of fuel.

For the British, the *danse macabre* of military disaster continued. Orders failed to get through, reports were late and inaccurate, battalions had lost confidence in their brigade command and support battalions, the infantry distrusted the armour, the artillery and engineers withdrew into a world of their own. Men who would willingly give their lives for a worthwhile cause withdrew their loyalty and obedience from their leaders, who in their eyes were unworthy of their trust and more than likely to waste their efforts through incompetence.

Opposite: Under attack from Allied fire, crew members of a German 'eighty-eight' rush to load and respond. Although originally intended as an anti-aircraft weapon, the 88mm (3.5in) proved highly effective as an anti-tank gun.

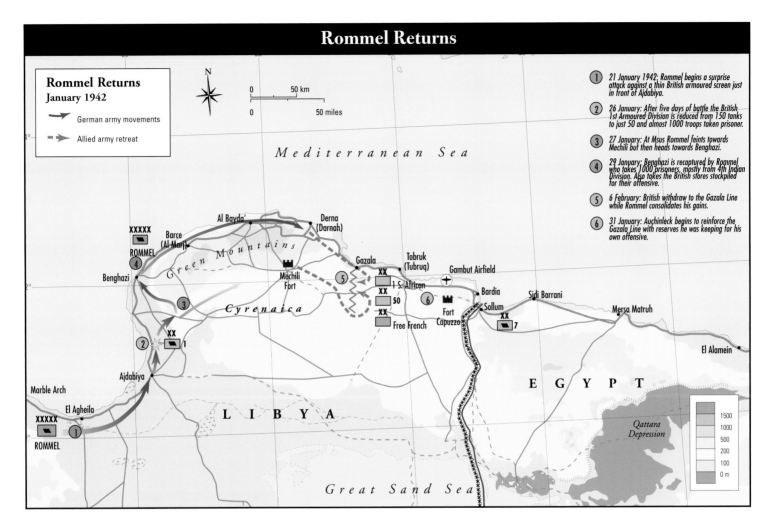

Rommel Returns

Rommel Returns
January 1942

➤ German army movements

➤ Allied army retreat

① 21 January 1942: Rommel begins a surprise attack against a thin British armoured screen just in front of Ajdabiya.

② 26 January: After five days of battle the British 1st Armoured Division is reduced from 150 tanks to just 50 and almost 1000 troops taken prisoner.

③ 27 January: At Msus Rommel feints towards Mechili but then heads towards Benghazi.

④ 29 January: Benghazi is recaptured by Rommel, who takes 1000 prisoners, mostly from 4th Indian Division. Also takes the British stores stockpiled for their offensive.

⑤ 6 February: British withdraw to the Gazala Line while Rommel consolidates his gains.

⑥ 31 January: Auchinleck begins to reinforce the Gazala Line with reserves he was keeping for his own offensive.

A plan for holding the *Panzerarmee* south of Mersa Matruh failed miserably. By the time it had been demonstrably shattered, Auchinleck had taken a step which many people, including Churchill, thought he should have taken much earlier: he sacked General Ritchie and took command of the battle himself. In doing so, he effectively saddled Ritchie with the all the blame for the preceding disasters.

Logistical Success

Rommel seemed to have the upper hand, but in truth the Allies were winning the all-important logistics war. It now took three weeks to ferry Axis supplies by road from the port at Tripoli. The port at Tobruk was not yet serviceable, thanks to the demolition efforts of the retreating Royal Navy.

Malta was still under pressure, however. In July 1942, six heavily laden transports departed from Gibraltar, while 11 set out from Alexandria. They were escorted by a battleship, two carriers and four cruisers from Gibraltar with a further eight cruisers and numerous smaller escorts. Only two supply ships got through – six were sunk, three were badly damaged, five cruisers were badly damaged and four destroyers were sunk.

In August 1942, with Rommel knocking on the gates of Cairo, one last ditch attempt was made to get supplies and fuel through to Malta. Operation Pedestal saw 14 merchant ships escorted by two battleships, three carriers (one sunk), seven cruisers (two sunk) and 33 destroyers (one sunk). Nine freighters were sunk, but five arrived in Malta, including the badly damaged tanker *Ohio*. Yet by now Allied air reinforcements had relieved the pressure on Malta, and from July 1942 over a third of Axis shipping

Above: In January 1942, Rommel's eyes turned towards Tobruk. The capture of the port intact would allow supplies to be shipped much closer to the front lines, easing the Afrika Korp's critically stretched logistics efforts.

Opposite: The Luftwaffe attempted to resupply North Africa, but for all of its efforts its lift capacity could not match a single convoy of merchant ships. Additionally, the lumbering Ju 52s were vulnerable to Allied fighters based on Malta.

Above: South African troops engage in house-to-house fighting in Sollum, following the German assault on the town in June 1941.

dispatched from Italy ended up on the bottom of the Mediterranean. Allied air forces had built up a great store of British and American fighters, fighter-bombers and bombers. Although the number of British planes in the sky gave eager *Luftwaffe* aces like Joachim Marseille the opportunity to build up vast scores, the ceaseless air combat was inevitably a drain on resources of fuel and skilled airmen.

Rommel was also now to be deprived of his flying artillery, the Junkers Ju 87, which was a sitting duck when pitted against modern aircraft types. The *Luftwaffe* was being inexorably driven from the skies. The advantage to the British was not yet apparent. By the morning of 29 June, the Axis had passed Mersa Metruh and were driving along the coast road through Fuka and on to El Daba. The two Panzer divisions and *Ariete* were driving southwest towards El Quseir. Across the front of the German advance ran a desert track. It connected the impassable Qattara Depression to the south, with the newly

Left: The battle for Tobruk came to a head before dawn on 20 June 1942. Here, German assault troops wait for the start of a highly effective attack, which rolled up the outer defences in a single day.

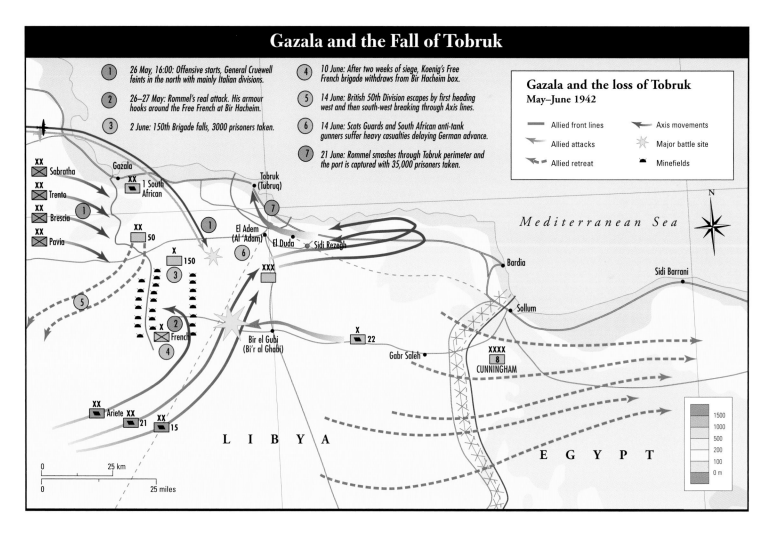

Gazala and the Fall of Tobruk

1. 26 May, 16:00: Offensive starts, General Cruewell feints in the north with mainly Italian divisions.

2. 26–27 May: Rommel's real attack. His armour hooks around the Free French at Bir Hacheim.

3. 2 June: 150th Brigade falls, 3000 prisoners taken.

4. 10 June: After two weeks of siege, Koenig's Free French brigade withdraws from Bir Hacheim box.

5. 14 June: British 50th Division escapes by first heading west and then south-west breaking through Axis lines.

6. 14 June: Scots Guards and South African anti-tank gunners suffer heavy casualties delaying German advance.

7. 21 June: Rommel smashes through Tobruk perimeter and the port is captured with 35,000 prisoners taken.

Gazala and the loss of Tobruk
May–June 1942

- Allied front lines
- Allied attacks
- Allied retreat
- Axis movements
- Major battle site
- Minefields

Above: The fall of Tobruk and the subsequent drive eastwards by the Afrika Korps *saw the British collapse, with the remains of the Eighth Army being driven back towards the Egyptian border.*

Opposite: Erwin Rommel was a commander of great dash, whose exploits in North Africa won him a Field Marshal's baton. But even he could not drive his exhausted troops further against the massively reinforced British lines in Egypt.

created defence post around the little railway station of El Alamein, of which few people at that time had ever heard.

Rommel's orders were short and clear. There was no reason to believe that these new British defences would be any more difficult to smash than the countless others now to their rear. Although their commander did realize that his troops were exhausted after the tremendous efforts of the past four weeks, he called on them for one last supreme effort. But Rommel's iron will was not to be enough. The Axis had already experienced a succession of heavy bombing raids, against which the *Luftwaffe* could send only an occasional lone Bf 109. Late on the afternoon of 1 July, the men of the 90th Light suddenly found themselves under a barrage, the like of which none of them had ever experienced. Heavy guns, howitzers, light and medium field guns, mortars, anti-tank guns, all contributed to a storm of fire which shook even Rommel, who came hurrying up in an armoured car immediately. The extent of the opposition to 90th Light's advance became evident. Auchinleck had found a way of stopping Rommel at last.

Fighting continued for an intense three weeks, at the end of which Rommel had been pushed back only a mile. The battle had revealed with blinding clarity the lack of cooperation throughout the Eighth Army. Its general amateurism compared poorly with the professionalism of the *Afrika Korps*, and the necessity for complete reorganization and thorough training was obvious. The first battle at Alamein produced one success and one failure for each side. Auchinleck had halted Rommel's drive for the Nile – but the *Panzerarmee* was still in existence and no one could foretell when it would strike again, and whether or not it would succeed.

Right: British infantry advance across open ground at the battle of El Alamein. Despite German weakness, the British under Auchinleck could not force the Axis forces back at the first Battle of El Alamein.

A Change in Command

Here, for the moment, both sides were forced to pause. Until resupply could be achieved, there was a lull in the fighting. Weary soldiers were given the opportunity to relax in their trenches, and read mail from home. But everybody knew the quiet could not last.

On 30 August, Rommel attacked again, at Alam Halfa. The four days of battle that followed decided the desert war. This time, Rommel faced a new opponent. Auchinleck had appointed Lieutenant-General Bernard Law Montgomery to command the Eighth Army. The change in British fortunes at this time has often been ascribed, not least by Montgomery himself, to his assumption of command. But one man, no matter how influential, could not win a war on his own.

The RAF had control of the skies, and bombed German supply dumps and headquarters units with impunity. Rommel was sick, as were many of his 17,000 veterans, who had fought in North Africa without a break for well over a year. The British refused to play the old game. Their armour did not expend itself on suicidal charges into German anti-tank guns, but waited, with artillery and air support, for the Germans to come to them. The British displayed none of the unsteadiness Rommel scented earlier

Map, page 150: General Bernard L. Montgomery had taken command of the Eighth Army after the first Battle of Alamein. Determined to drive Rommel out of Africa, he decided to wait until he had built up an overwhelming material superiority before moving. Under an artillery barrage of World War I scale, he launched the attack on 23 October 1942.

Map, page 151: Montgomery's initial attacks served to tie down and weaken the enemy. He launched his main tank attack on 2 November, which Rommel counterattacked. Both sides lost large numbers of tanks, but Montgomery had plenty of replacements. Rommel had none. The Axis forces withdrew in defeat, and the Eighth Army began the long march that would drive the Germans out of Africa.

that summer. For the moment, his Plan Orient was on hold. This grandiose scheme, endorsed by the Reich Chancellery, had been conceived of as a great pincer movement. Whilst the *Wehrmacht* thrust down through the Caucasus, the *Afrika Korps* would seize Suez. Once the two forces linked up, there would be an opportunity to drive eastwards until they met the Japanese. But even if Plan Orient had once been practical, its time had long passed.

Rommel applied for leave. Fêted in Berlin, where he stayed with the Goebbels family, he disconcerted his stand-in General Stumme with the statement that he would return if the British attacked. And attack they would, even if they were taking their time about it. As Rommel confided to his staff, 'if I were Montgomery, we wouldn't still be here.'

The Battle of El Alamein

The second battle of El Alamein was to take place just as Rommel had feared. Montgomery had a deep aversion, learned on the western front during World War I, to squandering the lives of his troops. He resisted Churchill's demands for immediate action until everything was in place and victory assured.

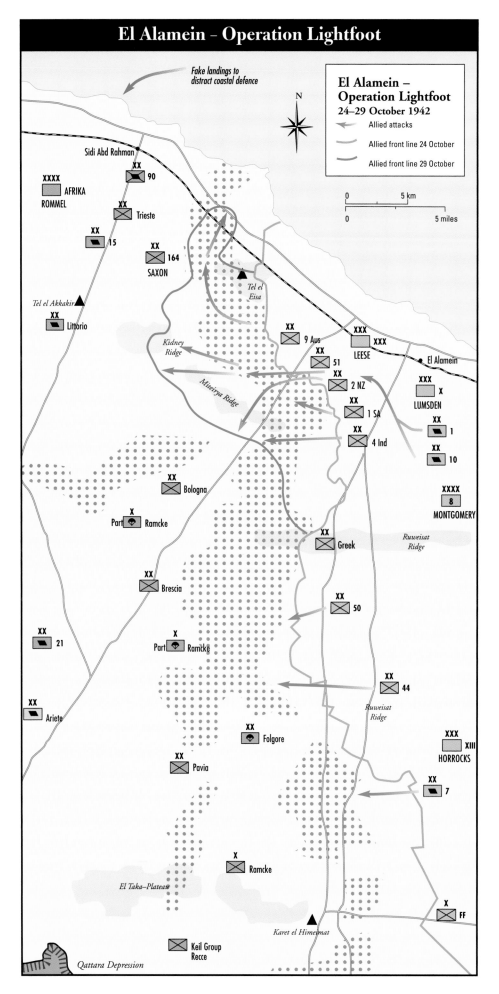

El Alamein – Operation Lightfoot

Fake landings to distract coastal defence

El Alamein – Operation Lightfoot
24–29 October 1942

Allied attacks
Allied front line 24 October
Allied front line 29 October

N

0   5 km
0   5 miles

AFRIKA ROMMEL
90
Sidi Abd Rahman
Trieste
15
164 SAXON
Tel el Eisa
Tel el Akkakir
Littorio
Kidney Ridge
9 Aus
LEESE
El Alamein
51
Miteirya Ridge
2 NZ
LUMSDEN
1 SA
1
4 Ind
10
Bologna
8 MONTGOMERY
Part Ramcke
Greek
Ruweisat Ridge
Brescia
50
21
Part Ramcke
44
Ariete
Ruweisat Ridge
Folgore
XIII HORROCKS
Pavia
7
Ramcke
El Taka–Plateau
FF
Karet el Himeimat
Keil Group Recce
Qattara Depression

On 23 October 1942, with dominance of the air, a substantial advantage in both infantry and tanks and an artillery barrage organized on a scale not achieved by the British Army since 1918, Montgomery launched the sort of classic set-piece battle at which he excelled.

The next eight days saw an intensive series of actions taking place between the coast and Miteiya Ridge. Rommel, not calling the shots for once, had to release his reserves to contain the British attacks, and was further disadvantaged as the *Luftwaffe* had completely lost out in the air battle. As a result, German armour could not call on the close-support usually provided by the Stukas.

In the meantime, Montgomery, with an immense logistical advantage, prepared his armour for a further thrust. This was launched on 2 November. Although the initial British tank force of 100 machines was virtually annihilated by the Axis anti-tank guns, Rommel impetuously launched his own massed armour counterattack, in the hope of exploiting a weak position in the English line. He found no weakness, and the *Afrika Korps* was that day broken in its repeated charges against unyielding Allied gunnery. By dusk, Rommel's Panzer divisions had only 35 operational tanks between them.

Rommel quickly realized that the African dream was over, and the only choice left open, if he wanted to save the remnants of his once proud formations, was to quickly extricate them from the threatened envelopment by the British armour. Although they didn't know it, Montgomery's attack at El Alamein marked the beginning of the end for Hitler and the Nazis.

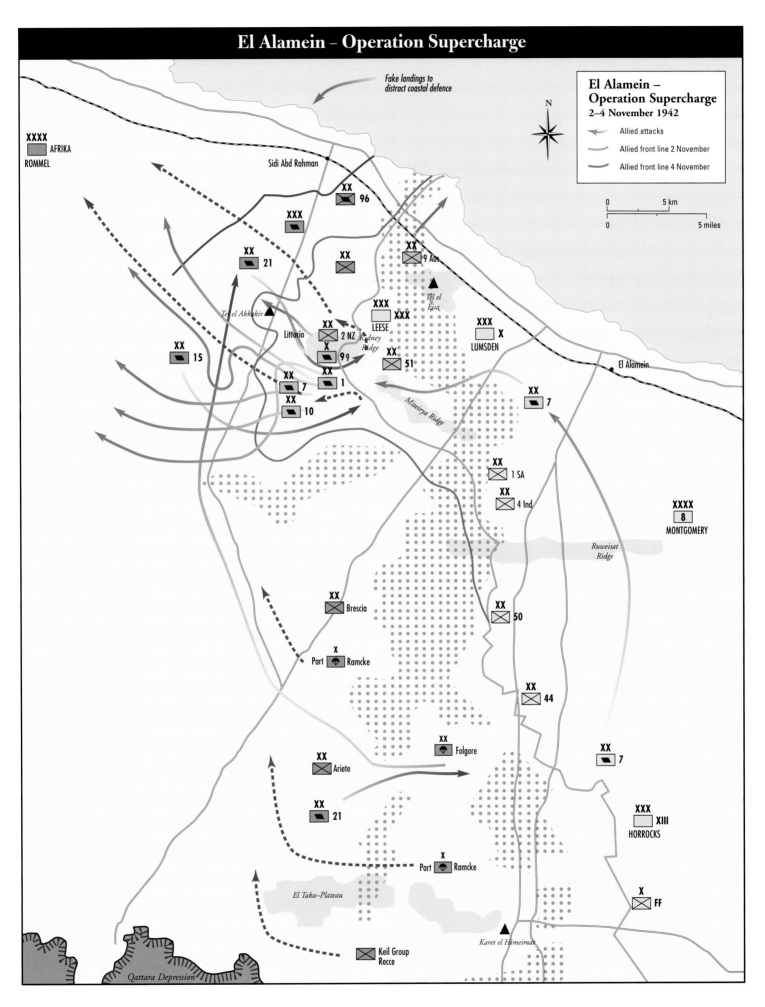

El Alamein – Operation Supercharge

El Alamein – Operation Supercharge
2–4 November 1942

- Allied attacks
- Allied front line 2 November
- Allied front line 4 November

| 0 | 5 km |
| 0 | 5 miles |

Fake landings to distract coastal defence

XXXX
AFRIKA
ROMMEL

Sidi Abd Rahman

XX 96

XXX

XX 21

XX

XX 9 Aus

Tel el Eisa

XXX
LEESE   XXX

XXX X
LUMSDEN

Tel el Akkakir

Littorio

XX 2 NZ   Kidney Ridge

X
99

XX 51

XX 15

XX 7   XX 1

XX 10

Miteirya Ridge

El Alamein

XX 7

XX 1 SA

XX 4 Ind

XXXX
8
MONTGOMERY

Ruweisat Ridge

XX Brescia

XX 50

X
Part   Ramcke

XX 44

XX Folgore

XX 7

XX Ariete

XXX XIII
HORROCKS

XX 21

X
Part   Ramcke

X FF

El Taka–Plateau

Karet el Himeimat

Keil Group
Recce

Qattara Depression

Operation *Barbarossa*

Adolf Hitler had long had plans for Russia. As early as August 1939, on the eve of the invasion of Poland, he said: 'I have sent my Death's Head formations eastwards. Poland will be depopulated and settled with Germans... the fate of Russia will be exactly the same.'

On 22 June 1941, Hitler launched the greatest invasion in military history – Operation Barbarossa. Three million German and Axis troops in three Army Groups attacked across the Russian border from the Baltic coast to the Romanian frontier. The Russians were taken by surprise. Stalin had been determined to do nothing that could provoke a German invasion until he had a chance to reorganize his own forces. Apparently unable to believe that Hitler would break their cynical alliance so soon, he saw to it that the USSR continued to deliver strategic materials to the Germans right up to the very night of the attack.

The *Luftwaffe* had been overflying Russian airbases for months before the invasion. Now the German air force scored the greatest victory in its history, wiping out the Red air force in a matter of days. Soviet bases were in the process of expansion, so many air regiments had their planes doubled up on the airstrips. Aircraft were packed together where a single bomb could destroy a whole squadron. If they got into the air, the Russians had neither the skill nor the aircraft to challenge the Messerschmitt Bf 109, and many German fighter pilots began to run up incredible numbers of victories.

Army Group Centre

Under the command of the icily aristocratic Field Marshal Fedor von Bock, Army Group Centre comprised two infantry armies and two Panzer Groups – in effect, tank armies – under Generals Hoth and Guderian. These were the armies whose commanders intended to reduce Napoleon's feat of arms of 129 years earlier to historical obscurity. They planned to reach Moscow in less than eight weeks, and to annihilate the Soviet army in the process.

In this hope, they were encouraged by Hitler, who had assured them, 'Before three months have passed, we shall witness a collapse in Russia, the like of which has never been seen in history. We have only to kick in the front door and the whole rotten Russian

Opposite: Operation Barbarossa, the German invasion of the Soviet Union, came as a surprise to Stalin, who had believed Hitler would adhere to the Soviet-German non-aggression pact. But anyone who had read Hitler's Mein Kampf *would have realized that Russia was the* Führer's *ultimate aim. It was Russia's vast steppes that would provide the* Lebensraum *which was a fundamental principle of the Nazi creed.*

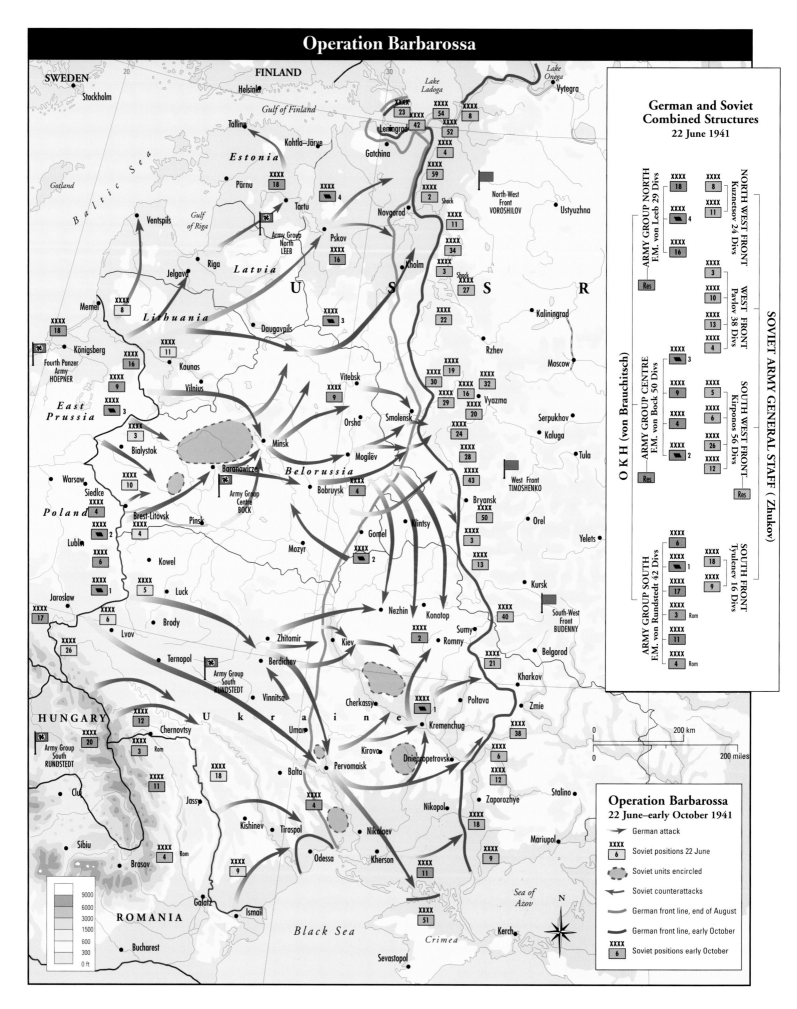

Operation Barbarossa

German and Soviet Combined Structures 22 June 1941

Operation Barbarossa 22 June–early October 1941

- → German attack
- Soviet positions 22 June
- Soviet units encircled
- Soviet counterattacks
- German front line, end of August
- German front line, early October
- Soviet positions early October

edifice will come tumbling down.' To Heinz Guderian, whose II Panzer Group included four Panzer divisions, this was the supreme moment of his military career. It was evident that he and Hoth between them commanded the most significant forces in the entire operation, and could well execute the most exciting and spectacular military feat of the century, perhaps of all history. And the first few days seemed to confirm the prospect.

Guderian's first task was to throw his Panzer Group across the River Bug on each side of the fortress of Brest-Litovsk, capture the fortress and then race with his armoured spearheads towards the city of Minsk. He would curve up to the city from the south to meet Hoth's spearheads coming down from the north. In this way, the Soviet front-line forces would be isolated in a huge cauldron. Once their supplies had run out, they would have little alternative but to surrender.

Above: German troops fight in the streets of Kiev. Caught by surprise, the Red Army could do little to halt the advance of the Wehrmacht, who swept through the ancient cities of the Ukraine and western Russia.

THE STATISTICS OF *BARBAROSSA*

To launch Operation *Barbarossa*, the Germans mobilized more than 150 divisions, including 19 Panzer divisions, which were supported by 1945 German aircraft and another 1000 Axis planes. They faced some three million men of the Red Army, which had another one million soldiers deployed across southern republics of the USSR and in the Far East, where they had recently beaten the Japanese in a series of border clashes. By the time the attack was launched in mid-June, enough fuel, ammunition and stores had been stockpiled to supply this vast force in a 600km (373-mile) advance. Half a million lorries waited in massed parks from East Prussia south as far as Romania, ready to rush those supplies forward on demand. To the modern mind, the only questionable, indeed alarming, figure to emerge from the tables of statistics is that for 'stabling': over 300,000 horses were to play an apparently essential part in this monumental military exercise.

Opposite: Three massive Army Groups struck on the morning of 22 June. Army Group North was directed at the Baltic States and Leningrad. Army Group South was to overrun the vast grainfields of the Ukraine. And Army Group Centre was poised like a spear to drive at Moscow, the heart of the Soviet Union.

'The war against Russia cannot be conducted in a chivalrous fashion. This struggle is one of ideologies and racial differences, and will have to be conducted with unprecedented, unmerciful and unrelenting harshness.'

Adolf Hitler, 1941

By 24 June, only 60 hours after the launch of the attack, 17th Panzer Division was driving into Slonim, over 140km (87 miles) from the frontier and halfway to the Germans' first objective. Three days later, on the afternoon of 27 June, the leading tanks of the 17th Panzer Division drove into Minsk to meet the spearheads of Hoth's III Panzer Group, which had covered 350km (217 miles) in five days.

Behind them, they had left pockets of Soviet troops which, unlike most of the French army the year before, showed little inclination to lay down their arms and surrender. There were four of these pockets: the fortress at Brest-Litovsk, six divisions around Bialystok, six more at Volkovysk, and another 15 between Novogrudok and Minsk itself. The task of first containing and then destroying them was assigned to the German infantry of the Fourth and Ninth Armies.

The trouble was that the infantry, trudging stolidly after the Panzer divisions, were now quite a long way behind. The roads shown on the Barbarossa maps proved in the majority of cases to be little but dirt tracks, which were quickly reduced to calf-deep dust, through which it was impossible to move at more than 5km/h (3mph). There was also a problem with supply. A large proportion of the half million lorries that were supposed to be bringing supplies and reinforcements were of French origin, captured during the 1940 campaign. Many were not capable of carrying heavy loads across rough country, and spare parts were in short supply. Moreover, they

Right: Spearheading the German drive were 19 Panzer divisions. Using the panzers' mobility to the full, the Wehrmacht *surrounded and cut off huge numbers of Red Army troops before driving onwards across the seemingly endless steppes.*

had already been driven halfway across Europe, and their useful mileage had been almost consumed.

Not surprisingly, arguments arose. Guderian and Hoth were convinced that they must immediately race further ahead, first to Smolensk and then to Moscow, confident that speed would prove the decisive factor in this campaign. On 1 July, in a burst of insubordination, the two Panzer commanders released units towards the next obstacle, the River Beresina. They were threatened with court martial for so doing by their immediate superior, General Günther von Kluge.

On the same day, Guderian's Panzers met the Soviet T-34 for the first time. A single tank blocked their advance for three hours, knocking out five Panzer IIIs. It was only removed when attacked from the rear by an 88mm (3.46in) flak gun. Fortunately for the Germans, no more T-34s were encountered in the area.

Pushing Forward

On 3 July, the order came for the next stage of the advance. From his unsanctioned bridgehead over the Beresina, Guderian launched the 18th Panzer Division towards the

River Dnieper, which was reached on 5 July. Here the division beat off a Soviet counter-attack and then waited until all three of the Panzer Group's corps were lined up along the river. It was not a safe position. Both flanks were exposed, the supply organization was becoming increasingly tenuous, and the support infantry was two weeks' hard marching behind them. No wonder Kluge remonstrated violently, and at first expressly forbade any attempt at further advance.

Yet every day that the Germans waited, the Soviet defences stiffened, and waiting too long would make the task of crossing the Dnieper become impossible for anything less than an army group. Eventually Kluge gave way. 'Your operations always hang by a thread!' he complained, but gave permission for the next stage. The next three weeks were occupied with the hardest fighting the Germans had yet experienced. For 10 days, II Panzer Group had three separate objectives to pursue. It was to bar the Soviet forces it had bypassed from escaping south or east. At the same time, it was to make contact with III Panzer Group fighting its way down from the northwest. Finally, it was to widen the German hold on the land east of Smolensk, turning it into a solid bridgehead for the final thrust towards Moscow.

Although advanced units of the 29th Motorized Division reached Smolensk on 16 July, fierce fighting still raged behind them, and there was as yet no sign of Hoth's III Panzer Group spearheads. On 29 July Hitler's adjutant, Colonel Schmundt, arrived at Guderian's headquarters, bringing with him Hitler's felicitations and the Oak Leaves to the Knight's Cross – Guderian was only the fifth man in the army to receive them. He also brought with him the first hint of changes of plan and emphasis.

Moscow was perhaps not so important after all. The rolling wheatlands of the Ukraine would provide the granary from which the ever-growing Axis armies could be fed. Moreover, down in that direction lay the Baku oilfields. Moscow could wait. Guderian for the moment must go no further east.

Army Group North

While Army Group Centre drove towards Moscow, Field Marshal von Leeb's Army Group North was aimed at the Baltic States and Leningrad. Group North consisted of two infantry armies containing 15 infantry divisions between them. The armoured punch was provided by IV Panzer Group, which comprised three Panzer divisions, three motorized infantry divisions and two infantry divisions. Three infantry divisions were held in support.

The fact that they had less of the *Wehrmacht's* mobile striking power than Army Group Centre was a matter of some irritation to von Leeb's staff – after all, they had further to go and, on paper, a much deeper enemy defence to penetrate. The differences did not extend to the two principals themselves. Leeb and von Bock were far too aristocratic to squabble – though they encouraged their subordinates to do so.

By midnight on 21/22 June, every unit was in position. At 3.05 on the morning of 22 June, Army Group North began the drive to Leningrad. The only early resistance encountered by the vital central thrust was quickly brushed aside, and by the evening of the first day the leading Panzers were 60km (37 miles) into Lithuania.

The 7th Panzer Division was racing along the main road from Kaunas to Daugavpils (Dvinsk) on the River Dvina. By the morning of the 26th, they had captured the two river bridges there. Counterattacks were beaten off, more Panzers came roaring in, and by the end of the day the city was firmly in German hands. The first objective of Army Group

Opposite: A flamethrower is used to sear the entrance to a Soviet bunker. Static Soviet positions such as these were rapidly cut off by the German armoured spearheads, and were then dealt with by the slower moving infantry that followed on foot.

North – bridgeheads across the wide River Dvina, 300km (186 miles) from East Prussia – had been achieved in five days. On 2 July, the Panzer Group set out on the 250km (155-mile) race to the Ostrov/Pskov area. Ostrov was captured by the 1st Panzer Division on 4 July. The 6th Panzer Division smashed a way through the northern extension of the 'Stalin Line' on the same day, and three motorized divisions of the Panzer Group had crossed the old Latvian-Russian border opposite Opochka and were also driving up towards Pskov. When, on 5 July, the mass of Soviet tanks held to the east were thrown into a counterattack, German armour had been thoroughly reinforced. By the end of the second day, only the wrecks of 140 Soviet tanks lay between the Panzer divisions and Pskov itself.

A Fragmenting Advance

The Panzer Group's infantry could not keep up. The terrain encountered on the Soviet side of the border was so marshy and impenetrable that even the motorized infantry was reduced to the pace of the marching columns, and they were just clearing Daugavpils, over 100km (60 miles) back. Things moved more quickly to the west. The roads in Lithuania, Latvia and Estonia were so much better than those in Russia that the Eighteenth Army was moving almost as fast as the Panzers. By 7 July, 12

Above: Dazed by the a massive artillery bombardment at Brest-Litovsk, a Soviet soldier surrenders to the Germans. Hundreds of thousands of captives were taken, but large numbers of Red Army men disappeared into the wilderness to continue the fight. These provided the nucleus of the partisan bands.

Soviet divisions had been destroyed, both Tallinn and Narva were under artillery fire and four divisions were driving towards the southern end of Lake Peipus.

To the commanders back in Germany – and to Hitler especially – the picture across the whole *Barbarossa* Front was one of increasing danger. Not only were the gaps opening between armour and infantry, they were also gaping widely between the army groups themselves. Even though the Soviet forces in these gaps ranged from confused to chaotic, they consisted of an apparently unlimited number of brave soldiers who seemed incapable of realizing when they were beaten.

Despite the anguished pleas of the Panzer commanders Reinhardt and Manstein, the idea of an immediate thrust into the heart of Leningrad would have to wait. Behind them, the infantry fought and marched, fought and marched again – and gradually their strength waned. Casualties were inevitably suffered, and battalions, regiments, even divisions had to be left behind to deal with pockets of resistance. Then in mid-July the orders came for units to be detached from the northern wing of Army Group Centre to fill the ominous gap between the two groups. The delay gave the Russian defenders the opportunity to strengthen their positions enormously. A German attack northwards was checked west of Lake Ilmen, largely by another immutable factor of warfare: after more than a month of constant fighting and forced marches, often in great heat, German infantrymen were suffering mounting exhaustion.

The assault ran into a Red Army counterattack. The storm of fire that erupted stunned both sides. Eventually, however, German training and efficiency prevailed. Four Panzer divisions broke through, and by 11 August were clear yet again for the drive on Leningrad – only to be held back by stiff Russian resistance.

Hitler now ordered Army Group Centre to release one of General Hoth's Panzer corps to help Army Group North. Driving up the west bank of the Volkhov, its leading tank units reached Ishora, only 17km (10 miles) from the centre of Leningrad. Its motorized infantry swung up to the east towards the River Neva and the shores of Lake Ladoga. The former capital of Russia was now surrounded.

It was not, however, yet occupied. The two leading divisions were soon enmeshed in a labyrinth of anti-tank ditches and straggling earthworks thrown up by the desperate Leningraders while the Germans had paused to regroup. By the evening of 10 September, German units had reached the Dugerdorf Heights, 10km (6 miles) southeast of the city. However, so many Panzers had been hit or had broken down that

Below: A Soviet KV-1 tank burns in a forest in Latvia. The Wehrmacht *was unpleasantly surprised when it encountered the latest Soviet tanks such as the T-34 and the KV-1, since their armour was very effective at turning aside the projectiles fired by standard 37-mm (1.41in) anti-tank guns. Only the heavier 50mm (2in) shells could knock out these tanks.*

the momentum of attack had been dissipated. German infantry crept up on their left during the following day, entered the Leningrad suburbs of Slutsk and Pushkin, and in the evening occupied the Summer Palace of the Tsars at Krasnoye Selo. But the impetus had gone. By now, the lure of the wheatlands of the Ukraine and the Baku oilfields had taken complete control of Hitler's mind. Like Moscow, Leningrad must wait.

Army Group South

There is some irony in the fact that by August 1941 Hitler had decided that the southern front of Barbarossa was the most important, for in order to capture it Field Marshal Gerd von Rundstedt had originally been given command of the weakest Army Group. His most powerful forces were in the north: Sixth Army under Reichenau, I Panzer Group under Kleist and Seventeenth Army under Stulpnagel. In the south, driving out of Moldavia, a single German army was accompanied by two Romanian armies, a Hungarian army corps and an Italian army corps, all armed with obsolete equipment and with a bare minimum of artillery and vehicles.

The attack, however, made excellent progress from the start. The opposing Russian commander, General Kirponos, committed his forces piecemeal as they became available. They were all destroyed in turn, though this was not the end of early resistance. In their first powerful thrust, I Panzer Group had shouldered the Russian Fifth Army aside and into the Pripet Marshes, where neither German armour nor vehicles could follow. With the astonishing resilience typical of bypassed Soviet troops, the Fifth Army reorganized and in mid-July struck southwest from Korosten, towards the Soviet Sixth Army driving up from below Berdichev. German expertise and their skilful use of the 88mm (3.46in) flak gun in an anti-tank role broke this attempt to snap off the invading spearhead, but the Fifth Army then retreated back into the marshes. For the next six weeks, both Kleist and Reichenau were uncomfortably aware of the threat hanging over their shoulders.

The key German drive continued down between the Bug and the Dniester. The main Soviet forces, commanded by the flamboyant but incompetent Marshal Budenny and his political commissar Nikita Khrushchev, concentrated around two important centres – Kiev and Uman. Avoiding both by cutting between them, Kleist's Panzer Group with the Sixth Army in close attendance drove down the land bridge between the rivers, and part of Reichenau's forces headed west. There, they were joined first by Stulpnagel's divisions and then by Schobert's coming up from Moldavia.

The ground was much harder here than further north, so infantry could move more quickly. The Russian Sixth and Twelfth Armies and part of the Eighteenth were thus isolated between overwhelming forces. By 3 August, they had been sealed in, and by the 8th they were being subjected to heavy artillery fire from every side. Two days later, their resistance ceased. Some 20 Russian divisions had been annihilated and 103,000 prisoners taken.

Meanwhile, the two Romanian armies had marched along the coast and begun a siege of Odessa. Although it was to cost the Romanians dearly, the 64-day siege prevented the large Russian garrison from playing a part in the drama unfolding in the heart of the Ukraine. Here, the largest concentration of Red Army troops lay at Kiev and in the area immediately to the north. On Hitler's orders, Guderian's Panzer Group was now driving down from Army Group Centre to meet Kleist, thus cutting off three complete Russian armies and the remnants of at least two more.

Above: Ukrainian peasants dig anti-tank ditches as Army Groups Centre and South combine to encircle Kiev. Over 600,000 Red Army soldiers were captured in the huge battle that followed – but the campaign took up valuable time, delaying the crucial drive on Moscow planned for the autumn.

Guderian had not, in fact, immediately obeyed the *Führer* because his eyes – and ambition – were still focused on Moscow. On 4 August, Hitler travelled forward to Novo Borosow and talked to his senior commanders. For the moment, he was sufficiently impressed by the arguments of Bock and Guderian not to insist upon the abandonment of the drive on Moscow. During the next three weeks, however, his attitude hardened, and on 24 August in a solitary interview with Guderian, he ordered him to lead his entire Panzer Group down to assist in the occupation of the Ukraine. During the next two days, *Panzergruppe Guderian* (as it had been renamed as a sop to Guderian's feelings) swung its axis through 90° and headed south.

A Landmark Defeat

A new army group – the Bryansk Front – had been formed by the Red Army high command, or *Stavka*. It had the specific aim of attacking Guderian's flank as it moved south. This reflected the arrival from the Far East of General Zhukov, who was already exhibiting his uncanny gift for divining an enemy's plans. Unfortunately, Marshal Shaposhnikov, the Red Army chief of staff, believed that Moscow was still Guderian's objective. He thus ordered the most powerful elements of the Bryansk Front to stay in the north, so they were unavailable to attack Guderian. Nonetheless, two armies of the Bryansk Front under General Yeremenko moved forward on 30 August to attack Guderian's left flank. Lack of coordination and, more importantly, of air cover – the Red air force had by now been virtually annihilated – left them at the mercy of the Germans.

By 2 September, Bryansk Front was in tatters, and eight days later Stalin was receiving direct appeals from both Budenny and Khrushchev for permission for their still large but disintegrating forces to be allowed to escape through the rapidly narrowing gap between Kleist and Guderian. Stalin dismissed his old revolutionary comrade Budenny and appointed Marshal Timoshenko to preside over the ensuing debacle. During the remaining days that the gap was open, Stalin insisted through Shaposhnikov that all fronts, all armies, all divisions should stand fast where they were.

Guderian's Panzers met Kleist's at Lokhvitsa on 15 September. Infantry and guns from Second Army to the north and from Seventeenth Army to the south came up to harden the ring, and by the evening of the 17th, the biggest encirclement of the Barbarossa campaign – perhaps the biggest in history – had been formed.

That night, permission was at last given for the remnants of the Soviet armies to attempt to break out to the east, but most had too far to go and lacked the heavy mobile equipment to smash through the waiting German ring. Budenny and Khrushchev were flown out. Major-General Bagramyan brought out about 50 men, but Kirponos and most of the staffs of the Southwest Front and of the Fifth Army were killed as they tried to escape, or were rounded up and captured. With them into graves, or German prison camps of the most appalling nature, went nearly 500,000 Russian soldiers. In terms of numbers, this was the biggest military catastrophe in Russian history.

Guderian and Kleist were jubilant, Rundstedt modestly gratified that the greatest single success of German arms had been won by the army group under his command. In that atmosphere of heady euphoria, few remarked that for all their triumphs and all the ground won, something had been lost, and that was time. Kleist at least was aware that time was passing. With admirable speed, he drew his Panzer Group back south to the area around Dnepropetrovsk. On 30 September, it erupted from a bridgehead over the Samara at Novomoskovsk and drove down to the Sea of Azov, neatly trapping three Soviet armies while Eleventh Army, now under command of General von Manstein who had been moved down from the Leningrad front, drove eastwards along the coast. Another 106,000 prisoners were taken, together with 212 tanks and nearly 700 guns.

The Moscow Offensive

Rain, wind and the first snow flurries brought a hint of the white chaos that would soon engulf the whole Russian front. By the end of October, Kleist's Panzer Group was edging its way slowly into Rostov. Although they did not know it, they were also edging into a Soviet trap. The Soviets had at last learnt the effectiveness of the traditional Russian tactic of trading space for time. Many of the units threatened with encirclement at Kharkov had been allowed by Stalin to retreat. They were now being reformed into the Soviet Thirty-Seventh Army in the angle of the Donets Bend.

On 19 November, they began to move forward into Rostov, joined by shock troops of the Ninth Army. It was the first time in World War II that the Germans had to face a major enemy attack, prepared and launched after adequate organization. By 28 November, I Panzer Group had been squeezed out of Rostov, back through Taganrog to the line of the Mius River. One of the immediate results was Hitler's anger, followed by Rundstedt's resignation. Guderian and Bock were facing a similar situation in front of Moscow. On 6 September, Hitler decreed that Moscow would be the next objective. Army Group North's breakneck advance had come to a sudden stop as it entered the swampy forests that surrounded Leningrad. Its Panzer Group was assigned to Army Group Centre,

'An advance towards the Ukraine, the Donets Basin and the Crimean Peninsula will give Germany all the food and coal it needs....My Generals know nothing about the economic aspects of war!'

Adolf Hitler, after senior officers questioned the diversion of forces from the drive on Moscow to the Ukraine

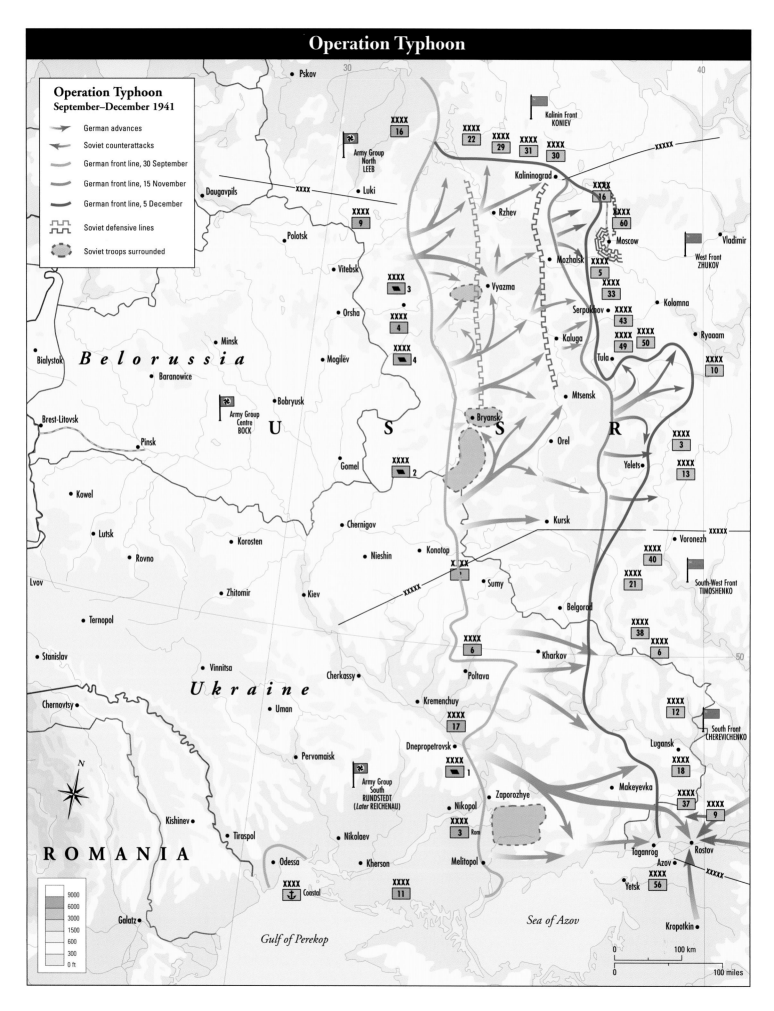

Operation Typhoon

Operation Typhoon
September–December 1941

→ German advances

← Soviet counterattacks

German front line, 30 September

German front line, 15 November

German front line, 5 December

Soviet defensive lines

Soviet troops surrounded

GERMAN SUPPLY FAILURES

The German supply network behind Operation Barbarossa had began to falter during the great advances of the summer of 1941. It proved impossible to sustain the front-line units using the primitive Russian rail and road network. The Russian railways used a wider track gauge than the German rail system, and it took longer than anticipated to convert them for use. It also did not help that the German logistics train had been filled out with captured vehicles from all over Europe. There were 2000 different vehicle types in service, with few interchangeable parts. Army Group Centre's spare parts inventory ran to over one million items. By early autumn, the *Luftwaffe* had been forced to ferry its own supplies forward in bombers – its fuel and other essential supplies were all held up in bottlenecks from Poland to the Smolensk–Moscow highway.

which now had three-quarters of Germany's tank forces at its disposal. In another giant battle of encirclement, Hoth and Hoepner's Panzers were to bypass Moscow to the north, while Guderian's Panzer Group would pass to the south. The tanks would link up east of Moscow, cutting the Soviet capital off from reinforcements and supplies.

Assigned the codename *Taifun* (Typhoon), the German drive on Moscow began on 2 October. The Russians had concentrated huge forces to bar the road to their capital, but these were smashed yet again. In two more great battles of encirclement, another 650,000 Russians were captured. The citizens of Moscow sensed which way the wind was blowing; party officials started burning documents and whole government departments were transferred east. Yet Stalin announced that he would be staying.

There were three reasons why the wily Soviet leader refused to abandon the Kremlin in late 1941. First there was the weather. On 6 October, German forces on the Moscow front awoke to find their tanks dusted with snow. Autumnal rains alternated with freezing nights, a seasonal phenomenon known to Russians as the *rasputitza* (literally the 'time without roads'). There were few metalled roads in the USSR. Most were wide dirt strips that now dissolved into a sticky quagmire, which even tanks were unable to cross. Germans on foot sank past the top of their jackboots. Airfields became unusable and the advance ground to a halt.

Stalin's second source of confidence came from his spy ring in Japan where, it was reported, Tojo's cabinet had definitely ruled out an attack on the USSR. Japan would attack America instead. The 750,000 Russian soldiers in the Far East were now available to reinforce the depleted forces fighting the Germans. Thirdly, the Red Army was replacing its staggering losses with unbelievable speed: 143 new divisions were mobilized between July and December, and 84 of the divisions destroyed in battle had been re-constituted.

Russia's Winter Ally

The *rasputitza* lasted for four weeks. Then, on 7 November, the temperature plunged and the liquid mud turned rock hard. The German advance began again with breakthroughs in the south as well as towards Moscow. At the end of the month, the 7th

Opposite: The headlong progress of the early advances slowed as Army Group Centre resumed the offensive against Moscow. Russian resistance had stiffened, but more ominously, the first signs of the ferocious Russian winter were appearing. From now on, the Wehrmacht *would have to fight the weather as well as the Red Army.*

167

Panzer Division established a bridgehead over the Volga canal. Its advance elements were soon within 20km (12 miles) of Moscow and in the cold, clear winter air the spires of the Kremlin were visible through binoculars.

Daytime temperatures around Moscow varied from -5 to -12°C (23 to 10.4°F) and the Germans found it increasingly difficult to keep fighting in the same uniforms they had worn through the baking heat of summer. Supplies of every kind were simply failing to arrive at the front, where battalions were reduced to a fraction of their authorized strength. Panzer divisions counted themselves lucky to have 50 tanks still running.

On 23 July General Halder, the army chief of staff, had reported to Hitler that the Soviet forces facing the *Wehrmacht* amounted to 93 divisions, of which 13 were armoured. Now, on 1 December his estimate had risen to 200 infantry divisions, 35 cavalry divisions and 40 armoured brigades, with at least another 70 mixed divisions deep inside Soviet territory. Eighteen divisions of excellently trained, well-equipped and warmly clothed long-service troops, with 1700 tanks and 1500 aircraft, were on their way to the Moscow front from the Far East. In early December, Stalin reviewed these Siberian divisions in Red Square. From the parade, they moved straight into the front line.

The Russians attacked on 5 December. The temperature plummeted to -15°C (5°F) and snow lay more than a metre thick in places. Unable to dig in properly, the undermanned German units were torn apart; the few serviceable German tanks were unable to manoeuvre in these conditions and the fuel was stuck hundreds of miles behind the front. The *Luftwaffe* was unable to help: its aircraft took an average of five hours to get airborne, even if the ground-crews kept fires lit under the engines to keep them from freezing. Russia's latest tanks, the T-34 and KV-1, had wide tracks and engines designed

Below: The first snows fell in early October, followed by rain, which turned the Russian countryside into one vast morass. When winter truly arrived in November, the Wehrmacht *found itself ill-equipped to deal with sub-zero temperatures, and soon frostbite was causing more casualties than enemy action.*

*Left: Soviet cavalrymen
enter a snow-bound
village west of Moscow.
Unlike the Germans, the
Red Army was intimately
familiar with 'General
Winter', and its
equipment was designed
to operate with minimal
maintenance in
temperatures as low as
-40°C below zero.*

to keep running even in Arctic weather. Russian guns and small arms were similarly robust, built to function in snow or mud, and the Red Army's soldiers wore thickly insulated uniforms. The hitherto victorious German army fell apart. It had suffered some 750,000 casualties between June and December, and losses soared once the full fury of winter descended. The army reported over 100,000 frostbite cases in December alone. Frostbite caused more hospitalization than Russian guns. Hypothermia would soon be killing more. Now Russian attacks were forcing them out of their hard-won positions, causing the German commanders to look over their shoulders and seek safer defences to the rear. Hitler would have none of this. Haunted by the spectre of Napoleon's retreat from Moscow, he would not allow the *Wehrmacht* to turn its back, even momentarily, on

the Russian capital. 'Where would they retreat to?' he asked. 'Is it warmer 50km or 100km to the west?'

There would be no retreat. The German army would stand fast, just as it had in World War I. When his commanders protested, he sacked them. The most senior to go was Brauchitsch, the commander-in-chief. Also sacked were the two Army Group commanders, Leeb and Bock, and, just before Christmas, Guderian. Thirty-five corps or divisional commanders were likewise dismissed, and Hoepner, who had commanded the IV Panzer Group in the north, was cashiered, then called back into the army as a private. Only Rundstedt, for whom Hitler to the end had great respect, was allowed to resign. Hitler, the former corporal, now took personal charge of the war in the East.

Russian Resurgence

For a time, it seemed as though the all-conquering *Wehrmacht* might suffer the fate of Napoleon's Grand Army, melting away in the Russian winter. Only Hitler's iron determination stopped the headlong retreat and destruction of his hopes.

Yet even Hitler's demonic will could not alter the facts. Though vast tracts of the Soviet Union had been occupied, the ambitious plans of the summer had come to nothing. The Red Army had been crippled, but it had risen from the ashes. More numerous than before, formidably equipped, and led by a new generation of highly capable commanders, it would be a far tougher opponent in 1942. Moscow had not been taken, and neither had Leningrad. The oilfields of the Caucasus remained out of reach.

For the first time, the myth of the invincibility of the German army had been broken. Though few knew it at the time, the defeat at the gates of Moscow had undermined the very foundations of the Thousand Year Reich.

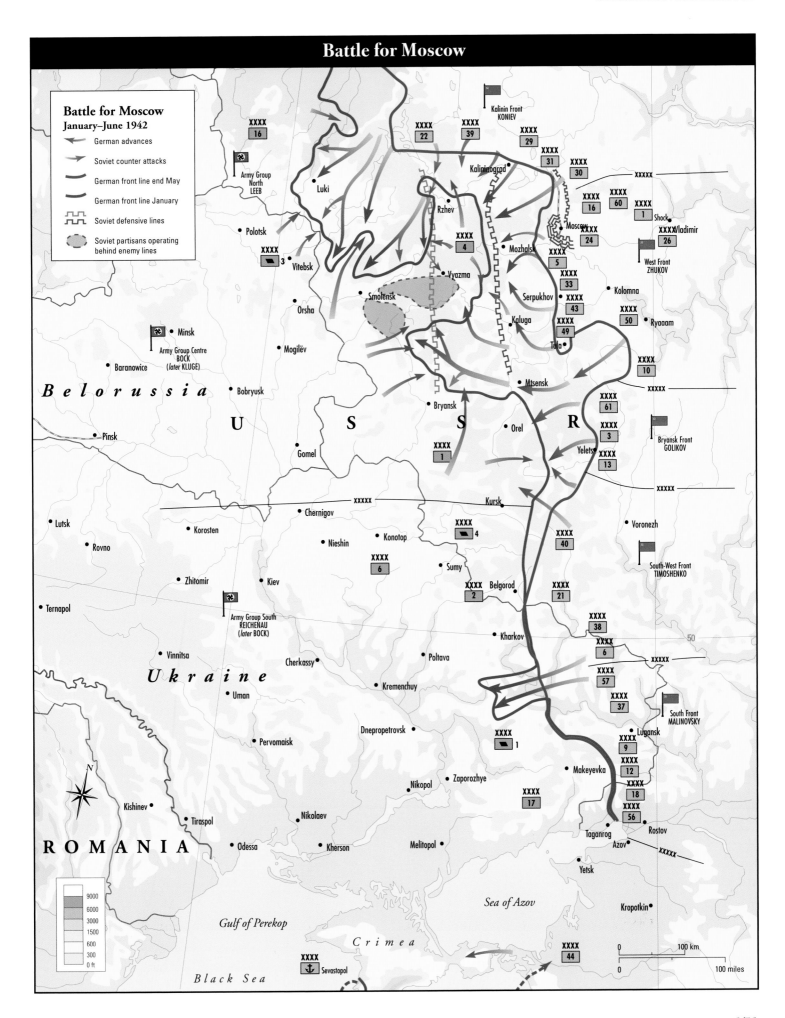

Battle for Moscow

Battle for Moscow
January–June 1942

→ German advances

→ Soviet counter attacks

German front line end May

German front line January

Soviet defensive lines

Soviet partisans operating
behind enemy lines

Kalinin Front
KONIEV

Army Group
North
LEEB

Luki

Polotsk

Rzhev

Kalininograd

Vitebsk

Vyazma

Smolensk

Orsha

Mozhalsk

Moscow

Serpukhov

Kaluga

Minsk

Army Group Centre
BOCK
(*later* KLUGE)

Baranowice

Mogilëv

Tula

Mtsensk

B e l o r u s s i a

Bobryusk

Bryansk

U   S   S   R

Pinsk

Orel

Bryansk Front
GOLIKOV

Gomel

Yelets

Lutsk

Chernigov

Kursk

Voronezh

Korosten

Nieshin

Konotop

Rovno

Sumy

South-West Front
TIMOSHENKO

Zhitomir

Kiev

Belgorod

Vinnitsa

Cherkassy

Poltava

Kharkov

U k r a i n e

Uman

Kremenchuy

Dnepropetrovsk

South Front
MALINOVSKY

Pervomaisk

Lugansk

Makeyevka

Nikopol

Zaporozhye

Kishinev

Nikolaev

Melitopol

Yetsk

R O M A N I A

Tiraspol

Odessa

Kherson

Taganrog

Azov

Rostov

Kropotkin

Sea of Azov

Gulf of Perekop

C r i m e a

Sevastopol

Black Sea

N

9000
6000
3000
1500
600
300
0 ft

0   100 km

0   100 miles

Kolomna

Ryaaam

Shock

Vladimir

West Front
ZHUKOV

171

Moscow to Stalingrad

The year 1942 did not start well for the *Wehrmacht*. Overextended in the great summer invasion of Russia, German armies had been checked for the first time in the last month of 1941.

Beaten back by fierce Soviet counterattacks from Leningrad to the Crimea, Hitler's War Machine was slowly freezing to a standstill. After being driven from the gates of Moscow, most of the generals who had made *Blitzkrieg* possible had been fired by the *Führer*. The former corporal had taken direct command of the armed forces. Hitler refused to consider the mere consolidation of 1941's huge territorial gains. He promised the German people that this year they would triumph.

Changed Priorities

Moscow was no longer the key: the massed Panzer and infantry formations were to drive southwestwards. They would seize the city of Stalingrad, a strategic city to be sure, but made even more important in Hitler's eyes because it was named after his hated rival, Joseph Stalin. From there, the Germans would be within striking distance of the real prize: the vital oilfields in the Caucasus.

The *Wehrmacht's* Panzers, however, were running short of fuel. Materially, Hitler's armies were dangerously depleted after the headlong advance of Operation Barbarossa, and losses from the fierce battles of the winter were far from being made good. Stalin also had something to prove. In January 1942, 12 German armies were locked in combat with 22 Soviet armies. On a front stretching from the Crimea to the Gulf of Finland, 141 divisions, including 11 from Axis allies, faced more than 300 Russian formations.

The very size of the war zone was in the *Wehrmacht's* favour. Stalin was trying not only to relieve Moscow and Leningrad, but also to destroy Army Group Centre. His generals knew what happened to commanders who failed, and Red Army offensives were launched all along the line. It was too much. Despite tattered uniforms stuffed with straw and newspaper, weapons that jammed in the arctic temperatures, and a grave lack of tanks or aircraft, the German army defended itself with extraordinary professionalism and courage. The fighting conditions were appalling, and favoured the Soviets, who were used to the rigours of the Russian winter. As the petrol froze in their fuel tanks, the

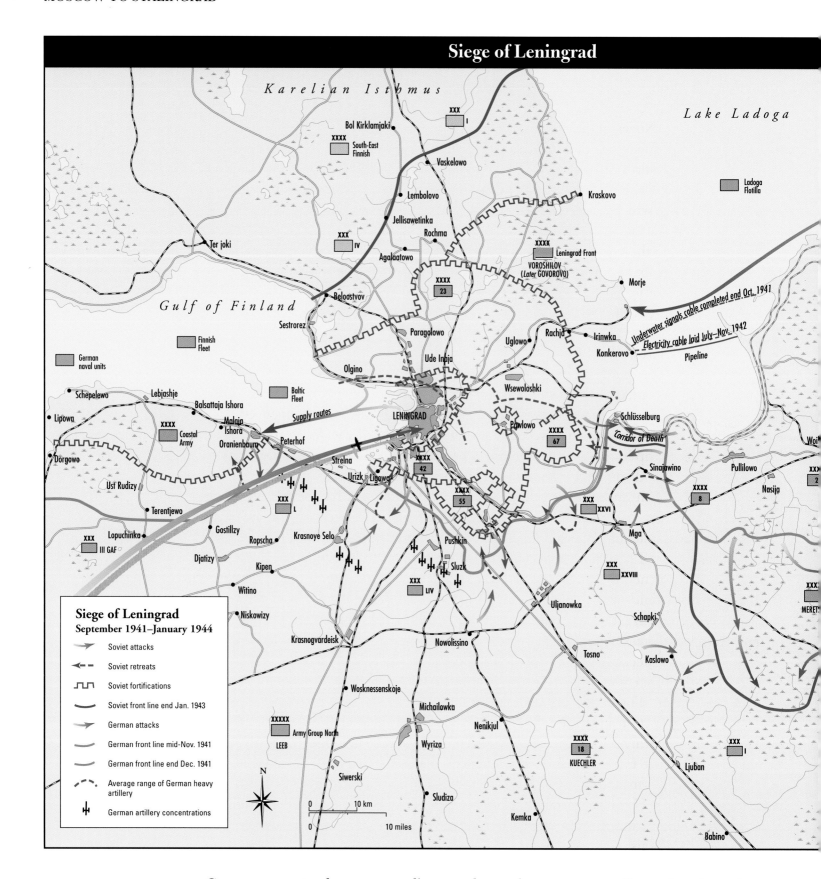

Siege of Leningrad

Siege of Leningrad
September 1941–January 1944

→ Soviet attacks

◄– – Soviet retreats

⊓⊔⊓ Soviet fortifications

⌣ Soviet front line end Jan. 1943

→ German attacks

⌣ German front line mid-Nov. 1941

⌣ German front line end Dec. 1941

⌐ ⌐ Average range of German heavy
artillery

⊢⊢ German artillery concentrations

Germans came to place greater reliance on horse-drawn transport. But as the winter drew on, they succeeded in stemming the Russian hordes. The stubborn German defence exposed the Red Army's lack of experience, its problems exacerbated by shortages of all kinds. By March, even Stalin had to admit that his great offensive was over.

Stalin's failure to relieve besieged Leningrad appeared to have doomed the city. Since Hitler had ordered that the cradle of the Bolshevik revolution be levelled, it seemed only

Summer supply route
from 'lifeline' road

Novaya-Ladoga

'Lifeline' road
completed
6 December 1941

Kisselaja

Wolkow

XXXX
54

Tscherenzovo

Pcheva

Oskui
XXXX
4

a matter of time before it fell. Its population swollen to over three million by refugees flooding into the city, Leningrad was cut off by Germans to the south and to the north by the Finns, eager to avenge the Winter War.

Communist Party chiefs anxiously calculated their food reserves. On 1 November, they realized there was enough food for only another week. Winter was also approaching, and there was so little fuel that buildings could not be heated – electricity was rationed to an hour a day. What followed was the most appalling siege in history, a long drawn-out agony in which nearly a million men, women and children died of cold and slow starvation – three times the *total* war dead suffered by Britain or the USA in the whole of World War II. Only the barest of supplies reached the embattled population. Throughout the winter and into the spring, the Germans kept a relentless grip on the city, stopping all Soviet attempts to break through.

The Spring Thaw

The fluid fighting of early 1942 isolated numerous pockets of the invaders. The Soviet Northwest Front broke through in the Valdai hills, encircling several divisions in turn. In each case, the trapped German troops were clustered around an airfield. With the *Luftwaffe* flying in supplies, they continued to defend their perimeters until relief was at hand, or – in the case of General von Seydlitz's six divisions in the Demyansk pocket – broke out. Seydlitz's men took a month to battle their way to safety across the snow. Their epic escape was sustained by parachute drops and an iron determination never to surrender.

The spring thaw halted operations on both sides. The *rasputitza* turned the steel-hard ground into impenetrable rivers of mud. Nothing could move, and the Germans were given the chance to breathe again. With the *Wehrmacht* still less than 300km (186 miles) from Moscow – a distance the Panzer divisions could cover in a week – the Soviets concentrated their forces around the capital. It was the obvious military strategy, and it was wrong.

The *Wehrmacht's* high command calculated that over the entire Eastern Front the Germans had lost 376,000 men killed and wounded during the Soviet winter offensive. Nearly double that number had been lost from frostbite and sickness. At the beginning of April 1942, the German armies in the east were 625,000 men under strength.

However, they had inflicted over 400,000 casualties on their enemies, and many soldiers puzzled over the Red Army's ability to take such punishment. What the Soviets lacked in military skill, they seemed determined to make up for with fanatical – and often futile – bravery. Goebbels damned them as mindless automata, an enduring image that survived long after 1945. But in its counteroffensive the Red Army had learned the true nature of its opponents. The ordinary Russian soldier discovered that the most outlandish atrocity tales fed to them by the commissars were not so incredible after all.

In their retreat, the Germans had ruthlessly enforced a scorched earth policy. In village after village liberated by the Soviets, they uncovered grisly evidence of German

Opposite: Hitler confidently expected that his armies would soon take Leningrad, the spiritual home of Soviet communism. But the terrain favoured the defenders, and the assault soon lapsed into a siege, which would last for more than 900 days.

'We were disheartened when we discovered in the winter of 1941 that the beaten Russians seemed quite unaware that as a military force they had almost ceased to exist; indeed, their non-existent armies were providing ever tougher resistance.'

Guenther Blumentritt, Chief-of-Staff of the German Fourth Army

Right: Dressed in winter camouflage, a Soviet infantryman waits in ambush in a birch forest on the Central Front, armed with a PPSh41s submachine gun. Although German equipment was generally well designed, it did not cope well with the Soviet winter. The standard German sub-machine gun, the MP40, often failed in snow and mud, and German troops often used captured PPSh41s. The PPSh41s was more crudely made, but could be relied on in almost any conditions.

atrocities. Buildings had been torched, livestock killed, women and children driven out into the snow to die – or summarily executed.

Many ordinary Russian peasants, brutalized by years of communist repression, had initially treated the Germans as liberators. However, any goodwill was quickly squandered by even greater German brutality. Large numbers of Russians took refuge in the forests and the steppes, where they joined the partisan armies fighting a no-quarter war with the occupiers.

For the coming campaigning season, Hitler needed to make good his losses, so he demanded his allies make up the numbers. Romania and Italy supplied half a million men in 1942. By German standards, they were poorly equipped and often badly trained, so they were mainly used to hold quiet sectors while the German formations led the attacks. By replacing German civilian labourers with slaves seized from Eastern Europe, by stripping battalions from divisions garrisoned in Western Europe, and by calling up the next year's conscription class a year early, the *Wehrmacht* was able to assemble 2.7 million men on the Russian front. This accretion of strength could not be repeated, so Hitler was betting everything on one roll of the die.

In material, too, the Germans were making considerable improvements, although even now the home economy was not on a total-war footing. The production of light tanks was halted and medium tanks were given heavier armour and bigger guns. The Panzer IV was equipped with a long-barrelled 75mm (2.95in) weapon, which had previously proved itself with the infantry in the anti-tank role. By so doing, the Germans to some extent overcame the nightmare posed by the appearance of superb Soviet T-34. At the same time, an increased number of cross-country vehicles allowed the *Panzergrenadier* infantry to follow more closely behind the tanks, and so exploit their successes. Thanks to the light armour and cannon fitted to their half-tracks, the troops were able to do some fighting without leaving their vehicles. Even so, it is important remember that the *Wehrmacht* still placed considerable reliance upon horse-drawn transport.

The German Summer Offensive

In Directive No.41, dated 5 April, Hitler stated: 'The enemy has suffered enormous losses of men and material. In attempting to exploit their apparent initial successes, they have exhausted during this winter the mass of their reserves, which were intended for later operations'. In this mistaken belief, Hitler set out his objectives for the

THE 'GUSTAV' RAILWAY GUN

Built originally to breach the Maginot Line, the 80cm (31.4in) 'Gustav' railway gun weighed over 1179 tonnes (1300 tons). It was carried by 25 special trains, and took up to six weeks to assemble on a prepared site. Over 1000 men under the control of a German army engineer unit dug through a small knoll to form a wide railway cutting, whose sides were raised to provide cover and protection for the gun. A further 500 men manned the weapon in action.

Gustav's shells weighed up to 10 tonnes (11 tons), and simply getting each shell and propellant charge to the breech was a major task requiring the use of lifting equipment. Projectile and charge then had to be rammed accurately and the whole barrel elevated to the correct firing angle. It all took time, and while the best firing rate was supposed to be one round every 15 minutes, in practice it was more like one shell per hour.

The gun had a maximum range of around 40km (25 miles), and all shots were observed by a special flight of Fiesler Storch spotter planes. At Sevastopol, one target after another was demolished by the gun, which pulverized Soviet coastal batteries, including the Molotov and Maxim Gorky forts, and the supposedly invulnerable underwater magazine beneath Severnaya Bay.

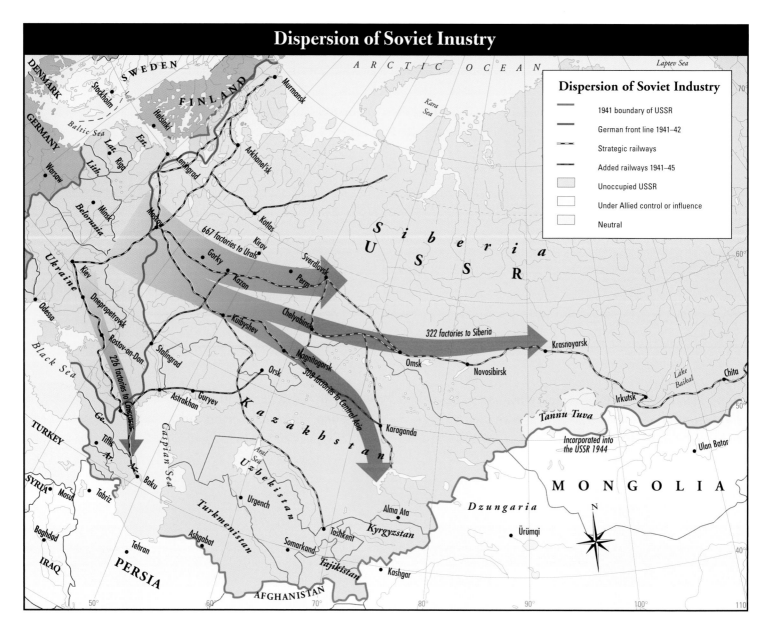

Dispersion of Soviet Inustry

Dispersion of Soviet Industry

- 1941 boundary of USSR
- German front line 1941–42
- Strategic railways
- Added railways 1941–45
- Unoccupied USSR
- Under Allied control or influence
- Neutral

Above: With so much of European Russia in enemy hands, the Soviets moved their major war industries to safety east of the Urals. This titanic effort was completed in an astonishingly short time, and Soviet industry was soon out-producing the Germans in key weapons like tanks, small arms and aircraft.

coming summer offensive, codenamed Operation *Blau* (Blue). He set his revitalized armies, now numbering some 215 divisions, the task of destroying the last remaining enemy formations, and as far as possible, capturing the main sources of raw materials on which the German war economy depended.

All available forces were to be concentrated on the southern sector. Their mission was firstly to annihilate the enemy on the Don. Then they were to swing north and take Stalingrad, followed by a combined assault to conquer the oil-producing areas of the Caucasus. Lastly, they were to capture the passes through the Caucasus mountains, giving access to the Middle East.

Hitler was not the only dictator planning a knockout blow. The return of warmer weather was the signal for another Soviet offensive, but the attempt to recapture Kharkov failed dismally. Ten days and nights of hectic thrust and counter-thrust in open country turned into a master class in *Blitzkrieg*. The advancing Russians were outmanoeuvred by the superbly coordinated German air and ground forces. The *Luftwaffe* air fleets under Ritter von Greim dominated the skies. Swarms of Ju 88s, Stukas and Heinkel 111s pounded the Russian positions, protected by the world's most experienced fighter pilots and reinforced by Germany's Axis allies.

Three Russian armies were surrounded and annihilated. Marshal Timoshenko was summoned to Moscow to explain the loss of another 200,000 men. As the German Sixth and Seventeenth Armies shattered the Russian offensive at Kharkov, the Eleventh Army under the command of General Erich von Manstein broke through the heavily fortified Soviet positions on the Kerch peninsula. By April 1942, the Soviets had ferried 250,000 men into the Crimea, together with considerable tank and artillery support. Yet as in the previous year, the forces were committed piecemeal against overwhelming German opposition.

At dawn on 8 May, Manstein crossed the Kamenskoye isthmus to assault the positions covering Kerch. The nine German divisions were outnumbered two to one, but as usual the *Wehrmacht* commanders placed their strongest forces at the weakest point in the enemy front line. The sheer weight of German metal forced the Soviets back from Feodosia. The Panzers, supported by screaming Stukas, then drove through the waist of the peninsula towards Kerch itself. Between 15 and 20 May, the Caucasus front imploded and the Soviets were driven into the Black Sea. They left behind 170,000 prisoners, 1138 guns and 258 tanks.

Sevastopol

Not wishing to belittle his victory, Manstein described his enemy in his memoirs in much more moderate terms than did the Soviet high command, which vigorously criticized their bad positioning, inertia, and lack of communication between air and land forces.

With its flank protected, Eleventh Army doubled back to storm Sevastopol, home of the Soviet Black Sea Fleet. Manstein had received strong reinforcements. To oppose the Russian garrison of 106,000 sailors, soldiers and marines, he could call on 204,000 men, 720 tanks, 600 aircraft, 670 guns and 450 mortars, including the *Wehrmacht's* general reserve of siege artillery.

Armageddon preceded the assault on the fortress. Operations commenced with a five-day barrage, which reminded some older members of the army staff of Verdun, 25 years

---

RUSSIAN INDUSTRIAL MIGRATION

In 1941–42, as the Soviet Union's key industrial regions were overrun by the invaders, whole factories were uprooted and shipped to the Urals, to the deserts of Kazakhstan or the frozen tundra of Siberia. Over 1.5 million wagonloads made the journey, and workers – many of them women – struggled to set up machine tools literally in the middle of nowhere. Not only did they get the factories working again, but they also did so with unbelievable speed.

The Yak fighter plant in Moscow was dismantled and taken to Siberia, where production resumed in only a week. By early 1942, this factory was building more aircraft per month than it had done on its original site. From a far inferior base – Russia produced only a quarter as much steel as Germany – the Soviets were, by mid-1942, already outbuilding the invaders, and supplying their armies with more tanks, guns and aircraft than the *Wehrmacht* was receiving.

Above: The German occupation of European Russia was brutal. Reprisals for partisan attacks saw entire villages destroyed, their inhabitants driven out onto the steppe or even killed out of hand.

before. Manstein's experts used every piece of artillery they could bring to bear. Included in the heavy artillery pounding the Russian positions was both the massive 'Karl', a siege mortar with a calibre of 60cm (23.6in), and the largest gun ever made, the 80cm (31.4in) 'Gustav' railway gun. The *Luftwaffe* also played its part, dropping more than 20,000 tonnes (22,050 tons) of bombs on Sevastopol in three weeks – more than it dropped on the whole of England during the Blitz.

After the barrage, the German LIV Corps moved against the defences. The Soviets defended every yard of territory through the first weeks of June, demonstrating a tenacity that would be repeated to resounding effect at Stalingrad later that year. By the third week, Manstein was sufficiently worried that he not only threw in his last reserves, but also begged for reinforcements from the Seventeenth Army. The Soviet Navy continued to perform miracles in resupplying Sevastopol across the Black Sea. This supply route had become a killing ground for the *Luftwaffe* and *Kriegsmarine,* as they intercepted the vital transports. The relief efforts were born of desperation and eventually the sheer weight of material thrown against the Soviet defences began to tell.

The Germans finally breached the defences on the night of 28/29 June. During the next three days, the Soviets organized a Dunkirk-style evacuation to rescue as many as possible of the men, women and children who had survived the 250-day siege. The Germans had won, but were left with a gutted city, its buildings destroyed.

Although von Manstein was awarded a field marshal's baton for taking Sevastopol, his Eleventh Army was so depleted that he would have to leave the drive on Stalingrad to the unimaginative but hugely ambitious General Paulus. Paulus, a staff officer with little operational command experience, knew exactly where his fame and fortune were to be made, and that was at Stalingrad.

The Don and the Volga

Hitler moved his HQ to Vinnitsa in the Ukraine to oversee the next stage of the campaign. Army Group South, re-named Army Group B, included the Second and Sixth Armies, Fourth Panzer Army and Third Hungarian Army. It was to advance into the bend of the Don river then on to the Volga at Stalingrad.

The other claw in a gigantic pincer movement would be a new formation. Army Group A, comprising First Panzer Army, Seventeenth Army and Third Romanian Army would link up with Army Group B somewhere on the steppe west of the Volga, hopefully trapping another vast haul of Russian prisoners. Having gutted the Soviet armies again, Army Group A would then lunge south and east to overrun the Soviet oilfields.

On 28 June, the great summer offensive began. Army Group B, under the recalled Field Marshal Feodor von Bock, attacked on a 150km (93-mile) front. The spearhead

Below: Three partisans armed with the PPSh-41 submachinegun listen to orders. The partisan war was brutal, with no quarter given by either side. The Soviets set up a partisan command to coordinate the actions of tens of thousands of guerrillas behind German lines. German security units, generally drawn from the SS or the police, were particularly brutal in their actions.

Right: The siege of Sevastopol was decided when the Germans made use of some of the heaviest artillery pieces ever made to flatten the city before it was finally taken by ground assault.

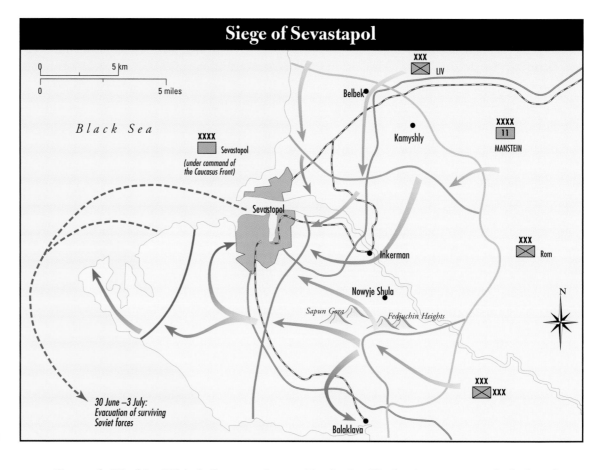

Siege of Sevastapol

Black Sea

Belbek

XXX
LIV

Kamyshly

XXXX
11
MANSTEIN

XXXX
Sevastopol
(under command of the Caucasus Front)

Sevastopol

Inkerman

XXX
Rom

Nowyje Shula

Sapun Gora   Fedjuchin Heights

N

XXX
XXX

30 June –3 July:
Evacuation of surviving
Soviet forces

Balaklava

Below: A flak crew provides security for troops advancing towards the Caucasus. Their weapons were as likely to be used against ground targets as against aircraft, as partisans regularly attacked the German lines of communication.

was General Hoth's Third Panzer Army. Paulus's Sixth Army extended the front a further 80km (50 miles) to the south. Two days later, Army Group A under General Wilhelm List burst over the Donetz bend and drove southwards to Proletarskaya and the Caucasus. The attacks were resoundingly successful. Hoth was in Voronezh by 3 July, though progress was not fast enough to satisfy Hitler and he replaced von Bock with Baron Maximilian von Weichs. Army Group B then poured down the Donets corridor to link up with von Kleist's armour pushing on Rostov. It seemed that the days of easy victory had returned.

The Russian forces were contemptuously swept aside. For the first time in many months, the ground favoured large-scale sweeping manoeuvres. Hundreds of miles of open rolling corn and steppe grass offered perfect country for the massed legions of German armour. Their advance was visible for miles: smoke from burning villages and dust kicked up by thousands of heavy vehicles signalled the irresistible onrush of a perfectly functioning war machine.

But then Hitler became too ambitious. He believed that the

Left: The crew of a 21cm (8.26in) Mrs 18 artillery piece load an enormous 113kg (250lb) shell as part of the bombardment of Sevastapol. Soldiers who had been frozen by the Russian winter only six months before were now being baked. Temperatures as von Kleist's panzer army approached the Caucasus mountains regularly exceeded 40°C, and tasks such as manning heavy artillery pieces became harder and harder.

Russians were finished and just needed one more devastating victory to bring the Soviet edifice low. On 13 July, aiming at another vast encirclement, he detached Hoth's armour, ordering it to swing southeast to link up with Army Group A's tanks, whose forces were now committed to an intense battle in the streets of Rostov. On 23 July, Rostov fell, but it ailed to yield the hoped-for booty. Stalin had finally learned the lesson of trading space for time, and he allowed his marshals to pull their forces back, rather than letting them be fatally surrounded. On the same day, Hitler issued the directive that arguably cost

Above: A German machine-gun crew take up position behind a wall on the outskirts of Stalingrad in the autumn of 1942. At this stage of the battle, many of the city's buildings were still intact.

him the war in the East, and with it sealed his empire's fate. Totally underestimating the opposing forces, he changed the plans for his two Army Groups. Rather than take Stalingrad and *then* attack the Caucasus, he opted to move on both objectives simultaneously. He compounded the error by making ruinous reductions in the forces available to the operations. The strategic reserve was sent to the four winds: 9th and 11th Panzer Divisions were assigned to General von Kluge, the *Grossdeutschland* Division was sent to Army Group Centre, *Leibstandarte*-SS was ordered to France, and the rested Eleventh Army was held back from taking part in the Caucasus drive.

A Stalling Advance

For the moment, everything still seemed to be going Hitler's way. The headlong advance across open country to the Volga was spearheaded by the Sixth Army, a veteran formation led in Poland and France by General von Reichenau, one of Hitler's strongest

supporters in the Wehrmacht. A vocal anti-Semite, von Reichenau had left his soldiers in no doubt as to their 'historic mission' to slaughter 'Asiatic inferiors', fighting talk that won him command of Army Group South when Hitler sacked von Rundstedt in December 1941. He did not live long to enjoy his promotion to field marshal, dying of a stroke soon afterwards. But his influence permeated the army he had led to victory for two years: the Sixth Army cut a swathe of destruction across Russia as it smashed its way east.

The only problems for the Germans were those of traffic control, for both Kleist and Hoth's Panzers arrived at the crossing of the Donetz simultaneously. In a series of acrimonious arguments, Kleist made it clear that he saw no reason why another Panzer army should be assigned to take the Caucasus. To prove the point, he speeded up his own pace once across the river and captured Proletarskaya.

But to the north, the advance had stagnated. Von Weichs had been left only with the Sixth Army to break through the Soviet forces barring the way to Stalingrad. He was forced to delay to await the arrival of the Italian Eighth Army, and lack of fuel stopped him employing all of his armour at any one time. Hitler relented, and sensing that Hoth's Panzers were doing more harm than good in the over-crowded roads south of the Don, he returned the forces to Army Group B on 30 July.

However, by that stage Hoth was already 140km (87 miles) south of Tsimlyansk, and strong Soviet forces were preventing a link up with Paulus. As Hoth's Panzers fought their way north, they were slowly being ground down, losing men and resources in a laborious war of attrition.

Map, page 187:
The German summer offensive made good progress, with one thrust heading for the Caucasus and its vital oilfields, while another was directed against the city of Stalingrad.

The End of Russian Retreat

The Sixth Army reached the banks of the Volga on 23 August. In spite of furious Soviet counterattacks, a defensive line was established upstream of Stalingrad. That night, Stalingrad was subjected to an air raid reminiscent of the heaviest London bombing. The bulk of the bombs dropped were incendiaries and the wooden buildings of the city burned in a spectacular holocaust. An assault on the city was now planned. But it was to prove an infinitely more difficult task, now that Stalingrad's defenders had had time to prepare the city's defences.

In the meantime, Army Group A had been making excellent progress. Six months after they had endured winter temperatures of -30°C (-22°F), German soldiers found themselves on the Kuban steppe, where the thermometer topped 40°C (104°F) in the shade. Inside the tanks of First Panzer Army, the heat was simply unbearable.

List's major worries were about supplies. It was impossible to satisfy the needs of 26 advancing divisions, some moving southwest, some south and some southeast – so much so that Colonel-General von Kleist jested: 'No Russians in front of us, no supplies behind

Below: Although the image of the Wehrmacht *which has passed into history is of a colossal mechanized juggernaut, the bulk of the forces involved in Russia were actually infantrymen, who marched for huge distances across the seemingly endless plains.*

us!' Jerry cans of petrol dropped from Ju 52 transports had to be brought up to the Panzers by camel transport.

The terrain slowed up fighting troops as well as supplies. Roads were rivers of dust, and the rivers were wide with unpredictable currents. Nevertheless, the SS *Wiking* Division forced the river Kuban in the face of intense resistance early in August. On 9 August, *Gruppe Ruoff* – Seventeenth Army and Third Rumanian Army under General Richard Ruoff – occupied simultaneously the port of Yeytsk on the Sea of Azov, Krasnovar on the Kuban and the blazing wreckage of the oil town of Maikop. Maikop's oil wells were so thoroughly sabotaged that they would not return to use until four years after the war.

Also on 9 August, First Panzer Army took Pyatigorsk at the bottom of the first foothills of the Caucasus, and patrols were sent out towards Astrakahn. On 21 August, a detachment of the elite 1st and 4th *Gebirgsjäger* mountain regiments planted the Swastika flag on the 5642m (18,510ft) summit of Mount Elbrus, and the rest of XLIX Mountain Corps advanced into the sub-tropical forests girding Sukhumi in Georgia. On the eastern side of the mountains, the river Terek was the last obstacle facing *Panzergruppe Kleist* in its breakneck advance.

Eventually the offensive reached what Clausewitz called the falling-off point, beyond which wear and tear take over from the initial drive and energy. Russian resistance was stiffening, and the German forces were now hundreds of kilometres past the last railheads. A desperate race followed, both sides hurrying forward ammunition, fuel, spare parts and more soldiers – always more soldiers – for one final battle before the *rasputitza* imposed nature's halt on campaigning.

Hitler, exasperated by the slow progress, removed List and took control of operations himself. Yet all the genius and dynamism with which he credited himself were unable to improve matters. With hindsight, it seems that Hitler may have been attempting the impossible, but Stalin was sufficiently alarmed by the series of reverses since the fall of Kerch to issue a famous order of the day on 28 July.

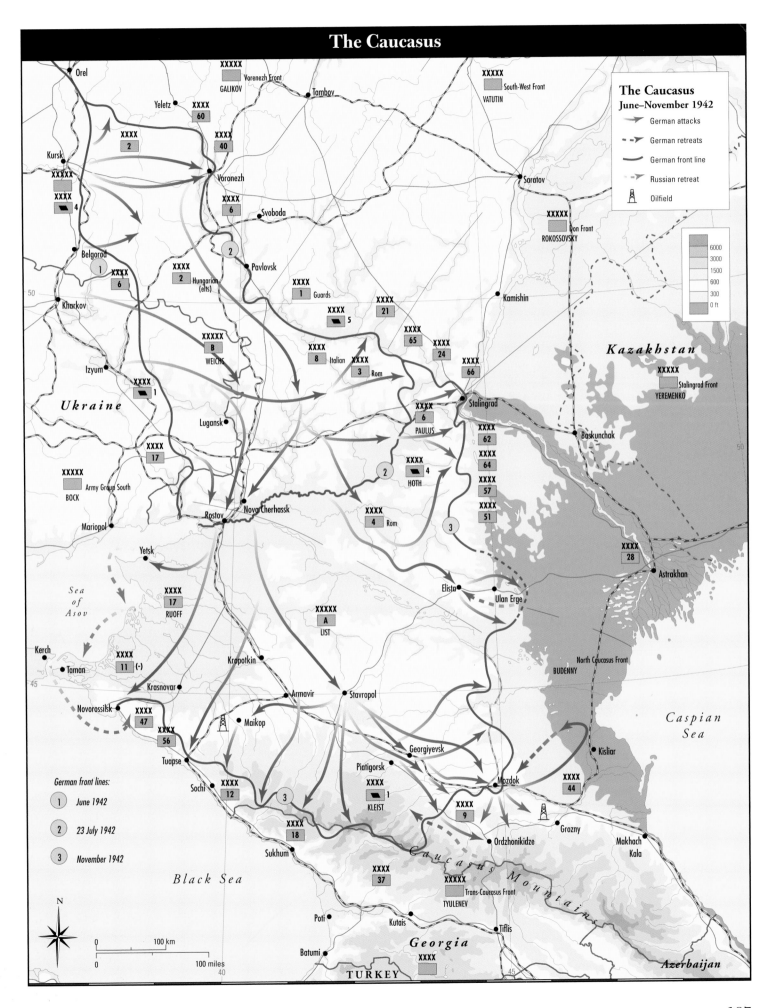

The Caucasus

The Caucasus
June–November 1942

→ German attacks
--→ German retreats
— German front line
-·→ Russian retreat
⛏ Oilfield

Orel
Yeletz
XXXX 60
XXXX 2
Kursk
XXXXX
XXXX 4
Belgorod
1
XXXX 6
Kharkov
Izyum
Ukraine
XXXX 1
Lugansk
XXXX 17
XXXXX
Army Group South
BOCK
Mariopol
Rostov
Nova Cherhassk
Yetsk

GALIKOV
Vorenezh Front
Tambov
XXXX 40
Voronezh
XXXX 6
Svoboda
2
Pavlovsk
XXXX 2
Hungarian (elts)
XXXX 1 Guards
XXXXX B WEICHS
XXXX 8 Italian
XXXX 3 Rom
XXXX 5
XXXX 21
XXXX 65
XXXX 24
XXXX 66
XXXX 6 PAULUS
Stalingrad

VATUTIN South-West Front
XXXXX
Saratov
Don Front
ROKOSSOVSKY
XXXXX
Kamishin
Kazakhstan
XXXXX
Stalingrad Front
YEREMENKO
Baskunchak
XXXX 62
XXXX 64
XXXX 57
XXXX 51
2 HOTH XXXX 4
XXXX 4 Rom
3
Elista
Ulan Erge
XXXX 28
Astrakhan

Sea of Asov
Kerch
Taman
XXXX 11 (-)
Krasnovar
Novorossilsk
XXXX 47
XXXX 56
Tuapse
Sochi
XXXX 12
3
XXXX 18
Sukhum

XXXX 17 RUOFF
Kropotkin
Armavir
XXXXX A LIST
Stavropol
Maikop ⛏
Georgiyevsk
Piatigorsk
XXXX 1 KLEIST
XXXX 9
Ordzhonikidze
Mozdok
XXXX 44
⛏ Grozny
Kisliar
North Caucasus Front
BUDENNY
Caspian Sea
Makhach Kala

Caucasus Mountains
XXXX 37
XXXXX Trans-Caucasus Front
TYULENEV
Black Sea
Poti
Kutais
Tiflis
Batumi
Georgia
XXXX
Azerbaijan
TURKEY

German front lines:
1 June 1942
2 23 July 1942
3 November 1942

N

0 — 100 km
0 — 100 miles

40
45
50

187

Right: While one man keeps watch, his comrades take the opportunity to have a meal. All supplies for the soldiers had to be brought across the Volga.

'Every inch of territory we concede strengthens the enemy and weakens the defence of our country. If we do not stop the retreat, we shall be left with no grain, fuel, metal, workshops, factories or railways. Therefore the moment has come to stop the retreat: not another step back!'

The Battle of Stalingrad

In Stalingrad, the order had the desired effect. The city had half a million inhabitants, and much of the civilian population had been marched out to dig trenches and anti-tank ditches. But these were not the only German worry. German intelligence had not warned the units taking part that Stalingrad sprawled for more than 30km (19 miles) along the Volga and that, in places, the western edge of the city was more than 8km (5 miles) from the bank of the river.

The time for taking the city by *coup de main* had passed. Paulus's makeshift attack could have succeeded only if it met an enemy that was not only beaten but whose morale was extremely low. From the very first engagements in the increasingly bitter street fighting, it was clear to the Germans that the Russians had recovered beyond anyone's expectations.

On 16 September, General von Richthofen, now commander of *Luftflotte IV,* wrote in his diary: 'With a little effort, the town should fall in two days'. Less than a week later, he noted, with more justification: 'September the 2nd. In the town itself progress is desperately slow. The 6th Army will never finish the job at this rate'.

The Russian soldiers, spurred on by patriotic propaganda, were now fighting in circumstances in which their own natural talents were an advantage, and their lack of armour and mobility did not matter. They fought from holes burrowed in rubble, from the blackened caverns of burned-out offices, from behind parapets of gaunt towering blocks; they fought for every yard of every street and every alleyway in the city.

Here, all the Panzers could do was to creep over the wasteland of a city devastated by their own efforts. Unable to see the hidden enemy, their fate was to be blasted by liquid fire, or their tracks blown off by grenades. Armoured vehicles are virtually defenceless once immobilized. And once the tanks were stopped, German infantry were mown down by machine-gun fire as they sought protection behind their vehicles.

In Berlin, Hitler was already proclaiming the victory in Stalingrad, and poured as many reinforcements as possible into the inferno. By contrast, the Russians fed in just enough troops to keep the Germans occupied, and to resist their best efforts. In the meantime, the mass of men and arms accumulating in reserve were being held back for a different purpose.

This was finally revealed on 19 November. The last of six major attacks by the Sixth Army had been repulsed, and the weary German troops were licking their wounds. Surprise was near total when the Soviets unleashed massive barrages north and south of Stalingrad. The Red Army had finally learned the lessons of *Blitzkrieg*. This time their attacks would be launched at the weakest part of the German line – Paulus' thinly held flanks, protected only by Romanian and Italian formations. The battle for Stalingrad had entered a new and desperate phase. General Paulus thought he had the city of Stalingrad within his grasp. But his confidence was shattered when he received alarming reports from the units guarding his flanks. Soviet forces were attacking in unbelievable strength.

To the north, German divisions were being engulfed by wave upon wave of massed Soviet armour, heavily supported by even larger numbers of aircraft and artillery pieces.

Below: The German 6th Army commanded by General Paulus reached the Volga at Stalingrad at the end of August. The Wehrmacht High Command expected the city to fall quickly, but the Soviet defenders fought street by street, building by building to thwart their expectations.

On 20 November, the Soviets attacked in the south, with equal effect. By 23 November, the encirclement was complete. Some 300,000 Axis soldiers were trapped inside Stalingrad.

Paulus reported that his Sixth Army had enough food for only a week and that fuel and ammunition was running low. His senior commanders begged him to order a breakout, but Paulus' superior, Field Marshal von Manstein, refused to hear of it. Hitler insisted that *'Festung Stalingrad'* – Fortress Stalingrad – hold out until relieved. The expression 'fortress' gave false comfort; the troops had no proper fortifications, just the holes in the frozen ground they had managed to excavate with their remaining explosives.

The temperature sank remorselessly. Blizzards swept across the steppe. Huddled in underground bunkers, the Sixth Army counted the days until a relief operation rescued them. Fighting rations were reduced to 200g (7oz) of horsemeat and 200g (7oz) of bread per day. Support troops received half that, and there was nothing at all for Soviet prisoners held inside the pocket. Yet the ordinary soldiers believed, against mounting evidence to the contrary, that Hitler would get them out. Manstein failed to relieve the trapped army. He sent Hoth to blast a way through the Soviet lines on 12 December, and in a week of desperate fighting, his Panzer corps got close enough to see the horizon lit up at night, flares rising and falling over the pocket. But the Soviets attacked the Italian and Romanian armies along the River Chir, north-west of Stalingrad. Another great breakthrough was achieved, and Hoth's relief force was compelled to turn away and meet the new threat. The Sixth Army was abandoned. Stalin ordered the pocket crushed in

Below: German prisoners-of-war after the capture of Stalingrad were tansported to the rear in the most appalling weather conditions. Few were to survive captivity.

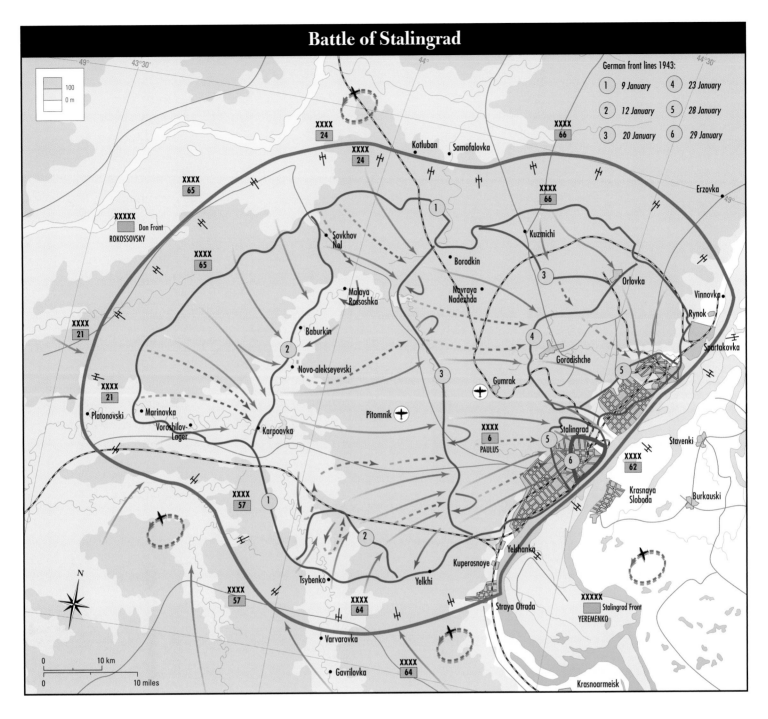

Battle of Stalingrad

German front lines 1943:

1. 9 January 4. 23 January
2. 12 January 5. 28 January
3. 20 January 6. 29 January

January, and a renewed Soviet Blitzkrieg broke into the perimeter west of the city. Some 25,000 sick and wounded Germans were evacuated, but a far greater number of men died as frostbitten limbs and wounds turned gangrenous. Basic medicines such as anaesthetic ran out. No rations were given to the wounded after 11 January. Hitler promoted Paulus to full general and then to field marshal, on the tacit understanding that no German field marshal had ever been taken alive. But Paulus refused to commit suicide, and surrendered himself and his staff on 30 January. Small parties of troops broke out onto the steppe, trying to make their way back to safety. Some were spotted from time to time by Luftwaffe reconnaissance flights. However, none made it back to the German lines.

Of the 300,000 German soldiers surrounded in Stalingrad, only 91,000 survived to surrender, and half of these would be dead before spring. Only 5000 would ever return from Soviet captivity, many of them not until the 1950s.

Above: The Sixth Army was quickly encircled: when Marshal Zhukov launched Operation Uranus on 19 November 1942, massive artillery barrages north and south of the city heralded equally massive attacks, which within four days had trapped Paulus' army in a ring of steel.

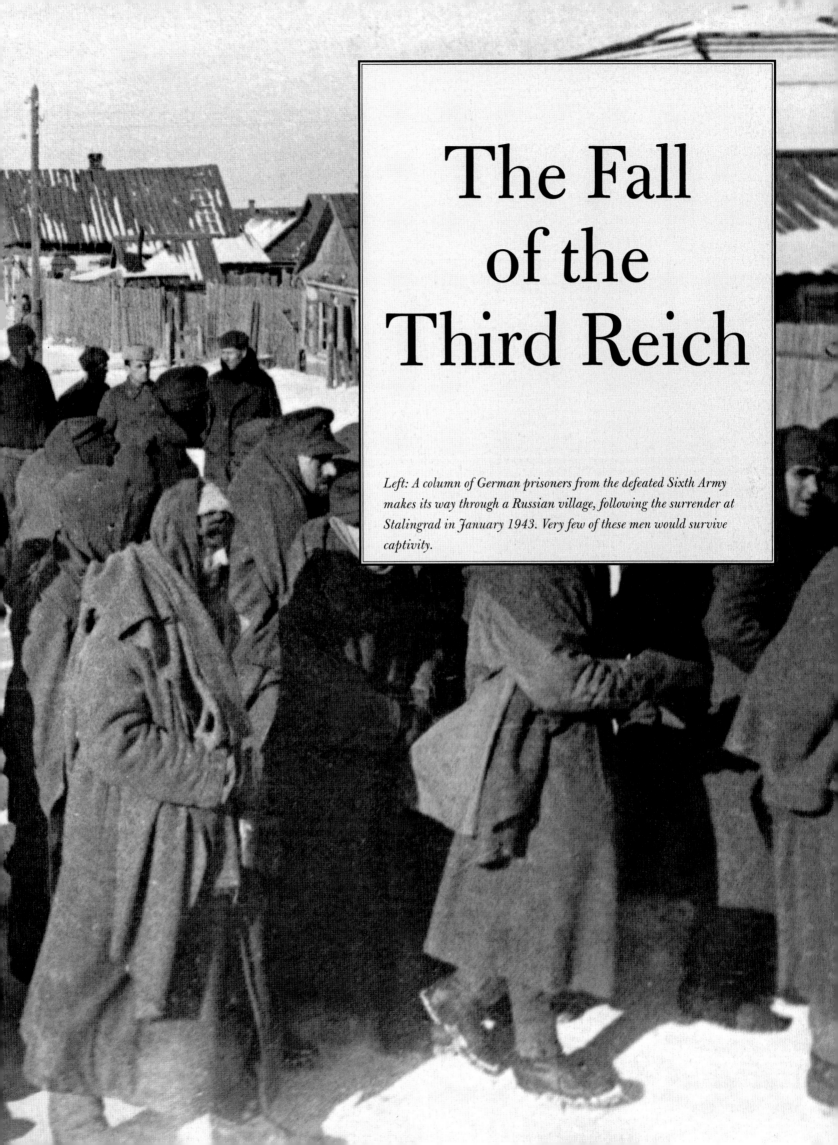

The Fall of the Third Reich

Left: A column of German prisoners from the defeated Sixth Army makes its way through a Russian village, following the surrender at Stalingrad in January 1943. Very few of these men would survive captivity.

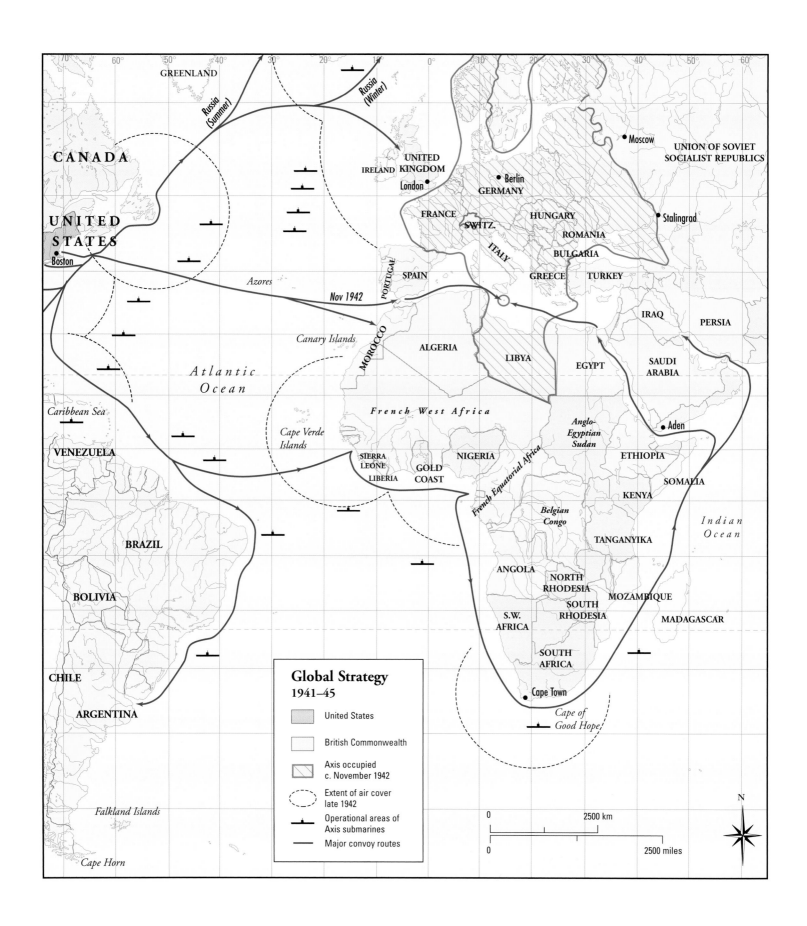

GREENLAND

Russia (Summer)

Russia (Winter)

CANADA

UNITED
STATES

Boston

Azores

Nov 1942

Canary Islands

*Atlantic
Ocean*

Caribbean Sea

VENEZUELA

BOLIVIA

BRAZIL

CHILE

ARGENTINA

Falkland Islands

Cape Horn

IRELAND UNITED
KINGDOM
London

FRANCE

SWITZ.

PORTUGAL

SPAIN

MOROCCO

ALGERIA

*Cape Verde
Islands*

French West Africa

SIERRA
LEONE
LIBERIA

GOLD
COAST

NIGERIA

GERMANY

Berlin

ITALY

LIBYA

HUNGARY

ROMANIA

BULGARIA

GREECE TURKEY

EGYPT

Moscow

UNION OF SOVIET
SOCIALIST REPUBLICS

Stalingrad

IRAQ

PERSIA

SAUDI
ARABIA

*Anglo-
Egyptian
Sudan*

ETHIOPIA

*Belgian
Congo*

French Equatorial Africa

ANGOLA

NORTH
RHODESIA

SOUTH
RHODESIA

S.W.
AFRICA

SOUTH
AFRICA

Cape Town

*Cape of
Good Hope*

Aden

KENYA

SOMALIA

TANGANYIKA

MOZAMBIQUE

MADAGASCAR

*Indian
Ocean*

Global Strategy
1941–45

United States

British Commonwealth

Axis occupied
c. November 1942

Extent of air cover
late 1942

Operational areas of
Axis submarines

Major convoy routes

0   2500 km

0   2500 miles

N

Beginning of the End

As 1942 drew to a close, it was clear that the rise of the Third Reich had reached its apogee. After the stunning successes enjoyed in the first years of the war, German advances had at first been slowed, and then reversed. The Allied war effort had grown in strength during the year. The entry of the United States into the war meant that the weight of American industrial power could be harnessed in the fight against Fascism.

A t the 'Arcadia' conference, held in Washington between December 1941 and January 1942 (their first summit as allies), President Roosevelt and Prime Minister Churchill had agreed that the main effort for the United States would be applied against Germany first, and then against Japan. Although it took time for the American armed forces to be available in strength, they had participated in their first combat in North Africa following the landings in French North Africa under the auspices of Operation Torch. Torch followed the British success at the second battle of El Alamein on 2 November 1942. El Alamein marked a turning point in British perceptions of the war – until that point, British forces had proved unable to inflict a meaningful defeat upon the Germans, and the victory by the Eighth Army raised morale considerably.

America Enters the Fray

American participation in Torch was controversial. It was proposed by Churchill at the 'Arcadia' conference, but opposed by the US Chiefs of Staff, who saw landings in North Africa as a diversion of effort that would prevent a quick assault against North West Europe. In February, General Dwight D. Eisenhower made clear that the best course of action for the United States was a build-up of American resources in Britain, followed by an invasion of France later that year. This was an over-optimistic assessment of what could be achieved in 1942, as Roosevelt was well aware. The President also felt that an early involvement of US troops in the European theatre of operations would be of considerable political advantage, both in reinforcing the 'Germany First' strategy, and demonstrating willing to the Soviet Union. As a result of these considerations, planning for a combined landing in North Africa got underway.

Opposite: The sea routes between the United States and Britain were of vital importance in supplying the Allies with men and munitions from North America. With its phenomenal industrial strength, the United States was the driving force behind the Allied war effort. Although Soviet industry was, in terms of military output, even more prolific, even the Red Army was dependent upon American factories for its trucks and jeeps. As the Soviets continued to push back the Wehrmacht *post-Stalingrad and inflict increasingly heavier casualties, the Anglo-American invasion of Europe became the prime focus for Allied strategy.*

The plan, now named 'Torch', called for three separate landings. The westernmost landing would be made by an all-American force near to Casablanca in Morocco; that in the centre would be carried out by American troops, while the Eastern Task Force would be mainly British, with a small US contingent. The landings took place before dawn on 8 November 1942, and met little resistance from the Vichy French forces. However, reinforcement of Tunisia by the Germans and Italians meant that Tunis could not be taken, and it became clear that it would not be until 1943 that the Allies would be able to launch a major effort to drive Axis forces from North Africa.

Defeat at Stalingrad

The German position was not only weakened in North Africa by the end of 1942, since events on the Eastern Front served to demonstrate that Hitler's notions of defeating the Soviet Union were perhaps over-optimistic. Grand plans for seizing Leningrad and the Caucasus oilfields had failed to come to fruition in 1942, and the German effort had been shifted to attacking Stalingrad, despite warnings from the German general staff that this represented a dangerous diversion to little strategic purpose. The German assault on Stalingrad was marked by savage street fighting as the advantage switched between the two sides. Although there were occasions when the Soviet situation appeared grim, the Germans simply could not break down resistance sufficiently to drive the Soviets from the city. Stalingrad's defence was the responsibility of Lieutenant-General Vasily Chuikov's Sixty-Second Army. Chuikov concluded that exploiting the constraints imposed on an army by fighting in a built-up area would make German co-ordination of their infantry, air power and armour – a hallmark of their successes to date – extremely difficult to attain. The battle started on 14 September 1942, beginning weeks of ferocious fighting.

While the battle raged, the Soviet high command had been busy preparing a counteroffensive. Over one million Soviet troops were gathered together to launch Operation Uranus, which was intended to encircle Stalingrad from north and south, cutting off the Sixth Army. The offensive began on 19 November and by the 23 November the Sixth Army was surrounded. Hitler refused to give permission for an attempt at withdrawal, and then forbade General Paulus to surrender. However, with his forces suffering attrition in the freezing conditions, Paulus met with Soviet emissaries on the 30 January 1943 to offer his surrender. Hundreds of thousands of men were marched into a captivity from which few would return.

The Battle of the Atlantic

One area of the war in which the Germans enjoyed a considerable advantage for much of 1942 was the conflict at sea. America's entry into the war provided a host of targets for U-boat commanders as the United States struggled to implement effective anti-submarine measures. From 12 January 1942, the U-boat fleet embarked upon what was known as the second 'Happy Time' as they operated with near-impunity off the east coast of America (the first 'Happy Time' had been while the British were struggling to address the threat posed by German submarines in mid-1940). The US Navy had serious difficulties in the first three months of the year, due to the lack of escorts and the lack of security measures employed by merchant shipping.

The German submarine arm enjoyed a further advantage in 1942. The British top-secret code-breaking station at Bletchley Park had succeeded in breaking the code for the

'Now this is not the end. It is not even the beginning of the end. But it is, perhaps, the end of the beginning.'

*Winston Churchill
10 November 1942,
after victory at Alamein*

U-boat fleet, and had exploited this to enable convoys to be routed away from the submarines as soon as radio intercepts revealed where the U-boats were in the Atlantic. A modification to the German Enigma machine as part of a routine security improvement ordered by Admiral Karl Dönitz meant that Bletchley Park was rendered 'blind', and the vital information about where the U-boats were congregating could no longer be divined. By July 1942, the U-boats had begun to target convoys in mid-Atlantic again. However, by this point, the battle had begun to tip, imperceptibly, in favour of the Allies again. The Royal Navy at last began to receive enough ships and equipment for the anti-submarine role, while the British Coastal Command started to employ long-range aircraft such as the Liberator. After the capture of Enigma material from the U-559, Bletchley Park was able to crack the new German code by December. The Battle of the Atlantic was, therefore, in the balance by 1943, with the British Admiralty predicting that early 1943 would be the critical phase of the struggle.

Year of Transition

Consequently, 1942 was a year of transition. German defeats in North Africa and the Soviet Union suggested that tide was beginning to turn in favour of the Allies, an impression bolstered by American entry into the war. It would be wrong, however, to suggest that a final victory against the Third Reich seemed an obvious outcome at the time. Hitler was still in control of mainland Europe; Allied bombing raids were by no means devastating, and the Battle of the Atlantic was delicately poised. Rather than a decisive change, the events of 1942 marked the first cracks in the defences of Germany, cracks which would be forced wider apart in the next two and a half years until the façade of a thousand-year Reich was brought crashing to earth.

Above: British Prime Minister Winston Churchill, US President Franklin Delano Roosevelt and Soviet premier Joseph Stalin had the second of three tripartite meetings at the Yalta Conference in the Crimea, 4–11 February, 1944. During this conference, the Allied leaders discussed Europe's postwar reorganization. This included such issues as the re-establishment of the nations conquered and destroyed by Germany, as well as how a defeated Germany would be divided into zones of control.

197

Collapse in the Desert

After the defeat at El Alamein, and the Anglo-American landings under the auspices of Operation Torch, it was clear that the German position in North Africa was becoming increasingly perilous. While resistance to the Anglo-American landings had been sufficiently fierce to delay the Allied advance, German forces were simply not strong enough to hold the invaders off forever.

While the Allies advanced from the west, it was quite clear to all parties that the *Afrika Korps* was in full flight from the Alamein battlefield, even if the Germans were withdrawing in reasonable order. The nature of Montgomery's pursuit ensured that the retreat did not turn into a rout, but Montgomery's reason for being careful was based upon the notion that he would rather be fully prepared for the next round of battles, and not outrun his supply lines in the process of pursuit.

Although Montgomery's controversial decision has been the subject of considerable debate since, the simple fact is that such retrospective analysis cannot alter the history of events in North Africa. The Eighth Army advanced methodically, driving the Germans and Italians back towards Tunisia. Montgomery's forces reached Sirte on 25 December, and spent the next few weeks ensuring that their supply lines were secure before the next phase of the advance.

On 12 January 1943, aircraft from the Desert Air Force began a series of preliminary raids in support of an offensive south of Buerat. The advance, by XXX Corps, was steady rather than spectacular, covered by constant air support. Progress on the ground was slow, with minefields and difficult ground conditions making movement difficult. This prompted Montgomery to instruct 51st Highland Division to press on as quickly as possible, although this was hampered by the fact that the division had not been provided with sufficient transportation under the original plan, which had other units in greater need. This was overcome to some extent by moving by day and night.

On 19 January, the 51st Division entered Homs. German intelligence of British movements concerned Rommel to the extent that he decided that it was necessary to abandon his defensive line. In fact, Montgomery's intentions were not as Rommel had

Opposite: Grumman Martlet and Supermarine Seafire fighters await take-off from the aircraft carrier HMS Formidable, *off the North African coast. Although not obvious from this picture, many British aircraft were painted with American markings during the Torch landings, to make it easier for the recently arrived US troops to tell the difference between hostile and friendly aircraft.*

Above: British troops relax prior to a training exercise in Tunisia. The British provided the majority of the forces in the North African campaign, even after the arrival of American forces under the auspices of Operation Torch.

anticipated. He made his main thrust along the coast road, rather than inland, aiming for Tripoli. By 21 January, the prize of Tripoli was in sight, and British formations pressed on as quickly as possible. On the night of 22/23 January, Rommel decided that the position was hopeless, and abandoned the city, leaving only small rearguard forces to protect the withdrawal. As it was, the first British forces entered Tripoli on 23 January, and found there was no opposition.

At midday, Montgomery received the surrender of the city from the Italian vice-governor. Rommel's army had been driven out of Egypt, Cyrenaica, and nearly all of Libya and Tripolitania, but although the Axis position in North Africa was now critical, there was still a great deal of fighting to be done.

Fighting in Tunisia

The reverses suffered in January 1943 caused considerable uncertainty on the part of the Axis powers at the end of the month, since it was not clear what could be done to prevent the Allies from gaining ultimate victory. Rommel fell back on the defensive positions of the Mareth Line, as the last of his army withdrew from Libya, reaching Tunisia on 13 February. This did not mean that the Germans had given up, however, for the next day, they launched an assault against the inexperienced American II Corps. The Corps Intelligence Officer had warned that there was the possibility that the enemy would attack in strength against Gafsa, and air intelligence officers agreed with this assessment. As a result, Lieutenant-General Sir Kenneth Anderson, the commander of First Army, had instructed that Gafsa was not to be held against a major attack, and that the Americans should pull back and defend in the hills around Feriana.

The Germans had been planning for the assault for over a week. Rommel had assessed that the Allies might strike against the coast from their position at Gafsa, and concluded that the best counter was an attack launched through Gafsa, with the aim of attacking the Americans before they were prepared for further action. The attack would drive through Gafsa, then the American troops in open country beyond and in the hills to the west. There were a number of difficulties, however, since Rommel and Colonel-General Jürgen von Arnim endeavoured to persuade each other to release their mobile forces (a sign of the numerical problems faced by the Germans), but had failed in their efforts. Von Arnim would not release his mobile troops to support Rommel, since he was anxious to

Below: Battle-weary Afrika Korps troops trudge through the desert between battles. The Germans suffered from a lack of motorised transport, and movement in daylight hours became increasingly dangerous as the British gained air superiority. After the campaign had ended, Rommel concluded that any army fighting under near-constant air attack would be unable to overcome its opponents.

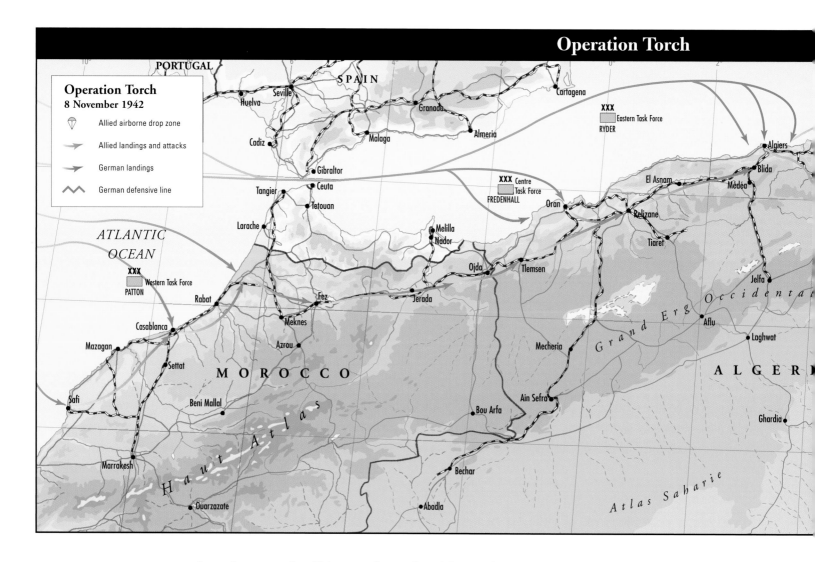

Above: Operation Torch was the first major Anglo-American operation of World War II, and saw four separate landing operations along the North African coast. A complication came in the form of the French troops defending Morocco and Algeria, since they were nominally opposed to the Allies as the result of the terms of the Vichy treaty. Although some resisted, most did nothing to oppose the landings, and the Allies made a swift advance until they came into contact with German forces in Tunisia.

launch an attack of his own through Faid to Sidi Bou Zid. Von Arnim's attack began first, just as predicted by US II Corps' intelligence, and went well. By 06:00 of the first morning, German troops were five miles west of the Faid Pass. American defensive efforts were not helped by a failure of communications which meant that their artillery's pre-planned defensive fireplan was not brought down on the enemy as intended. German air attacks supported the advance, and although the Americans did their best, they were unable to prevent German forces from linking north of Sidi Bou Zid by 10:00.

The success of the advance prompted Rommel to order that the attack on Gafsa should begin on 15 February, although the American and French troops there left for Feriana, in accordance with Anderson's instructions. A counter-attack by the American Combat Command C ran into difficulties and only just managed to withdraw, losing a battalion of tanks in the process. Combat Command A was left isolated, and although it was finally ordered to withdraw during the night of 16 February, some 1400 troops were captured during the course of the next day.

Anderson had meanwhile decided that US II Corps should hold Feriana, Kasserine and Sbeitla, without attempting any more counterattacks. This demanded several complicated movements for the units of First Army, but these were accomplished with little interference from the enemy. On 17 February, Anderson gave permission for Feriana and Sbeitla to be abandoned, and by the afternoon, Rommel's forces had entered the former, and also Thelepte, as well as Gafsa and Tozeur; Sbeitla and Sidi Bou Zid followed into German hands shortly afterwards. While the Germans held the initiative,

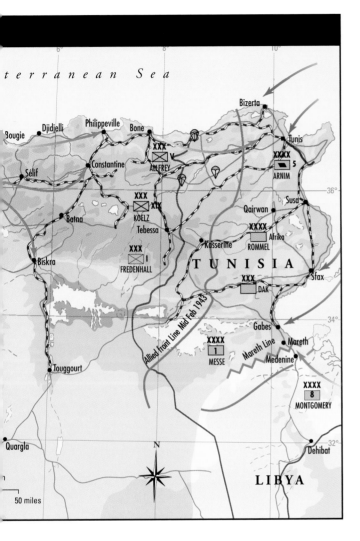

orders came from the Italian supreme command (which had overall responsibility for Axis forces in North Africa) ordering a move northwards, with the aim of attacking V Corps. Neither Rommel nor von Arnim agreed with the order. Von Arnim was concerned that the proposed move would in fact put his forces in contact with the enemy's reserves at the strongest point; Rommel, meanwhile, chose not to protest, but instead ordered the *Afrika Korps* Assault Group to capture the Kasserine Pass.

The Kasserine Pass

Following Rommel's instructions, a reconnaissance of the Kasserine Pass was carried out by German forces on 18 February, convincing the Americans that an attack there would soon be forthcoming. The commanding officer of the US 26th Infantry Regiment, Colonel Alexander N. Stark, was ordered to take control of a variety of units in the vicinity, to be known as Stark Force. The Germans attacked Stark Force on 19 February, with the aim of capturing and sealing the pass. An intense German effort thrust against the inexperienced American forces, and by mid-morning next day, the American defence began to collapse. A withdrawal to Djebel el Hamra was carried out, with considerable amounts of equipment left behind intact for the Germans to capture. In the face of these successes, the Allies were concerned about the position, and could not call on a great amount of air support as the weather was so poor as to prevent much flying.

A German advance on Thala and Djebel el Hamra on 21 February was blocked by Combat Command B at the latter location, but the British 26th Armoured Brigade was slowly pushed back to around four miles south of Thala. As the armoured brigade passed through the positions of the defending infantry, German tanks broke into the position, and only an *ad hoc* defence by the 17th/21st Lancers and two batteries of field guns firing over open sights as anti-tank weapons stopped the assault. The Germans withdrew at about 22:00, and an improvised defensive plan, including the grouping of British and American artillery into a single force, was drawn up. The situation appeared extremely dangerous, but in fact the pressure was about to be reduced. It seemed apparent to the Germans that they were not going to be able to break through, and by the afternoon of 22 February, Rommel made clear that he thought that there was little point in continuing the offensive. There were several reasons for these conclusions. First, Rommel was convinced that the losses sustained by the Allies had been heavy, and meant that they would be unable to take to the offensive for some time. Second, Rommel noted that the

'The total destruction or capture of all enemy forces in Tunisia, culminating in the surrender of 248,000 men, marks the triumphant end of the great enterprises set on foot at Alamein and by the invasion of North West Africa.'

Winston Churchill, 3 June 1943

DESERT AIR POWER

The use of air power proved critical to success in the desert campaign, and laid the foundations for Allied air operations in Italy and Normandy. Initially, the British found that the years of inter-service rivalry after World War I meant that air support for the Army was almost totally lacking, while the Army did not fully understand what could and could not be done with aircraft in support of land forces. This reached a nadir when the Army demanded that the RAF bomb individual tanks as they sped across the battlefield.

Fortunately, while the spirit of cooperation had been lacking at the most senior levels of the two services, the commanders in the desert campaign realized that air support was important, and developed a highly effective system. This required the RAF to gain control of the air, use fighter-bombers in support of Army operations and attack German supply lines. By the end of the desert war, the Allies had absolute air supremacy, enabling them to bring firepower to bear against key German targets in support of the advance of ground forces.

Kasserine area was unsuited to further mobile operations (particularly now the ground had been made more difficult by the weather); far better, he concluded to break off the offensive and turn attention to southern Tunisia for a blow against the Eighth Army. As a result, orders were given that the German forces should return to their start points. By the morning of 24 February, the Kasserine Pass was in Allied hands once more, after what had been a particularly fierce and bloody introduction for the Americans to what the Germans were truly capable of.

The Battle of Medenine

In the immediate aftermath of the Kasserine Pass, Rommel was given command of all Axis forces in Tunisia, but this new appointment came too late for him to prevent von Arnim's proposed attack northwards toward Medjez el Bab. Rommel expressed the view that von Arnim's plans were totally unrealistic, and was not surprised when the attacks ended in failure. Although over 2500 prisoners were taken in

Map, page 206:
The Battle of Kasserine Pass was the first clash between American and German troops. The inexperienced Americans were roughly handled by Rommel's forces, and for a time, the situation appeared critical. However, the defences held, and Rommel withdrew once it became clear that he would not achieve a breakthrough.

the attacks, the Germans lost over 70 of their tanks, which they could ill afford.

The offensive had another negative element in that it delayed preparations for Rommel's next planned attack, against Montgomery's position at Medenine. As it became clear that the Germans were building their strength in the area, Montgomery grew extremely concerned. Signals intercepted and decoded at Bletchley Park gave away Rommel's overall intentions, and information gathered from local reconnaissance patrols and prisoner interrogation made it clear that a major attack was in the offing. More men and equipment were rushed to the area, so that by early March, the British strength at Medenine had been more than quadrupled. The Germans seem to have been blissfully unaware of the increase in British strength, and when they finally attacked on 6 March, they were in for an unpleasant surprise.

The British defences had been carefully established, and rested upon two key components – a heavy defensive fireplan for the artillery, and the use of anti-tank guns located in the forward area. Anti-tank gun strength was bolstered by flying 100 of the new 17-pounder guns to North Africa, where they were fitted on to 25-pounder field gun carriages in the absence of carriages designed for the 17-pounder. When the Germans advanced, they were allowed to reach within 100 yards of the anti-tank guns, which then opened fire. The German tanks suffered heavy losses under the assault of the anti-tank guns, and matters were not helped by the heavy defensive artillery fire that made it almost impossible for the German infantry to advance. By 17:30, it was clear that there would be no breakthrough, and Rommel called off the attack.

The Mareth Line

Rommel's failure at Medenine convinced him that the time for German and Italian forces to abandon North Africa had come, and he determined to inform Hitler and Mussolini of this fact. Taking sick leave on 9 March, he flew to Italy, where he discovered that Mussolini had no appreciation of how dangerous the situation was. He continued his journey to Berlin, where Hitler demonstrated an even greater lack of awareness of the German situation, talking not of withdrawal, but of operations against Casablanca to throw the Allies out of Africa.

While the two dictators were demonstrating their lack of understanding of how grave the situation had become, Montgomery made plans to break through the German defensive positions on the Mareth Line, with a start date of 20 March.

Three days before the attack, US II Corps, now under the command of the inimitable Lieutenant-General George S. Patton, launched a supporting attack in the area of Gafsa. The attack began well, and Gafsa was taken without a fight as the enemy fell back; however, over the next three days, stubborn German defence prevented the Americans from moving to cut the coast road. On 23 March a German counter-attack in the El Guettar sector overran American forward positions before being thrown back. Although a relatively inconclusive engagement, the attack used up yet more of the German armoured reserve that could have been employed in the struggle for the Mareth Line.

Montgomery's attack began on 20 March as planned, using troops from X and XXX Corps, with 160,000 men, 600 tanks and over 1400 guns. The plan involved a main effort in the form of a frontal assault on the enemy defensive positions, but this made only a small dent in the Axis lines before being driven back by the end of 22 March. The second element of the attack, a flanking march by the New Zealand Corps against

Below: A flight of Hawker Hurricane IID fighter-bombers from the RAF patrol over the desert. The Hurricane IID was armed with two 40mm cannon for use against German armour, and proved extremely effective. However, the weight of additional armour protection and the guns had a drastic effect on the aircraft's top speed, making it vulnerable. Despite the success of the guns, the RAF moved on to using rocket projectiles when the fighting moved to mainland Europe.

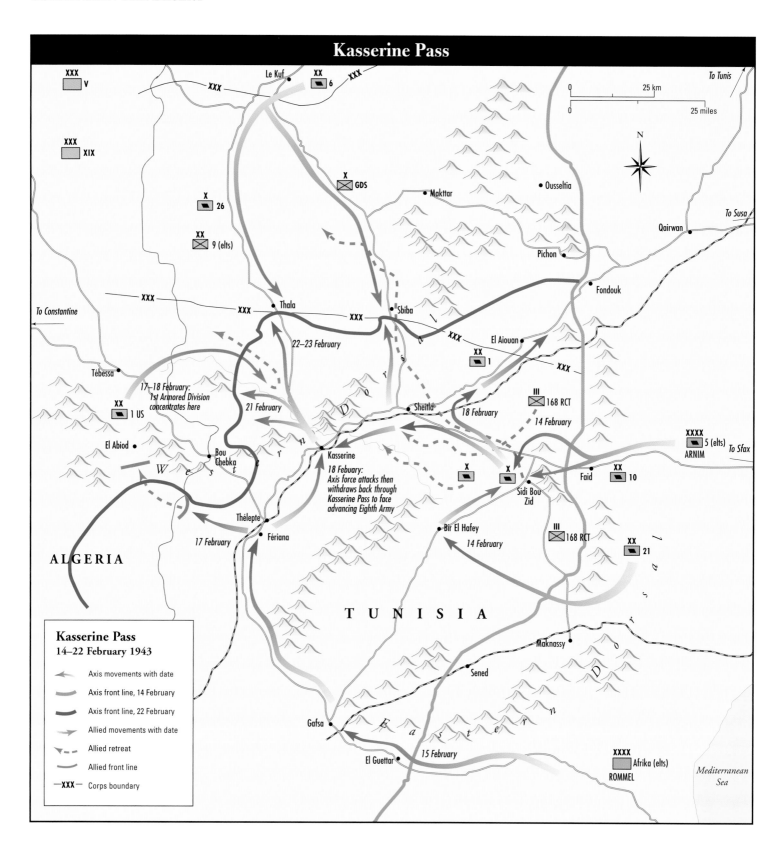

Kasserine Pass

El Hamma, initially enjoyed more success, but was then held up. After clearing the coastal approaches, the attack was stopped at the hill gap known, rather oddly, as Plum. The Plum Gap was reinforced by 21st Panzer Division and four infantry units brought down from the Mareth Line and it was soon clear that the New Zealanders would not be able to progress. As a result, Montgomery recast his plan, concentrating all his forces on the inland flank, where it appeared that a renewed attack might break through. X Corps and the 1st Armoured Division made a move inland to support the New Zealanders on

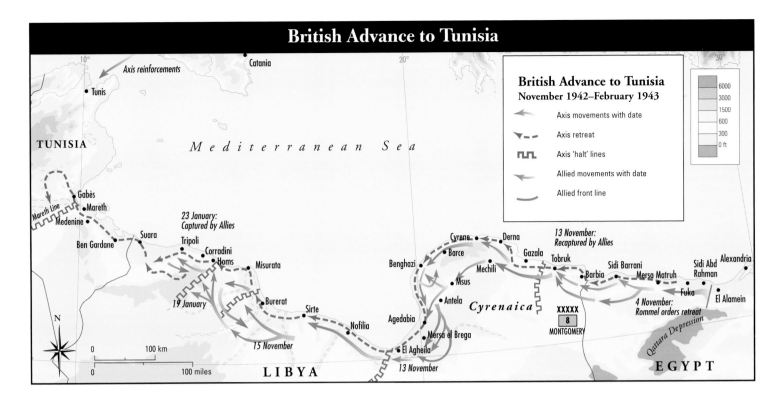

British Advance to Tunisia

British Advance to Tunisia
November 1942–February 1943

← Axis movements with date

▼-- Axis retreat

ⅡⅡ Axis 'halt' lines

← Allied movements with date

⌣ Allied front line

23 March, while 4th Indian Division was given the task of clearing the Hallouf Pass – taking this would reduce British supply lines by over 100 miles – then moving along the hills to the flank of the Mareth Line, presenting a new threat to the Axis forces.

The movement of the New Zealanders was detected by Axis reconnaissance, and further snippets of information about movement gleaned from observers located in the hills suggested that a major attack against the desert flank of their position was in the offing. This prompted von Arnim to instruct the Italian forces holding the Mareth Line to pull back; this in turn meant that the Plum Gap would only be held as long as it took for the non-mobile units in the Mareth Line to withdraw.

The attack began at 16:00 on 26 March, supported by heavy air cover and artillery. The 1st Armoured Division passed through the leading troops at about 18:00 and, advancing through the night, had reached the edge of El Hamma by dawn on 27 March. A German counter-attack checked the advance for 48 hours, giving most of the Mareth Line garrison the opportunity to retreat to the Wadi Akarit position. Montgomery now paused for a week to prepare for the next phase of the attack.

While the British were attacking, Patton's II Corps renewed their assault towards the coast and the Axis rear areas, attacking from El Guettar on 28 March. In a desire to act quickly, Patton was ordered to attack without waiting for the infantry to clear the German anti-tank gun positions, but after three days of fighting, the Americans had advanced no further. While the attack may not have taken much ground, it forced the diversion of 21st Panzer Division to this sector, reducing German armoured strength in the area of the Wadi Akarit.

A frontal attack at nightfall on 5 April by 4th Indian Division carried the ground ahead of it, with over 4000 prisoners being taken by dawn the next day, by which time the 50th and 51st Divisions had launched attacks of their own. While the 50th Division had been stopped, the 51st broke into the German lines. This offered the opportunity of a rapid exploitation by X Corps' armour, but there was a delay in moving the armour forward, which meant that the chance passed. Montgomery instead intended to put in a

Above: The British advance to Tunisia marked the end of an often painful campaign against the Germans. The advance began in earnest with the victory at El Alamein, with Montgomery pursuing the retreating Afrika Korps in a careful and methodical fashion that later came in for some criticism. Despite this, the Eighth Army pursued the Germans all the way to the Mareth Line, and then broke through, ready for the final push against Tunis.

Above: A British 5.5-inch gun fires as part of a night-time artillery barrage against the Mareth Line. Robust and reliable, the 5.5-inch gun was one of the mainstays of the Royal Artillery, and remained in use with the British Army for many years after the war.

decisive blow the next day, but when daylight came, it was clear that the enemy had simply slipped away. Without reinforcement, holding Wadi Akarit became more and more difficult, so the Axis troops began to withdraw to Enfidaville. As the Axis forces joined to defend the last remaining foothold in North Africa, plans were drawn up by the Allies to ensure victory.

The Final Act

By the last three weeks of the North African campaign, the growing numerical superiority of the Allies began to tell. While the Germans and Italians had 13 by now understrength divisions and 130 tanks, the British and Americans had 19 fully effective divisions, supported by over 1100 armoured vehicles. The Allies had three times as many artillery pieces as their opponents, and enjoyed almost complete dominance in the air. As ever, the key test for the Allies would be to translate this superiority on paper into actual supremacy on the field of battle.

For the Axis powers, retaining a foothold in North Africa was crucial, no matter how small the area occupied was in comparison with the territory held when the *Afrika Korps* was at the height of its power. Hitler and Mussolini understood that if they could hold on in Tunisia until the summer or autumn of 1942, they might be able to delay an Allied invasion of Europe until a time when amphibious operations would be made far more difficult by poor weather (also hindering the use of air support to ground troops). As a result, the Germans carried out a great deal of work aimed at improving the defences on high ground, with the aim of bogging down the Allied assault.

For the Allies, the best approach to Tunis was clearly through the Medjerda valley, by clearing the hills on either side of Medjez el Bab (a task which would be in the operating areas of First Army's V Corps and Patton's US II Corps). If this was achieved, it offered the prospect of opening a considerable gap for armour to exploit in a way that would not be possible elsewhere. As far as Montgomery's Eighth Army were concerned, their narrow front along the coastline gave possible access to Tunis or Cap Bon. However, since Sir Harold Alexander (Commander-in-Chief Middle East) was hoping to take the Tunisian ports quickly, the first option was far preferable – if the ports could be seized in short order, this would allow an invasion of Sicily to take place during the summer. As a result, he ordered Anderson's First Army to launch an attack on 22 April against the Axis forces between Medjez el Bab and Bou Arada, with US II Corps attacking in the direction of Bizerta. Eighth Army was to carry out a series of holding attacks around Enfidaville, with the aim of diverting attention from First Army in the days leading up to the offensive.

This instruction was complicated by the fact that Montgomery appears to have regarded giving primacy to First Army in this attack as an unacceptable step, denying Eighth Army the chance to win the final victory in the North African campaign. As a result, he proposed to carry out an attack by four divisions (three infantry and one armoured) which would aim to punch at least 20 miles into enemy lines – hardly the holding attack that Alexander had intended for Eighth Army. Montgomery's plan may have been inspired to some extent by a desire for his army to round off its North African

GENERAL GEORGE S. PATTON

George S. Patton was born in 1885, and graduated from West Point in 1909. Patton was appointed as an aide to General Pershing in the punitive expedition against Mexico in 1916, and was still serving as Pershing's aide when America entered World War I. He accompanied Pershing to France in May 1917. When in France, Patton transferred to the Tank Corps, and was promoted to command of the 304th Tank Brigade.

The end of the conflict saw the dissolution of the Tank Corps, which prompted Patton's return to the cavalry. In the interwar period, Patton's career progressed through the usual round of command and staff appointments, until, in July 1940, he was promoted to brigadier-general and assumed command of the 2nd Brigade, 2nd Armored Division at Fort Benning, Georgia. Promotion to major-general followed less than a year later, and he took command of his division. Patton was given command of the Army's newly formed Desert Training Center on 1 April 1942, before being assigned to the planning for Operation Torch. He was then appointed as commander of the Western Task Force during the invasion of North Africa, in which capacity he led the American forces that took French Morocco. Following the mauling of US II Corps at the Battle of Kasserine Pass on 19 February 1943, Patton was appointed to lead this formation, a role he held until the end of the desert conflict.

Right: The last phase of operations in North Africa came with the assault against the capital, Tunis. A series of attacks launched by Eighth Army to the southeast and the recently arrived invasion armies from Operation Torch met with fierce resistance, but the weight of numbers ranged against them began to tell on the Axis troops, who were forced to fall back towards Tunis.

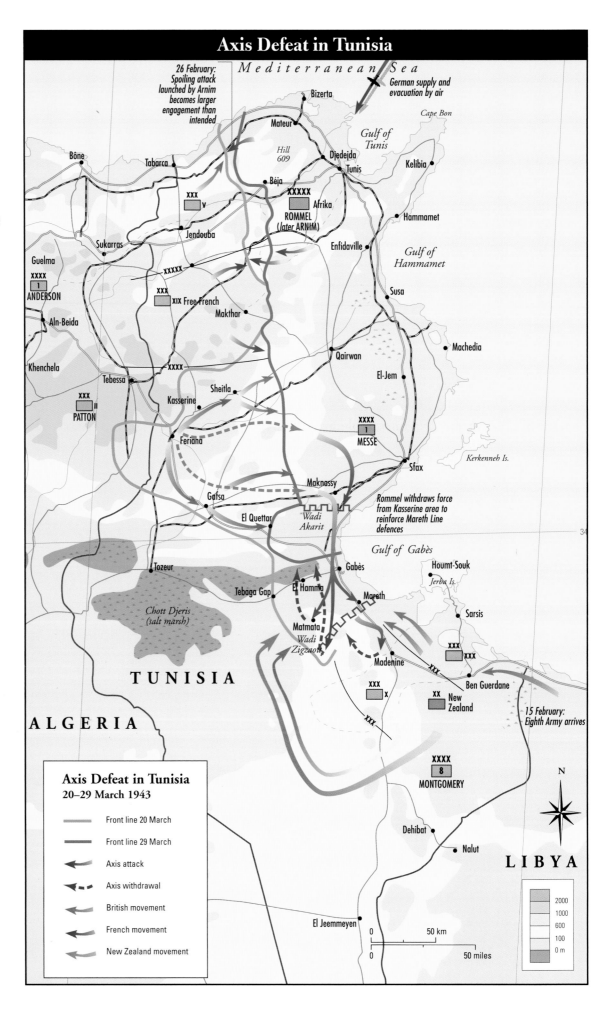

Axis Defeat in Tunisia

Mediterranean Sea

26 February: Spoiling attack launched by Arnim becomes larger engagement than intended

German supply and evacuation by air

Bizerta

Mateur

Cape Bon

Bône

Tabarca

Gulf of Tunis

Djedejda

Hill 609

Tunis

Kelibia

Béja

XXX V

XXXXX Afrika ROMMEL (later ARNIM)

Hammamet

Sukarras

Jendouba

Enfidaville

Gulf of Hammamet

Guelma

XXXX 1 ANDERSON

XXXXX

XXX XIX Free French

Susa

Aln-Beida

Makthar

Machedia

Khenchela

XXXX

Qairwan

El-Jem

Tebessa

Sheitla

XXX II PATTON

Kasserine

XXXX 1 MESSE

Kerkenneh Is.

Feriana

Maknassy

Sfax

Gafsa

El Quettar

Wadi Akarit

Rommel withdraws force from Kasserine area to reinforce Mareth Line defences

Gulf of Gabès

Tozeur

Gabès

Houmt-Souk

Jerba Is.

Tebaga Gap

El Hamma

Mareth

Sarsis

Chott Djeris (salt marsh)

Matmata *Wadi Zigzaou*

Madenine

XXX

XXX XXX

XXX

TUNISIA

XXX x

XX New Zealand

Ben Guerdane

ALGERIA

XXX

15 February: Eighth Army arrives

XXXX 8 MONTGOMERY

Dehibat

Nalut

N

LIBYA

Axis Defeat in Tunisia
20–29 March 1943

Front line 20 March

Front line 29 March

Axis attack

Axis withdrawal

British movement

French movement

New Zealand movement

El Jeemmeyen

0   50 km

0   50 miles

2000
1000
600
100
0 m

campaign in glorious fashion, but it would also deliver Cap Bon to the Allies before the enemy could turn it into a last redoubt. Alexander decided that he could afford to allow Montgomery to carry out the attack he proposed, but this had the unfortunate side effect of ensuring that resources were not concentrated within First Army area to the extent originally planned.

Bouncing the Enemy

Montgomery's plan was based upon the supreme confidence amongst his army as to what could be achieved against the Germans, and he made clear his intention to 'bounce' them out of the Enfidaville position. However, as intelligence was gained about the strength of enemy defences, he moderated his tone. A heavy attack would be launched, but without grandiose notions of a rapid advance. Unfortunately, this did not fully communicate itself to X Corps (Lieutenant-General Sir Brian Horrocks), and the plan worked out by the corps was rather optimistic. X Corps were under the mistaken impression that there were only around six enemy battalions facing them, when there were, in fact, 23. Although these units were below strength, they were still quite capable of putting up stiff resistance. Furthermore, only the 4th Indian Division had any preparation for fighting in the mountainous conditions facing them, with the 2nd New Zealand, 50th and 56th Divisions totally lacking the training required to be fully effective; worse still, the terrain was unsuitable for 7th Armoured Division's tanks, which meant that the employment of British armour would be hampered.

Below: German soldiers inspect the wreck of a crash-landed P-38 Lightning fighter. The Lightning was the most advanced fighter in front-line service with the US Army Air Force in 1942. While it was not as manoeuvrable as German and Italian fighters, the Lightning proved extremely effective, and came to be known as 'the fork-tailed devil' by German pilots.

Horrocks' plan called for 4th Indian and 2nd New Zealand Divisions to assault into the hills, cutting across the enemy's rear and heading for the coast. Once this was completed, Horrocks envisaged an advance that would gather in momentum as the enemy was defeated, aided by penetration from armoured units. A competent commander, Horrocks was well aware of the adage 'no plan survives first contact with the enemy', and made clear to his subordinates that the success of his scheme depended upon the strength of the enemy being as anticipated; as we have seen, it was not.

On the night of 19/20 April 1943, the assault began, as 4th Indian Division attacked. Enemy resistance was extremely fierce, and by daybreak, very little of the ground necessary for the next phase of the operation had been taken completely. Rather than breaking through into the enemy's rear area, the offensive had been brought to a near halt in the outer fringe of the Axis defence lines. This presented Horrocks with an uncomfortable choice – he could either try to press on, with the likelihood of significant casualties, or he could stay where he was, with a similar probability of casualties, but with greater opportunity of damaging the enemy as they counter-attacked. Whatever decision Horrocks reached meant that instead of the swift advance intended, a slower, attritional battle would develop instead.

During the course of the day, 50th Division took Enfidaville, but the rest of the corps could not make any decisive showing on the battlefield. Montgomery, therefore, sat down to refine his plan to address the situation now facing him, but it was clear that the main effort in the assault must now pass to First Army and US II Corps. The preliminary offensive on 18 April to put these formations into position for the offensive between Medjez el Bab and Bou Arada had made some gains. US II Corps was left facing the last enemy positions

Left: Tank crew from a Free French unit study map coordinates before moving off into the Tunisian desert, March 1943.

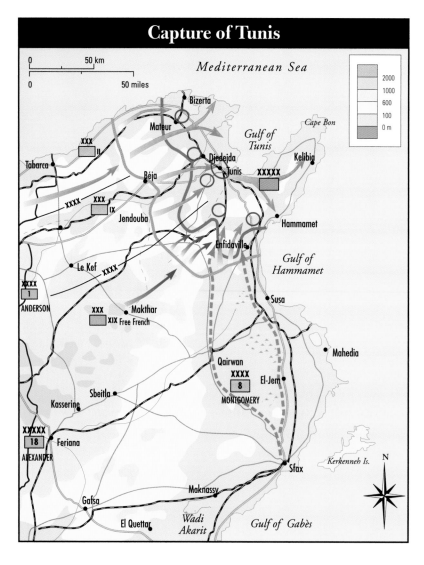

Capture of Tunis

Mediterranean Sea

Capture of Tunis
April–May 1943

- Front line mid-April
- Front line 3 May
- Axis withdrawal
- British movement
- French movement
- Concentration of Axis surrenders 7–13 May

blocking the way to Bizerta, while First Army was faced with the possibility of breaking through the German defences if it could drive the enemy from the hills on either side of the river Medjerda. Further south, First Army faced the Goubellat plain, which was lightly held, and which offered good opportunities for exploitation as long as the enemy could be prevented from sealing the plain at its eastern end by withdrawing in strength to the broken ground between Kasr Tyr and Sebkret.

Alexander therefore had three key areas in his offensive, of which the most important was that for which British V Corps was responsible. If Longstop Hill and Peter's Corner were taken, then a direct approach on Tunis could be made. That this was most important was clear not only to Alexander, but to the Germans, who made plans for a series of attacks that aimed to disrupt the offensive. These attacks began on 20/21 April, on both V and IX Corps' fronts. The Germans became stuck in the positions of 1st and 4th Divisions, and their attack on 46th Division was particularly serious, since that formation was meant to launch the first assault of the offensive the next morning.

However, the preponderance of numbers began to tell on the Germans. Although their attack affected 46th Division, only one of that formation's brigades was late in joining the offensive on the morning of 22 April. All of V Corps was able to advance to its start line, while even in 4th Division's lines, where the German advance reached within half a mile of divisional headquarters, the attack was rebuffed. In brutal terms, a weakened attacking division ought to have stood little chance against two strong divisions with a brigade of tanks in support – and it did not. More than 30 German tanks were destroyed in the fighting, with British losses less than half that. The spoiling attacks, therefore, did not make a material difference to the British advance; they did, however, succeed in weakening the German mobile forces to a notable extent immediately before they were required to assist in the defence against an enemy offensive.

The British Advance

Although the German attacks were pushed back, this did not guarantee success for the attacking formations the next morning. As General Anderson had predicted, the anti-tank defences ahead of IX Corps proved particularly difficult, and prevented the corps from breaking through the German lines and heading to the north. In the crucial sector, that of V Corps' advance against the high ground around Peter's Corner, it was essential that Longstop Hill be captured, since if the Germans were allowed to remain in control of its peak, they would be able to fire upon both British and American forces.

The task of assaulting Longstop Hill was given to 78th Division, while 1st Division descended upon Guriet el Atach in the centre, and 4th Division secured the right flank at Peter's Corner. During the night of 22/23 April, British infantry seized the western slopes of Longstop Hill, but could not take the western summit. Early the next day, a battalion of the Argyll and Sutherland Highlanders continued the assault, in the face of fierce resistance. The battalion commanding officer was killed, and Major John Anderson took over; even though his force had been reduced to just over 40 men, they carried the summit and held it, a feat which won Anderson the Victoria Cross (he was killed in action in Italy later in 1943). Fighting on Longstop went on for three more days until the last Germans were cleared out.

Von Arnim realized that his position was becoming increasingly untenable, and sought to counter-attack, but although this started promisingly, it was thrown back by 30 April, with a notable cost in armour. Although the British and Americans were still advancing, it became evident that the general offensive was beginning to break down as individual formations undertook a variety of localized attacks. General Alexander decided that he needed to take decisive action to prevent the attack from stalling. The solution appeared to lie in ending Eighth Army's activities around Enfidaville, since it appeared that the operations here were unlikely to achieve anything of substance, and moving formations from Eighth Army to First Army.

In fact, Montgomery was reaching similar conclusions. Advised by Horrocks that while Eighth Army would break through in the end, there would be very little left of it afterwards, Montgomery offered 7th Armoured and 4th Indian Divisions, along with 201st Guards Brigade, to Alexander so that they could reinforce First Army.

The transfer of some of Montgomery's best troops to First Army did not escape the attention of the Germans, and while von Arnim knew what was coming (an assault in the

Opposite: The final push in Tunisia began on 6 May 1943, and was marked by far less resistance from the Axis forces than had been encountered previously. Tunis was entered the next day, and after five more days of fighting, the Axis forces surrendered.

Below: A formation of American troops march along a road in Algeria in a picture clearly staged for the camera. Resistance in Algeria and Morocco was relatively light, and the Allies made swift advances after the Torch landings; however, once they drew nearer to Tunisia, they encountered far stiffer opposition.

*Right: General
Eisenhower and other
allied leaders on a
reviewing stand,
awaiting a march past by
Allied troops. Lieutenant-
General Sir Kenneth
Anderson, the commander
of British First Army, is
standing directly behind
Eisenhower, while
General Sir Harold
Alexander, the
Commander-in-Chief
Middle East, is to
Anderson's right. The
French officer standing
next to Eisenhower is
General Henri Giraud,
the commander of French
forces in North Africa.*

Medjerda valley), there was little he could do to
stop the offensive, such was the paucity of
resources available to him in contrast to those
possessed by the Allies. Alexander intended to
launch the final blow against the Axis forces with
a massive assault down the road from Medjez el
Bab to Tunis on 6 May. This would be
conducted along a relatively narrow frontage,
before the attacking forces split, with half turning
to the north to assist US II Corps in taking
Bizerta, while the remainder would turn to the
south to isolate the base of the Cap Bon
peninsula. Once this was complete, the force
would then round up the remaining enemy
troops. Any Axis forces that sought to evacuate
Tunisia would have to brave the Mediterranean,
which was firmly under control of the Royal
Navy. The final push began at 03:00 on 6 May
1943, and by 09:30 the 4th Indian Division had
punched a large hole in the enemy defences, and
just before 10:00, the lead elements of 7th
Armoured Division began to drive through the
gap created, but did so with rather more caution
than was strictly necessary. Nonetheless, the next
day saw the armoured cars of the 11th Hussars
enter Tunis, followed by tanks and infantry who
secured the city's capture. Meanwhile, US II
Corps had reached Bizerta, and discovered that
the Germans had left; by now the Axis forces had
reached their limit. Mass surrenders began all
along the line, and resistance broke into isolated
pockets of men determined to continue the fight
for a while longer.

On 12 May, von Arnim surrendered to 4th
Indian Division, while the Italian commander,
Field Marshal Messe, capitulated the next day. At
13:16 local time, General Alexander signalled
London with a simple message:

> 'Sir, it is my duty to report that the
Tunisian campaign is over. All enemy resistance
has ceased. We are masters of the North African
shores.'

The war in North Africa was over, the first
theatre-wide defeat inflicted upon Hitler's Reich
by the Western Allies.

The War in Italy

Once Axis forces had been defeated in North Africa, attention turned to invading Sicily as a prelude to a full invasion of the Italian mainland. Plans had been in place since early spring 1943, and some historians contend that the problems encountered by Eighth Army around Enfidaville were connected with the fact that Montgomery's attention was diverted between operations in North Africa and the need to plan for the assault on Sicily.

The origins of the plans stemmed from the Casablanca Conference of January 1943, at which Roosevelt and Churchill had discussed the next steps in Allied strategy. It was clear from the outset that there was disagreement between the two parties. The Americans wished to turn to an invasion of France, arguing that operations elsewhere were a pointless diversion from the ultimate goal of defeating the Germans. The British demurred. Conscious of the massive casualties sustained trying to defeat the Germans in France between 1914 and 1918, the British saw a campaign to knock Italy out of the war as being an extremely attractive alternative. Churchill, employing one of his favourite phrases, spoke of Italy as being the 'soft underbelly' of Europe, through which the Allies could drive into the heart of the continent. An invasion of Italy might also persuade neutral Turkey to join the war on the Allied side, a tempting prospect given the well-won reputation of Turkish troops, and their numbers.

Despite strenuous opposition from the US Army Chief of Staff, General George C. Marshall, Roosevelt was prepared to compromise with his ally. It was quite clear that the strength required to invade France was not yet near being achieved, yet to stop fighting until the requisite forces were in place for such an invasion was unacceptable for two reasons. First, the Allies would lose the momentum that they had managed to build during the latter stages of the North African campaign; second, to leave the burden of all fighting on land to the Soviet Union would be guaranteed to cause serious complaints from Stalin as the Germans were able to turn their full attention to the East once more.

As a result, it was agreed that the Allies would invade and occupy Sicily as a possible precursor to an invasion of Italy, although a decision on whether or not this course of action would be taken would be left until later. Eisenhower was appointed as supreme

Opposite: Two German paratroopers carry out observation of enemy positions from amongst the rubble of an Italian building. The Germans proved extremely adept at making strong points amongst the wreckage of buildings, nowhere more effectively than at Monte Cassino after the medieval monastery was reduced to rubble by air attack.

commander, despite the fact that American forces were in a minority in the Mediterranean theatre, but his deputies were all British – General Sir Harold Alexander, Air Chief Marshal Sir Arthur Tedder and Admiral of the Fleet Sir Andrew Cunningham. The plan, drawn up while the North African campaign was in its last stages, called for an attack on or around 10 July 1943. Montgomery's Eighth Army would land on the southeast corner of Sicily, while Patton's Seventh Army would land to the left of the British to protect the flank. With his flank secure, Montgomery would drive up the east coast of the island to Messina. The plan was not popular with American commanders, who suspected (rightly) that Montgomery was trying to relegate them to a supporting role, so that he could take the credit. Montgomery's general demeanour had not endeared him to the Americans, and the problems of command relationships that would later appear during the campaign in Northwest Europe originated from the plan for the Sicilian campaign.

The major concern for all parties, though, was not who gained the glory from the campaign, but whether the defenders of the island would fight. There were around 200,000 Italian troops, supported by 30,000 Germans. The Axis troops were commanded by General Alfredo Guzzoni, the commander of the Italian Sixth Army. Guzzoni was a competent general (not always a feature of the generals in Mussolini's army), but as insurance, the German troops maintained another chain of command that was headed by Field Marshal Albert Kesselring, the Commander-in-Chief South. While the Allies were confident that they could seize Sicily, there was very little idea of how fierce the resistance would be. That could only be discovered when the invasion was under way.

'Forward to Victory! Let us knock Italy out of the war!'

General Sir Bernard Montgomery, message to Eighth Army, 2 September 1943

Operation Husky

On 9 July 1943, 2500 ships and landing craft, carrying an invasion force of over 160,000 men drawn from the US Seventh and British Eighth Armies headed for Italian waters, with the aim of making the landing on Sicily in the largest amphibious operation mounted up to that time. The fleet steamed past Malta, a demonstration of just how important it had been that the island had held out against Axis air attacks, since had Malta fallen, the seas would have been completely covered by Italian and German air power, making the invasion impossible. As the day drew on, the invasion force was first gently buffeted by the wind, then thrown about with increasing violence as it rose in intensity. For a short while it appeared that General Eisenhower would have to call off the invasion, but after pondering the matter he decided that he would go ahead.

In Tunisia, a fleet of transport aircraft had been awaiting Eisenhower's decision; once it came, they lifted off, towing the gliders of the British 1st Airlanding Brigade towards Sicily. Unfortunately, they flew straight into the path of the storm, and chaos ensued as they reached Malta, with aircraft being driven off course while the gliders were tossed

about in the gale. The same fate befell another 200 transport aircraft carrying over 3000 US paratroops, and the airborne operation fell into confusion as aircraft wandered across the sky, unable to maintain their course in the teeth of the storm. This led to tragedy – while 40 of the glider tugs turned back, 69 released their gliders well short of the correct point, and the fragile transport craft fell into the sea, causing many fatalities among the airborne troops. While the American paratroops remained in transport aircraft until the dropping zone, they fared little better – the navigational problems caused by the weather meant that very few of the transports dropped their cargo in the correct place. Only 200 men landed in reasonably close proximity to their objectives, and such was the confusion that the American airborne commander, General James M. Gavin, was for some time convinced that he had been dropped into mainland Italy by mistake. The only positive note about the confused air landings was that the enemy had been fearfully confused as well. There were so many reports of paratroops and glider landings that the Germans

Above: German troops participate in a training exercise near Salerno, prior to the Allied invasion of Italy. The tank is a Panzer Mk IV, which remained an important type until the end of the war, although it came to be overshadowed by the later Panther and Tiger tanks.

and Italians were initially convinced that Sicily had been invaded by at least 20,000 and possibly even 30,000 airborne soldiers – in fact, there were just over 4500.

Mercifully for the invasion, the wind dropped away overnight, and as the invasion fleet approached the beaches it was clear that the landings could go ahead as planned, although the US Seventh Army, due to land on the west of Sicily, were some way behind schedule as a result of the weather conditions. Eighth Army were on time, and discovered very little opposition as they came ashore. The Italians defending the invasion area had surmised that any attempt at making a landing in the weather they were experiencing would be lunacy, so relaxed once the Allied transport aircraft had left. The first assaulting troops landed without opposition, and stormed up the beaches to seize the coastal defences. As it became clear what was happening, some desultory Italian artillery fire was experienced, but this was suppressed by naval gunfire support provided by six British battleships sitting offshore ready to deal with any such eventuality.

It was not long before the advanced elements of the forces ashore in eastern Sicily were moving inland – by 08:00, the town of Cassibile was in the hands of the British 5th Division, making the arrival of XIII Corps and elements of XXX Corps rather easier than might otherwise have been the case if the defenders remained in place. The Americans did not enjoy similar fortune. The defenders in western Sicily were alive to the fact that an invasion was under way, and opened fire on the invasion craft as soon as they fell within range of the coastal gun batteries. These were engaged and neutralized by naval gunfire, and the Americans went ashore with relative ease. At Licata, American soldiers found an abandoned command post, and as they entered it, heard the telephone ringing. An Italian-speaking war correspondent accompanying the troops, Michael Chinigo, answered it. An Italian officer anxiously enquired whether it was true that the Americans had landed. Chinigo informed the officer (in Italian) that the story was ridiculous. Satisfied, the Italian rang off.

By mid-morning, the invading forces were firmly ashore, and their leading elements were pushing inland, aided by the fact that the American airborne troops had overcome the problem of not landing in the right place. A number of *ad hoc* groupings of paratroops who had met up with one another as they tried to reach their intended drop zones set about causing havoc behind the Italian lines. This greatly aided the forces moving inshore from the beaches, since the flow of reserves to the invasion area was hampered by the activities of the paratroops.

The British airborne formations also tried to make the best of a poor situation. Only about 100 of the 1500 men who were supposed to have landed made it onto the island,

Invasion of Sicily

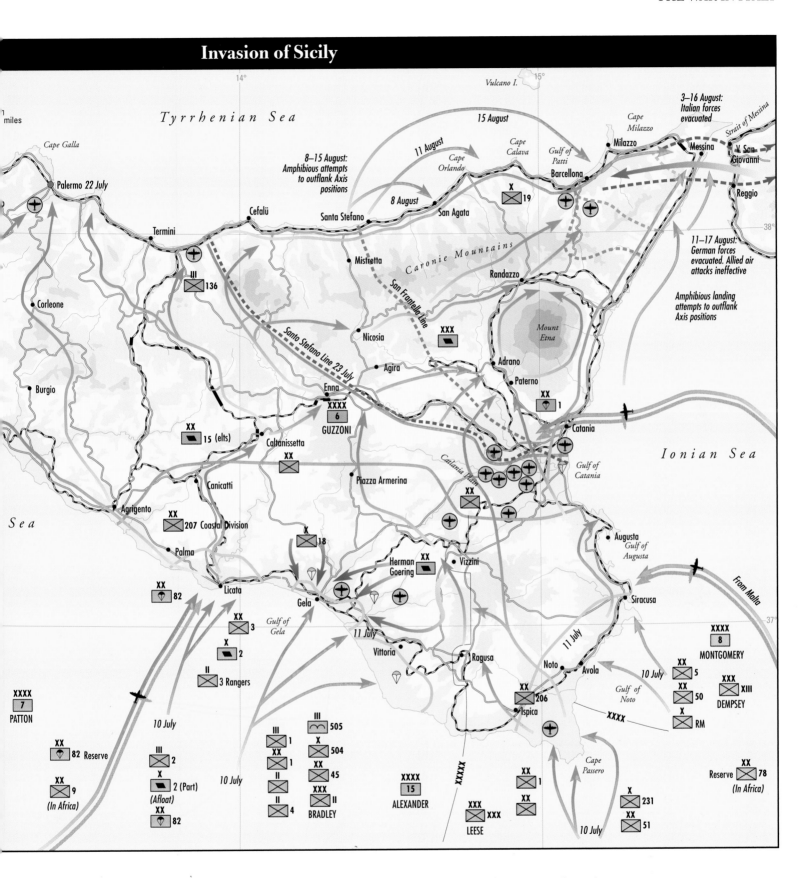

but this did not prevent them from seizing the Ponte Grande bridge over the River Cavadonna. The Italians made numerous attempts to dislodge the airlanding brigade's survivors, but it was not until late in the afternoon of 10 July that they finally succeeded. By this point, only 15 of the British troops were left, and seven of them were killed in the Italian assault. Undaunted, the eight survivors split into two groups – two men took up positions on a nearby hill and prevented the Italians from moving by sniping at them at

Right: British troops make their way through the wreckage of an Italian building. The leading man is armed with a Thompson sub-machine gun, while his colleagues are all equipped with Lee Enfield .303-inch rifles. In urban areas, the compact size of the Thompson, coupled with its rate of fire, made it a popular weapon.

Map, page 226: The invasion of Italy began smoothly, with little opposition provided by defending Italian troops in the very south, but the Germans put up fierce resistance, particularly around Salerno. After some hard fighting, the beachhead was firmly established by the end of September, and the Allies moved northwards, towards the German defensive positions around Cassino.

every opportunity, while the remaining six made their way back to the invasion area, in the hope of finding friendly troops. This they did, and promptly led a mobile column from 5th Division to the bridge, from which the Italians were removed in short order. This opened the way for an advance into Syracuse, marking the first major success of the campaign.

The Americans ran into some difficulties around Gela, particularly after the German Hermann Göring Division entered the fray. Disruption to communications meant that the Germans were unable to coordinate with the Italians, and this perhaps hampered their activities. While the Germans caused problems for the Americans, they could not break through to attack the landing beaches, and as night fell, it was clear that the Allies were safely ashore in some numbers.

The second day of the Sicily campaign demonstrated that the battle to take the island would not be easy, as the Germans and Italians began to show a more coordinated response to the attack. An assault by 60 German tanks came within two miles of the beaches, and all unloading operations had to stop as every man in the area grabbed his weapon and ran to defensive positions. The tanks were slowly forced back, at which point ships standing offshore began to fire in support of the troops, now that the danger of fratricide from their shells was removed. Powerful though the German tanks were, they were no match for the broadside from a ship, and pulled back as quickly as they could.

There was also tragedy when aircraft bringing reinforcements to the American sector were engaged by anti-aircraft fire after they had been mistaken for German bombers. Twenty-three were shot down and another 37 badly damaged; over 200 men were killed. The following day, the Germans made an airdrop of their own, landing reinforcements at Catania. This marked the start of a major German reinforcement of the island; while the troops were arriving, the Allies continued their advance.

The Drive on Palermo

For the rest of July, the two Allied armies pushed forward, with the rivalry between Patton and Montgomery increasing as they moved further north. This was most notable when British XXX Corps was held up near Lentini, prompting Montgomery to order a change of direction around the base of Mount Etna, to enable an assault on Messina from the west. To achieve this manoeuvre, XXX Corps' commander, General Sir Oliver Leese, had to use Route 124, a road running from Vizzini to Caltagirone. The road was in the American sector, but Montgomery sent Leese up the route without bothering to inform

the Americans of the fact that his troops would be joining them. This led to a situation where both American and British units, who had been told that they would be working independently of one another, found themselves attacking the same objective, namely the town of Enna. Despite initial confusion, all went well.

However, Montgomery's action irritated Patton, not least since it meant that the role of the Americans in providing flank protection became more important, and denied them the chance to participate in taking Messina. Patton was not as angry as he might have

Invasion of Southern Italy

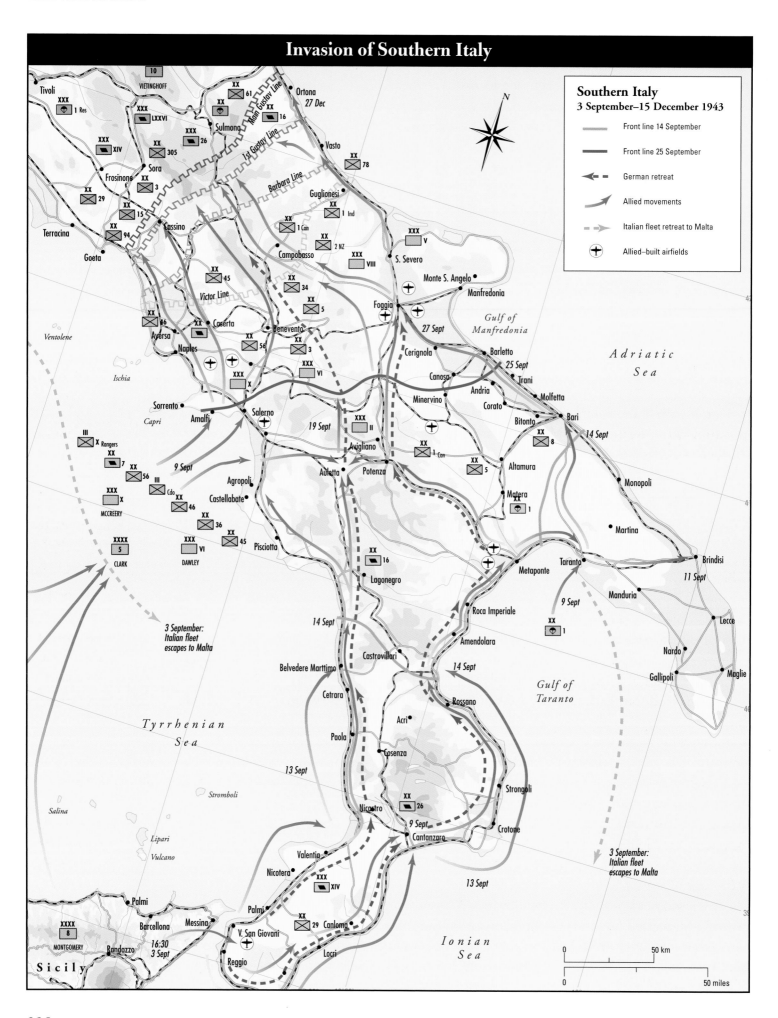

Southern Italy
3 September–15 December 1943

— Front line 14 September
— Front line 25 September
◄-- German retreat
◄— Allied movements
◄-- Italian fleet retreat to Malta
✈ Allied–built airfields

been, however, since he was already considering taking Palermo, the island's largest city. After personally asking General Alexander to order him to take Palermo (although the request verged on being a demand), Patton was more content. The US 2nd Armoured and 3rd Infantry Divisions were tasked to drive on the city, and after covering 100 miles in four days entered Palermo on 22 July. There had been very little resistance on the way, and the only enemy troops the Americans encountered in Palermo were Italians who were simply waiting to surrender. The Germans in the city had abandoned it some days before, sabotaging the harbour by scuttling over 40 ships, but US Army engineers had it working at over half capacity within a week, a remarkable achievement.

Patton's drive on Palermo now left him in a position to advance on Messina, and he determined that he should arrive there before the British, informing his subordinates that the pride of the US Army was at stake. The task of advancing on Messina would be much more taxing than taking Palermo, since the terrain through which Seventh Army had to pass was mountainous, and the roads could easily be blocked by the Germans. The advance, therefore, was slow, and stalled at Troina, where a whole US division and heavy air attacks were needed to clear out the defending Germans on 6 August. Spurred on by Patton's advance, Montgomery also drove his troops forward. By the middle of the month, both British and American units were on the outskirts of Messina; on 17 August, an American patrol entered the city, to be joined a little later by British armour. The city was deserted, since the Germans had pulled back across the Strait of Messina to the mainland.

It transpired that Kesselring had taken the decision that the position in Sicily would be untenable in the end, and that the island was not worth sacrificing a large number of Germans for. As early as 8 August, he gave orders for an evacuation, and by the time that Messina fell, 40,000 troops and their equipment had been withdrawn successfully. Although the Allies had failed to stop the Germans from escaping, they had succeeded in their primary aim – after 38 days of fighting, Sicily was in Allied hands. Attention could now turn to Italy itself; not least because of a dramatic development during the course of the Sicilian campaign – Mussolini had been deposed.

The End of Mussolini

By the middle of July, it seemed obvious that the Anglo-American invasion of Sicily would succeed, and discontent with Mussolini mounted. Anger was increased when an Allied bombing raid on Rome on 9 July destroyed not only the railway marshalling yards that were the target, but killed and wounded 4000 civilians. It seemed clear that such disasters would continue as long as the war went on. The only obstacle to ending the

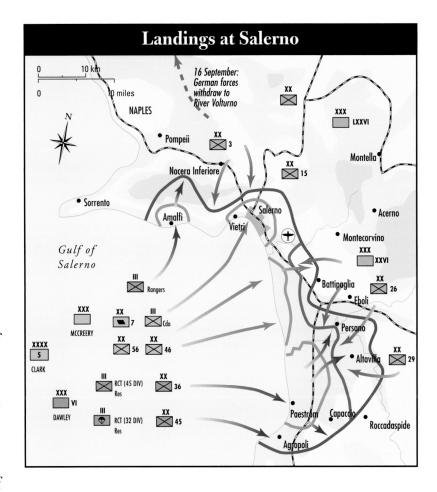

Landings at Salerno
9–16 September 1943

▬▬▬	Allied front line 9 Sept.
▬▬▬	Allied front line 11 Sept.
▬▬▬	German front line 14 Sept.
◄—	German movements
—►	British movements
—►	U.S. movement

Above: The landings at Salerno were met by particularly heavy opposition from the Germans. A build-up of reinforcements and the provision of greater air support reduced the pressure on the Allies, and by the end of the month they were able to move out from the Salerno area.

'The dominant aim should be to kill Germans and make Italians kill Germans on the largest scale possible in this theatre.'

Winston Churchill, 5 September 1943

conflict seemed to be Mussolini, so the Grand Council of the Fascist Party did something that would have been unimaginable with the German Nazi Party – it held a meeting, decided that the leader was taking them to ruin, and voted to replace him. Mussolini was taken into captivity in a state of utter amazement, while a new government, headed by Field Marshal Pietro Badoglio, made less-than-convincing announcements that Italy would remain allied to the Germans.

Hitler was certain that this step meant that the Italians would soon surrender, and gave orders that Mussolini should be rescued from wherever he was being held, a mission that was later carried out by commandos landing in gliders, who recovered the Italian dictator and took him to Berlin. He also told his generals to prepare to disarm the Italian Army, to prevent the defection of the country to the Allied cause. Hitler was right to be suspicious. Mussolini was deposed on 25 July; on the 26th, Badoglio announced that Italy remained an unshakeable ally of Germany; and on the 31st he sent emissaries to meet with the Allies to negotiate peace.

Excited by these developments, the Allies started to negotiate, and to plan for an invasion of the mainland. The invasion was planned with the complicity of the new government, who were anxious to ensure that the Germans could not simply remove them and install a government of their own. It was agreed that the Allies would land at Salerno on 9 September, just a few hours after the Italians would announce that they had surrendered. Anticipating this, the Germans made plans to sacrifice most of Italy, and retire to hold a line in the north of the country running from Pisa to Rimini.

MUSSOLINI

Mussolini's early life gave little clue that he would go on to lead his country for 21 years. A rebellious youth, Mussolini was often in trouble, and continued his penchant for upsetting the authorities by becoming editor of a socialist newspaper. He broke with the socialists over the issue of Italian entry into World War I, giving the conflict his full backing. He enlisted and reached the rank of sergeant by the end of the war. Mussolini then returned to political activism, but this time at the head of his own movement, the Fascists.

He achieved power in 1922, and secured his position through a mixture of populism and ruthlessness. Mussolini attempted to make Italy a significant European power, seeking new colonies in Africa. This culminated in the conquest of Abyssinia in 1936. By this point, Hitler's similar views had provided Mussolini with a notable ally, but one who was soon to dominate the Italo-German relationship.

Italy entered the war only after the fall of France, and endured a series of military reverses, often requiring assistance from the Germans to prevent humiliation. The Allied invasion of Italy led to Mussolini being deposed in September 1943. Rescued from imprisonment by a daring German commando raid, he was installed as the puppet leader of German-held northern Italy. When the German position collapsed, Mussolini's time had run out – he was captured by partisans and executed, a humiliating end for a man who had cast himself as the father of a great Italian nation.

The Italian Campaign

The invasion of Italy began with a landing by Eighth Army on the 'toe' of the country on the morning of the Italian surrender. The only Italian troops they encountered offered to assist with the unloading of their landing craft. A few hours later, Lieutenant-General Mark Clark's US Fifth Army (which contained British troops as well as Americans) came ashore at Salerno, where they were to face much harder opposition in the form of the Germans. To complete the invasion, the British 1st Airborne Division was landed at Taranto and captured the port.

The eight German divisions under Kesselring's command could be expected to put up stiff resistance, and they did. Counter-attacks began on 11 September, and dislodged British formations from the Molina Pass the next day. The attacks were of such ferocity that serious consideration was given to abandoning the beachhead in the southern sector, although this was dismissed when the Royal Navy provided gunfire support that prevented further German gains, even though the enemy had come to within a mile of the beaches by the time they were forced to stop. Reinforcements were brought in over the course of the next few days, and between 13 and 16 September, the fighting was notably fierce. The construction of landing strips in the beachhead meant that air support could be provided to the hard-pressed troops, and the situation began to ease. Meanwhile, the British 1st Airborne Division had captured Taranto, and once reinforced began to move out towards the other Allied troops. The link-up of the Eighth Army, 1st Airborne Division and Fifth Army took place on 20 September, by which time the beachhead was well established as the Germans were pushed back.

The Allies began to advance on Naples, and the Germans were forced to fall back. On 1 October, the Allies reached the city and entered it unopposed. Alexander ordered that armour from both the Fifth and Eighth Armies should pursue the enemy. By 5 October, the Allies were on the River Volturno. Some newspapers made optimistic assessments of

Above: In a picture that appears to have been posed especially for the camera, two German soldiers discuss the situation before them during the Italian campaign.

229

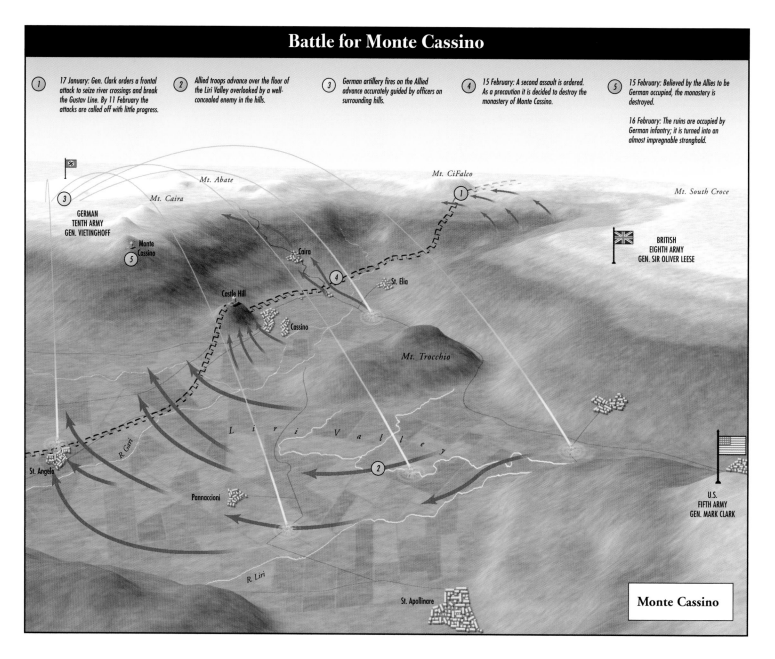

Battle for Monte Cassino

① 17 January: Gen. Clark orders a frontal attack to seize river crossings and break the Gustav Line. By 11 February the attacks are called off with little progress.

② Allied troops advance over the floor of the Liri Valley overlooked by a well-concealed enemy in the hills.

③ German artillery fires on the Allied advance accurately guided by officers on surrounding hills.

④ 15 February: A second assault is ordered. As a precaution it is decided to destroy the monastery of Monte Cassino.

⑤ 15 February: Believed by the Allies to be German occupied, the monastery is destroyed.

16 February: The ruins are occupied by German infantry; it is turned into an almost impregnable stronghold.

Mt. CiFalco
Mt. Abate
Mt. Caira
Mt. South Croce
GERMAN TENTH ARMY GEN. VIETINGHOFF
Monte Cassino
Caira
St. Elia
BRITISH EIGHTH ARMY GEN. SIR OLIVER LEESE
Castle Hill
Cassino
Mt. Trocchio
L i r i   V a l l e y
R. Gari
St. Angelo
U.S. FIFTH ARMY GEN. MARK CLARK
Pannaccioni
R. Liri
St. Apollinare

Monte Cassino

Above: The battle of Monte Cassino was crucial to the progress of the Italian campaign, since if the Allies did not break through, the route to Rome would be blocked. An attritional battle developed, and it was only after the fourth major assault by Allied troops that a breakthrough was achieved.

how soon it would be before Allied troops entered Rome – but their guesses were wildly inaccurate as the Allies had to face the reality of the situation on the ground.

The Germans had a number of advantages in defending their positions in addition to the high quality of their troops. The narrow mountain passes which had to be traversed as the Allies progressed northwards were relatively simple to defend, and this slowed down the advance considerably, along with careful demolition of bridges and communications links as the Germans withdrew. A further obstacle to the advance came with heavy rainfall early in October, about a month before it was normally due. The precipitation caused landslides and waterlogged the ground, making a swift advance impossible. Kesselring used the opportunity to prepare for a fighting withdrawal to a new defensive position some 15 miles north of the Volturno, which was carried out on 16 October. This defensive position, the Gustav Line, was to present a major obstacle to Allied efforts, since it had to be breached before any advance on Rome could be contemplated. Alexander, reporting on the situation to Churchill, expressed the view that the advance on Rome would be difficult and something of a 'slogging match' as the Allies attempted to break through the German positions.

Alexander's plan for the Gustav Line was to start with an assault along a 10-mile front by the British 46th Division near Minturno. The 46th Division went into battle on 4 January 1944, and managed to take some ground overlooking the German positions, giving it an advantage. Hard fighting continued across the line for several days, and it was not until 17 January that the British managed to establish a bridgehead across the mouth of the River Garigliano, and it took a further 10 days of struggle for this to expand to include Monte Juga. An American attempt to cross the river ended in disaster with most of the US 36th Division being lost in the attempt. Overall, while the Allies made some ground, the defenders still held the advantage.

Anzio and Cassino

On 22 January 1944, a landing was made at Anzio, due south of Rome, with the aim of cutting the German lines of communication between the Italian capital and Cassino. Some 36,000 men were landed and captured the port intact, aided by the fact that a large number of the troops who would have been defending it had been moved to the Gustav Line. This was followed by the bitter struggle for Cassino, which depending upon the preferred nomenclature was the site of one long battle, or four shorter ones. The fighting was intense and was arguably the nearest that the Western Allies came to fighting a World War I-style battle where manoeuvre was all but impossible. Cassino had to be taken, or the advance northwards would be halted. The task of taking it would be very difficult indeed, since the town had numerous fortifications, and was overlooked by a hill on which sat the famed medieval monastery, potentially a perfect defensive location.

Below: The Anzio landings were made on 22 January 1944, with the aim of cutting German lines of communication between Rome and the position at Monte Cassino. The landing was successful, helped by the fact that many of the troops who would normally have been defending the area had been moved to bolster the defences elsewhere in Italy. Fierce German counter-attacks nearly dislodged the Anglo-American landing force, and it took until May for the Allies to break out from the beachhead.

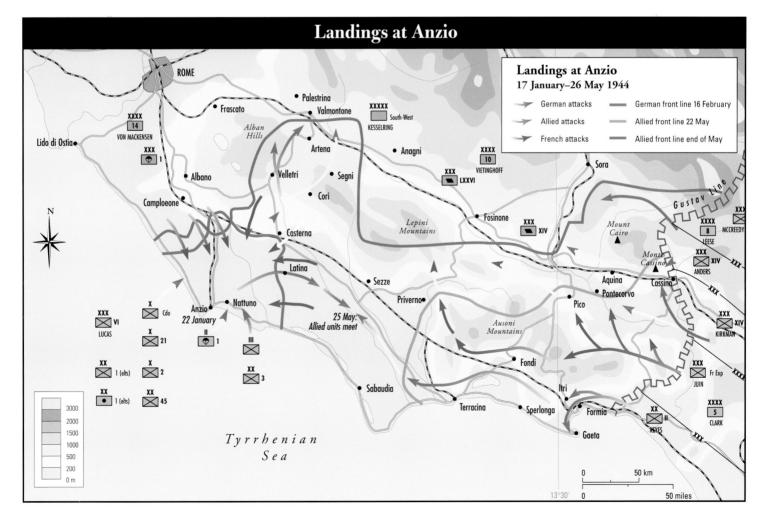

Landings at Anzio

Landings at Anzio
17 January–26 May 1944

→ German attacks   ━ German front line 16 February
→ Allied attacks   ━ Allied front line 22 May
→ French attacks   ━ Allied front line end of May

The first fighting at Cassino occurred between January and February 1944 as the Allies launched their attack into the teeth of the German defences. The Germans could not be dislodged, and the attack swiftly came to a halt. This set the pattern for the next month as the Allies made numerous attempts to advance, but found the sheer face of Monte Cassino an almost impossible obstacle to overcome. Ground was traded between the two sides on a regular basis, until the Allies tried a different tack.

On 15 March, a massive aerial bombardment was launched against Cassino, in an attempt to shatter the German defences. The historic monastery was destroyed in the process (every building in the town was either demolished or damaged in the raid), and it

Below: Armed with an MG42 machine gun, two German paratroopers man a defensive position in the ruins of the monastery at Monte Cassino.

appeared that the way for an advance was now clear. However, the Germans simply moved from their well-made defensive positions into the ruins of the monastery, and became even harder to dislodge. Once again, bitter fighting occurred, with regular trading of small patches of ground. A third attempt to take Monte Cassino failed after a week, and a fourth attempt was made in early May 1944.

On this occasion, the better weather and the fact that the Allies had massed an overwhelming number of troops meant that they were able to carry the hill. The monastery fell to the Polish II Corps on 18 May, and once this was in Allied hands, the Gustav Line had been unlocked. This finally meant that the Allied advance on Rome could continue, after five months of savage fighting – hardly the swift advance to the Italian capital that had been predicted by excited journalists when news of the Italian surrender came through eight months before. The landings at Anzio met with similar problems. As at Salerno, the Germans made determined efforts to reach the beaches and drive the Allies back into the sea. On 19 February, the Germans came perilously close to doing just that, and they were driven off with some difficulty. Further attacks followed, but did not imperil the Allied position. Nevertheless, a stalemate persisted at Anzio until 23 May, when the Allies broke out from the beachhead.

Within two days, US 1st Armoured and 3rd Infantry Divisions had joined with the US II Corps, which was pushing forward to Rome. General Clark had decided that his army was to have the glory of taking Rome, and duly entered it on 4 June 1944, much to the irritation of the British, Polish and French troops who thought that their efforts at breaking through at Cassino (thus making the advance on Rome possible) at least merited equal publicity; as well as making himself unpopular with the troops, Clark was disobeying Alexander's orders that his main effort should be to ensure the capture of Valmontone.

On to the Gothic Line

The capture of Rome did not mean that the campaign in Italy was at an end, since there was still much fighting to do to dislodge the Germans from the north of the country. Several units were withdrawn to support the Normandy campaign, which made Alexander's task more difficult. He now had to break through the last German defensive line (the Gothic Line) just to the south of the Lombardy plains. Success here would give access to Austria and the Balkans, and was a prize that Kesselring was anxious to deny the Allies.

The Allied offensive began on 25 August. Eighth Army, now commanded by Lieutenant-General Sir Oliver Leese after Montgomery's departure for 21st Army Group in Normandy, carried out the attack, and progressed well to begin with. Unfortunately, the weather intervened once more, and coupled with supply problems, the offensive slowed. Throughout September, a series of attacks along the length of the Gothic Line gained some ground, but nothing of significance. As the offensive slowed, Kesselring redeployed his forces to meet the threat now posed by Fifth Army's approach from the west, and the advance here was brought to a near halt.

By early November, a stalemate had been reached again. The campaign could not be restarted until the spring, and yet more Allied forces were removed from the theatre and sent to the Western Front. Many of the units in Eighth Army left as well, detailed to assist with the restoration of order to Greece after the German withdrawal and the outbreak of civil war there.

Maps, following pages: Once Cassino had been taken, the Allies had to fight their way northwards, against heavy German opposition. After the break-out from Anzio, the Allies were able to make a major push towards Rome, although General Clark's decision to take the city (on 4 June 1944) was fiercely criticized for his perceived wish to put personal vanity ahead of the Allied effort against Valmontone. Once Rome fell, the Germans continued to put up steady resistance, and the campaign ground to a halt in November 1944. The Allies restarted their campaign in April 1945, and the by now seriously weakened German troops fell back. The execution of Mussolini by partisans may have been of no military significance, but symbolized the hopelessness of the Axis position. On 25 April, a surrender was agreed, and the Italian campaign was brought to an end on 2 May 1945.

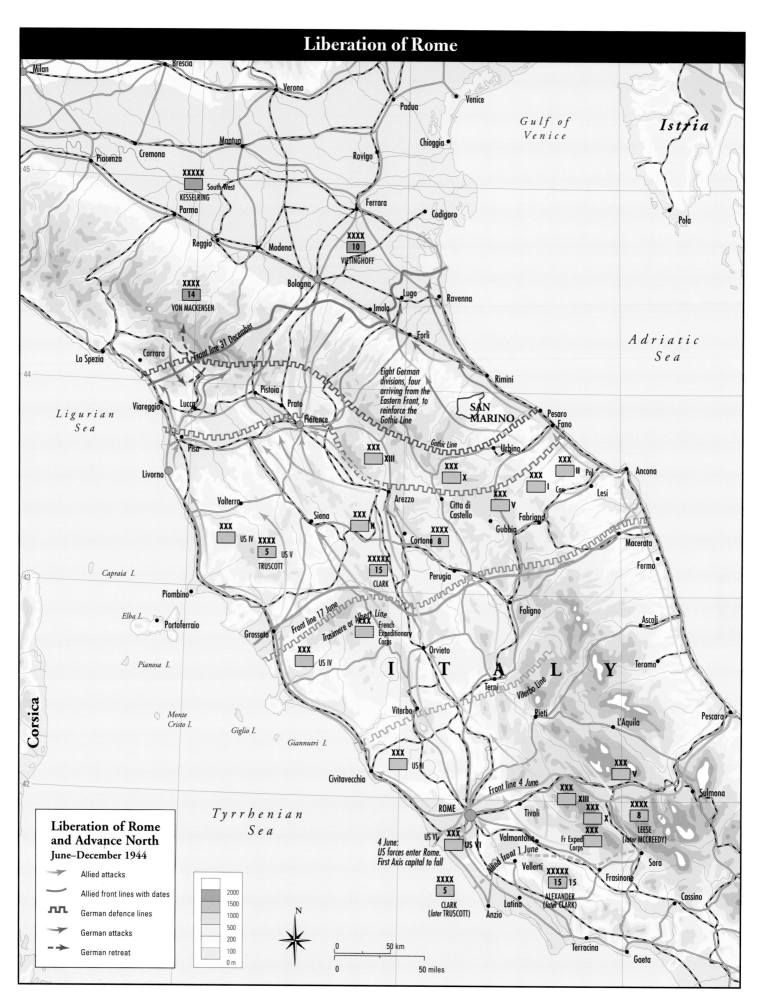

Liberation of Rome

Milan
Brescia
Verona
Padua
Venice
Gulf of Venice
Istria
Piacenza
Cremona
Mantua
Rovigo
Chioggia
Pola
45
XXXXX
KESSELRING
South West
Parma
Ferrara
Codigoro
Reggio
Modena
XXXX
10
VIETINGHOFF
XXXX
14
VON MACKENSEN
Bologna
Imola
Lugo
Ravenna
La Spezia
Carrara
Front line 31 December
Forli
Adriatic Sea
44
Pistoia
Prato
Rimini
Eight German divisions, four arriving from the Eastern Front, to reinforce the Gothic Line
Viareggio
Lucca
Florence
SAN MARINO
Pesaro Fano
Ligurian Sea
Pisa
Gothic Line
XXX
XIII
Urbino
XXX
II
Pol
Ancona
Livorno
XXX
X
XXX
I
Can
Lesi
Volterra
Arezzo
Citta di Castello
XXX
V
Macerata
XXX
US IV
Siena
XXX
M
XXXX
Cortona 8
Gubbia
Fabriano
Fermo
XXXX
5 US V
TRUSCOTT
XXXXX
15
CLARK
Perugia
Ascoli
Capraia I.
43
Piombino
Foligno
Elba I.
Portoferraio
Front line 17 June
Trasimere or Albert Line
XXX
French Expeditionary Corps
Orvieto
Teramo
Pianosa I.
Grosseto
XXX
US IV
Monte Cristo I.
Giglio I.
Giannutri I.
I T A L Y
Terni
Viterbo Line
Rieti
L'Aquila
Pescara
XXX
US II
Viterbo
Front line 4 June
XXX
V
Corsica
42
Civitavecchia
ROME
Tivoli
XXX
XIII
XXXX
8
LEESE
(later MCCREEDY)
Sulmona
Tyrrhenian Sea
4 June: US forces enter Rome. First Axis capital to fall
US VI
XXX
US VI
Valmontone
Fr Exped Corps
XXX
X
XXX
Sora
Allied front 1 June
Vellerti
XXXXX
15 15
ALEXANDER
(later CLARK)
Frasinone
Cassini
XXXX
5
CLARK
(later TRUSCOTT)
Latina
Anzio
Terracina
Gaeta

Liberation of Rome and Advance North
June–December 1944

→ Allied attacks

⌣ Allied front lines with dates

⊐⊏ German defence lines

→ German attacks

⇢ German retreat

2000
1500
1000
500
200
100
0 m

N

0   50 km

0   50 miles

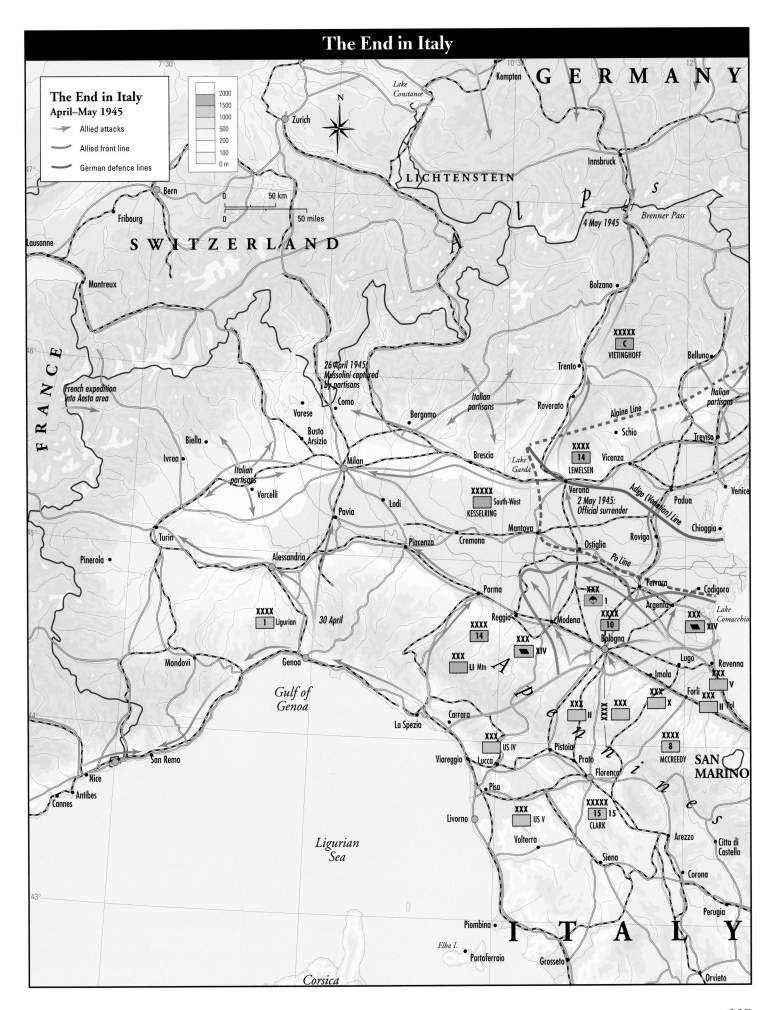

The End in Italy

The End in Italy
April–May 1945

→ Allied attacks

Allied front line

German defence lines

2000
1500
1000
500
200
100
0 m

0   50 km

0   50 miles

GERMANY

Kempten

Lake Constance

Zurich

N

Innsbruck

LICHTENSTEIN

A l p s

Brenner Pass

Bern

4 May 1945

Fribourg

SWITZERLAND

Bolzano

Lausanne

A

Montreux

l

p

Belluno

s

XXXXX C VIETINGHOFF

Trento

Italian partisans

26 April 1945: Mussolini captured by partisans

Roverato

Italian partisans

Como

French expedition into Aosta area

Varese

Bergamo

Schio

Alpine Line

Treviso

Biella

Busto Arsizio

Brescia

XXXX 14 LEMELSEN

Vicenza

Ivrea

Milan

Lake Garda

Verona

Padua

Venice

Italian partisans

Vercelli

Lodi

XXXXX South-West KESSELRING

2 May 1945: Official surrender

Adige (Venetian) Line

Pavia

Cremona

Mantova

Rovigo

Chioggia

Turin

Piacenza

Ostiglia

Po Line

Ferrara

Codigoro

Alessandria

Parma

XXX 1

Argenta

XXX XIV

Lake Comacchio

XXXX 1 Ligurian

30 April

Reggia

XXXX 10

Pinerola

Modena

Bologna

XXXX 14

XXX XIV

Lugo

Ravenna

Mondovi

Genoa

XXX LI Mtn

A

XXX X

Imola

XXX V

Forli

p

XXX II Pol

Carrara

e

XXX II

XXXX

XXX

Gulf of Genoa

La Spezia

n

XXXX 8 MCCREEDY

SAN MARINO

XXX US IV

Pistoia

Prato

i

San Remo

Viareggio

Lucca

Florence

n

Nice

Pisa

Antibes

Cannes

XXX US V

XXXXX 15 15 CLARK

e

Arezzo

Citta di Castello

Livorno

Volterra

s

Corona

Ligurian Sea

Siena

Perugia

Piombina

ITALY

Elba I.

Portoferraio

Grosseto

Orvieto

Corsica

The Final Phase

While the Italian front was in limbo during the winter, the Allies replaced those units that had been sent elsewhere so that they began 1945 with a strength of over 600,000 men. In addition, supplies of ammunition, armoured vehicles and tracked amphibious vehicles were sent to the theatre, the latter a particularly welcome addition for a campaign that was beset with frequently waterlogged ground impassable to conventional vehicles. On 9 April 1945, the Allies resumed the offensive, with Fifth and Eighth Armies heading towards Bologna. The Germans, worn down and considerably weaker than before, were unable to hold the advance back, despite fierce resistance at the outset.

Kesselring had been injured in a car accident, and it was left to his successor, General Heinrich von Vietinghoff, to recognize that the position was becoming near untenable. He requested permission to fall back to the line of the River Po, but as was common by 1945, Hitler peremptorily rejected this. Vietinghoff ignored the nonsensical order, and told his men to withdraw. This sparked the collapse of the German position. British paratroops took Milan and Genoa, while a band of partisans found Mussolini and his mistress near Lake Como.

Nominally reinstalled as Italian dictator by Hitler after the rescue mission by German commandos, Mussolini had been little more than a puppet of the Germans ever since. This mattered not a jot to the partisans, who executed Mussolini, his mistress and other members of his entourage, and then displayed the corpses hanging upside down in the town square.

Lake Garda, Verona, Trieste and Turin all fell next, and the Germans were on the brink of surrender. Negotiations between the head of the SS in Italy and the US Office of Strategic Services had begun as early as February, but Hitler's obstinate refusal to accept the idea of capitulation meant that nothing had happened in this regard. Finally, despairing of the *Führer*, the German commanders decided that they would ignore him on this subject again. Proper negotiations began, and on 25 April 1945, orders were given for German and Italian Fascist forces to surrender at 12:00 noon on 2 May. The war in Italy was over.

Opposite: An American soldier, armed with an M1 Garand rifle, takes careful aim from his position in a ruined house in Cisterna. Cisterna fell on 25 May 1944, as the American VI Corps drove the defending Axis troops from the town.

The Russians Advance

The German failure to overcome the USSR by 1943 meant that factors other than just martial skill and good fortune came into play on the Eastern Front. In a total war, the ability of one side to out-produce the other could be of huge significance, particularly if this could be coupled with a vast source of manpower for the front line. The Soviet Union had both the capacity to out-produce the Germans, and the men and women who could make full use of that equipment at the front.

Soviet industrial potency was one of Stalin's major achievements, even though the cost in human terms during the 1930s had been horrific as those suspected of not cooperating had been purged; sometimes even those who had given wholehearted support to Stalin's vision found themselves arrested and consigned to the *Gulag* or execution. The reason for Stalin's drive towards mass industrialization had been simple – he knew that one of the primary causes of Russia's failure in World War I had been the appalling lack of material required to fight a modern war. Some Russian troops had found themselves equipped with a derivative of the Winchester Repeating Rifle more commonly seen in the American West since the middle part of the nineteenth century; they had been the lucky ones, since many soldiers had been forced to acquire their weapons by taking them from dead or wounded colleagues. Stalin had been determined that the USSR should never again find itself in a similar position, and this was one of the key factors in his ambitious plans for industrialization of a nation that had previously been considered as backward.

'Feeding Mars'

Industrialization was carefully thought out, with the creation of huge industrial complexes deep in the Soviet interior, as exemplified by the city of Magnitogorsk. In 1928 it had 25 inhabitants; by 1932 there were 250,000 people living there to support the industrial city that had risen from the barren land. The location of such complexes, involving the relocation of thousands upon thousands of workers, had been carefully chosen – far to the east of the Urals, in Siberia or Central Asia, well out of range of attack

Opposite: A Soviet propaganda poster exhorts the population to greater efforts in the fight against the Nazis. The Soviet Communist Party made considerable use of such posters, and it was natural that the skills of the artists would be turned to encouraging the populace in warlike endeavours, drawing on sentiments of patriotism and idealism to convey their message.

Above: Soviet troops go into action riding on the rear deck of a T-34 tank. The Red Army regularly used tanks as a means of transporting troops up to the front line, with the 'tank riders' dismounting just before contact was made with the enemy.

by any likely enemy. While this was the case for heavy industry, light industry had not been in as happy a position in 1941, since much of that sector was well within the compass of an invading enemy. As a result, the State Defence Committee ordered a mass exodus of factories and workers, evacuating industries to the heartland of the USSR. While this caused considerable disruption during 1941, by 1942 production had begun to increase dramatically.

As an illustration of just how impressive the manufacturing achievement of the USSR was, the simple fact that Russian factories produced around twice as much war material as German industry in 1942, despite the fact that Soviet industry had access to only around a third of the steel and coal supplies available to Hitler that year, serves as a telling example. The reason for this lay in careful development of industrial capacity, so that a factory that produced tractors as its main business would also turn out some tanks; when war came, the ratio of tank to tractor production was reversed, so that a rapid build-up in Red Army tank strength could be guaranteed. While production for agriculture would inevitably fall considerably, it did not disappear entirely, enabling a balance to be struck between feeding the front line with armaments and feeding the nation as a whole.

As a consequence of Stalin's vision, Soviet industry was able to produce nearly 240 million tons of munitions in 1942, a dramatic increase on the 1940 figures – and even more impressive when the disruption caused by evacuating industry is taken into account. The overall output from Soviet industry was prodigious. Between 1943 and 1945, over 80,000 aircraft, 73,000 armoured vehicles and 324,000 artillery pieces had been made; as an example, the Ilyushin Il-2 'Sturmovik' attack aircraft was built to the tune of 36,000 examples, making it the most heavily produced aircraft in history (a figure which is almost certainly never to be beaten).

While it would be ridiculous to claim that industrial output was all that was required to defeat Hitler on the Eastern Front, the ability to produce almost unimaginable amounts of war material, coupled with the massive strength of the Soviet armed forces, needs to be appreciated when making any assessment of the fighting that took place from 1943 onwards – the sheer scale of men, machines and other equipment involved is difficult to grasp, but without industrial capacity, victory on the Eastern Front would have been impossible to achieve.

The Precursors to the 1943 Campaigns

Following the success of Soviet operations around Stalingrad and the crushing of the German Sixth Army, the Russians continued with their offensive operations, continued to advance, eager to exploit their success. On 29 January 1943, Operation Gallop was launched, with General Vatutin's Sixth and First Guards Armies attacking along the entire German front, with considerable success. The front collapsed rapidly, and the Soviets pushed deep into the German rear area. Vatutin's main effort began two days later, with troops moving in support of the Voronezh Front's attack towards Kharkov, which had also begun on 29 January. This too had punched a huge gap in German lines. Although the Germans recovered their poise to a considerable degree and put up stiff resistance, they were unable to stop the onward march of the Soviet forces, until by 14 February, they were in danger of being surrounded in front of Kharkov itself. German commanders were uncertain of how best to defend against the possibility of disaster, and were not aided by Hitler's insistence that the city be defended to the last man. As a consequence, German resistance became fragmented, and after particularly heavy street fighting on 15 and 16 February, Kharkov was retaken.

This freed Vatutin to reorganize his plans for his forces, and he aimed to seize crossings over the river Dnieper, although this move was risky – it would stretch the overextended Soviet forces over a much wider area than originally planned, making it difficult to ensure that supplies could be maintained. Stalin was concerned by the possible dangers, but granted permission for the plan to be enacted. While Vatutin moved on towards the Dnieper, the newly created Central Front, under General Rokossovsky, began operations towards Smolensk, with the aim of encircling German Army Group Centre. Although the attack began well, the need for

Map, page 243: Success at Stalingrad marked a turning point for the Soviets, although it took time before the victory was fully exploited. After the Soviets had retaken Kharkov, the Germans appreciated that they were in for much hard fighting. Although the Russians had sustained huge casualties, they were still capable of offensive action, and were beginning to inflict serious damage upon the Germans.

T-34 – THE BEST TANK OF THE WAR?

The T-34 is one of the legendary weapons of World War II, and small numbers still remain in use even 60 years after the end of the conflict. The T-34 went into production in 1940, and struck an effective balance between armour protection, speed and armament, using a 76.2mm (2.9in) high-velocity gun. The tank was kept a closely guarded secret and proved an unpleasant surprise for the Germans in 1941.

By 1943, as the tide of the war in the East turned in favour of the USSR, the T-34 was the mainstay of the Soviet armoured formations, and was undergoing continual improvement. In 1944, a larger, 85mm (3.3in) gun was fitted to the vehicle, ensuring that it remained capable of dealing with all but the heaviest of German tanks. As well as being a thoroughly capable tank, the T-34 was available in huge numbers, enabling Soviet tank forces to dominate the battlefield.

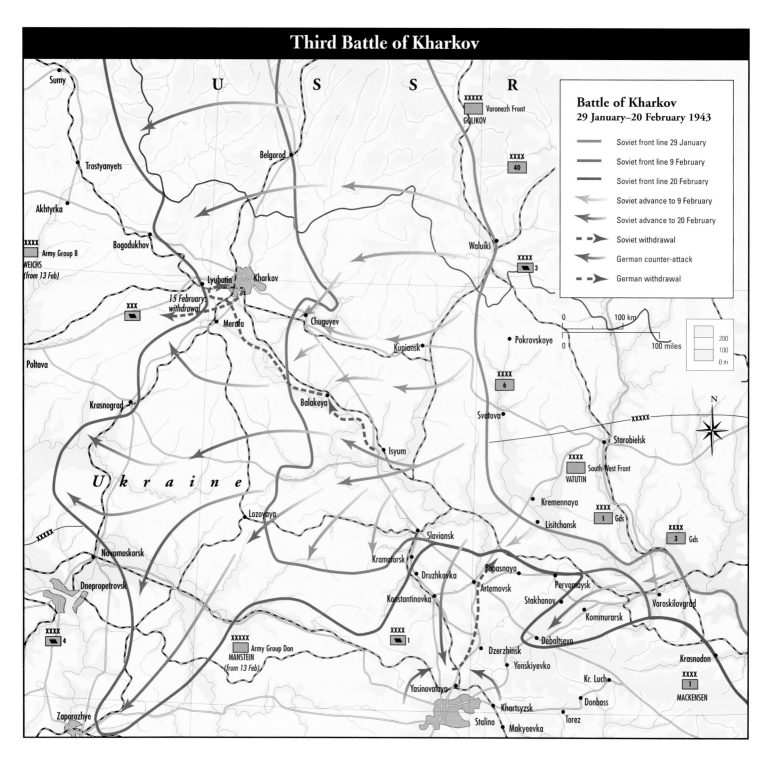

Third Battle of Kharkov

Battle of Kharkov
29 January–20 February 1943

- Soviet front line 29 January
- Soviet front line 9 February
- Soviet front line 20 February
- Soviet advance to 9 February
- Soviet advance to 20 February
- Soviet withdrawal
- German counter-attack
- German withdrawal

0   100 km
0   100 miles

200
100
0 m

Above: The Third Battle of Kharkov came as the Soviets were anxious to exploit their success at Stalingrad. A Soviet offensive forced the Germans back all along the line, and the Voronezh Front drove towards Kharkov.

Rokossovsky to employ men and armour redeployed from around Stalingrad represented a risk – if they could not reach the front in time, the attack would fail. The poor weather and the effect this had on the rather limited transport network meant that the reinforcements were not available for the proposed start date of the Central Front's offensive, which had to be put back by 10 days to 25 February. By this time, it was clear that operations by the Soviet Western and Kalinin Fronts would not be able to achieve success, and the fact that Central Front's offensive was meant to be carried out in conjunction with these two fronts meant that the scope of Rokossovsky's operations had to be recast so that they were less ambitious. However, the Germans had managed to hurry troops to the area, and this meant that they were able to counter-attack. By early March, Rokossovsky had been forced to switch to the defensive in positions north of Kursk.

Fourth Battle of Kharkov

The initial successes of the Soviet offensive caused considerable concern to Field Marshal Erich von Manstein, the commander of Army Group Don. Manstein was well aware that the length of front under his control was too great for the forces available to him, and the need to shorten the line was pressing. He therefore managed to persuade Hitler, after much argument, that he should withdraw from the salient around Rostov and the Donbas area to a better position on the River Mius. Even this withdrawal was insufficient to meet the threat posed by Vatutin's advance, and Manstein decided that the position was on the verge of becoming untenable. The Dnieper crossings were in serious danger, and if the railway junction at Dnepropetrovsk were taken as part of the drive to the Dnieper, Army Group Don would be cut off without supplies.

Manstein's solution was one of the most daring moves of the entire war in any theatre. Rather than pull back to protect his supply lines from the onrushing Soviet forces, he chose instead to launch a counter-attack. Although this plan was dangerous, Manstein assessed that the enemy would, by now, have become worn down by the high tempo of operations in recent weeks, not least because their supply chain would be far more fragile than it had been at the outset. The offensive began on 20 February, with an attack by the SS Panzer Corps against Vatutin's Sixth Army. Over the course of the next few days, the Germans made rapid progress against the Russians, who were poorly positioned to meet what was an almost entirely unexpected counter-attack. By 25 February, Vatutin's forces were exhausted, and he went over to the defensive, enabling Manstein to launch the second phase of his campaign.

A drive into the left flank of the Voronezh Front began in the first week of March, and the Germans closed in on Kharkov once more, until by 10/11 March the city was on the point of falling into German hands once more. After a few more days' fighting, Kharkov was firmly under German control, and Manstein's daring had averted disaster. The counter-attack came to a halt as the arrival of additional Soviet troops stabilized the front just prior to the spring thaw that brought operations to a

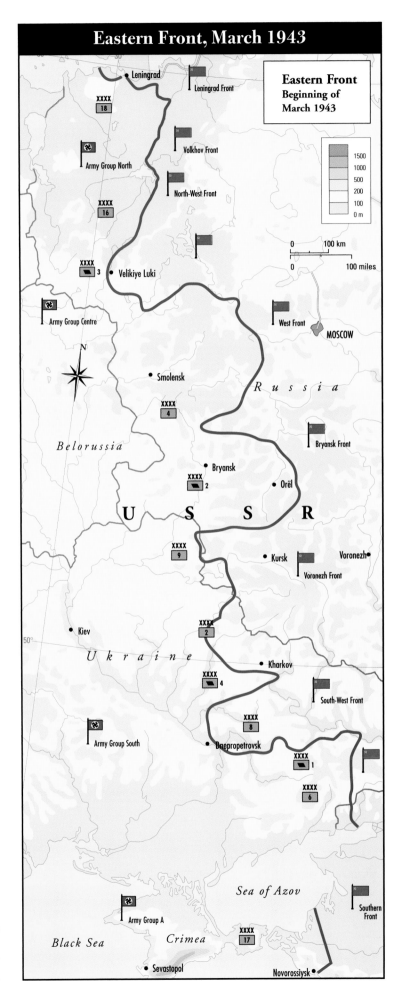

Eastern Front, March 1943

Eastern Front
Beginning of
March 1943

halt for the time being. Despite the brilliance of Manstein's counter-attack, the Germans could not be said to have been in an enviable position by April 1943, since they had suffered huge losses. Three German armies had been annihilated in the fighting between November 1942 and the halt in late March 1943. While the Russians had also suffered grievously, they were far better positioned to bring newly formed units into the line.

A further negative factor for the Germans, and one which they were to come to appreciate over the next few months was that the Red Army began to put into practice a number of the key lessons learned in the first 18 months of the war. Stalin finally recognized that he could take credit for the success of operations without controlling them totally, and his mistrust for his generals, so high in the 1930s, dissipated as they began to deliver success. As a result, Stalin abandoned the monolithic command structure centred around him, and turned the high command into something more than just a glorified staff which would implement his every wish. While Stalin remained firmly in control, he made some significant changes that brought the generals firmly back into the planning process.

General Georgy Zhukhov was appointed as Stalin's deputy, making him the most powerful Soviet general, while Colonel-General Aleksander Vasilevsky was handed the role of chief of staff at the high command. These changes were followed by a total reorganization of the Red Army's command structure. Previously, political officers appointed to ensure that the army acted with the utmost loyalty had taken an undue part in planning. Since the overwhelming majority of these officers had no idea about how to organize a battle, they were a considerable obstacle to effective operations, demanding unrealistic goals for operations with the implication that commanders who did not accede to these demands would be removed. Zhukhov made sure that this was overturned at once, and the political officers, while still deeply involved in planning, did

Above: A Soviet sniper takes aim from his position at the foot of a ruined building. The fact that the man has not made any effort to camouflage his position suggests that this may be a propaganda photograph, rather than an image from actual fighting.

Opposite: Two partisans, seen operating around Leningrad in the summer of 1943. The picture demonstrates how the partisans drew their forces from all age groups, presenting the Germans with a massive security problem as they attempted to quell resistance.

Right: The retaking of Kharkov by the Soviets left the German Army Group Don under serious threat, prompting Field Marshal Manstein to launch a daring counter-attack. He assaulted the Soviets on 20 February 1943, forcing the Russians back over the River Donets. Kharkov fell into German hands again, bringing the 1942–43 winter campaigns to an end, as both sides were exhausted.

Opposite: The end of Manstein's counter-offensive left a significant salient in the Russian lines, centred on the town of Kursk. Hitler decided that this offered an opportunity to destroy the two Soviet fronts (Central and Voronezh) that held the area, and set in train plans for what was to become the biggest tank battle in history at Kursk.

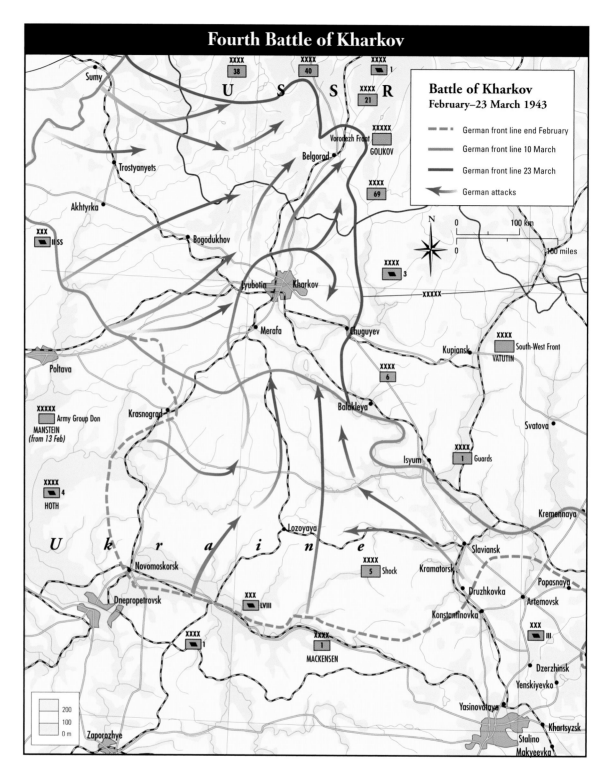

not have the authority to overrule Red Army officers. The sum of these developments was to leave the Germans facing an enemy that was improving its equipment, strategy and tactics with a much better command structure than before, a problem that would become all too apparent once the effects of the spring thaw lifted and the operations of summer 1943 began.

On to Kursk

The end of Manstein's counter-offensive against Kharkov left the Soviets holding a significant salient, centred on the town of Kursk. In another of his optimistic visions, Hitler concluded that this offered his troops the ideal opportunity to destroy the two

Soviet army fronts (Central and Voronezh) holding the area. This did not take account of the fact that the Soviets would recover from the demands made upon them by the post-Stalingrad operations, and Hitler only made matters worse by his insistence upon a course of action that he proclaimed would deliver the decisive blow for which he was aiming.

Hitler was convinced that many of the problems that had confronted his troops since Stalingrad had been caused by the lack of armour capable of dealing with the Soviet T-34. However, there was hope, since the Germans had developed two new tanks, namely the Panzer Mark V (better known as the Panther) and the large Tiger tank. Hitler argued that these armoured vehicles were the key to the offensive. If enough of them were made available to his forces around the Kursk salient, success would follow. To aid matters further, he pointed to the fact that more self-propelled guns, an integral part of German offensive tactics in that they supported the advance of the infantry, were coming off the production lines. The validity of these thoughts was questionable, but Hitler would not be dissuaded from his intended course.

This failed to take into account the fact that while Panthers, Tigers and self-propelled guns were indeed coming off the production line, they were not being produced in anything like the numbers to guarantee success against the Soviets. This prompted Hitler to postpone his planned offensive until enough were available, a move loaded with risk. By delaying the attack he granted the Soviets more time to recover from the winter's fighting and to increase their strength. This in turn meant that it would be more difficult to make a breakthrough, even with the new weapons in which Hitler invested so much faith.

The German generals were less than impressed with the idea of an offensive when Hitler presented it to them in early May 1943. Not unreasonably, they queried whether the resources for such a venture would be available, and they made clear their concerns about Hitler's decision to postpone the attack while waiting for new tanks. The generals made it very clear that the Soviets were almost certainly going to build far stronger defences around Kursk, given that it was an obvious weak spot in

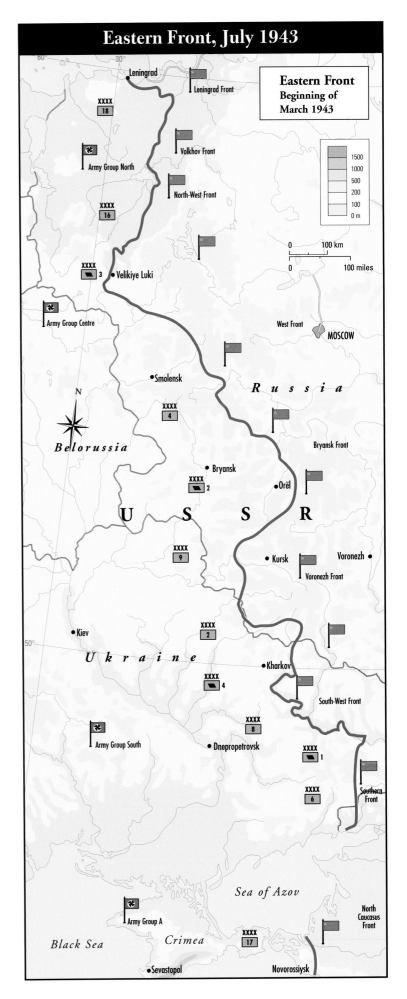

Eastern Front, July 1943

Eastern Front
Beginning of
March 1943

Above: Soldiers from the SS Totenkopf Division make their way towards the front lines at Kursk, July 1943. Massive troop concentrations were to fight a savage battle that saw huge losses on both sides – but these were losses that the Soviets could absorb, and which the Germans could not.

their line, and that every day that passed to allow German forces to grow stronger was a day in which the Soviets did the same. Not for the first time, nor for the last, Hitler simply refused to listen. He was presented with a number of alternative options, designed to maintain the German position, but was fixed upon his own idea. General Heinz Guderian, the inspector-general of Panzer forces, presented bitter opposition to the idea of any offensive in Russia, be it around Kursk or anywhere else.

Guderian was well aware that the Axis position in North Africa was on the verge of total collapse, and that the majority of the troops still in Tunisia would inevitably be captured and unavailable for redeployment. He also suggested that once North Africa was lost, the Allies would turn their attention to opening a second front in Western Europe, leaving the Germans facing the unwelcome prospect of a war on two fronts against allies who seemed able to conjure up massive amounts of equipment, despite the losses inflicted upon them.

To Guderian, this dangerous strategic situation suggested that any attempt to go on the offensive in Russia would be absurd. Rather than squander large amounts of Germany's armoured strength in another attritional battle in the East, Guderian argued, the Panther and Tiger tanks upon which Hitler was pinning so much hope should be kept for facing the invasion forces in the West. He contended that the logical conclusion was that German troops in the USSR should adopt a defensive posture, and not gamble on offensive action at all. Hitler listened to Guderian's views and then ignored them totally, pressing on with the plan, and committing the Germans to another major attritional battle.

To make matters worse for the Germans, Soviet intelligence-gathering capabilities were improving. Unlike in June 1941 when the German attack had come as an almost complete surprise, by May 1943, the Soviets were much better at divining German intentions. Indeed, it is possible that Zhukhov had enough information to suggest that Kursk would be the venue for the next German offensives before some of Hitler's generals were aware of the fact. Unsurprisingly, Zhukhov made sure that his troops would be prepared for the assault that would follow.

Operation Citadel

As part of Zhukhov's preparations, troops were brought in from other fronts to defend the salient, while plans were made to follow up a German attack with a huge counter-offensive along the entire southern part of the front. By early July, the Germans had concentrated nearly 3000 tanks and assault guns around the salient, but while this force was being built up, the Soviets quietly prepared a series of strong defensive positions. Seven defence lines were constructed between April and July, while Zhukhov moved reserves opposite the largest German troop concentrations to ensure that they could not have a decisive effect when thrown into battle against the Soviet lines. As well as the seven major defensive positions, the Russians set up a further line of defence well behind the salient, to deal with the possibility of a German breakthrough.

As a result, a huge force stood directly opposite the Germans by the start of July. There were nearly one million men and 3300 tanks in position, while another 380,000 men and 600 tanks were held in reserve. While these figures seem incredible, they do not represent the entire strength of the Soviet position – the 1.38 million men and 3900 tanks

'[Hitler's] interest in anything technological led him to exaggerate the effect of armament. For example, he imagined himself to be able with the help of a few battalions of self-propelled artillery or Tiger tanks to redress situations where only the engagement of several divisions held out any hope of success.'

Field Marshal Erich von Manstein

SOVIET HEAVY TANKS

In addition to medium tanks such as the T-34, the Soviets developed a number of heavier vehicles that were designed to take on enemy tanks, as well as to provide support to the infantry. The first of these was the T-35, which, despite its designation, was produced several years before the T-34. The T-35 proved slow and difficult to manoeuvre; when they faced the Germans in 1941, they proved very vulnerable.

The T-35 was followed by the more successful KV-1. This was used as an assault tank, designed to lead the attack and break through German lines, whereupon the more mobile T-34s would exploit the success. The KV-1 was much better than the T-35, and was developed into the KV-85, with an 85mm (3.3in) gun as its main armament, and the KV-152, armed with a 152mm (5.9in) howitzer. While the KV-1 and KV-85 were a handful for German defences, they were succeeded in production by the IS series of heavy tanks, which first entered service in mid-1943. The IS-2, introduced in early 1944, was the most notable, armed with a massive 122mm (4.8in) gun that could defeat any German tanks it encountered. It remained the most powerful tank in the world for a decade after the end of the war.

Below: By early July 1943, the Germans had 3000 tanks and assault guns around the Kursk salient. The Soviets, aware of an impending attack, prepared incredibly strong defensive positions. Nearly two million Soviet troops and 5000 tanks faced the Germans, setting the scene for one of the largest battles in military history.

represented just the tactical level defences against and assault. The operational line behind the salient had a further 500,000 men and another 1500 tanks available to it, ready for deployment where required. To make matters worse for the Germans, the Red Air Force (strictly Frontal Aviation) was present in large numbers to provide direct air support against the attack.

As a result, Hitler's decisive offensive was to begin with the attacking forces heavily outnumbered by their opponents. These sat in strong defensive positions that would take huge effort to overcome, and they had massive reserves to come to their aid if required, or to exploit the developing situation on the battlefield – a recipe for potential disaster, rather than the decisive victory that Hitler insisted would follow.

The Clash of Battle

Army Group South carried out a number of preparatory operations on 4 July to secure the starting positions for Operation Citadel, with the attack itself due to begin at 04:30 the next morning. At this point, the German guns opened fire all along the Central Front, while aircraft joined in the bombardment on the Voronezh Front. Shortly after 05:00, the first reports of tank and infantry attacks were made by Soviet front line positions. Fourth Panzer Army committed 700 armoured vehicles to the assault against the Soviet Sixth

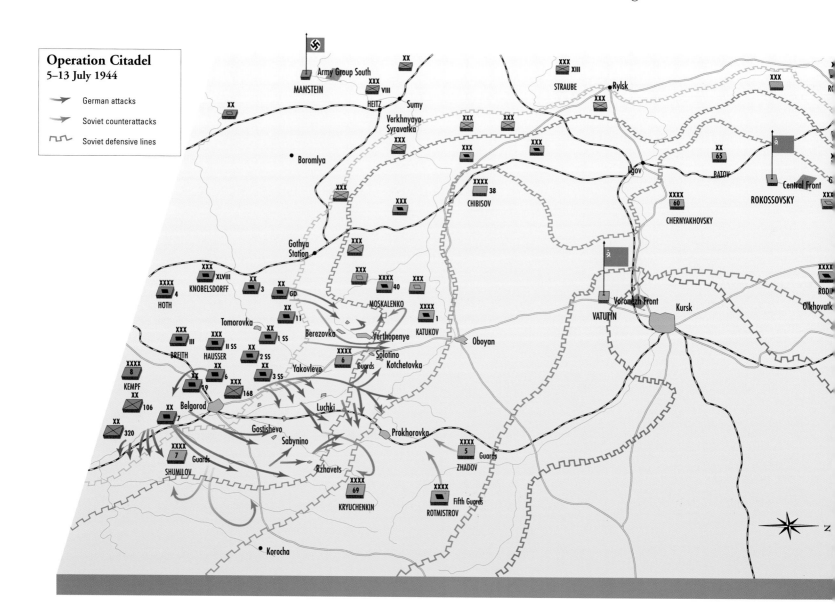

250

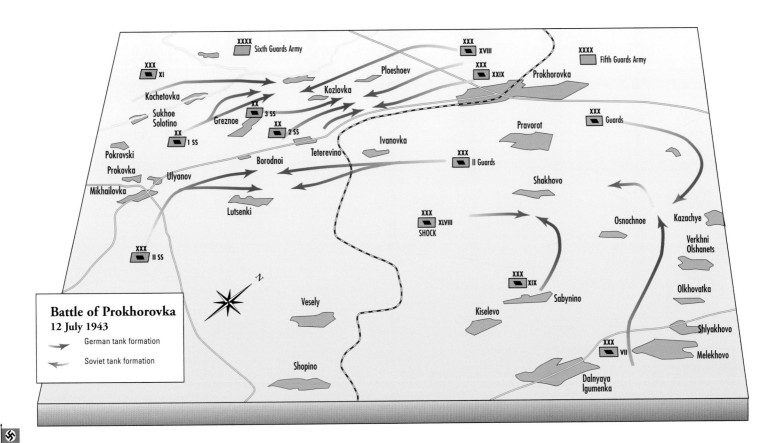

Battle of Prokhorovka
12 July 1943

→ German tank formation

← Soviet tank formation

Guards Army, with tanks packed 40 or 50 per kilometre of line in most sectors, rising to as many as 100 per kilometre elsewhere.

The Germans managed to gain ground to a depth of four to six miles, and Rokossovsky secured agreement from Stalin that the Twenty-Seventh Army would be sent forward to assist. However, when it became clear that the situation on the Voronezh Front was even more serious than that facing Central Front, Stalin withdrew his offer and sent the forces there instead. By 18:00 on 6 July, both sides were pouring men and material into the battle, with the armour of both sides moving on a scale never seen before or since, moving in formations up to 200 strong on both sides of the front. Some 4000 Soviet and 3000 German tanks and assault guns were now on the verge of entering the battle, which continued with ever greater ferocity; the Soviet high command estimated that nearly 600 German tanks were destroyed or disabled on the first day of the fighting.

Attack was followed by counter-attack, and the Germans managed to make a number of gains, so that by the morning of 7 July they were threatening the high ground near Olkhovatka, which gave command of the battlefield. Rokossovsky promptly reinforced the approaches to Olkhovatka, and fighting of rarely paralleled intensity broke out as the Germans tried to attack against anti-tank guns, mines, armour and artillery, with both sides suffering fearful losses as they went. By 10 July, the Germans were regrouping after the first five days of combat, and it was clear that the climax of the battle

Above: By nightfall on the first day of Kursk, the Germans had managed to advance around seven miles. By 11 July, II SS Panzer Corps had reached Prokhorovka, a small village that swiftly became the location of the largest tank battle in history. The Soviet commander, General Vatutin had concluded that the Germans would attack at Prokhorovka, and reinforced his positions there. The end result was an enormous battle on 12 July, in which over 1000 tanks participated. After 36 hours' fighting, the Germans were brought to a halt.

was approaching. Despite having made a penetration of nearly 20 miles towards Oboyan, the Germans had been unable to break through to the necessary depth, and were about to shift the axis of their attack towards Prokhorovka, a small village which had a railway junction as its most notable feature. Within 24 hours, it had become the site of the largest tank battle the world has ever seen.

Climax

In response to the German moves and the increased threat to Prokhorovka, armour and troops were moved to strengthen the Voronezh Front, being placed in blocking positions. If the Germans could break through here, they would be in a position to unhinge the Soviet defences. General Vatutin saw the threat as an opportunity, however. He was well aware that the Germans had suffered massive losses in the course of the battle so far, and felt that if the Germans were to attack against Prokhorovka, they would have to move units from their flanks to support the attack. This reduction in strength on the flanks appeared to offer an ideal opportunity to counter-attack, with the aim of encircling the German forces.

At dawn on 11 July, the Germans attacked Prokhorovka and Oboyan, with a massive battle taking place between Fifth Guards Tank Army and three SS divisions. The battle for Prokhorovka was in the balance by nightfall, and the Soviet relief attack to the north against the Orel bulge was timely, but the main struggle took place at the village itself. Fifth Guards Tank Army was sent into the fray once more, counter-attacking vigorously. Yet again, the battle was fierce with huge casualties on both sides. The Germans had lost more than 300 tanks (including 70 Tigers), while around 50 per cent of the Fifth Guards Tank Army had been destroyed. Yet despite the heavy losses, the Soviets had achieved their aim. The German attacks had been halted, while the Russians still had reserves in hand to use if required.

The Germans continued probing attacks for three more days, but it was clear that they were not going to be able to break through at Prokhorovka, nor were they going to be able to bypass it. By this point, the battle was over, since developments elsewhere had seized Hitler's attention.

On 10 July, an Anglo-American invasion force landed in Sicily, with the obvious implication that Italy would be next to be invaded. Hitler feared that the Italians would capitulate as soon as the Allies invaded, and decided that he had no alternative but to reinforce his units in the West, at the expense of Operation Citadel.

Hitler gave orders for the transfer of a number of units to the Western Front. In a number of instances, the units that were to head west found their transfer was complicated by the need to extricate themselves from the battle before they could obey their instructions. With the reduction of strength that this move entailed, the Germans had no option but to carry out a fighting withdrawal and head back to their start points of 5 July. To all intents and purposes, the Battle of Kursk was over.

Aftermath

As the northern element of the German attack at Kursk ground to a halt the Soviet Western Front (General Sokolovsky) launched Operation Kutuzov, an attack against Second Panzer Army. The German forces were distracted by their own offensive, and taken by surprise. Their defences were quickly overrun, and as it became obvious that Soviet units would soon be in a position to cut the lines of communication of General Walther Model's Ninth Army, the Germans were forced to defend vigorously before finally checking the attack. This was not the end of the fighting, however.

Operation Kutuzov was quickly followed by an offensive towards Orël by General Popov's Bryansk Front. Orël was the key road and rail junction in the region, and, as was always the case, the prospect of losing such a key communications point was a major concern to the Germans. After a week's fighting, the Soviets took Orël, and continued their advance; by the middle of August, the German positions on the northern shoulder of the Kursk Salient became untenable, and had to be abandoned.

The Germans fell back to prepared defensive positions some 75 miles away to the west, having failed in their objectives for the northern shoulder of the offensive against Kursk. A similar dismal result was to befall the Germans in the southern sector as the Steppe Front (General Koniev) and Vatutin's Voronezh Front launched their own offensive (Operation Polkovodets Rumyantsev), with the aim of destroying the southern shoulder of the salient as a precursor to an advance towards Belgorod and Kharkov.

When Operation Rumyantsev began on 3 August, the Germans were again taken by surprise. They had correctly assessed that both the Steppe and Voronezh Fronts had taken heavy losses during the fighting at Kursk, but totally underestimated the Russians' ability to bring replacements into the line. As a result, they had not prepared to meet an enemy attack, and were taken completely by surprise when the blow fell upon them. The offensive thus enjoyed considerable early success. By nightfall on the second day, Belgorod was back in Soviet hands. This success allowed an advance towards Bogodukhov and Kharkov, with a German counter-attack proving futile. The Soviets

'Whenever I think of this attack, my stomach turns over.'

Adolf Hitler on Operation Citadel to General Heinz Guderian, May 1943

253

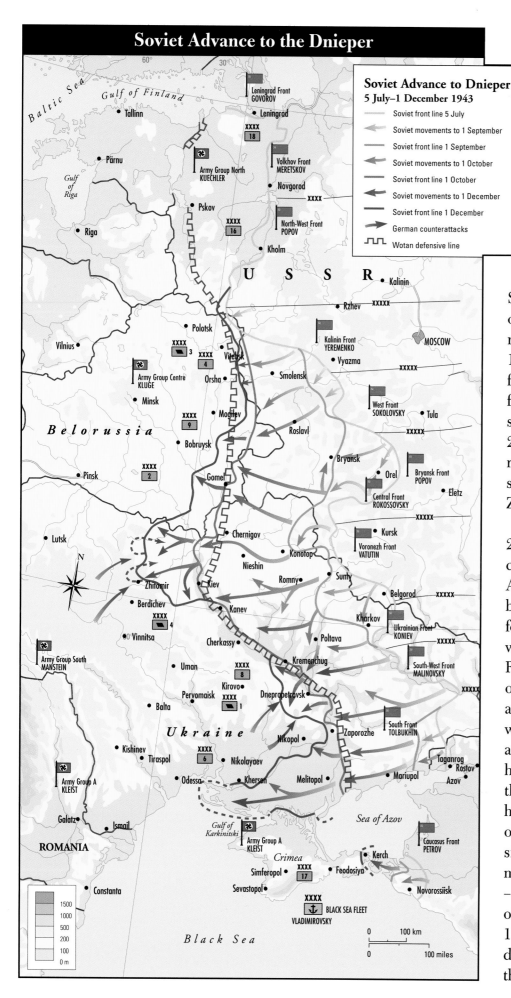

Soviet Advance to the Dnieper

Soviet Advance to Dnieper
5 July–1 December 1943

- Soviet front line 5 July
- Soviet movements to 1 September
- Soviet front line 1 September
- Soviet movements to 1 October
- Soviet front line 1 October
- Soviet movements to 1 December
- Soviet front line 1 December
- German counterattacks
- Wotan defensive line

advanced inexorably upon Kharkov, which changed hands for the fourth – and final – time in the war on 21 August.

As Operation Rumyantsev progressed, Rokossovsky's Central Front launched an offensive of its own from its positions around Kursk. Central Front acted as a link between the two offensives to the north and south of its positions. Alongside this attack the Southwest and South Fronts began offensives of their own against Army Group South. As a result, by the middle of September 1943, Army Group South had been forced back across the Dnieper. The first bridgehead across the river was secured by a Soviet advance party on 23 September, with the main force reaching the river along a frontage stretching from Gomel to Zaporozhye.

The offensive continued, and by 25 October, the Soviet advance had cut off German forces in the Crimea. Another German counter-attack battered some of the Soviet advanced forces around Krivoi Rog, but this was not enough to prevent the Russians advancing on Kiev. The offensive here began on 3 November, and the city was back in Soviet hands within 48 hours. As Christmas approached, the Germans were left holding just a few small sections of the western bank of the Dnieper, hoping to hold on until the Soviet offensive had exhausted itself. Initial signs that the Russians had lost momentum were misleading, though – they had no intention of slackening off their pace for the remainder of 1943, and were to bring further disaster upon the Germans before the year was out.

Left: A German non-commissioned officer carries two land mines. He is armed with a single hand grenade and probably a pistol for personal protection. The Germans made considerable use of mines on all fronts, with the aim of destroying Soviet tanks and attacking formations, thus reducing the enemy's forces to more manageable proportions.

Opposite: The events following Kursk came as a massive blow to German forces on the Eastern Front. The Soviets followed up their success at Kursk with Operation Rumyantsev in early August 1943, in which the Germans found themselves outnumbered by nearly 3:1, facing nearly 700,000 Russians. The Soviets advanced quickly over the coming months as they drove on to the Dnieper, and as the year drew to a close, Soviet troops lined the river banks, waiting to make their next move against an increasingly stretched enemy.

The Balkans, 1942–45

For much of the war, the Balkan theatre saw little in the way of conventional fighting. However, there were substantial numbers of resistance fighters at work in Yugoslavia, Greece and Albania, all aiming to overthrow German occupation. The Balkan area was also notable for the fact that Hitler's minor allies were to be found there, in the form of Bulgaria, Romania and Hungary, although each had a different perspective on their relationship with Hitler and with each other. These subtleties were not appreciated by the Soviets, who regarded them simply as allies of the Nazis, and therefore to be defeated.

If the Germans thought that they would have an easy time in Yugoslavia after their rapid victory there in 1941, they were swiftly disabused of this notion. Unbeknown to them, a leading member of the pre-war Yugoslav Communist Party, Josip Broz, was determined that the country should rise against the Nazi invaders. At the time, Broz was living in Zagreb under the name of Babiç. Although the new puppet government of Croatia was attempting to round up all communist activists, Broz had considerable practice at avoiding the authorities. The previous government had spent some time attempting to locate, with a similar lack of success, a 'Comrade Tito', the *nom de guerre* by which Broz would become known for the rest of his life.

The Yugoslav Partisans

The invasion of the USSR prompted Tito to issue a call for a national revolt against the 'Fascist hordes', issued on 4 July 1941. The partisan war began almost immediately, with acts of sabotage across the country, most notably in Serbia and Montenegro; in the latter, the Italian occupying forces were routed. The German response to the uprising came in the form of reprisals in which thousands of people were killed; this only encouraged more to join the Partisans.

Tito expected that the conflict to liberate Yugoslavia would be a long and difficult one, and he was quite correct. The task was complicated considerably by the presence of another resistance group, the Çetniks, headed by a former army officer, Draça Mihailoviç.

Opposite: Two RAF aircrew prepare to drop supplies to Yugoslav Partisans. The RAF established a number of 'special duties' squadrons to carry out supply runs to underground organizations and to drop liaison officers into occupied territories to advise and assist the resistance in their struggle against the Nazis.

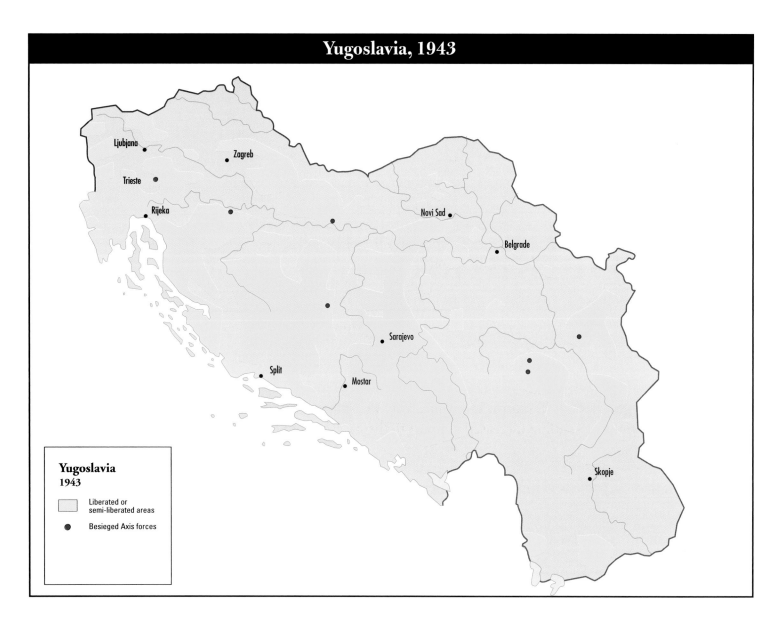

Yugoslavia, 1943

Yugoslavia
1943

Liberated or
semi-liberated areas

● Besieged Axis forces

Above: The nature of the countryside in Yugoslavia meant that it was impossible for the Germans to control all of the country. This allowed Tito's Partisans to run large parts of Yugoslavia themselves as 'liberated areas'. While German offensives meant that the amount of territory held by Tito's forces fluctuated, the Partisans always managed to remain a viable combat force, and never lost great swathes of territory.

Although Tito endeavoured to establish a united front with the Çetniks, it soon became clear that this was an unlikely alliance. Mihailoviç was an ardent royalist, aiming for the restoration of the *status quo*, while Tito hoped to see the establishment of a communist state after the Germans had left. The Çetniks had the advantage to begin with, in that a British liaison officer was sent to support them. The liaison officer arrived before a second meeting between Tito and Mihailoviç, but was excluded from the talks, leaving him poorly informed about the Partisans. The negotiations between the two sides collapsed, and it became clear that the Çetniks saw the Partisans as being their principal enemies ahead of the Germans. This led to a situation in which the Çetniks began to work alongside the Germans and Italians, with the aim of destroying Tito's movement.

German Offensives

Owing to the nature of Yugoslavia's terrain, it was extremely difficult for the Germans and Italians to control all the territory in the country. This meant that it was possible for the Partisans to control large swathes of territory, running them as liberated areas with their own administrative structures.

The Germans were determined to crush the Partisans, and launched a series of offensives, beginning in Serbia in September 1941 and lasting until December. The

Partisans were driven back from much of the territory under their control, falling back on the liberated town of Foça in Bosnia. The Germans followed this offensive with a second, beginning on 15 January 1942, and this drove Tito's forces out of Foça by 10 May as they advanced across the countryside. The Partisans fell back again across the high ground around Mount Kozara, which the Germans found impossible to take. Their offensive then merged into a third assault, beginning in April, prompting Tito to lead his forces out of eastern Bosnia and nearer to Croatia. The retreat started on 24 June 1942, and was to cover 150 miles before it was complete. Unlike conventional military retreats, this withdrawal was marked by considerable success, since the Partisans captured the towns of Jajce and Bihaç as they went. By capturing Bihaç, the Partisans gained control of a large amount of liberated territory, in which Tito was able to hold a political congress, the Anti-Fascist Council for the National Liberation of Yugoslavia. The council arranged elections and laid down a manifesto for the future direction of the Partisan movement. This had a positive effect on Partisan morale, and raised their profile in the West.

The Çetniks had enjoyed all the support of the British and Americans up to mid-1942, receiving liaison officers in mid-1941. The Çetniks had ensured that relatively little information about the Partisans reached London, by controlling the radio transmissions of the liaison team. The Allies, including the Soviets, had already recognized the right of the exiled royalist government to return, and Mihailoviç was a member of their cabinet; not aiding the Çetniks or sending increased support to their rivals would be politically difficult. All of this militated against Allied help being sent to Tito, but by the end of 1942, enough information had reached London to provide a better picture of how successful the Partisans had been. It also became clear that the Çetniks were collaborating with the Germans and Italians in many areas, while in others they were largely inactive. These factors were particularly relevant to Allied considerations by the end of 1942, since planning for the invasion of Sicily and then, possibly, Italy was well under way. It was quite evident that it would be beneficial if Axis forces could be tied down in Yugoslavia by increased Partisan activity, denying the enemy the opportunity to

Below: German paratroops take up positions during the raid on Tito's headquarters at Drvar. They were unsuccessful in their aim of killing or capturing the Partisan leader, who managed to escape. Several days of bitter fighting left most of the paratroops who had led the raid dead or wounded, with nothing to show for their sacrifice.

Above: German soldiers guard Partisan prisoners, taken during one of the Axis offensives against Tito's organization. Despite making massive efforts to destroy the Partisans, the Germans never quite succeeded in achieving their goals, leaving large areas of Yugoslavia under Tito's control.

redeploy a number of divisions to the new battlefront. However, while it was clear that the Partisans were a major force in Yugoslavia, the decision over what, if any, help should be despatched was still being made when the Germans launched yet another assault in January 1943, in response to a decision by Hitler that the danger of the Allies invading the Balkans was such that the Partisans' constant interference with communications and supply routes had to be stopped. The Germans employed over 150,000 troops in five divisions, while the Italians employed three divisions of their own. In addition, some 18,000 Çetniks and troops loyal to the puppet regime in Croatia were used. The German and Croatian troops attacked from the north and east, while the Italians approached from the west and south. Tito ordered a retreat to east Bosnia, with the intention of crossing into the mountains of Montenegro. To achieve this, the Partisans had to pass through enemy territory across the River Neretva, where 12,000 Çetniks were waiting for them.

As the Partisans reached the Neretva, fierce fighting broke out as they encountered Çetnik and Italian forces. The Partisans inflicted severe damage on the Italians, and utterly routed the Çetniks to the extent that they were never able to reconstitute themselves as a major force. Tito's forces successfully crossed the river, and headed into Montenegro, pursuing what was left of the Çetnik forces at they went.

The Germans were far from impressed at the results of the offensive, blaming the Italians and the Çetniks for the failure. A fifth offensive was planned, and began in the third week of May 1943. Just as the offensive began, the first Allied liaison officers arrived, in time to witness the capabilities of the Partisans first hand. The Germans attacked with the support of an Italian division, along with Bulgarian troops and elements of the Çetniks, a total of some 120,000 men. The Germans managed to trap Tito's forces in the Montenegrin mountains. Tito decided to attempt a break-out, and used his 3rd Division to hold the Germans off while the 1st, 2nd and 7th Partisan Divisions fought their way out. The battle was particularly hard, since the Germans had correctly assessed where Tito would try to break out – but they were unable to stop him. By the middle of July, the Partisans had evaded the German attempt to encircle and destroy them, but had lost 8000 fighters in the process.

TITO

Born Josip Broz in 1892, Tito had been a prominent communist activist in the years prior to the German invasion of Yugoslavia (and it was during these activities that his alias of Tito was created). His influence over the Partisan movement was incalculable, since he appreciated that victory over the Germans would not be achieved in a short time.

Tito established political structures within the Partisan movement, and held a national assembly in 1942, to demonstrate that the Germans did not have control of all of the country. Although the Western Allies initially supported the Çetnik movement as the resistance to the Germans, they switched their allegiance to Tito's far more effective Partisans in 1944.

As the military situation throughout Europe deteriorated for the Germans, the Partisans made more and more gains, taking Belgrade on 20 October 1944, supported by the Red Army. Tito became president of Yugoslavia in the aftermath of the war, and remained fiercely independent of Stalin, refusing to become a mere satellite of the USSR. When Tito died in 1980, it marked the start of the disintegration of Yugoslavia, which many argue was held together solely by the strength of his leadership.

Changing Fortunes

The loss of 8000 men was a blow to Tito, but the liaison officers had been convinced that the Partisans were a viable organization and worthy of support. As a result, a full British military mission under the command of Brigadier Fitzroy Maclean was sent to Tito's headquarters in September 1943. This was a particularly auspicious month for the Partisans, since as well as the arrival of the British mission, Italy surrendered. Although the Germans maintained their position in the north of Italy, this had a major effect in Yugoslavia. The Partisans took the opportunity to round up 10 Italian divisions, relieving them of their equipment; a proportion of the Italian troops decided that they wished to fight alongside the Partisans, and three Italian Partisan divisions were set up as a result.

The Partisans were able to liberate territory under Italian control, creating further problems for the Germans, who had to try to fill the vacuum left by the capitulation of their allies. The Partisans took advantage of the situation to increase the size of their army by 80,000.

In addition, the arrival of British support meant that there was a steady flow of medical supplies and other equipment; in addition, it was possible to evacuate wounded Partisans to North Africa and other Allied-held territory, thus removing a major logistics burden from the Partisans, who did not have to ferry their wounded with them as they moved across the countryside.

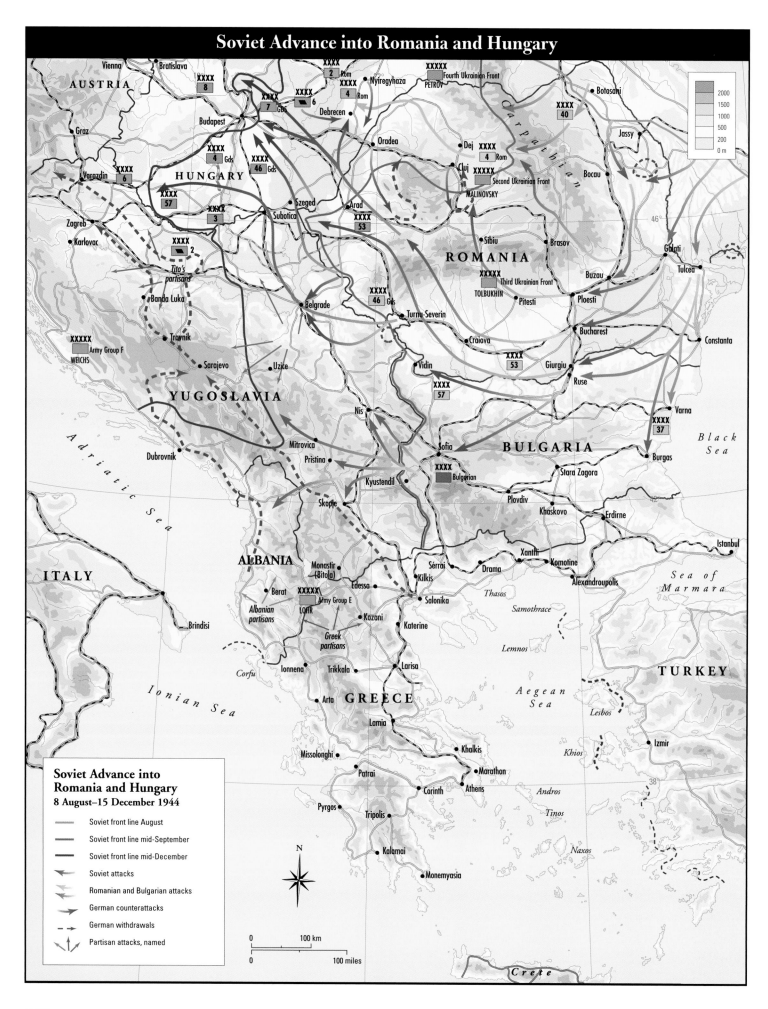

Soviet Advance into Romania and Hungary

Soviet Advance into Romania and Hungary
8 August–15 December 1944

Soviet front line August
Soviet front line mid-September
Soviet front line mid-December
Soviet attacks
Romanian and Bulgarian attacks
German counterattacks
German withdrawals
Partisan attacks, named

0   100 km
0   100 miles

N

The Final Offensives

By the end of 1943, Tito had an army 300,000 strong, controlling around two-thirds of Yugoslavia. Once again, Hitler decided that the threat posed by the Partisans had to be addressed, but the approach taken to the sixth offensive was very different. Rather than trying to destroy the Partisans through one major operation against their main body, the Germans instead launched attacks in several parts of the country, aiming to overwhelm individual Partisan groups by sheer weight of numbers. Although the Germans made some gains, the whole campaign began to peter out in mid-January 1944, by which time it was clear that World War II was entering a decisive phase. The Russians were advancing all along the Eastern Front, while the campaign in Italy had seen Allied landings at Anzio. It was quite clear that the German position in Romania would soon be under threat, and Hitler determined to remove the Partisans with a final effort.

The seventh offensive was duly launched in April 1944, with fighting in a variety of locations. All of these skirmishes were overshadowed by a daring German airborne assault on Tito's headquarters at Drvar in Bosnia. Early in the morning of 25 May, the headquarters complex was attacked by German bombers, the precursor to a glider assault. The glider-borne troops established firm defensive positions, while paratroops and more gliders were dropped in. Tito's escort held the Germans off, and help was sent for. Tito took the opportunity to escape, but fierce fighting raged through the town for the next two days as the Germans sought to capture their now departed quarry. When German infantry arrived in Drvar, they found that only one-sixth of the airborne troops had survived the operation. By this time, Tito had been flown out of Yugoslavia to Italy, before moving to the island of Vis where he set up a new headquarters. Although the Germans obtained some propaganda value from the raid, displaying captured uniforms, papers and equipment, this could not hide the fact that their plan had failed.

Hitler's focus now turned away from the Balkans to France, since the Allied landings in Normandy occurred just days after the abortive attempt to kill or capture Tito. As the pressure on the Germans increased in the West, the Russians made their presence felt as they advanced on Romania.

Romania

By early August 1944, Soviet offensives in the north and centre of the Eastern Front were going well, and planning for an attack into Romania was begun as soon as it was clear that no redeployment of forces to support other attacks would be required. The plan that emerged called for 2nd Ukrainian Front to attack German and Romanian defences to the north west of Iasi, and once a break-in had been achieved, the exploitation forces would cross the River Prut behind the German Sixth Army (now reconstituted after the original Sixth Army had been lost at Stalingrad). The 3rd Ukrainian Front would make an attack at Bendery, breaking through enemy lines to allow it to link up with 2nd Ukrainian Front. This would allow the Soviets to encircle all German forces in the Kishinev area, while the other forces would head south towards Bucharest and the oilfields at Ploesti.

The offensive began on 20 August 1944. The attack at Bendery was held up by two German divisions, but in the northern sector, only Romanian forces stood in the way of the advance. Many of the Romanian troops did not have any desire to support the Germans, and many units offered nothing more than token resistance before they retreated or surrendered. Despite this, the Germans were initially convinced that the Soviet threat was not particularly serious, and planned to fall back on to a ridge to the

Opposite: As the Soviet armies advanced through 1944, it was natural that they would turn their attention to the Balkans, seeking to deal with Germany's allies in Romania, Hungary and Bulgaria. Bulgaria and Romania were not eager to fight the Soviets, and detached themselves from Hitler with alacrity and changed sides. This did not prevent the Russians from invading both countries and destroying the German formations still there, while Hungary proved a difficult battleground, particularly the attempt to seize Budapest.

Above: Soviet troops, riding on T-34 tanks, enter Bucharest on 31 August 1944. The Romanian population had grown increasingly weary of the alliance with Germany, and the Nazi attempt to assassinate the king (to prevent him from capitulating) alienated them even more; however, the arrival of Russian troops was met with concern and ambivalence, as can be seen in the less than ecstatic welcome being given to these soldiers.

south of Iasi where a defensive line (the Trajan Line) had been erected. However, it soon became clear that the Soviets were doing better than anticipated, and their armour seized the high ground behind Iasi without any resistance. This undermined the German plan, and the German commander, General Hans Friessner, was forced to order a withdrawal to the Prut. The following morning saw the 3rd Ukrainian Front make a breakthrough at Bendery, and the danger of encirclement rose rapidly for the German forces.

As the Russian advance continued, it was clear that the Romanian front had all but collapsed. This precipitated a political crisis in Bucharest. King Carol II took the opportunity to sack his government, and made clear his intention to seek an armistice with the Allies. The German response was to send 6000 SS troops to the capital, where they discovered that the Romanians were quite happy to turn their guns on their supposed allies and put up vigorous resistance.

Friessner came to the conclusion that the situation was so desperate that the only chance of maintaining the German position in Romania was to remove the king. He promptly ordered an assassination attempt against Carol II on 24 August, led by dive bombers attacking the royal palace. The dive bombers failed in their task of killing the monarch, but managed to kill or injure many civilians. The attempt to kill their king and the casualties caused by the bombing only served to turn the Romanians against their erstwhile allies – Romania declared war on Germany the next day.

Friessner now faced complete disaster, so ordered all units under his command to retreat to Hungary, then to block the mountain passes in the Carpathians and

Transylvanian Alps as they went. This was far more complex than it sounded, since Sixth Army was now trapped in two pockets on the eastern bank of the Prut, making withdrawal unlikely. As the other German forces pulled back into Bulgaria, their movements caused concern in Sofia. Bulgaria was a member of the Axis, but had not declared war on the USSR. The government feared that allowing German troops to make use of their territory would be considered a hostile act by Moscow, so Bulgarian troops set about disarming the Germans as soon as they entered the country, sending the Germans to internment camps. While the Bulgarians were trying to ameliorate the effect of their alliance with Germany, the Soviets were busy completing their advance – Ploesti fell into their hands on 30 August, and Bucharest the next day.

As Soviet forces started occupying Romanian territory, the Fourth Guards Tank Army was sent to destroy the remains of the German Sixth Army, which was now attempting to escape from the pockets into which it had been forced by the fighting. The Russians had air superiority, and were able to make considerable use of their aircraft to hamper movement of German convoys. By 26 August, what was left of Sixth Army managed to break through a series of Soviet cut-off positions, opening a narrow corridor to the Prut. This was the only possible escape route for the Germans, and as thousands of men tried to gain the relatively safety of the river as a preliminary to withdrawing across it, they found that the Soviets had concentrated their artillery and armour against the corridor in a bid to prevent their escape.

The results were predictable. Heavy Soviet fire caused huge numbers of casualties, and forced the surviving Germans to plunge into the Prut with the aim of swimming to the west bank. Unfortunately for the Germans, they discovered that what they thought was the bank was in fact an island in the middle of the watercourse. Some Germans attempted to swim from here to the west bank, only to find that the Fourth Guards Tank Army was waiting for them. The Soviets attempted to secure the surrender of the remnants of the German force by sending emissaries to negotiate; however, as command and control had completely broken down amongst the Germans, they did not receive a response. As a result, the island was shelled, forcing the Germans to leave the island for the waters once more. Thousands were killed as they attempted to cross, and most of the others were taken prisoner. When the shelling ended, it was clear that Sixth Army had been completely destroyed in the fighting. Out of a strength of 275,000, the army had lost at least 125,000 dead by the start of September, with another 150,000 captured.

Bulgaria

The Soviets were now in a position to exploit the Romanian transport network and turned their attention to Bulgaria. Despite the best efforts of the Bulgarians to stay out of the war with Russia, this proved impossible. Attempts to negotiate with the Soviets failed, and although the Bulgarian government proclaimed that it was no longer at war with the Western Allies, the Russians could not be convinced. They announced that Bulgaria was a possible refuge for retreating Germans, and that this could not be tolerated; on 5 September 1944, they declared war.

The 3rd Ukrainian Front crossed the border on 8 September, and this prompted the Bulgarians into a new step – the next day, they announced that they were now at war with Germany, fighting alongside the Soviets, in one of the swiftest defections in military history. The effective surrenders of Romania and Bulgaria left the Russians with a front that was 425 miles long, stretching from the Hungarian border to the Aegean Sea.

'The proposal to save the Balkans from communism could never have been made good by a "soft underbelly" invasion, for Churchill himself had already cleared the way for the success of Tito … [who] had been firmly ensconced in Yugoslavia with British aid long before Italy itself was conquered.'

General Albert C. Wedemeyer

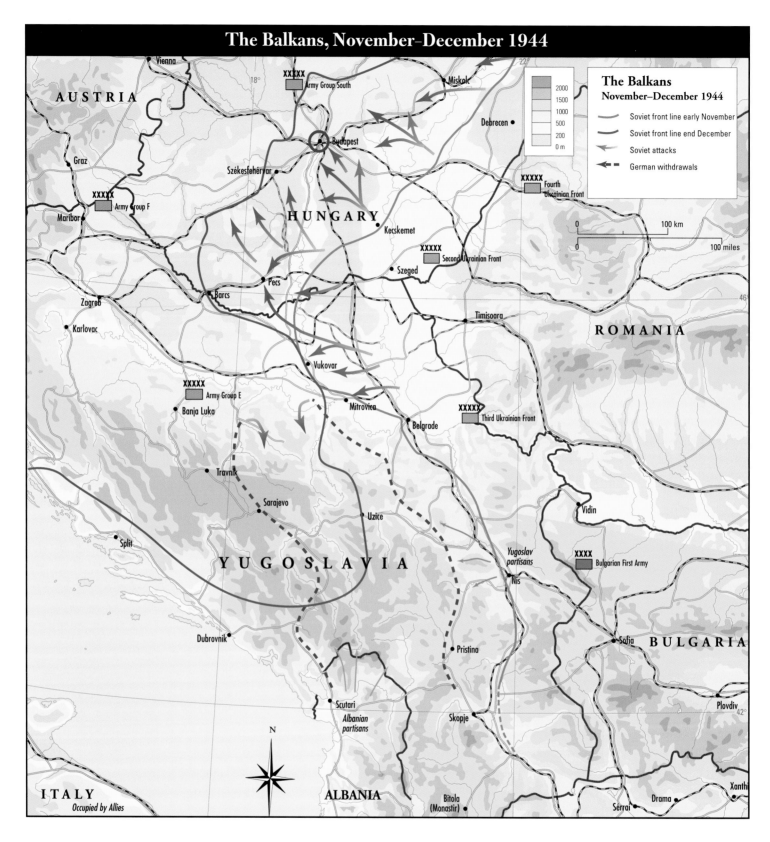

The Balkans, November–December 1944

The Balkans
November–December 1944

Soviet front line early November
Soviet front line end December
Soviet attacks
German withdrawals

The Germans were now forced to reorganize to meet the threat posed along this immense extent of front, and it was obvious that one of the solutions to the problem was to withdraw from Greece. The decision to do this was helped, oddly, by the failure of an Allied plan to assist Tito's Partisans to push into Serbia so that they might link up with the Red Army. Air attacks against communications links, aimed at blocking the routes by which German forces might leave Greece and southern Yugoslavia so as to block the Partisans, caused confusion when the Partisans failed to make anything like the progress

Left: Bulgarian troops set up defensive positions, awaiting the arrival of Soviet units. The machine gun is a World War I vintage Schwarzlose MG05, originally made for the Austro-Hungarian Army. Although old by 1944, it was tough and reliable, and still a viable combat weapon.

Opposite: The Soviet advances during mid- to late 1944 succeeded in driving the Germans from most of their positions in the Balkans. Belgrade was liberated on 31 August 1944, although fighting with German units remaining in Yugoslavia continued until the very end of the war, while the advance in Hungary culminated with the encirclement, and then capture, of Budapest after several weeks of hard fighting.

anticipated. Hitler and his generals reached the conclusion that the air attacks must be designed to trap German units in Greece, so that they could not be redeployed.

Hungary

Events in Romania led to considerable concern in Hungary as to the future. Romania and Bulgaria had been fierce rivals in the interwar period, with a number of territorial disputes arising from the Versailles settlements causing tension. The threat now presented by the Russians persuaded the Hungarian Army that it should launch an attack into Romania, which it did on 5 September 1944. The Soviets responded by turning more of their units towards Hungary. This in turn prompted panic in Budapest, and on 7 September, the government announced that unless the Germans sent the equivalent of five Panzer divisions to defend the country, the Hungarian government would be forced to act in its own interests, a clear indication that following a path similar to Romania and Bulgaria was imminent. Sufficient German forces were available to meet the demand from those pulling back from Romania. Hitler was concerned that the Hungarians would be unconvinced by the level of support that they were receiving if the Germans fell back any further, and ordered a halt to the retreat. This would have left the

Above: A jubilant Bulgarian leads the celebrations welcoming the Red Army into the outskirts of Sofia. The Bulgarians had become increasingly uncomfortable with their alliance with the Germans, and although they had not been at war with the USSR, this had not prevented the Russians from declaring war; rapid political manoeuvring saw the Bulgarians denounce their allies and declare war upon them within a matter of days in September 1944.

Germans in a highly disadvantageous position, and representations that withdrawal to a line some 40 miles west of the Muresul (as had been planned) would be far more sensible were accepted. The relative slowness of the Soviet moves towards the border (caused by increasing reliability problems with trucks and armour that needed attention after hard going over the previous weeks) meant that this vacillation was not as immediately problematic as it might have been.

As 2nd Ukrainian Front made its way forward, orders reached it from the high command that it was to carry out three separate attacks – one was to target Budapest, the second Debrecen and Miskolc, while the third was to head for Debrecen as well. The plan was too ambitious, since the Russians were having supply difficulties (Romanian railways were of a totally different gauge to Soviet rail lines, forcing greater reliance upon lorries). The second of the planned attacks, by Sixth Guards Tank Army from Oradea to Debrecen, began on 6 October, but was checked by the Germans, who then counter-attacked. A massive tank battle saw three Soviet corps cut off and destroyed, but although this was a dramatic success, it could not be regarded as anything other than a postponement of ultimate Soviet success.

On the day that the counter-attack at Debrecen began (10 October), other elements of the Red Army came within 10 miles of Belgrade, and as it became clear that the position there was untenable, the decision to evacuate the Yugoslav capital was taken; by this time, the folly of leaving German troops in Greece for a moment longer had been recognized, and the Germans began to withdraw from the country.

Greece

For nearly three years, the Germans had been confronted by a Greek resistance movement made up of communist and pro-royalist groupings, each subdivided into groups and factions. The movement was complicated by the fact that all of these groups greatly mistrusted one another. While there may have been mistrust amongst the pro-communist and pro-royalist factions towards other members of their group, there was outright enmity between the two generic factions. The only thing more certain than the fact that the Greek royalists and communists detested one another to the point of open hostilities being likely was that their hatred of the Germans would be sufficient to prevent them from embarking upon a civil war before the German occupation ended. As the Germans retreated, the situation collapsed as royalists and communists turned on one another.

On 12 October 1944, British troops landed in Greece, with the intention of assisting the exiled government to return to power. They found themselves present at the start of a bitter civil war. Although Greece was completely liberated by 4 November 1944, fighting would continue for some years as the two sides struggled to gain the upper hand until the royalists triumphed in 1948.

Budapest and Vienna

The increased risk of Soviet intervention in Hungary had alarmed the government in Budapest considerably, prompting its demand for at least five Panzer divisions to assist

Left: An Albanian farmer looks on as a British soldier searches a German prisoner. While taking control in Albania was a smooth operation, the British occupation of Greece faced far more difficulties from the warring Greek factions than it did from the Germans, most of whom had been withdrawn before the British landed.

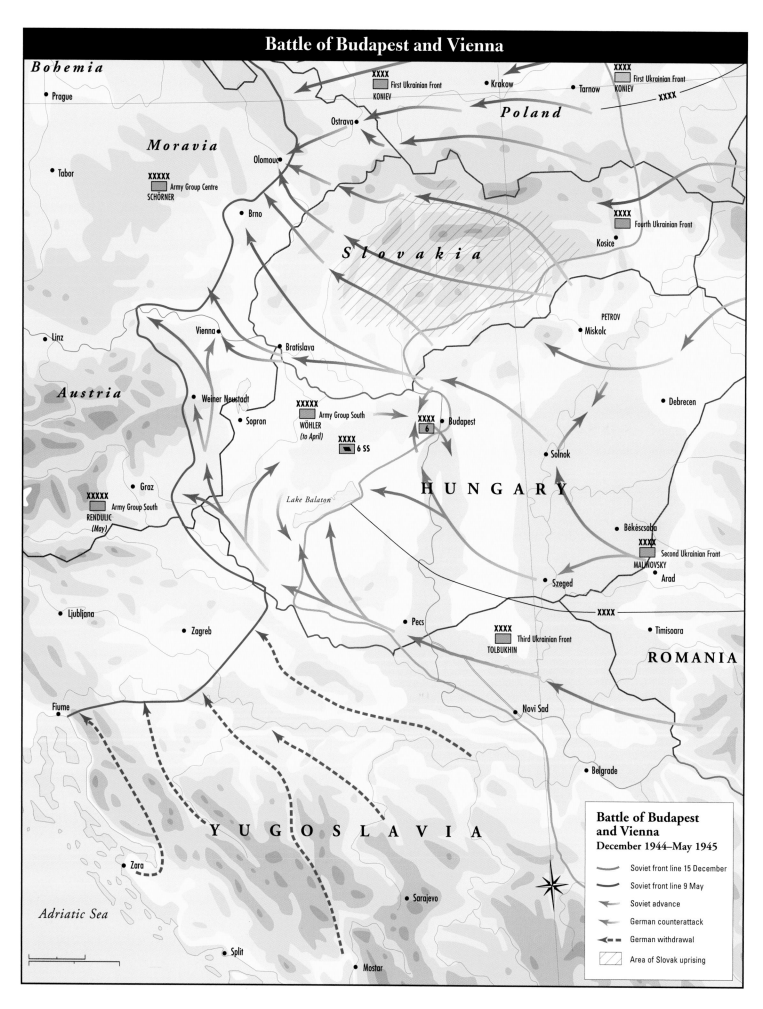

Battle of Budapest and Vienna

Bohemia

- Prague

Poland

XXXX First Ukrainian Front
KONIEV

- Krakow

- Tarnow

XXXX First Ukrainian Front
KONIEV

XXXX

- Ostrava

Moravia

- Tabor

XXXXX Army Group Centre
SCHÖRNER

- Olomouc

- Brno

Slovakia

XXXX Fourth Ukrainian Front

- Kosice

PETROV

- Miskolc

- Linz

- Vienna

- Bratislava

Austria

- Weiner Neustadt

- Sopron

XXXXX Army Group South
WÖHLER
(to April)

XXXX 6 SS

XXXX 6 Budapest

- Debrecen

- Solnok

H U N G A R Y

Lake Balaton

- Graz

XXXXX Army Group South
RENDULIC
(May)

- Békéscsaba

XXXX Second Ukrainian Front
MALINOVSKY

- Arad

- Ljubljana

- Zagreb

- Pecs

XXXX

- Szeged

XXXX Third Ukrainian Front
TOLBUKHIN

- Timisoara

R O M A N I A

- Fiume

- Novi Sad

- Belgrade

Y U G O S L A V I A

- Zara

Adriatic Sea

- Sarajevo

Battle of Budapest and Vienna
December 1944–May 1945

— Soviet front line 15 December
— Soviet front line 9 May
← Soviet advance
← German counterattack
◄‑‑ German withdrawal
▨ Area of Slovak uprising

- Split

- Mostar

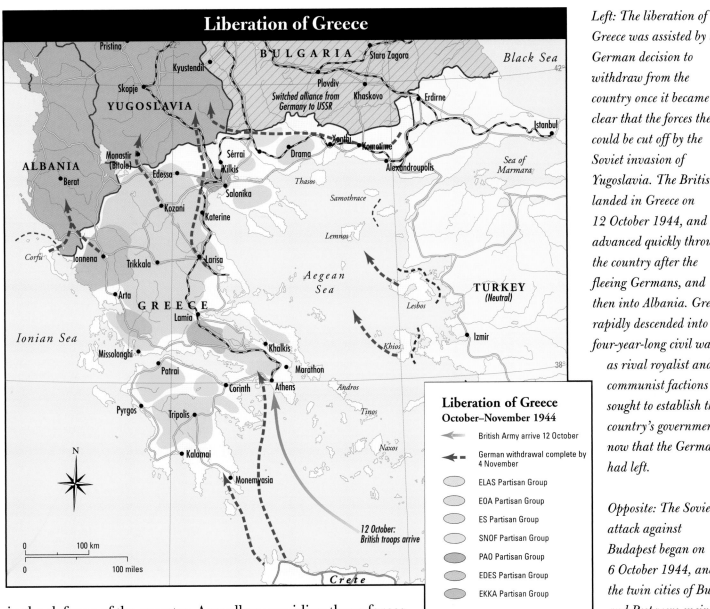

Liberation of Greece

Liberation of Greece
October–November 1944

→ British Army arrive 12 October

⇠ German withdrawal complete by 4 November

ELAS Partisan Group

EOA Partisan Group

ES Partisan Group

SNOF Partisan Group

PAO Partisan Group

EDES Partisan Group

EKKA Partisan Group

12 October:
British troops arrive

Left: The liberation of Greece was assisted by the German decision to withdraw from the country once it became clear that the forces there could be cut off by the Soviet invasion of Yugoslavia. The British landed in Greece on 12 October 1944, and advanced quickly through the country after the fleeing Germans, and then into Albania. Greece rapidly descended into a four-year-long civil war as rival royalist and communist factions sought to establish the country's government now that the Germans had left.

Opposite: The Soviet attack against Budapest began on 6 October 1944, and the twin cities of Buda and Pest were encircled on 24 December. The layout of Pest meant that it was easy to defend, and it took until 12 January 1945 until the Germans were dislodged from the city. Buda was equally difficult to take, and the Russians were forced to advance street by street until the Germans surrendered on 13 February. The Russians then moved on to Vienna, which fell on 13 April 1945 after a week's fierce fighting.

in the defence of the country. As well as providing those forces, Hitler tried to encourage the Hungarian leader, Admiral Horthy, by promising to give Hungary those parts of Romania that it claimed as its territory. This was popular with the Hungarian population in general, since nationalist sentiments towards the Romanians were high. Horthy was not convinced, however, wondering exactly how Hitler proposed to overturn the disasters that were now enveloping his forces. Horthy opened secret negotiations with the Russians, prior to the offensive of 6 October 1944. While the attack against Debrecen ran into serious difficulties, the Soviet approach to Budapest was easier. Within three days, Soviet forces were less than 70 miles away from Budapest, causing panic in the capital.

Horthy's lack of resolution in dealing with the Russians persuaded Hitler that a change in leadership was required in Budapest, and a team of SS commandos, led by Otto Skorzeny, kidnapped Horthy's son in an attempt to stiffen the Hungarian leader's resolve. Horthy stepped down instead, and the pro-Nazi Ferenc Szálasi was installed in his place on 16 October. Although German success in slowing the Soviet advance may have demonstrated that the Germans were not beaten yet, it did not mark anything like a turning point. The Russian advance resumed, and by the end of the month, Russian tanks were within 50 miles of Budapest.

General Malinovsky asked for five days to prepare his 2nd Ukrainian Front for the attack against Budapest, but was ordered to attack immediately by Stalin. The assault moved slowly, being joined by 3rd Ukrainian Front as it went. The twin cities were duly surrounded by Christmas 1944, as 2nd and 3rd Ukrainian Fronts linked up.

The Russians dealt with Pest first, but the layout of the city – large, easily fortified factories and streets that were difficult for tanks to operate in – meant that the task of an attacking force was extremely difficult. As it became clear that moving down the streets of the city was to invite certain death, the Russians took a brutally simple approach. They advanced one building at a time, blasting the defenders out with artillery and tank fire, with bitter hand-to-hand fighting characterizing the attack. Finally, on 12 January 1945, Soviet forces reached the city's racecourse. This had been used to fly supplies in to the Germans, and its loss meant that the defenders could not hold out for much longer, and they surrendered on 18 January. Buda was equally difficult to take, since its topography meant that the streets were narrow passages up cliffs and hills, hard going for any attacker. The Soviets pushed in to the city from 20 January, but although many of the Hungarian troops defending the city either surrendered or defected, the Hungarian Arrow Cross youth movement provided hundreds of fanatical boys willing to fight against the Soviet attackers. This opposition, in which youths used their knowledge of the city to outflank the Russians, sniping at them or launching small-scale attacks, forced the Russians to adopt another methodical approach. The Soviets brought up assault guns, and forced their way through the streets by the simple expedient of destroying any building that stood in their way. By 12 February, it was clear that resistance was hopeless, and around 16,000 German troops attempted to break out. They were trapped in the Lipotmezo valley the next day and annihilated on 14 February. By this time, Buda had fallen. The German escape attempt meant that organized resistance collapsed, and the remaining defenders surrendered at 10:00 on 13 February 1945.

By 23 March, the Germans had taken up positions to the west of Lake Balaton, but it was clear that they were in serious difficulties, and 3rd Ukrainian Front took the key road junction in the Bakony Forest. This meant that the Germans would be forced to move along the shore of the lake to withdraw, and left them in danger of imminent encirclement. It became clear to General Hermann Balck (commanding the once-more rebuilt Sixth Army) that his troops were beginning to lose their will to

GENERAL DRAÇA MIHAILOVIÇ

Mihailoviç was a Yugoslav Army officer, in charge of the Operations Bureau of the General Staff when the Germans invaded in 1941. He left Belgrade for Serbia after the defeat, and established the Çetniks, a small resistance group that immediately gained recognition in Britain and then the USSR and America. However, it soon became clear that the Çetniks were far more opposed to communism than to Nazism, and this prompted the collapse of efforts to link Tito's Partisans and the Çetnik movement in 1941.

Fighting between the two parties left the Partisans victorious, and Mihailoviç decided to alter his strategy. He abandoned fighting the Germans in the hope that they would destroy Tito and the Partisans, and this soon evolved into a policy of collaboration with the Nazis. By careful management of the information sent back to London, Mihailoviç managed to conceal this fact for a while; once the Allies discovered his collaboration, they switched their support to Tito. Devoid of support, Mihailoviç was unable to sustain operations, and his treachery guaranteed that he had no place in the post-war government; instead, he was tried for treason and executed in 1946.

Left: Partisans crowd around the corpses of dead Çetniks. The Çetniks and Partisans loathed one another, and the picture demonstrates the depth of feeling of the Partisans. This contempt was in many ways understandable, since the Çetniks had collaborated with the Germans in an attempt to ensure the destruction of the Partisans, abandoning their supposed role as a resistance organization seeking to free Yugoslavia.

fight, and wished to withdraw as quickly as possible to avoid being encircled. Balck reported this to Berlin, causing consternation, but his comments were accurate. The Russians launched the final phase of their operations in Hungary on 24 March, and within the space of four days had reached the Austrian border, with the Hungarian troops under German command beginning to desert. The Russians reached Vienna on 7 April, and although fighting continued for the next six days, there was little danger of the battle turning into another Stalingrad or Budapest. Resistance in the rest of Austria continued until early May, when the majority of German forces surrendered not to the Russians, but to Patton's US Third Army, which had entered Austria some days before.

The Last Act

The last major activity in the Balkans came in Yugoslavia. The Soviets entered the country on 11 October 1944, and their arrival prompted the collapse of German resistance in Belgrade. As the Partisans and the Red Army approached, the Germans carried out a fighting withdrawal, the futility of remaining in the city to be wiped out being obvious. By the end of 1944, Serbia, Montenegro, Macedonia and much of Bosnia had been liberated, with the Germans on the back foot everywhere else in the country.

The dramatic changes in Yugoslavia were demonstrated on 7 March 1945, when Tito formed a provisional government, in which he included some members of the exiled royalist administration (although he was to leave them there for as short a time as possible before replacing them). The final act in the Balkans came, appropriately enough, on 8 May 1945, when Zagreb was liberated at around the time that the full German surrender was signed. A few isolated pockets of German resistance continued to fight for another week, but were overcome. The war in the Balkans was over.

Victory at Sea

From late 1942, the war at sea against Germany was dominated by the struggle against the U-boats, with relatively little in the way of surface action taking place. The struggle beneath the waves of the Atlantic was crucial to the outcome of the war, and the bland alphanumeric descriptions of some convoys across the ocean now stand alongside more familiar names of battles as a testament to the defeat of the Third Reich in this environment.

On 19 December 1942, convoy ONS154, made up of 45 ships escorted by Royal Navy Escort Group C1, set sail. The escort group was inexperienced, and had not been given the opportunity to work up on an exercise before leaving. In addition to this, in an attempt to direct the convoy away from appalling weather in the North Atlantic, the convoy was given a course that took it straight into the jaws of two U-boat groups totalling 20 boats. The first sighting of ONS154 was made by *U-154* on 26 December, and the first attack came that night, when *U-356* made two runs through the convoy sinking four ships. *U-356* was sunk by the escorts, but this was to be their only success. The following day, *U-225* sank a tanker, then on the 28th, a total of 13 U-boats closed in on the convoy. At least five got amongst the ships, and within the space of two hours, nine vessels had been sent to the bottom. Relief came on 31 December, with the arrival of the destroyer HMS *Fame*, but it was quite clear that the Germans had won this particular battle – 14 ships had been sunk for the loss of just one U-boat.

As the climax of the battle of ONS154 was being reached, convoy TM1 set sail from Trinidad, heading for Gibraltar. It consisted of nine oil tankers, and was protected by the rather weak escort of four ships. Bletchley Park's signals intercepts located a group of six submarines patrolling between the Azores and Madeira, clearly lying in wait for convoys such as TM1. The U-boat group was unaware of the convoy's approach, but *U-514* spotted it on 3 January 1943.

Late that evening, *U-125* attacked and fatally damaged the tanker *British Vigilance*, and although contact with the convoy was lost as *U-125* made good its escape, an inspired piece of planning by Admiral Dönitz meant that TM1 was not allowed to evade the

Opposite: The crew of a Royal Navy destroyer watch the explosion of a depth charge rolled from the stern of the vessel on top of a suspected U-boat contact. The seaman bending forwards in the foreground of the picture is preparing another depth charge for use.

*Right: Between January
1942 and February
1943, the advantage in
the Battle of the Atlantic
swung between the Allies
and the Germans, with
the U-boats enjoying
considerable success at the
start and end of this
period. However, as the
air gap between
Newfoundland,
Greenland, Iceland and
Britain was closed by the
provision of long-range
aircraft, the German
advantage began to ebb
away, never to be
regained.*

Battle of the Atlantic IV
January 1942–February 1943

— Change and operational control UK to US, August 1942

— Extent of air escort cover

- - UK escort stations to July 1942

☐ Major convoy routes

• Allied merchant ships sunk by U-boats

⚓ U-boats sunk

▨ Territory under Allied control

▨ Territory under Axis control

☐ Neutral territory

clutches of the submarines. Another group of U-boats was placed across the last known course of TM1 just in case the convoy was continuing in the same direction. It was. On 8 January, *U-381* made contact, and four more submarines were sent to join in. That night, *U-436* sank two tankers before being damaged by the escorts, *U-552* crippled two more ships and an hour later, *U-442* sank another. Over the next three days, the pack managed to sink 77 per cent of the convoy, along with another vessel sailing independently, but which was unlucky enough to blunder into the way of the pack.

Casablanca

The events of ONS154 and TM1 gave Churchill and Roosevelt much to discuss when they met at Casablanca on 14 January 1943, in the pleasing afterglow of Operation Torch. Although the landings in North Africa had been an outstanding success, there was little doubt that the Battle of the Atlantic was going less well.

The conference went smoothly, and it was agreed, to the irritation of the Anglophobe Admiral Ernest King (the US Navy Chief of Staff), that the Atlantic should be reinforced. Churchill told Roosevelt that to win the battle, 65 escorts, a dozen escort aircraft carriers and as many B-24 Liberators (to be used as long-range anti-submarine aircraft) as possible were required. While agreement was reached, it took time to deploy these resources, and the struggle between the convoys and the submarines remained of major concern.

There were some good points for the Allies in early 1943, since appalling weather in the Atlantic meant that the U-boats found it extremely difficult to locate convoys. Worldwide shipping losses were reduced to 261,000 tons. While the loss of TM1 was a serious blow, only one North Atlantic convoy – HX222 – was attacked, and lost only one ship. This respite was short-lived, however, since on 29 January, convoy HX224 was sighted and once a wolf pack of submarines had been formed over the course of the next three days, three ships were sunk. In return, a Coastal Command Flying Fortress sank *U-265*. A survivor from

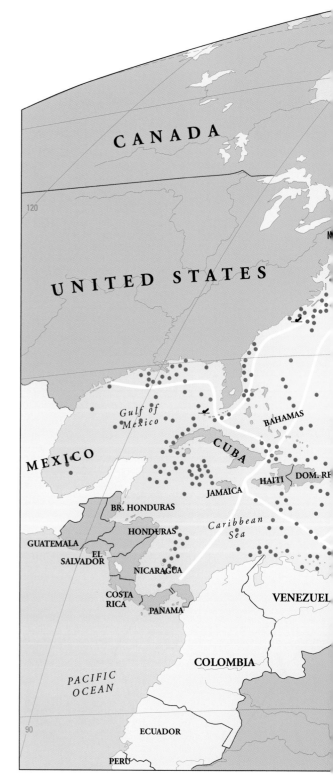

one of the merchantmen was rescued by a U-boat, and revealed that another convoy, SC118, was following on the same route. As a result of this a pack of 20 U-boats was formed for use against SC118.

On the morning of 4 February, the wolf pack closed in. The first action came when the destroyer *Vimy*, under Lieutenant-Commander Richard Stannard VC, sank *U-187*. By

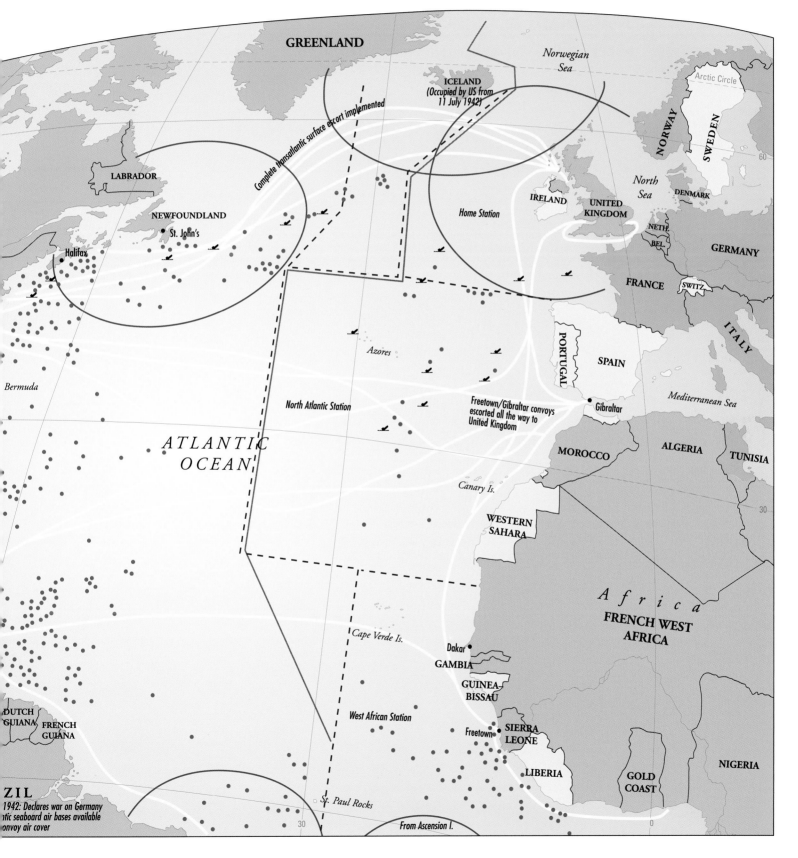

'Dominating all our power to carry on the war, or even keep ourselves alive, lay our mastery of the ocean routes and the free approach and entry to our ports.'

Winston Churchill on the Battle of the Atlantic

the afternoon five U-boats were in contact with the convoy. While heavy air cover prevented attacks on the 5th, on 6/7 February, the U-boats struck, *U-402* sinking six ships in four hours. Air cover returned at daylight, and a Fortress from 220 Squadron sank *U-624*, while *U-609* was sunk by the Free French corvette *Lobelia*. However, on the night of the 7th, *U-402* sank a seventh victim. When the battle was broken off on 9 February, SC118 had lost 13 ships, while three U-boats had been sunk and another four seriously damaged. This was one of the hardest fights of the battle so far.

For Admiral Sir Max Horton, the worrying aspect of the battle was that the losses had been inflicted despite an unusually large escort (including five destroyers). However, while the British were worrying over the losses to SC118, Admiral Dönitz – who was appointed head of the German Navy at the end of January – was equally concerned with the losses and damage inflicted upon his submarines. While it may not have appeared to be the case at the time, it was obvious that while the Germans had the upper hand, they were not having things all their own way, and were concerned about the possible effects of effective Allied convoying.

For the Allies, matters got worse when convoy ON166 was attacked by 21 U-boats on 21 February. The initial attack went badly – *U-225* was sunk, then next day, *U-606* was also lost, mainly as a result of an incorrectly sealed conning tower hatch. The crew managed to get the submarine to the surface, where it was rammed by the USCG cutter *Campbell*. The submarine stayed afloat long enough for the survivors to stand on deck eating sausage and drinking champagne while awaiting rescue; one of the crew, perhaps emboldened by the drink, took the opportunity to punch the unpopular first lieutenant. Despite the experience of the escort group, 14 ships, or 22.2 per cent of the convoy, were sunk. Only the skill of the escorts prevented a worse fate from befalling the convoy, and it was evident that the battle was reaching a peak.

The Height of Battle

For the Allies, the crisis point came with attacks on four successive convoys – SC121, HX228, SC122 and HX229. On the night of 6/7 March, *U-566* and *U-230* made contact with SC121, sinking one merchantman. A Force 10 gale the next day caused contact to be lost, but it was soon regained. Over the course of the next three days, 12 more ships were sunk.

The havoc caused by the wolf packs led to HX228 being ordered to evade to the south, but the instruction was intercepted by the Germans and a pack sent in against this convoy as well. On

SUBMARINE TECHNOLOGY

Perhaps the most critical element of the Battle of the Atlantic was technological development, particularly in the area of anti-submarine warfare. When the war broke out, the British relied almost entirely upon ASDIC (or sonar) to detect submerged U-boats, but had failed to appreciate that the Germans preferred to attack on the surface at night, and would only fire their torpedoes from beneath the waves if there was no other alternative. This was overcome by the use of radar mounted on escort vessels, while the employment of patrol aircraft forced the Germans to submerge for long periods to avoid being depth-charged.

This led to experiments to improve the endurance of a submarine operating underwater, and led most notably to the *Schnorchel* (Snorkel), a device which, as the name suggests, allowed the submarine to take on air for the operation of its diesel engines while beneath the waves. Although this proved a reasonably effective means of improving the submarine's endurance, the Germans were not satisfied, and began development of closed-cycle engines that could operate without the need for *Schnorchel*. However, the war ended before these could be brought into full service.

10 March, HX228 was spotted by *U-336*. HX228, unlike SC121, was exceptionally well escorted by four destroyers, five corvettes and the American Carrier Support Group TU 24.4.1 (also known as Escort Group 6). This contained the escort carrier USS *Bogue* and two destroyers. The weather prevented *Bogue* from flying her aircraft to begin with, which meant that she could not play a part in the convoy's defence.

The battle began when *U-336* was located and driven off. *U-444* remained in contact and guided in *U-221* which sank two ships. Within a few hours, *U-336* (again), *U-86*, *U-406* and *U-757* had also joined in, sinking two more ships. One of the victims was the *Brant County*, carrying munitions. The explosion that ripped the merchantman apart also damaged *U-757*. It was at this point that the battle turned against the U-boats. HMS *Harvester* sighted *U-444* on the surface and attacked. The submarine submerged, but was forced to surface by depth charge attack and *Harvester* rammed her. As the two hit, the submarine scraped along *Harvester*'s keel, and became wedged under the propellers. *U-444* broke free, and remained afloat, only to be rammed again and sunk by the French corvette *Aconit*.

During the morning, *Harvester*'s damaged propellers stopped, *U-432* spotted the stricken ship, and sank her. *Aconit* saw the smoke from the sinking *Harvester*, and hurried to the scene. *Aconit* obtained an ASDIC contact, and depth-charged *U-432*. The submarine surfaced, and was finished off by ramming. On 12 March, *Bogue* was able to launch aircraft, and the U-boats stayed submerged. The arrival of aircraft from RAF Coastal Command to cover the convoy made it too dangerous for further attacks, and the U-boats withdrew. The battle ended with four merchantmen and one destroyer lost, with two U-boats sunk and two seriously damaged.

The Climax

While SC121 and HX228 were fierce battles, they were relatively minor compared to those involving SC122 and HX229. SC122 left New York on 5 March, covered by a US Navy destroyer, a frigate, five corvettes and an armed trawler. HX229 left on 8 March, accompanied by Escort Group B4.

Eight U-boats were deployed against SC122, followed by a newly formed pack of 18 more. Another 11 boats were sent after HX229. After problems caused by the weather, the eight-boat pack (Group Raubgraf) was guided in by *U-653* on 16 March, not against SC122, which had been driven past the group by a gale, but HX229. Three ships were

Above: U-boat crew members monitor the instrumentation above their positions. The U-boats offered a cramped and unpleasant working environment for their crews, who either baked in tropical conditions or froze in arctic temperatures, depending upon where their vessels were operating.

sunk that night; the following morning, five more were sent to the bottom. The 18-boat group (Stürmer) arrived on the scene on the 17th, by which point SC122 had arrived in the area, providing the wolf packs with a host of targets. This caused considerable confusion at U-boat HQ, but gave the submarines unprecedented opportunities. *U-338* sank four ships from SC122, then accounted for a fifth later in the day. Two more of HX229's ships went down at lunchtime, and it appeared that the convoy was absolutely at the mercy of the pack. The losses already sustained were serious enough, but complete disaster was prevented by the intervention of RAF Coastal Command.

Two Liberators, flying from Northern Ireland, arrived over SC122 on 17 March, and kept the U-boats underwater for the course of the day. Another Liberator covered HX229, and had a busy time, depth-charging *U-221* and *U-608*, then attacking another, unidentified, boat with machine guns and cannon once its depth charges had been expended.

Two merchantmen were lost from HX229 while air cover changed over, and during the night SC122 lost two more ships. After this, though, the two convoys lost just three more ships. Heavy air escort forced a dozen U-boats to break off.

Above: A U-boat crew bring a torpedo aboard. After reliability problems at the start of the war, German torpedoes were improved and the U-boats swiftly became a serious threat to Allied shipping.

On the afternoon of the 18th, the destroyer HMS *Highlander* found HX229. By the morning of 19 March, no U-boat had been accounted for by the escorts or air cover, but by this stage the convoys had entered the Western Approaches, where the shorter-range aircraft of Coastal Command were able to join in the fray, sinking *U-384* which was still tailing the convoys.

The arrival of the convoys was met with some gloom, since it appeared that the Germans were winning in the Atlantic. In fact, the provision of air cover had demonstrated the way forward once resources were available to bring enough aircraft to bear.

Finding the Answers

It appeared that, despite all the efforts of the long-range aircraft, convoys and escort groups, the Germans were about to disrupt the vital ocean link between Britain and America. In the first 20 days of March 1943, 95 ships were sunk. These apparently devastating losses all took place against the backdrop of a conference where Allied military leaders discussed their next step. If they could not find the answer, they feared, they might lose the war.

The conference began badly, when Admiral King made clear that he was going to withdraw all US Navy forces from the transatlantic convoy routes (this was just one of the reasons why Churchill later argued that the war at sea would have been simplified if someone had shot the admiral). The solution that arose to this problem was to create a Canadian operational command in the Northwest Atlantic, which would come into operation in May. While King's news was unwelcome, it was in fact less important than it might have been. The conference was presented with evidence from Professor Patrick Blackett of Coastal Command's Operational Research Section that analysis showed that a force of 200 very long-range (VLR) aircraft might be expected to save at least 400 ships. At this point, Coastal Command had just two operational squadrons of Liberators, with a third forming. The Canadians had formed squadrons of crews that had no aircraft, while every single American Liberator not in the Pacific Theatre was employed on bombing duties. King had subverted the Casablanca agreement that 80 VLR aircraft should be assigned to the Atlantic by keeping his VLR aircraft in the Pacific. An irritated Roosevelt overruled King and ordered that 60 US Navy Liberators would be used to cover the North Atlantic; the Army Air Force would deploy another 75 for anti-submarine duties. In addition deliveries to the RAF would be expedited, so that 120 Liberators would be available.

The first 20 aircraft from this massive increase in resources arrived in the last 10 days of March. The Atlantic air gap, where convoys had been forced to brave the mid-Atlantic beyond the range of any friendly aircraft, had finally been plugged.

Raised Spirits

The British Admiralty also began to understand the reason for the apparent failure of convoys at about this time as well, and realized that matters were not as bad as they first appeared. With the introduction of convoys, sailings by individual merchantmen had been reduced to such a low level that the U-boats had very few targets to attack. This meant that they were bound to attack convoys; given that there were so few German submarines engaged on independent operations, the size of the attacking packs was bound to be larger, enabling them to cause serious problems for the escorts.

The answer to the problem was air cover. U-boats had to submerge or risk being depth-bombed – thus imposing all the difficulties of trying to operate underwater for long periods that faced submarines of that era. The Admiralty began to appreciate that increasing numbers of VLR aircraft helped but using escort carriers was also of considerable assistance. On reflection, the view that the great German victory against SC122 and HX229 was the harbinger of doom was quite misleading. Pessimism was misplaced, and it was the jubilation of the Germans at the apparent breakthrough achieved against the four unfortunate convoys that was premature.

These suspicions were confirmed in April 1943. Between 4 and 7 April, an attack was mounted against HX231, a convoy of 61 merchant ships. The escort group beat off a

'[The Tirpitz] exercises a vague general fear, and menaces all parts at once. It appears and disappears, causing immediate reactions and perturbation on the other side. If she were only crippled and rendered unseaworthy the entire naval situation throughout the world would be altered…'

Winston Churchill, January 1943

'The submarine weapon has not been broken by the setbacks of 1943. On the contrary, it has become stronger. In 1944 ... we shall smash Britain's supply.'

Admiral Karl Dönitz, December 1943

concerted attack. *U-635* was sunk by a frigate, while an RAF Liberator accounted for *U-632*. Between them, the air and sea escorts damaged another four boats so badly that they had to head for home. For three ships sunk, this was hardly a decent return for the Germans. By May the U-boats found that the situation had turned dramatically for the worse.

ONS5

On 29 April, convoy ONS5 was sighted by the U-boats, and ran into the largest pack of the war, made up of 40 submarines. A ship was sunk that night, but the battle was truly joined on 4 May. Six ships were sent to the bottom. The next day, a Royal Canadian Air Force Canso (the Canadian version of the Catalina flying boat) sank *U-630*. That evening, the U-boats sank seven ships, but the escorts damaged an equal number of submarines. Then, on 5 May, *U-192* was sunk by HMS *Pink* and all attacks attempted on the convoy were driven off. After dark, four merchantmen were sunk, but now the escorts gained the upper hand. HMS *Loosestrife* pounded *U-638* with depth charges and destroyed it. HMS *Vidette* located *U-125*, and used her Hedgehog anti-submarine mortar to good effect, blowing the submarine to pieces. *U-531* was sunk by HMS *Oribi* after ramming. Fog descended, but the sloop HMS *Pelican* used her radar to find *U-438* and sank that as well. At 09:15 on 6 May, U-boat HQ called off the attack. Twelve merchant ships had been sunk, but crucially, the U-boats had suffered a devastating blow. No escorts were lost or seriously damaged, but eight U-boats had been sunk in the course of the action – two having collided – while another five were so seriously damaged that they limped home in a sorry state.

On 16 May, another convoy, HX237, made port having lost just three merchantmen, with the escorts having accounted for *U-89*, *U-186* and *U-456*, while *U-402* and *U-223* were seriously damaged. A pack had been decimated for little return.

Victory

The next convoy of note was SC130. The convoy ran into fog, and might have collided with an iceberg but for the alertness and quick thinking of the crew of the destroyer *Vidette*, which warned the shipping away. The next problem came in the form of a pack of 33 U-boats, which were detected by signals intercepts. Nothing was found on 18 May, but next evening HMS *Duncan* ran down a radio bearing just in time to see a U-boat submerging. At first light, RAF Liberators arrived and reported submarines all around the convoy. In the course of the next 12 hours, the U-boats made repeated attempts to force their way into the convoy, but ran into the escorts. *U-381* made one too many attempts, and was pounced upon by the *Duncan* and HMS *Snowflake*, which sank the submarine with a fusillade of Hedgehog bombs. Later that day, the 1st Escort Group joined the convoy, adding a cutter and three frigates to the convoy's strength. This did not deter the U-boats, which attacked again. *U-954* was despatched by a Liberator, *U-209* was sunk by the escorts, and an RAF Lockheed Hudson joined the fray to sink *U-273*. On the 20th, *U-258* was surprised on the surface by another Liberator, and went to the bottom as a result of the attack. On 21 May, the pack was called off. The submarines had not sunk a single ship from SC130; indeed they had not fired a single torpedo. In return five U-boats had been lost. The blow struck against the U-boats had been immense, not least because as well as their reduced success in convoy operations, the Germans had found their submarines under attack elsewhere.

While VLR aircraft were enjoying successes, shorter-range ones operating in the Bay of Biscay were gaining the upper hand there as well. The introduction of centrimetric radar meant that it was impossible for the radar warning equipment fitted to U-boats to warn of the approach of an aircraft, and U-boats had to cross the bay submerged both by day and at night. However, they also needed to charge their batteries. This meant surfacing, and Dönitz's answer to the air threat was to order U-boats to shoot it out with attacking aircraft with their anti-aircraft guns. However, while this increased the problems for the attacking aircraft, it left the submarines dangerously exposed.

Seven U-boats fell to Coastal Command in May as a result of operations in the bay, and it was clear that the tide of battle had turned. Despite the gloomy predictions of early March 1943, the Admiralty had in fact managed to acquire almost all the tools it needed to defeat the U-boats by this time. The only element missing was air power. When they became available in sufficient numbers, aircraft completed the 'tool kit' needed. The balance turned in favour of the Allies. By 22 May 1943, 31 U-boats had been lost. On 24 May, Dönitz radioed his surviving commanders, and commented on how difficult their struggle had become. He told them that only U-boats could fight the enemy offensively, and that the hopes of the Third Reich rested upon them. The same day, Dönitz ordered his U-boats out of the North Atlantic to the easier waters south of the Azores. Despite his exhortations, he knew something that his determined crews did not. They had lost.

The End of the U-Boats
The victory against the U-boats was the result of three years and nine months of incessant struggle, but although the Germans had to all intents and purposes lost the Battle of the Atlantic, this could not be taken for granted. The Allies now had to maintain their dominance over the U-boats until the end of the war, recognizing that the Germans would continue to try to regain the upper hand.

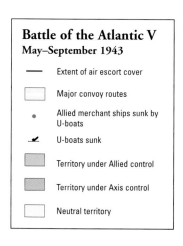

Battle of the Atlantic V
May–September 1943

— Extent of air escort cover

☐ Major convoy routes

• Allied merchant ships sunk by U-boats

⌐ U-boats sunk

▨ Territory under Allied control

▨ Territory under Axis control

☐ Neutral territory

The technological war between submarine and aircraft therefore intensified, as the Germans endeavoured to produce submarines that could operate effectively underwater, and as the Allies attempted to make sure that their technology was adequate to prevent such boats from becoming a serious threat. The Germans succeeded in developing the first true submarine – one that could operate effectively while submerged – but it was already too late. Continuing attacks by Allied forces meant that the U-boats were always at a disadvantage, no matter how innovative the technology employed.

Designs for Type XXI and Type XXIII submarines, able to use new engine technology that allowed underwater operations for a considerable time, appeared in June 1943. Earlier U-boat types had often been limited to single-figure speeds underwater, the Type XXI and Type XXIII could offer submerged performance of 18 knots for 90 minutes, or 12–14 knots for anything up to 10 hours. This was a promising development, but there was a major problem. Production of the new designs would be slow, and it meant that the first two Type XXIs would only be ready at the end of 1944, with mass production beginning in 1945, for full service entry in 1946. Naval production was reorganized by placing it under Albert Speer, the head of the Ministry of Arms and Munitions. Innovative solutions to production problems, such as building the submarines in sections and then assembling them at the coast, were introduced, and these methods meant that the first Type XXI was able to enter full service in 1944, with sufficient numbers in service by the autumn of that year for a proper campaign to be mounted.

While this was a good plan, in practice things were different. Disruption caused by Allied bombing had a profound impact. Production was delayed by at least four weeks after the air raids on Hamburg during August, and it was obvious that further attacks would destroy the submarine-building plan before it had even begun. A new factory near was built near Bremen but this took time to construct. In addition, getting the submarines from the factory to

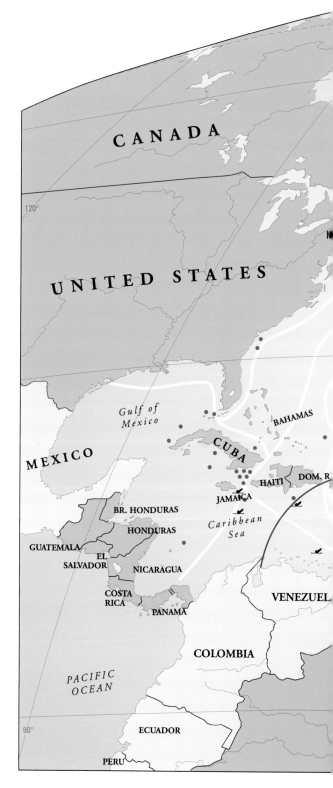

the coast demanded the use of the canal network, which was under severe attack by late 1944. On 23 September 1944, an RAF attack on the Dortmund–Ems canal aqueduct caused such damage that traffic was brought to a complete standstill, and it was not repaired until November, whereupon the RAF came back and destroyed it again. The submarine plan would have been a cause of considerable concern had it been

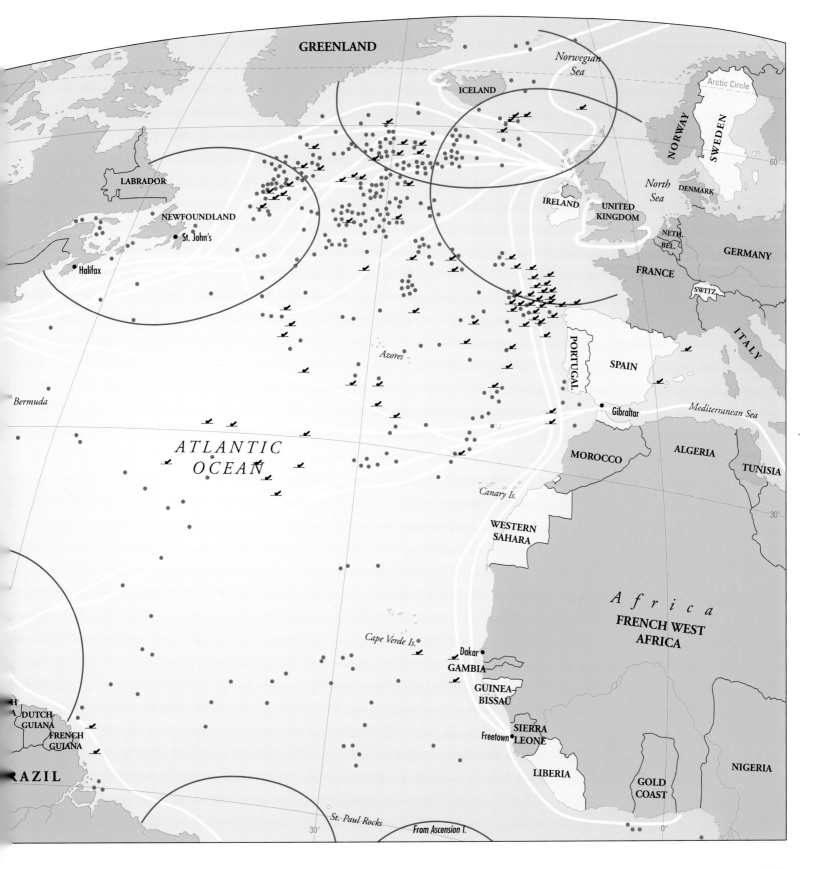

Right: Tirpitz *is seen at anchor in July 1942. Although* Tirpitz *remained moored in Norwegian fjords rather than putting to sea for much of the war, the ship remained a serious potential threat to Allied shipping. After being damaged in an attack by midget submarines and then in air attacks by the Royal Navy,* Tirpitz *was finally sunk by Lancaster bombers from the Royal Air Force in 1944.*

implemented by a nation not facing the sort of difficulties confronting the Germans in 1943 and 1944, but would in fact never be able to deliver the boats required to achieve the effect needed. Once the Allies had the lead over the German submarine arm, they were never to surrender it.

Surface Action

In stark contrast to the U-boat arm, the German surface fleet came nowhere near to influencing the outcome of the war, and after the sinking of the *Bismarck* in 1941, Germany's ships posed little threat to the overall superiority of the Allies. However, the threat posed by the remaining surface ships was a concern to the British, particularly in the shape of the battleship *Tirpitz* and the battlecruiser *Scharnhorst*. The two ships remained a nuisance, since although safely bottled up in harbour, it was clear that they could attack both North Atlantic and Arctic convoys.

The *Tirpitz* problem exercised the Admiralty for some time, until it was decided that the way to deal with the threat was through an attack by midget submarines, known as

X-craft. These carried two large charges of explosive that could be placed on the sea bed directly beneath their targets. Six X-craft were towed towards their target by full-sized submarines on 11 September 1943, but two slipped their tow lines *en route,* and another broke down when the time came to part company with the towing submarine. The remaining three entered the fjord in which *Tirpitz* lay on 20 September, and after a difficult journey in past obstacles and torpedo nets, two laid their charges beneath the battleship. The two craft to make it through (the fate of the third is uncertain) may have managed to lay their charges, but they could not escape. The crews were forced to scuttle their craft and were taken prisoner; both submarine commanders (Lieutenant Godfrey Place and Lieutenant Donald Cameron) were awarded the Victoria Cross for their daring.

When the charges detonated, the *Tirpitz* was badly rocked by the force of the explosions. All her engines were put out of action, the rudder and steering gear were badly damaged, and several hundred tons of water poured into the ship. While this guaranteed that *Tirpitz* would be unable to put to sea for months, the fact that the ship remained afloat meant that the Allies could not be certain as to whether the attack had succeeded.

While the Admiralty worried about the threat still posed by *Scharnhorst* and *Tirpitz,* convoys to Murmansk were suspended. They were resumed in November, and within a matter of weeks, the *Scharnhorst* sought to intervene. However, this was not without design on the part of the British admiral Sir Bruce Fraser, the Commander-in-Chief Home Fleet. Fraser reasoned that the Germans would wish to attack a convoy on the Murmansk run, after the suspension of the summer, and would sortie in force against the next convoy to appear. Fraser therefore ensured that the convoy was unusually well protected, sending 14 destroyers, two sloops and a minesweeper to escort the chosen convoy, coded JW55B.

German reconnaissance aircraft located convoy JW55B on 22 December 1943, and *Scharnhorst* and its accompanying destroyer flotilla left harbour during the late afternoon of Christmas Eve, under the command of Rear Admiral Erich Bey. Bey was completely unaware of the fact that as well as the escort vessels, a further naval squadron was in distant support, in the form of Admiral Fraser's flagship – the battleship HMS *Duke of York* – plus the cruisers *Jamaica, Norfolk, Sheffield* and *Belfast,* along with their attending destroyers.

Although the Germans became aware that there was a possibility of heavy surface escort to the convoy, the *Scharnhorst* did not turn about and head for safety. Unfortunately for Bey, the British knew of his location, while he had no idea of where anything other than the convoy was. At about 09:20 on 26 December, *Scharnhorst* was engaged by *Norfolk, Sheffield* and *Belfast,* and Bey turned away, without exploiting the superiority of his ship's guns. The cruisers raced to cut off *Scharnhorst's* approach to the convoy, and succeeded in forcing Bey to turn straight into the direction from which Fraser was approaching. At 16:17, the radar on *Duke of York* located *Scharnhorst,* and at 16:50, *Duke of York* and *Jamaica* opened fire, while the other cruisers closed in and attacked from the other beam.

At 18:20, *Scharnhorst* was forced to slow as the result of a shell hit, and by 19:30 she was dead in the water, with the ship's secondary armament firing defiantly at the out-of-range British ships. *Scharnhorst* was sent to the bottom by torpedoes from Fraser's destroyers at 19:45, and only 36 members of her crew were rescued.

The *Tirpitz*, meanwhile, had remained firmly in port, and the Admiralty sought to sink her by air attack. The first raid, launched by carrier aircraft in April 1944, achieved six hits on the ship in the first assault, followed by another eight in the second wave. Other raids had to be aborted because of bad weather until, on 17 July 1944, a further attack was made. All went well until the attacking formation was spotted and a smokescreen thrown over *Tirpitz*. Unable to see their target, the British aircraft could not bomb accurately, and only one bomb fell near to the ship. A further set of raids was mounted in August, under the codename Goodwood (a confusing choice, since this was the name of an operation by the Army in Normandy at around the same time). Goodwood I and II were unsuccessful, but Goodwood III succeeded in hitting *Tirpitz* with two bombs – however, one failed to explode, and the damage caused by the other was minimal.

At this point, the RAF intervened in proceedings. Lancaster bombers from 9 and 617 Squadrons launched two attacks, one from a temporary base in Russia (and which was unsuccessful) and the second from Britain. On this raid, on 12 November 1944, at least two of 28 5443kg (12,000lb) 'Tallboy' bombs found their mark, and the ship capsized, causing fearful casualties amongst her crew, many of whom were trapped in the hull. 617 Squadron later returned to finish off the *Lützow* in the same manner, although as the ship settled on the bottom of the fjord with her decks still above water, the Royal Navy (jokingly) claimed that the RAF could not claim that the ship was sunk, merely that her lower decks were awash.

The End

While still firmly on the back foot, the U-boats did not have a completely disastrous 1944, in that the number of sightings made by enemy aircraft declined. This owed much to the widespread use of the *Schnorchel*, a development that worried the Allies. The Allied anti-submarine effort had been based upon the fact that the most effective way to counter the U-boats was to locate them when surfaced and sink them, or to force them to stay underwater for long periods, with a concomitant reduction in the amount of time that the submarine could remain at sea. The use of the *Schnorchel* meant that the air threat was considerably reduced. Furthermore, the U-boats were unable to make use of their radio when submerged, which denied an array of information to Bletchley Park, and prevented location of submarines by signals interception.

From September 1944, though, the U-boats were switched towards British home waters, reducing the risk to Atlantic convoys still further. They began to make their presence felt from November. Casualties caused by the U-boats rose, and the fact that the boats were operating in inshore waters meant that it was extremely difficult to use anti-submarine detection devices properly, since these were optimized for ocean-going warfare. Fortunately for the Allies, even this offensive was a case of too little too late. The Type XXI and Type XXIII submarines caused no little concern with their underwater speed and endurance, and caused some losses; but it was too late for them to make a difference. Everywhere, the German Army was in full retreat, and the Allies were approaching the Third Reich on two fronts. The end of the war was fast approaching. While U-boat operations from Norway continued as late as April 1945, there was nothing these submarines could do to alter the outcome of the war, which had become inevitable. In British home waters, 10 merchant ships and two escort vessels were sunk, in exchange for 23 U-boats. Allied bombing reduced the U-boat bases to chaos, forcing the U-boats to head for the Baltic. There, the last five weeks of the war saw the

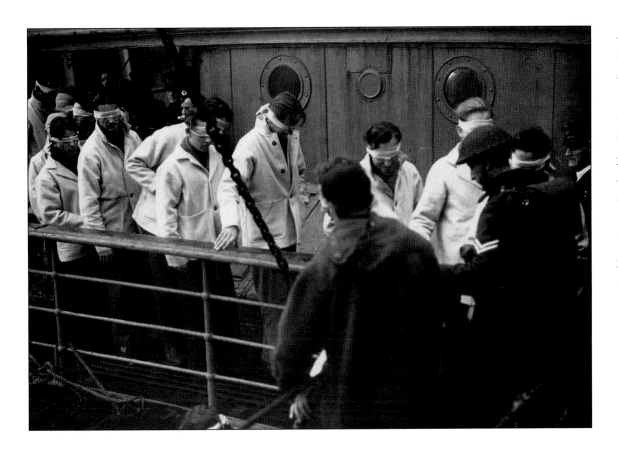

Left: Survivors from the Scharnhorst *are brought ashore at a British port. The prisoners have been blindfolded for their movement through the port facilities to make sure that security is not compromised. The Germans are all dressed in British clothing, provided to replace their own garments lost when their ship went down.*

destruction of 83 U-boats by a whole variety of aircraft. Coastal Command strike wings were joined by rocket-firing Typhoons from 2nd Tactical Air Force, wreaking havoc amongst the unfortunate submarines. The last U-boat to be lost was *U-320*, so badly damaged by a Catalina on 7 May that it sank two days later.

The Final Reckoning

Despite initial hopes, the U-boats did not win the war for Germany, for a variety of reasons. Most notably, there were never enough U-boats available to make the sort of concerted effort against the convoys that was needed. The work of the large wolf packs towards the height of the campaign in later 1942 and early 1943 demonstrated what could have been achieved had enough been available to swamp the defences of the convoys. By the time sufficient U-boats were available, the British had dramatically increased the number of escort vessels and managed to combine these with long-range aircraft that kept the U-boats underwater, or attacked them as they transited the Bay of Biscay. The entry of the United States into the war meant that the shipbuilding might of the US yards would always make it impossible for the Germans to sink more ships than the Allies could build – while inflicting so much attrition on Allied shipping that Britain would be starved into submission was a possibility before American war production had geared up, once the US shipyards were at their wartime capacity, this was a forlorn hope.

Improved technology, more escorts and the combination of air and sea power meant that the task of the U-boat crews became ever more difficult, culminating in defeat when the defences became just too strong. As for the surface fleet, the Germans caused some embarrassment in the early phases of the war, but once the *Bismarck* was sunk, their surface units presented very little threat. While the key battles of the war were largely fought on land after 1943, winning the Battle of the Atlantic was a fundamental requirement for Allied victory, the value of which was fully seen in 1945.

The Air War Against Germany

World War II was marked by the rise of air power, particularly the employment of strategic bombing against the enemy homeland. Bombing did not bring the Third Reich to its knees as the interwar theorists might have suggested that it would, but was an important factor in the final defeat of Nazi Germany nonetheless.

Although much of the Royal Air Force's doctrine in the 1920s and 1930s had been based around the effectiveness of strategic bombing, when war broke out in 1939, RAF Bomber Command was ill-prepared to mount a bombing offensive against Germany. As well as the practical difficulties of sending bomber aircraft against Germany, concerns over whether attacks on towns would provoke German retaliation led to a situation where Bomber Command was used for raids against military targets. When early attacks met with disaster upon being intercepted by fighters, it was decided to move over to night raids instead. As bombers were not equipped with anything other than the most rudimentary navigation equipment, and since most RAF navigators had not been trained to navigate with any accuracy at night, it was hardly surprising that bombing raids were ineffective.

A further obstacle to effective bombing came from the fact that the bomb loads of the RAF's main aircraft of the day (the Wellington, Whitley and Hampden) were not large enough to achieve an adequate concentration of bombs to the extent required for a truly effective offensive; nor did they have the fuel supplies to carry them to the heart of the Reich. This had been appreciated in the run-up to the war, and orders for 'heavy' bombers had been placed. The first of these designs, the Short Stirling, arrived in service in August 1940, and was followed by the Avro Manchester and Handley Page Halifax. By early 1941 there were three squadrons of each type, but this was still not regarded as being a sufficient level to launch the sort of bombing offensive that could have a major impact on Germany. The older bombers had to bear the brunt of the offensive, which

Opposite: RAF armourers prepare a 1000lb bomb for loading onto the Lancaster bomber in the background. The Lancaster was the most versatile bomber in the European theatre of war, and the mainstay of the RAF's bombing effort from 1943 onwards.

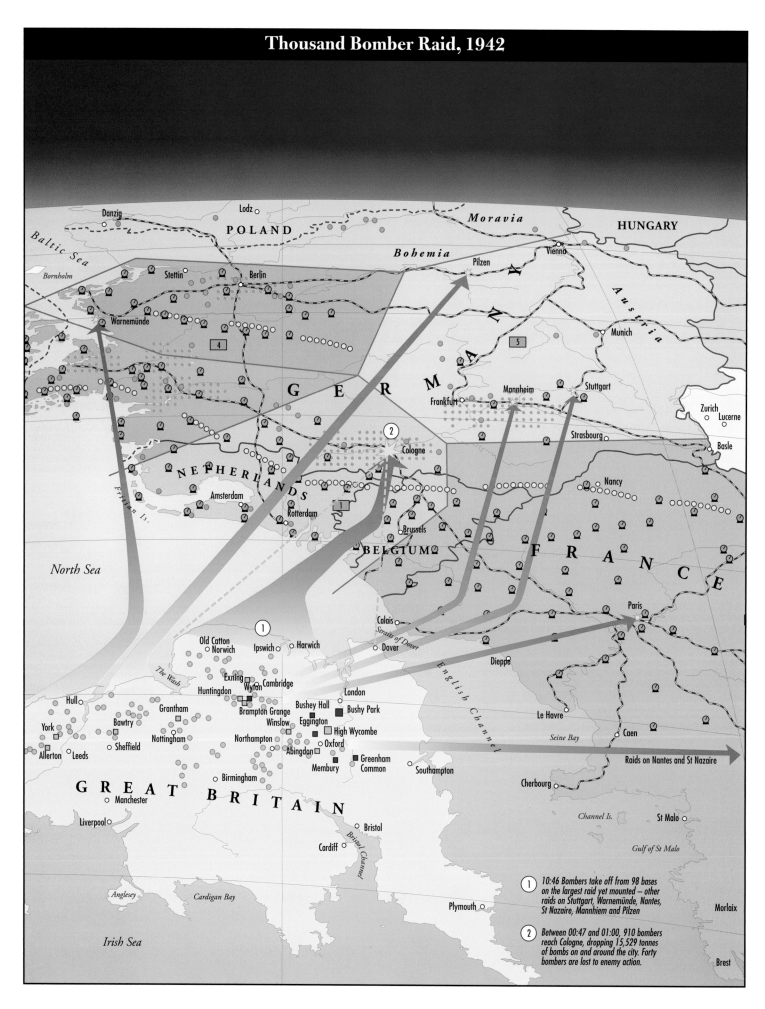

Thousand Bomber Raid, 1942

① 10:46 Bombers take off from 98 bases on the largest raid yet mounted – other raids on Stuttgart, Warnemünde, Nantes, St Nazaire, Mannhiem and Pilzen

② Between 00:47 and 01:00, 910 bombers reach Cologne, dropping 15,529 tonnes of bombs on and around the city. Forty bombers are lost to enemy action.

Raids on Nantes and St Nazaire

meant that so-called fringe targets had to be attacked. To make matters worse, the Manchester's Rolls Royce Vulture engines proved to be appallingly unreliable – the disaster of losing an otherwise sound airframe from the front line was solved by replacing the two Vultures with four Rolls Royce Merlins, creating the Avro Lancaster; however, the redesign meant that the first squadron was unable to re-equip until the end of 1941.

The problems of accurately striking targets at night meant that Bomber Command turned to the notion of area bombing as the means to achieve the desired effect of destroying German industry, although this inevitably meant that entire German towns would be attacked, with the associated risks to civilians. This approach was beginning to be adopted by early 1942, when Air Marshal Sir Arthur Harris was appointed as the Air Officer Commanding-in-Chief of Bomber Command. Harris was a firm believer that area bombing would win the war, and if it was carried out on a sufficient scale, the employment of ground forces would not be necessary, since the Third Reich would be driven to its knees by air attack.

The Millennium Raids

The turning point for Bomber Command, from which point it developed into a key weapon of war, might be said to have arrived in mid-1942, when Harris sent over 1000 aircraft to bomb Cologne as part of Operation Millennium on the night of 30/31 May. The raid was launched mainly for propaganda purposes, with the aim of demonstrating that Bomber Command could carry out devastating attacks against major targets. To make the tally of aircraft up to the important 1000 figure, Harris was compelled to draw upon training units, a risk that paid off when the attacking force lost just 40 aircraft. The attack on Cologne was followed up by two more on Essen and Bremen, but it was quite evident that the disruption caused to Bomber Command's training schedule by such large raids, along with the subsequent maintenance demands, outweighed the value of the attacks, even if they made for effective public relations opportunities.

Opposite: Shortly after assuming command of RAF Bomber Command, Air Chief Marshal Sir Arthur Harris launched three raids against Cologne, Essen and Bremen in which over 1000 bombers took part. To achieve this strength, Harris had to make use of aircraft from training squadrons, and it was to be some time before raids nearing this scale could be repeated.

Thousand Bomber Raid
30/31 May 1943

↗	Main RAF night attacks
□	Main Headquarters
▫	Group Headquarters
◉	Bomber Command airfields
✳	Targets bombed
—	Fighter Division boundary
▓	Fighter Division
◔	German radar station
●	German night fighter station
○○	Searchlight batteries
▣	Anti-aircraft batteries

Left: German flak gunners sprint for their 88mm anti-aircraft gun. German anti-aircraft defences were particularly strong, and took a heavy toll of bombers, particularly on daylight raids. However, it required a large number of anti-aircraft guns firing an even greater number of shells to guarantee a hit on a single bomber.

Harris was also more concerned about correcting the inaccuracy of bombing, and gave instructions that the development of navigation aids should be prioritized, to allow more aircraft to reach their intended target. Refinements to tactics so as to concentrate more aircraft over the target were also introduced, and had an almost immediate effect. However, one of the most significant contributions to improving the accuracy of bomber attacks was initially opposed by Harris. During the Blitz on Britain during the winter of 1940–41, German bombers had been guided to their destinations by a pathfinder force, which had marked the targets with special bombs. It was suggested that this would be a profitable line of approach for Bomber Command to adopt – a pathfinder force, equipped with target-marking bombs instead of conventional ordnance, could provide a clear indication of the aiming point for the main bomber stream following them. Harris was opposed to the plan on the grounds that he was not convinced that creating an elite force within Bomber Command was a good idea. However, he was overruled at a high level within the Air Staff, and on 15 August 1942, the Pathfinder Force (later to be designated as 8 Group) was formed under the command of Air Commodore Donald Bennett. By the end of 1942, the Pathfinder Force had begun to have an effect in terms of increasing the number of aircraft that located and bombed the correct target, while the a new radio navigation device for bombers, codenamed Oboe, had been installed in Mosquito light bombers, enabling them to navigate very precisely to their targets. Although Harris had improved the quality of his force immeasurably during the course of 1942, it was still not quite in a position to launch decisive attacks against Germany. However, by the end of the year, a further significant development had taken place. The US Army Air Force's first bomber units had arrived in Britain, enabling 'round-the-clock' bombing to commence. There were many trials and tribulations to be overcome in 1943, but the progressive development of the Allied bomber force into a major weapon

Right: A formation of B-17 Flying Fortresses drops its bombs over a target in Germany. The close formation was designed to allow the bombers to provide mutual fire support against enemy fighters, using their array of machine guns to stop the Germans from getting through. This proved to be an inadequate solution, however, and the provision of long-range escort fighters was needed to deal with German fighter attack.

of war gathered pace, and began to have a telling effect upon Germany, even if not quite in the manner envisaged by those who had proclaimed that victory could be brought about entirely by the application of bombing.

The 'Mighty Eighth'

With the agreement that the United States would follow a 'Germany first' policy, it was a logical step for American bombers to be sent to Britain. VIII Bomber Command was to be the UK-based bomber force, as part of the Eighth Air Force. The first elements, in the form of the command's staff, arrived in February 1942, led by Major-General Carl A. Spaatz, but it took until May before the first combat units arrived, flying in B-17 and B-24 bombers. The first operation was flown against Rouen on 17 August, escorted by RAF Spitfires, and was followed by another raid two days later. The use of escorts was contrary to American doctrine, which held that the heavy armament of the bombers would be enough to protect them from fighter attack, an idea that was to be severely tested over the next 12 months. The rest of 1942 was taken up with relatively short-range raids against targets in occupied Europe, with the intention of carrying out the first raids on Germany in 1943. By the end of the year, however, there were increasing concerns about German fighters – the German pilots had swiftly evolved tactics that enabled them to conduct highly effective frontal attacks against the bombers, exploiting the fact that the forward-firing armament of both the B-17 and B-24 was relatively light, relying upon single hand-held guns rather than power-operated gun turrets. Although it seemed that the notion of carrying out unescorted raids needed to be abandoned, the lack of fighters with sufficient range to accompany the bombers all the way to the target meant that there was no other alternative.

The Battle of the Ruhr

The policy of carrying out round-the-clock bombing of Germany was reaffirmed at the Casablanca Conference in 1943, with a directive being sent to Harris that he was to undertake a campaign that would lead to 'the progressive destruction of the German military, industrial and economic system' and which was also to reduce the morale of the German people so that 'their capacity for armed resistance is fatally weakened'. Harris chose to concentrate upon the latter aspect of the directive, which, he felt, was best served by area bombing, which as well as damaging and destroying German industrial centres had, in Harris' phrase, the effect of 'dehousing the German worker' with a concomitant reduction in his or her morale.

Harris duly set about increasing the tempo of the night offensive with an attack against the industrial cities of the Ruhr valley, in an assault that was to become known as the Battle of the Ruhr. The first operation was carried out on 5/6 March 1943 against Essen, marked by the first wide-scale use of Oboe to aid navigation. The aid was important, since the bomber crews were faced with the difficulty of finding their targets when confronted with the haze of pollution rising from the factories. The raids on the Ruhr continued for the next six weeks, culminating in one of the most famous air operations in history – Operation Chastise, which became far better known as the Dambusters raid.

The Dambusters

The choice of dams as a target for bombing had been raised prior to the war. It seemed fairly obvious that breaching the Ruhr valley dams would have several effects, both in

'It is true to say the heavy bomber did more than any other single weapon to win this War.'

Sir Arthur Harris, Despatch on War Operations, October 1945

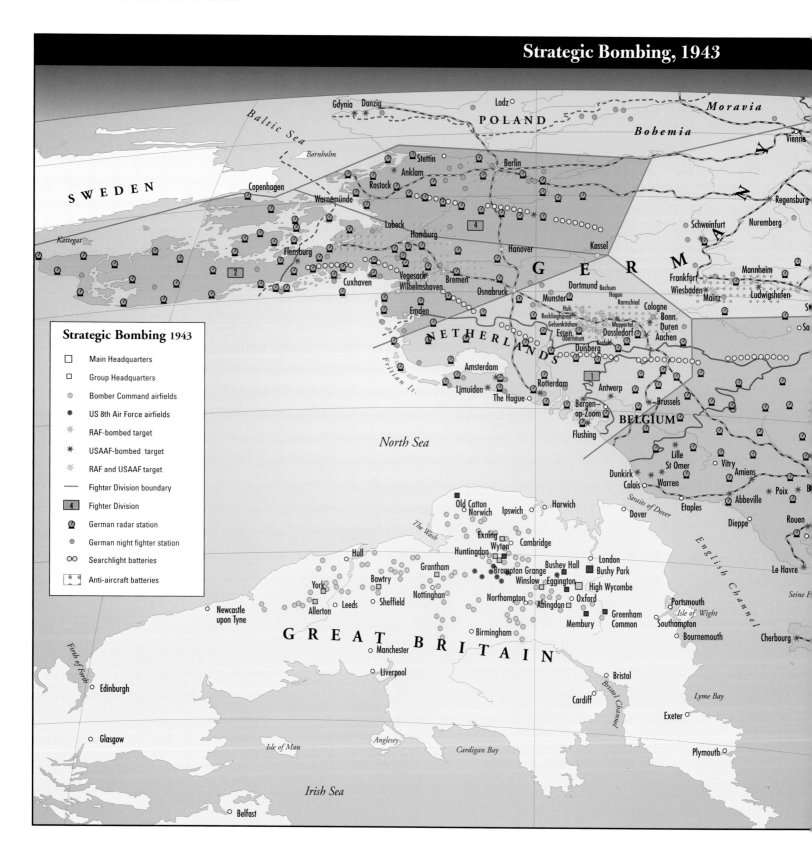

Strategic Bombing, 1943

Strategic Bombing 1943

☐ Main Headquarters
☐ Group Headquarters
● Bomber Command airfields
● US 8th Air Force airfields
✳ RAF-bombed target
✳ USAAF-bombed target
✳ RAF and USAAF target
— Fighter Division boundary
4 Fighter Division
⊕ German radar station
● German night fighter station
∞ Searchlight batteries
▦ Anti-aircraft batteries

terms of the sheer physical destruction caused by the release of millions of gallons of water, and the need to restore the dams to full working order before production in the area could restart.

The difficulty with targeting the dams lay in the fact that destroying them was far from simple. Bomb aiming was simply not accurate enough to deliver the required weight of explosive onto the dam to destroy it, while the use of torpedoes could be made impossible by installing netting that would prevent the weapons from striking the wall of

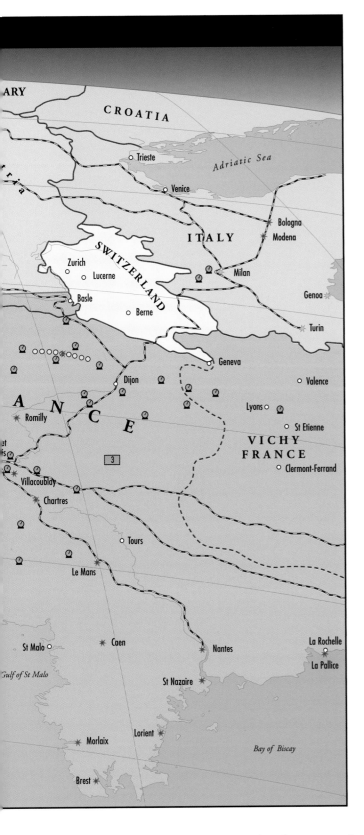

the dam. The solution came in a revolutionary idea from the scientist Barnes Wallis, who proposed a special bomb, to be dropped at low level to achieve the desired result. The idea behind the bomb was simple, but appeared at first glance to be slightly eccentric. Wallis worked out that to breach a dam, it was imperative that the bomb used detonate right against the wall, with the water held behind the dam being used to magnify the force of the explosion. To place the bomb exactly where required, Wallis hit upon the idea of bouncing the weapon across the surface of the lake; it would hit the wall, and because of the backspin applied to it, would sink to the bottom of the lake while remaining in close contact with the dam.

While Wallis was refining his design, a special RAF squadron, number 617, was formed under the command of Wing Commander Guy Gibson. Gibson's squadron undertook a great deal of low-level flying, and improvised a solution to both maintaining the required height of 60 feet above the water and dropping the bomb at the correct distance from the dams. The first problem was solved by using spotlights in the belly of the aircraft angled so the beams converged at 60 feet, while improvised bombsights made from nothing more advanced that a few pieces of wood with nails driven into them were devised to release the weapon accurately.

The raid was launched on the night of 16/17 May 1943, with 19 aircraft taking part. The Möhne and Eder dams were breached, and the Sorpe dam was hit. The destruction of the dams was achieved at high cost, with eight of the attacking force being lost, along with all but one of the 56 aircrew aboard. The raid caused considerable damage through flooding, but a massive German repair effort managed to minimize the effect of the attack on industrial output. Controversy over whether the raid was a success or not has been ongoing, although there is little doubt it provided a massive boost for British morale as the nature of the daring attacks became more widely known.

Left: From 1943 onwards, strategic bombing operations against Germany and targets in occupied territories were carried out by both day and night by the British and American bomber fleets. American operations were hampered by the lack of escort fighters until late in 1943, but once these were provided, they allowed effective operations against the German capital to be undertaken.

Above: German fire-fighters battle against the results of an RAF bombing raid against Cologne in 1943. In the area bombing campaign, great use was made of incendiary bombs to raze large sections of German cities to the ground, and there was often little that the German emergency services could do to quell the flames.

Hamburg

The Dambusters raid was followed by a more conventional attack as Harris turned his force against Hamburg, with the city being subjected to four attacks between 24/25 July and 3/4 August 1943. Harris chose the city as the target for a sustained attack given its importance to the German war effort, particularly submarine production. The attacks saw the use of a new device codenamed Window – which took the form of millions of thin tin-foil strips dropped from the attacking bombers, with the aim of jamming German radar sets by sending back thousands of spurious radar returns.

The first bombs began to fall on Hamburg just before 02:00 on 25 July, as the Pathfinder Force released a mixture of illuminators followed by 250lb target indicators to highlight the aiming point to the following waves of bombers. The leading aircraft unloaded incendiaries to set fires to the many timber buildings in Hamburg. As the emergency services rushed to put out the many small fires started, the next wave of aircraft dropped high explosives, bringing down buildings, shattering water mains and killing around 4000 rescue workers. The devastation caused by the first raid was immense, but was merely the start of the city's sufferings. On 27 July, Bomber Command returned, with over half of the bombs dropped being incendiaries. These quickly turned Hamburg into a vast fire, in which the air became superheated. To feed itself, the fire sucked in oxygen from around its outer edges, creating a massive and terrifying firestorm, carrying blazing timbers further into the city and causing yet more fires and beginning the process again – by the end of the raid, a massive conflagration had been started, and winds of up to 150mph ripped through the streets, causing huge casualties. Many civilians in air raid shelters were suffocated, while those who managed to escape had to brave the firestorm. Many leapt into nearby canals, the only way in which they could survive the fire raging around them. By the next morning, over 6000 acres of the city had been reduced to ashes, and still Harris was not finished. Another raid took place two days later, the bomber crews guided in by fires still alight from the previous attacks, and a second firestorm was caused. A final attack was then carried out, causing a third firestorm, despite the torrential rain that fell throughout the duration of the raid.

By the end of what came to be known as the Battle of Hamburg, over 60 per cent of the residential accommodation had been destroyed, and nearly 600 factories were knocked out. The German armaments minister, Albert Speer, feared that another six similar raids in succession would force Germany to surrender. However, despite the immense casualties caused, with over 41,000 killed and 37,000 severely wounded in the raid, Hamburg's manufacturing output recovered within six weeks. Bomber Command did not return, for the truth was that it simply could not sustain attacks of this nature, as it did not have the resources to do so. As his command recovered from its intensive efforts, Harris turned his thoughts to attacking Berlin, the most difficult target, with the aim of striking the decisive blow that would win the war.

The Daylight Offensive

While Harris was attacking Germany at night, the US Army Air Force increased the tempo of its operations, launching its first attack on Germany on 27 January 1943, attacking Wilhelmshaven. Experience in 1942 had shown the need for fighter escort, but

Left: The grisly aftermath of the raid on Dresden in 1945 – the remains of just some of the victims are piled up on a funeral pyre, ready for cremation. The scale of destruction wrought by the attack on Dresden demonstrated the level of lethal efficiency that Allied bombing could achieve, and raised serious doubts amongst some of the Allied leaders about the ethics of a campaign directed against cities.

Right: The Dambusters raid of 16/17 May 1943 was one of the most daring attacks of World War II, with the use of the famed 'bouncing bomb' to destroy two major German dams and inflict damage on two more. Losses from the raid were heavy, with eight aircraft out of nineteen failing to return.

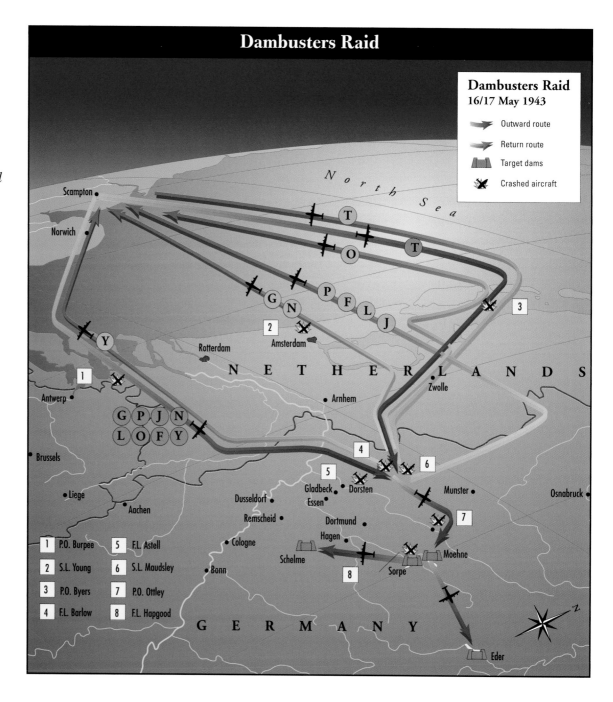

this was problematic as aircraft with adequate range to cover operations deep into Germany were not available. Although P-47 Thunderbolts carrying additional fuel in drop tanks could cover the bombers for much of their flight, the first major raid deep into Germany demonstrated how important fighter escorts were. Attacks against Regensburg and Schweinfurt on 17 August 1943 led to the loss of 59 bombers out of 200, which would be unsustainable if continued. The solution lay in the North American P-51 Mustang, a fighter originally designed for the RAF. Fitted with a Rolls Royce Merlin engine, the P-51 had a range of over 2000 miles when carrying external fuel tanks, and they made the difference almost as soon as they arrived in December 1943. The presence of escort fighters meant that it became possible to make the *Luftwaffe*'s fighter force one of the targets of the bombing campaign. By early 1944, the Eighth Air Force had begun to mount large-scale attacks against German targets, with the first visit to Berlin being made on 6 March 1944. By this point, Bomber Command's campaign against Berlin was drawing to a conclusion.

The Battle of Berlin

Harris was extremely confident that large-scale attacks against Berlin would paralyse the German war effort, and bring about a swift end to the war. As a result, Harris launched 16 major attacks against Berlin, beginning on the night of 18/19 November 1943. The city was an extremely difficult target, and the Battle of Berlin did not produce the results Harris had predicted. In the course of 9111 sorties against the capital, 587 aircraft were lost along with over 3500 aircrew killed or missing. Harris was forced to end the assault, but not before a disastrous raid on Nuremberg on 30/31 March 1944, in which over 100 bombers were lost as the *Luftwaffe* night-fighter force set about them. To Harris' intense irritation, he was ordered to turn his attention to bombing transportation targets in both Germany and France in support of the forthcoming invasion. His arguments that his crews would not be capable of attacking such targets were disproved when trial attacks ordered by the Air Staff demonstrated that his bombers were more than able to destroy railway lines and key transport nodes. Attention thus turned away from the bombing of German cities and to French and Belgian targets; before this occurred, the Americans attempted to inflict large-scale attrition on the *Luftwaffe* as part of its bombing campaign.

The Final Raids

From August 1944, the Americans began to carry out heavy attacks against the German oil industry, and a host of industrial targets across the Third Reich. The potency of the escort fighters meant that the Germans found it extremely difficult to inflict damaging levels of attrition on the bomber forces, while they sustained notable losses themselves as the battle escaped them. Although night fighters had more success at dealing with the RAF's attacks, these were increasing in efficacy – by early 1945, Bomber Command's level of accuracy was such that it was able to drop its bombs at night more accurately than the Americans could in daytime – a feat that no one would have thought possible just five years previously. The most controversial episode of the entire bombing campaign occurred in February 1945, with the British raid on Dresden. Huge numbers of casualties were caused by an extremely effective attack that devastated the city, and the effect of the raid was to highlight some of the serious ethical questions about targeting cities and, inevitably, their populations. Although there was never a policy of terror bombing of Germany, critics have subsequently argued that this was, in effect, what occurred. By April 1945, the number of viable targets for the bombers to strike had dwindled considerably. RAF bombers began to undertake daylight raids again, the threat of the *Luftwaffe* having all but disappeared as the German fighter force ran out of fuel. The RAF concluded its campaign with a raid on Hitler's mountain retreat at Berchtesgaden by 617 Squadron. As a sign of the dominance of the bombers over Germany, this was difficult to beat.

The bomber campaign against the Third Reich proved to be extremely costly and, after the war, controversial as the sheer scale of the casualties sustained during the course of the air assaults was appreciated. The fact that the Germans did not surrender as a direct result of the attacks has been taken as a sign that the campaign was a failure, but this is too simplistic a view. The bomber campaign tied up a substantial amount of manpower and resources, while disrupting production and diverting industrial output towards defensive weapons rather than items that could have been put to use on the Eastern or Western Fronts. While a controversial campaign, the air war against the Reich played its part in bringing down Hitler's regime.

The Liberation of France

The turn of the tide in favour of the Allied cause during late 1942 and early 1943 meant that it was inevitable that the Americans and British would have to consider an invasion of mainland Europe to drive German forces out of the occupied countries, and then to inflict a final defeat on the Third Reich. As well as the simple practical necessity of a land assault in Europe for the defeat of the Reich (despite the claims of air power proponents, strategic bombing did not appear to be about to win the war by itself), political considerations had to be taken into account.

Stalin had made no secret of the fact that he took the opening of a second front to be a sign of good faith from Britain and America, and although the assault on Italy could be said to represent just such a development, Stalin was not convinced that this demonstrated the full commitment of the Western Allies to relieving the burden on the Red Army (despite the fact that the invasion of Italy caused Hitler to withdraw units from the Battle of Kursk at a critical point to reinforce the wavering morale of his ally). In fact, there were few doubts on the Anglo-American side that an invasion of France was required to bring about the defeat of Nazi Germany. Just as in World War I, the decisive field of battle in the West would be France, not Italy or anywhere else, even if the pressure that could be applied from these areas would make a substantial contribution to the overall outcome of the war.

Early Notions

In fact, the Americans had been extremely keen on an invasion of France almost from the outset of their involvement in the war. While the United States could not present an immediate threat to the German position on mainland Europe in early 1942, this did not prevent them from making planning assumptions about how they could best assist in bringing about an early conclusion to the conflict. America was at a disadvantage to begin with, since its isolationist policy in the interwar period meant that its army was relatively small. Although the American Army was larger than those of many other nations, it would still take time to build up its strength before it could be pitted against an army the size of

Opposite: A young French woman joins the celebrations as Allied troops march through Paris, marking the liberation of the city after four years of German occupation.

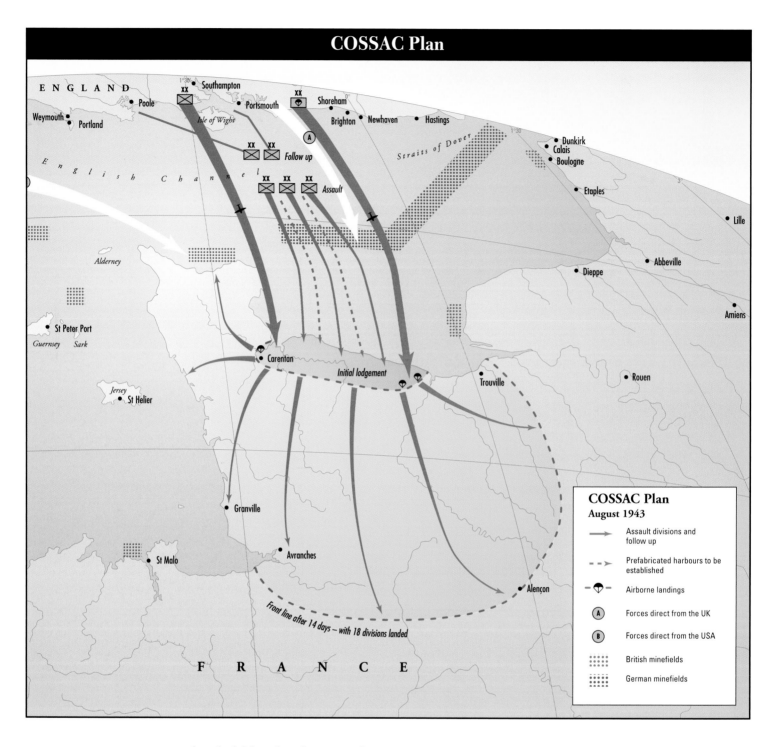

COSSAC Plan

Above: Planning for the invasion of France began in 1943, well before the appointment of General Eisenhower as Supreme Allied Commander. Major-General Morgan, appointed as chief of staff to the yet-to-be named commander, oversaw the development of the plan.

that held by the Germans in Europe. In addition, it was obvious that the demands of fighting both in Europe and the Pacific Theatre would have an effect on the pace of the build-up of American capabilities for intervening in the war against Germany. The Germans were not slow to recognize this fact, and came to the conclusion that it would not be until early 1943 that American troops could arrive in Britain, the only place from which an invasion to open a second front could be launched. It was therefore logical for the main German effort to remain on the Eastern Front, particularly since the Russians were at this point (early 1942) proving more difficult to break down than had at first been anticipated – Stalingrad and Kursk were yet to come.

While the main German effort would remain in the East, Hitler appreciated that it would be necessary to establish substantial defences along the coastline of occupied Europe to deal with any invasion attempt. Hitler formally recognized this in March 1942, issuing a directive ordering construction of an immense line of fortifications stretching from the Franco-Spanish border up to the North Cape in Norway. For reasons that are not altogether clear, Hitler was convinced that the British would attempt a landing in Norway as their first priority. While his rationale that the British would want to be in a position to protect their Arctic convoys from the depredations of U-boats had some merit, the dynamics of Allied decision-making clearly escaped him. There was little chance that the British or Americans would see Norway as an obvious point for invasion, given that it was so far away from the United Kingdom, with all the logistical problems that this would present in contrast to an attack on France. Nonetheless, Hitler gave instructions that the Norwegian coastline was to be given top priority in the construction of shore defences, and his instructions were carried out to the letter – by the end of 1943, Norway's coastline was the most heavily fortified in the world. The effort placed into building the Norwegian defences meant that the French coastline received relatively little attention. Construction work began at a comparatively leisurely pace, which meant that the defences at Dieppe were only partially completed when British and Canadian troops staged a landing there on 18 August 1942.

The Impact of Dieppe
The Dieppe raid failed, although it provided a great number of valuable lessons for the future. In response to the operation, Hitler issued another directive giving greater priority to the construction of fortifications along the French coast. However, while he instructed that the work should be undertaken quickly, those responsible for implementing the order were unconvinced. A major raid had been driven off with half-completed fortifications manned by inexperienced and over-age reservists, all of which

Left: General Eisenhower talks with an American soldier on a visit to pre-invasion manoeuvres. His deputy, Air Chief Marshal Tedder, is at the left of the picture (in the fur-lined jacket), while General Montgomery can just be seen over Eisenhower's shoulder.

Above: A Churchill tank sits forlornly on the beach at Dieppe after the disastrous raid there in 1942. Many lessons were learned from Dieppe, and the planning staffs took meticulous care to ensure that such scenes would not be repeated when the invasion itself took place.

implied that the pace of building did not need to be frenetic, as even half-finished fortifications would make it problematic for an invading force to break through.

This attitude had changed by autumn 1943. The landings in Tunisia, Sicily and Salerno demonstrated that the Allies were more than capable of carrying out successful amphibious operations. Hitler was moved to order the creation of a series of fortifications that would ensure that any invasion was defeated 'before, if possible, but at the latest upon the actual landing'.

COSSAC

Anglo-American invasion planning began after the meeting between Prime Minister Churchill, President Roosevelt and their Combined Chiefs of Staff at Casablanca in January 1943. Two months later, the Trident Conference in Washington laid down that the landings should take place on 1 May 1944 under the codename Overlord. Planning responsibility was given to the Chief of Staff to the Supreme Allied Commander (COSSAC), the British general Sir Frederick Morgan. Morgan's title was rather misleading, since no supreme commander had then been appointed. Undaunted, Morgan and his Anglo-American staff set about working out the details of an invasion.

The first task for COSSAC was to work out where the invasion should take place. Three locations in France appeared to offer the best choices – the Pas de Calais, Normandy and Brittany. The Pas de Calais had several advantages, most notably that it offered the shortest route across the Channel. However, the area's topography was far from ideal, and it was such an obvious area for assault that the Germans had begun to fortify the region with some vigour, a step that had not been missed by Anglo-American intelligence. Also, the exits from the beaches around the Pas de Calais were restricted, making it difficult to move armour and heavy equipment forward – landings would also have to be made on the Belgian coast or at the Seine estuary ports to allow such material to be landed. Finally, the Kentish ports were simply not big enough to accommodate the whole landing fleet, which would demand that some vessels sail from Portsmouth and Southampton – a journey of over 100 miles within range of German shore batteries.

Brittany enjoyed a brief period of favour amongst the American planners, on the grounds that it had good beaches for landing. As with the Pas de Calais, though, Brittany was rejected. First, it was clear that logistical difficulties presented by its being far to the west of the Low Countries, extending the supply lines as the Allies broke out and headed for Germany, were far from encouraging. In addition, the Royal Navy representatives on COSSAC were aghast at the thought of landing in Brittany. They pointed out that the weather on the Atlantic coast was often appalling (and when it was not appalling it was bad), and then went on to highlight the hazardous nature of the waters. Such strong reasons against using Brittany as the landing site meant that only Normandy was left.

That is not to say that Normandy was chosen by default – rather that the disadvantages of a Normandy landing were far less than those presented by the other choices. Once the location for the landings had been decided upon, more detailed preparations could be undertaken. The number of American troops arriving in England increased, and the training regime for all Allied soldiers in the United Kingdom became more intense as the men were prepared for the invasion. Landing craft were built, maps prepared and specialist tanks that could swim, clear mines or fire heavy demolition charges were constructed. By May 1944, there were over three million soldiers, sailors and airmen from Britain, America, Canada, New Zealand, Australia, Poland, France, Belgium, Norway, Holland and Czechoslovakia in England waiting for the instruction to launch an invasion.

By this time, COSSAC had a supreme commander to work for. On 7 December 1943, General Dwight D. Eisenhower was appointed Supreme Allied Commander for the invasion. One of his first tasks was to deal with the clashing egos of his subordinate commanders. As they included Bernard Montgomery and George S. Patton, this was a far from easy task. Montgomery in particular was to prove a regular source of anguish to Eisenhower, since it was quite evident that the British general thought that he should be in command of all operations in Europe after the landing (rather than just for the first phase) and made little effort to disguise this fact.

BRITISH VERSUS GERMAN TANKS

One of the most notable features of the war was the superiority enjoyed by German tanks on the Western Front, particularly over British tanks. While the Germans saw tanks as being ideal for fast, mobile all-arms warfare, the British showed signs of confusion over how to employ theirs. This meant that while the Germans developed a range of fast, heavily armed and well-protected tanks, the British went through a process which provided either relatively slow, heavily armoured but inadequately armed tanks or fast, lightly armed and lightly armoured vehicles that were no match for their opponents. By 1944, the main British tanks were the Cromwell and Churchill, joined by large numbers of American M4 Shermans.

Although the German Panther, Tiger and upgraded Panzer IV tanks were able to defeat their opponents in a one-on-one engagement, the numerical supremacy enjoyed by the Allies meant that they were often able to overwhelm the Germans by sheer weight of numbers.

Finally, by early June 1944, everything was ready. The invasion was planned to be launched on 5 June, but poor weather forced a postponement of 24 hours. Despite only slightly better weather the next day, Eisenhower issued the orders for the invasion. During the night of 5/6 June 1944, over 250,000 men launched one of the largest and most complex military operations the world has ever seen – securing a foothold in Normandy as the first element in bringing about the defeat of Hitler's forces in the West.

The Other Side of the Hill

Hitler's rising concern about the defences in France led to him sending Field Marshal Erwin Rommel (one of his favourite generals) to inspect the so-called Atlantic Wall.

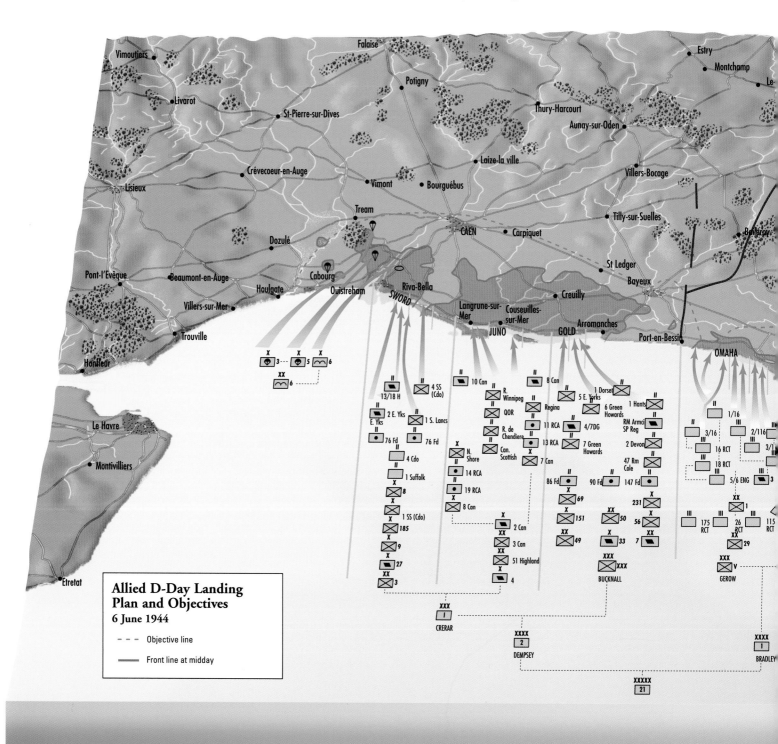

Allied D-Day Landing Plan and Objectives
6 June 1944

- - - Objective line

——— Front line at midday

Rommel was also appointed commander of Army Group B, with operational command over the German forces in northern France, on 1 January 1944. By this point, it was clear that the Allies would be in a position to launch an invasion in the near future, although no one knew exactly when, or even more importantly just where, it would be.

Rommel was immediately in dispute with the Commander-in-Chief West, Field Marshal Gerd von Rundstedt, over the way in which the coast should be defended against an invasion. Von Rundstedt wished to allow the Allies to land before attacking them with six panzer divisions as they were establishing their beachhead. Rommel was unconvinced – having experienced the effect of air attack on armoured columns in his time commanding the *Afrika Korps*, he was convinced that the panzers would be

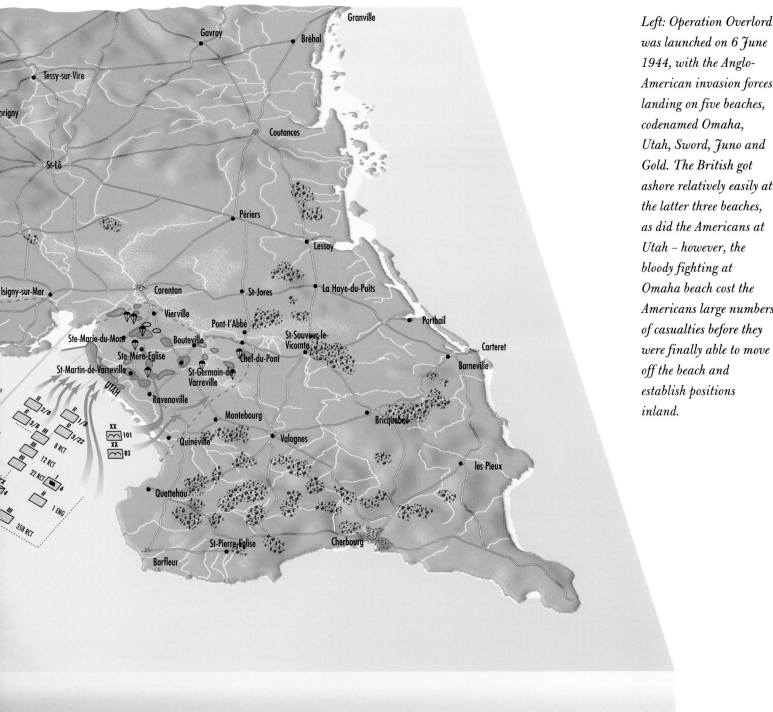

Left: Operation Overlord was launched on 6 June 1944, with the Anglo-American invasion forces landing on five beaches, codenamed Omaha, Utah, Sword, Juno and Gold. The British got ashore relatively easily at the latter three beaches, as did the Americans at Utah – however, the bloody fighting at Omaha beach cost the Americans large numbers of casualties before they were finally able to move off the beach and establish positions inland.

destroyed by bombing (and naval gunfire) as they headed for the beachhead. They might not even manage to make it into battle with the enemy. Rommel argued that the only way of defeating the invasion was to destroy the landing forces as they came ashore.

This bitter dispute between von Rundstedt and Rommel led to Hitler suggesting a compromise – the panzers would be placed under his direct control, and he would give the order to move them in the light of events. While this was accepted, it meant that operational control in the face of an Allied landing became more rigid than it needed to be, and opened the possibility that the panzer reserve might not be able to be deployed in time. Although Rommel did not prevail in regard to the armoured reserve, his views on the need for strong fortifications were accepted. By spring 1944, the defences were at last beginning to be built.

D-Day

The first major actions in the invasion were not carried out by troops from the seaborne invasion force, but by members of the French Resistance and the men landed shortly after midnight on 6 June by an aerial armada of transport aircraft and gliders. The air drop was marked by confusion as paratroopers landed miles from their drop zones (and often miles from other elements of their units), but displaying the initiative expected from airborne troops, they set about attacking the Germans anyway. The air drops were followed by the actual landing of the amphibious force. The landings went relatively smoothly, with the exception of that at Omaha beach. For a while, it appeared as though the landing would have to be suspended, but Brigadier-General Norman Cota, the assistant divisional commander of 29th Division, managed to make sense of the confusion on the beach. Cota brought together a company-sized force of men on the beach, made up of Rangers, engineers and infantrymen. Cota led them from the beach to a fold in the bluffs, which protected them from machine-gun fire.

Cota next sent his men to attack German positions. By 11:00, they had captured the Vierville exit to the beach, and within half an hour of this, more determined attacks had captured the St Laurent exit and the Americans could finally begin moving off the beach in strength. Elsewhere, the British and Canadians had moved forwards from Sword, Juno and Gold beaches, while American forces at Utah beach had endured a far less torrid time than their comrades at Omaha.

The German reaction proved to be confused. The first parachute landings were interpreted as supply drops to the Resistance, and only appreciated for what they were some time later, when it became clear that the Resistance appeared to be receiving enough equipment to arm every man, woman and child in France twice over. The appearance of the invasion fleet was at first assessed as a diversionary move. Von Rundstedt could not be shaken from his view that the Pas de Calais was the real landing area, and nor could Hitler. There appeared to be evidence of an invasion force approaching the Pas de Calais, and it was not until some time later that it was realized that this was a deception – in fact, the radar contacts that suggested ships approaching had been caused by RAF aircraft dropping bundles of aluminium foil to produce spurious signals on German radar screens.

Hitler was reluctant to order the release of the armoured units, although 21st Panzer Division's commander had begun to engage the airborne troops around the Orne bridges on his own initiative. By nightfall on 6 June, the German response was more coordinated, but the Allies were firmly ashore.

Break-out

Establishing a beachhead was just the first step. Once ashore, the Allies then had to break out into the countryside beyond. This proved difficult. A major reason for this lay in the topography of the Normandy countryside. Between Capriquet and the Cotentin peninsula lay *bocage* – narrow, sunken lanes surrounded by tall, thick hedges that led to small, well-built villages or individual stone farmhouses. All of these features meant that *bocage* was an almost perfect terrain to defend.

Allied first attempts to exploit the success of their landings met hard resistance all along the line as the Germans began to recover their poise. The experience of the British 7th Armoured Division at Villers-Bocage served to demonstrate the nature of the bitter struggle that would follow. Montgomery wished to use the 7th Armoured Division (the famed Desert Rats) to punch through the gap in the area of Villers-Bocage, enabling it to link up with the 51st Highland Division, and then encircle the key city of Caen. On 10 June, 7th Armoured moved from Tilly towards Villers-Bocage, which was defended by the Panzer Lehr Division – understrength, but still a formidable opponent. The attack

Above: American troops head for the shore in a landing craft. Hours of practice went into the amphibious assault, which paid off on D-Day itself as the landings went ahead successfully, allowing the Allies to establish a lodgement on the coast of France.

Right: After the D-Day landings and the securing of a lodgement inland, the Allies turned their attention to breaking out into the countryside beyond. The Americans were assigned the task of clearing the Cherbourg peninsula in the west before sweeping round to link with the British, who headed towards Caen.

Break-out Plan

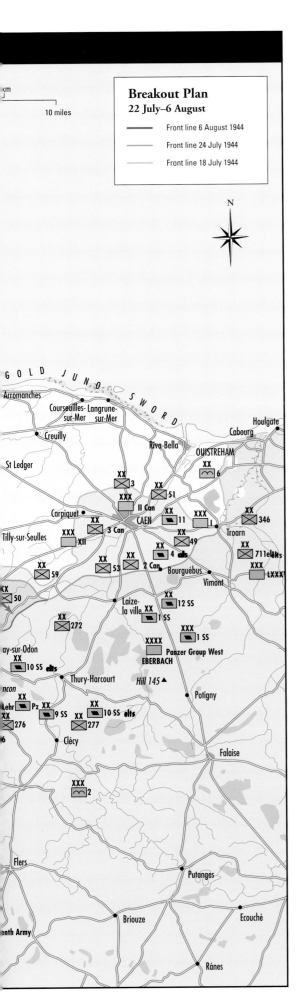

Breakout Plan
22 July–6 August

—— Front line 6 August 1944
—— Front line 24 July 1944
—— Front line 18 July 1944

was conducted on a narrow front, which aided the Germans, who might not have been able to resist an attack all along their overextended line. A bitter battle developed. It took three days for the lead elements of 7th Armoured to enter Villers-Bocage, and shortly after they passed through the town, they were ambushed by a lone Tiger tank commanded by Michael Wittmann, a panzer 'ace' from the Eastern Front. Wittmann destroyed the lead tank, cut off an easy escape route for the column by also destroying the rear tank, and began to move along the column picking off the British tanks as he went. A rescue force in the form of tanks from the 8th Hussars was mauled before a shot from an anti-tank gun knocked a track from Wittmann's vehicle, rendering it immobile. He escaped on foot (later succumbing in the battle when an air strike delivered by RAF fighter-bombers destroyed his tank), but left carnage behind him. A counter-attack that afternoon by the Panzer Lehr Division drove 7th Armoured Division back to Tilly; in the fighting, the British lost 25 tanks, 28 other vehicles and a large number of men. The pattern was to be repeated as the Germans fought doggedly over every inch of French soil. The British forces faced a considerable proportion of the German Army, making their advance difficult and costly. By the start of July, neither the Allied nor German high commands were content – the Allies were not progressing as quickly as they had hoped, while German efforts at a counter-offensive had failed. On 3 July, Hitler removed von Rundstedt from his command, replacing him with Field Marshal Gunther von Kluge. Von Kluge had an unfortunate reputation as a 'yes man', possibly one of the reasons for Hitler's choice. Most generals found Hitler's increasingly unrealistic demands to hold fast in the face the Allied advance impossible.

20 July

On 20 July 1944, Hitler held a planning meeting at his headquarters in East Prussia. Hitler's bunker was being strengthened, so the meeting was held in a large wooden hut instead.

Above: RAF groundcrew load 60lb rocket projectiles onto a Hawker Typhoon fighter-bomber. The Typhoon became famous for carrying out rocket attacks on German tanks and transport, and was one of the most effective weapons platforms available in Normandy, the notorious inaccuracy of rockets notwithstanding.

The meeting began without Field Marshal Wilhelm Keitel, the head of the German high command – the *Oberkommando der Wehrmacht* (OKW). Keitel's absence was explained when he arrived a few moments later with Colonel Count Claus von Stauffenberg, the representative of the Training and Replacement Command, who was scheduled to provide a report on the raising of new divisions. Keitel introduced von Stauffenberg, and he took his place at the conference table, placing his distinctive yellow leather briefcase beneath it. After a few moments, he muttered an apology to the man next to him, explaining that he had to go and make a telephone call. A few minutes later, as Keitel began wonder where von Stauffenberg had gone, there was a huge explosion.

Men came running. The first survivors began to emerge, and finally Keitel appeared, supporting Hitler as the two men left the wreckage. Hitler was bleeding from wounds on his face, his arm was temporarily paralysed and his legs contained hundreds of fragments of the conference table. It was clear that there had been assassination attempt, and Hitler sent officers to look for evidence of a bomb. The search party deduced that the explosion must have occurred under the map table around which the conference was being held.

Suspicion was already falling on von Stauffenberg. He had disappeared, apparently to a nearby airfield, and pieces of his distinctive briefcase were retrieved from all over the remains of the conference room. In the middle of the afternoon, copies of signals from

Berlin reached Hitler. He was incredulous to learn that an unscrupulous group of officers and politicians had assassinated the *Führer*, and that the government had declared a state of emergency. For a few hours it appeared as though the coup might succeed – Hitler was at an isolated location, and all those commanders loyal to Hitler were, naturally, at the battlefront.

Fortunately for Hitler, his run of luck had not ended with his survival. Just after 18:30, the *Führer* received a telephone call from Josef Goebbels, the propaganda minister. With some difficulty, Goebbels explained to the still-deafened Hitler that he had a Major Renner with him. Renner was the leader of the only combat unit then in Berlin, the Grossdeutschland Battalion. Goebbels explained that Renner was confused – he had received one set of orders instructing him to place members of the government under house arrest and another telling him to arrest Field Marshal Witzleben (who had taken authority in Berlin under the terms of the signal announcing Hitler's death) and von Stauffenberg. Goebbels wondered if Hitler would like to talk to Renner. Hitler said he would. He told Renner that he was to restore order in Berlin, and to shoot anyone who stood in his way. By midnight, von Stauffenberg and three other conspirators were dead. A wave of arrests and executions followed. Rommel, now implicated in the plot, was given the choice of suicide, followed by a state funeral, or a public trial, execution and a similar fate for his family. Rommel chose a capsule of fast-acting poison. The bomb plot thus cost Germany one of its most capable commanders, and had one further important effect – it reinvigorated Adolf Hitler.

Only an hour or so after the blast, Hitler was entertaining Mussolini to lunch. He spoke excitedly about how his survival clearly demonstrated his true destiny and that of Germany. Divine providence meant that whatever the current unfavourable circumstances facing Germany, the Third Reich would triumph in the end. A further effect of the bomb was that Hitler no longer trusted his generals, with one or two notable exceptions, and took an ever greater degree of control over military operations. He began to accept even less advice from the Army, and displayed an unwillingness to listen to any suggestions that contradicted his own perceptions of the situation on the battlefield. This was to have important repercussions for the future conduct of the war. The current situation, though, was bad enough, and the Allies finally started to make the breakthrough they had been looking for after weeks of bitter fighting.

Goodwood and Cobra

By early July, the invasion forces were no more than 15 miles inland at any point. Although few people were commenting openly about it, fears of a stalemate increased. By the second week in July it seemed as though Montgomery was the only commander

ALLIED AIR SUPPORT

The importance of air support had been fully recognized in the desert war, and this had prompted the Allied air arms to develop extremely effective cooperation methods with the surface forces. These predominantly used fighter-bombers to attack targets on the battlefield, or supply columns. The most famous of the aircraft employed in this role were the Hawker Typhoon and Republic P-47 Thunderbolt. Robust and well armed, these two types caused havoc amongst German ground units, with the Typhoon gaining a particular reputation for destroying tanks with rockets. The domination of Allied air power over France meant that it was extremely difficult for the Germans to counter the effect of enemy air attack, and this caused them no little difficulty in their attempts to stop the Allied advance across France.

with any sense of optimism left, as he planned to make the decisive breakthrough. On 10 July, he issued instructions for the break-out from Normandy. General Omar Bradley's US First Army would attack towards Avranches, after which the lead element of US Third Army (VIII Corps) would strike into Brittany. To assist this general advance, General Sir Miles Dempsey's British Second Army would attack through the open countryside to the east of Caen. This attack, Operation Goodwood, was to start on 18 July, with Bradley's offensive, Operation Cobra, starting the next day. However, until St Lô was captured, it was impossible for Bradley to start his attack, and this was only achieved on the morning of 19 July. As a result, it was necessary to put Cobra back until 24 July.

On the afternoon of 19 July, just as it appeared that success had been achieved, Goodwood's armoured element ran into heavy resistance, and was halted short of Bourguébus Ridge. Heavy rain the next day brought the attack to a total standstill. Although it appeared that Goodwood had failed it had in fact achieved Montgomery's aim of drawing in German armour away from the Americans. Thirteen German divisions now faced the British, while nine were opposite the Americans; only two of these nine divisions were armoured, giving the Americans a notable superiority.

Although it began later than intended, Operation Cobra was conducted according to the original plan. This was that the attack was to start with the carpet-bombing of the German forces in front of the US VII Corps, who would advance towards the Germans' main line of resistance and seek to break through. At the end of the first phase of Cobra it was hoped that the Americans would be in a position push into Brittany to seize the ports.

Cobra was meant to begin at 13:00 on 24 July with the bombing attacks, but a heavy overcast sky above the battlefield prompted the decision to call the attack off. Some bombers did not receive the recall message; over 300 dropped their bombs, and one unit released theirs on elements of the 30th Division. Bradley was furious, not just because of the casualties, but because he feared that it would alert the Germans to the offensive. As it happened, the Germans did not change their plans. The commander of the German Seventh Army, General Paul Hausser, did not appear concerned when he reported the events of the day to von Kluge.

A Second Attempt

Cobra began again the next day with an air attack just after 09:30, fighter-bombers being followed by 1500 bombers. These dropped over 3048 tonnes (3000 tons) of bombs, and were in turn followed by 380 B-26 medium bombers that added another 1422 tonnes (1400 tons) of high explosive to the fray. The German defences were shattered. Over 1000 defenders were killed, and a similar number wounded or so badly dazed that they were incapable of resistance. Many of the German troops nearest to the American positions were not affected by the bombs, however, and once again, bombs fell short, killing 111 men, including Lieutenant-General Lesley McNair, the head of US Army Ground Forces, and wounding 490.

The ground assault started at 11:00, running into stiff resistance in areas where bombing had not inflicted much damage. This meant that the first day proved to be disappointing for the Americans, who gained about a mile rather than the three that were anticipated. The advance continued, at which point Hitler intervened with orders for a counter-attack.

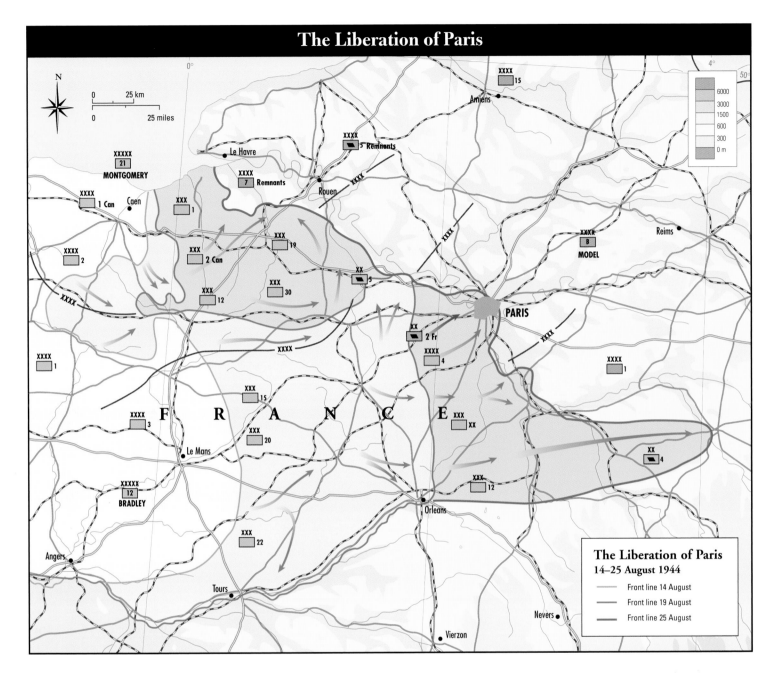

The Liberation of Paris

The Liberation of Paris
14–25 August 1944

Front line 14 August
Front line 19 August
Front line 25 August

The Mortain Counterattack

The attack was to be launched around Mortain, striking at Avranches. Avranches was the key to the American advance, since it was the supply hub for Patton's Third Army. Hitler believed that an attack here would dislocate the entire American effort, and allowed himself to imagine that the forward American divisions would be cut off, and then could be destroyed. The counter-attack began on 7 August and penetrated almost 10 miles into American lines. Some American units were indeed cut off, and for a while it seemed as though Hitler's plan might work. However, a more tangible form of intervention from above came the next morning. As dawn broke on 8 August, the weather was fine. By the middle of the morning, the sky was filled with British and American fighter-bombers. The advance had to stop as the Germans sought cover, and for the next three days they would only attack at night. Bitter fighting followed, but the Germans made no significant gains. The attack had failed.

On 8 August, the first elements of Patton's Third Army reached Le Mans. Eisenhower ordered them to turn north and head towards the British sector. Meanwhile, the

Above: The liberation of Paris proved controversial amongst the Allies, since it was not a primary objective for General Eisenhower. Political pressure from General de Gaulle, and the generally favourable situation, persuaded Eisenhower that he could afford to divert forces to retake the city, a task that was completed by the end of August 1944.

317

Above: Weary but satisfied American troops have a cigarette while awaiting transport to take them to the rear for a few days' rest. The picture was taken in October 1944, and the three soldiers in question had been at the front line since 12 June. The ferocity of the combat in Normandy took its toll on both sides, and it was necessary to give troops some time for rest and recuperation.

Canadian II Corps was planning to make a thrust towards Falaise. If this succeeded, they would be able to link up with the Americans and cut the Germans off. Consequently, just after nightfall on 8 August, 1000 heavy bombers attacked the flanks of the Falaise corridor. The Canadians then advanced along the corridor, marking the start of Operation Totalise.

The Germans counter-attacked just before midday on 9 August. They were stopped by 14:00, but just as the Canadians and the Polish forces accompanying them were about to resume their advance, the sky was filled with 500 B-17 Flying Fortresses from the USAAF. The intention was to repeat the bombardment of the night before, but this went disastrously wrong. Many bombs fell short, killing friendly forces and damaging or destroying many tanks. The next day, a Canadian battle group managed to lose its way and blundered into two panzer groups. To make matters worse, the Poles were engaging the panzers, and took the Canadians under fire as well. Although Totalise was still making ground, it was in serious danger of grinding to a halt as opposition became stiffer. The Americans, on the other hand, were having a better time, and were pushing on towards Argentan. The prospect of linking up with them added new impetus to the British forces, and a development of Totalise was swiftly put in train.

Operation Tractable

The new plan, Tractable, was intended to strike a decisive blow against the Germans. It began with a massive artillery bombardment closely followed up by 300 tanks and four infantry brigades. At this point, disaster struck, when many of the 800 heavy bombers called upon to provide air support began dropping short of the Germans and onto the advancing Allied forces. Although the troops pressed on, the dust and smoke kicked up by the bombing and the artillery was intense and visibility was almost nil. Inevitably, tanks and armoured personnel carriers collided with one another in the confusion and the advance fell into disarray. The debacle was compounded when the armour encountered a narrow stream in its way. While the stream itself was too narrow to cause the tanks difficulty in fording it, the problem lay in the fact that the banks were too steep for tanks to even attempt to traverse it. Eventually, armoured engineers dropped fascine bundles into the stream and the armour moved on – but the advance had slowed irreversibly. Once again, the Canadians found themselves making a slow, hard advance, eventually entering Falaise on 15 August.

Although the Allies were now gaining the upper hand, Hitler was totally convinced that they could still be defeated by launching a series of counter-attacks. Von Kluge was ordered to maintain pressure on Avranches. It was at this point that von Kluge's predominant characteristic of obeying Hitler's every order deserted him. He decided that Hitler's orders were completely ridiculous, and informed Berlin that his forces were no longer strong enough to defeat the Allies. Without waiting for a reply, von Kluge ordered the troops in the pocket to begin a withdrawal.

The End in Normandy

Hitler was furious, and sacked von Kluge immediately. The unfortunate field marshal poisoned himself rather than make the journey home to face Hitler's wrath and probable execution. On 17 August Field Marshal Walther Model, a loyal Nazi who would obey orders, was appointed in von Kluge's stead. Model's loyalty may not have been in doubt, but nor was his intelligence. As soon as he took over, he appreciated that the position was hopeless, and that von Kluge had been right. However, Model was clever enough to withdraw while using the remnants of his armour to make thrusts against both Falaise and Argentan. He knew that these would fail, but he could claim to have carried out Hitler's instructions to the letter. By 19 August, the Germans were in a dire state – artillery and air strikes were decimating their retreating columns; two days later, those forces remaining in the pocket were trapped as the jaws of the trap closed. Free French forces raced for Paris. The city fell to the French forces, and by 29 August, American troops were marching down the Champs Elysées as part of the liberation celebrations.

Operation Dragoon

While the fighting in Normandy was going on, the Allies sought to open a second front in France, by landing in the south of the country. The plan had been endorsed at the Tehran Conference, but no firm date was given for the operation (codenamed Anvil) since it swiftly became clear that providing enough shipping for both it and the Normandy landings was impossible. Eisenhower, who was not convinced about the wisdom of the operation taking place alongside the Normandy landings, secured agreement that it should take place after Overlord, and as late as 11 June, Churchill was pressing for the landings to be abandoned in favour of landings in the Balkans.

'The battlefield at Falaise was unquestionably one of the greatest "killing grounds" of any of the war areas ... Forty-eight hours after the closing of the gap, I was conducted through it on foot, to encounter scenes that could be described only by Dante. It was literally possible to walk for hundreds of yards at a time, stepping on nothing but dead and decaying flesh.'

General Dwight D. Eisenhower, Crusade in Europe

Roosevelt rejected this suggestion, telling Churchill a landing in the Balkans would be deeply unpopular in the United States. The message was quite clear – it was an election year in America, and Roosevelt was politely informing the prime minister that he had no intention of doing anything unpopular. Churchill made desperate attempts to convince Eisenhower to modify the plan; Eisenhower refused. Churchill joked bitterly that as he had been dragooned into accepting, the plan should be renamed Operation Dragoon. Oddly, the joke was taken as being an expression of seriousness, and the landings were given the codename of Anvil/Dragoon as a recognition of Churchill's offhand remark.

The invasion fleet assembled in a variety of locations in the Mediterranean and the landings began with commandos coming ashore on the night of 14 August. They were followed by parachute and glider-borne assaults which aimed to seize the vital intersection at Le Muy. Some of the paratroopers were dropped outside their intended landing zone, right on top of the headquarters of the German LXII Corps. As was now common with paratroops who found themselves miles from where they ought to be, the soldiers made a quick assessment of the situation, worked out how best to inconvenience the opposition and set about doing it. They attacked the headquarters, preventing it from coordinating the defences on the beaches against the seaborne attack. Le Muy fell the next day. The main landings took place at 05:50 on 15 August, and made good progress. On 17 August, orders for the abandonment of southern France (apart from the ports) were issued by the German high command, and the forces there began to retreat.

Below: A motley collection of members of the French Resistance pose for the camera in a town somewhere in France. The men are mainly equipped with British rifles, and a Bren light machine gun can be seen on its bipod to the bottom right of the photograph. These weapons had almost certainly been dropped to the Resistance by British aircraft.

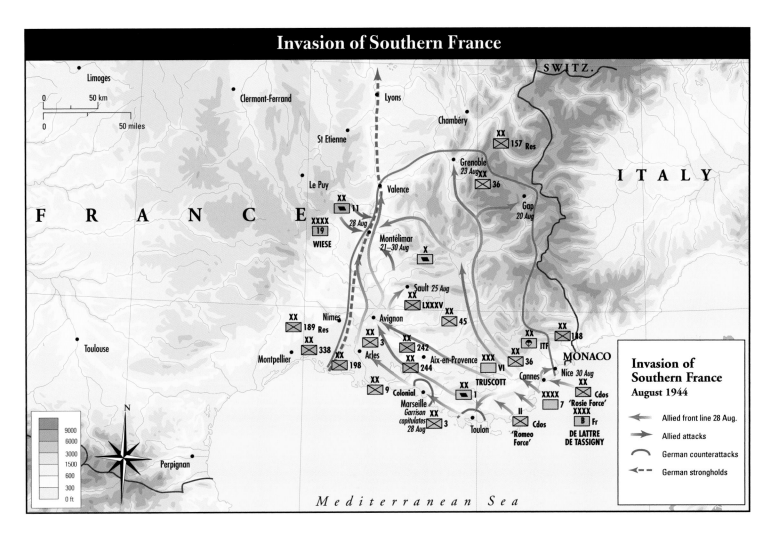

Invasion of Southern France

Invasion of Southern France
August 1944

Allied front line 28 Aug.

Allied attacks

German counterattacks

German strongholds

The Franco-American advance proceeded smoothly; Marseilles surrendered on 28 August, and leading elements of General Lucian K. Truscott's VI Corps entered Lyon on 3 September to the acclaim of the population, overjoyed that the Germans had been forced out. By the time Truscott had reached Lyon, the Allied forces in the north had rapidly exploited their breakthrough. Montgomery launched Operation Kitten, an advance to the Seine on 16 August, forcing the Germans to carry out a phased withdrawal across the river to escape complete destruction. As the Germans fell back, heading for the Belgian and German frontiers, they were pursued by the Allies. By the first week of September, the Allies began to outrun their logistics, so they halted along a line from the Meuse to Maastricht and then south from Aachen to the Swiss border. While plans for the next stage of operations were being drawn up, Truscott's forces linked up with Patton on 11 September, trapping the last 20,000 men of the German rearguard, who surrendered. While the operation in the south of France actually increased logistical problems, Anvil/Dragoon succeeded in ensuring political stability in the south of France, which had been was one of the key concerns for the Americans when they had insisted upon the operation over Churchill's objections.

By the end of August 1944, the Allies had succeeded in their aim of driving the Germans back. Most of France was liberated, and once the logistic system had been restored, the advance would continue into Germany. Although the Germans had been compelled to pull back, their resistance remained fierce. It was quite obvious that they would remain a formidable enemy as the Western Front was pushed ever closer to the German border as the final reckoning between the Allies and the Axis powers drew near.

Above: The controversial invasion of southern France (Operation Anvil/ Dragoon) was carried out despite British opposition. Originally planned as a means of dividing the efforts of the Germans, the operation went ahead even after they had begun to withdraw north, since it was deemed necessary by the Americans as a means of ensuring the maintenance of order and the restoration of government in the south of the country.

Northwest Europe, August 1944 – April 1945

The Allied armies arrived on the banks of the River Seine after only 80 days, and while Paris was being retaken, the bulk of Allied forces started to cross the river, aiming to keep in touch with the retreating Germans. There was concern that if the pursuit fell some distance behind, the Germans could use the time to prepare strong defensive positions that would inevitably hamper the drive towards Germany. Memories of the defences along the Somme, the Marne, the Aisne and the Meuse from World War I returned to the minds of the senior officers, many of whom had experienced the effectiveness of these positions at first hand.

US First Army (Lieutenant-General Courtney Hodges) was the first to drive on after crossing the Seine, and fought a series of sharp engagements as they pursued the Germans, taking St Quentin by the end of August, and then Mons and Tournai. Patton's Third Army conducted a similarly rapid advance to the Meuse, but was forced to halt on 31 August when it ran out of petrol. Montgomery's 21st Army Group, meanwhile, moved in preparation for the capture of Le Havre, Dieppe, Boulogne and Calais, before heading into Belgium. XII and XXX Corps from the British Second Army crossed the Seine and after overcoming stiff resistance began a drive to Amiens, gathering momentum as they went. At dawn on 31 August, the leading tanks of the 11th Armoured Division were in Amiens, and by the end of the morning had secured the river crossings over the Somme. The next day saw units from XXX Corps in Arras and Aubigny on the River Scarpe, followed the next day by Lens and Douai. Although the British had to fight their way into all these locations, German resistance was relatively light. A rest was ordered on 1 September, so as to allow an airborne operation to seize Tournai prior to the arrival of Hodges' US First Army. In fact, First Army moved so quickly that Tournai fell before the parachute drop could take place, and the British were now instructed to drive on Brussels. The Guards Armoured and 11th Armoured Divisions were tasked with

Opposite: An American infantryman shows off a variety of captured German weapons that he has collected. He has three MP40 sub-machine guns slung over his right arm, and is carrying two MG42 machine guns in his left hand. The MG42 later formed the basis for the American M60 machine gun.

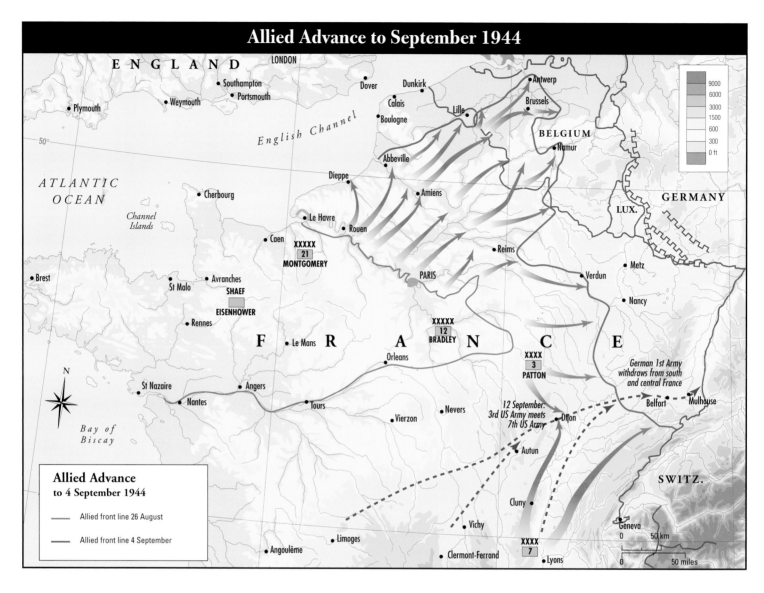

Allied Advance to September 1944

Above: After the difficult task of breaking out from Normandy was complete, the Allies enjoyed considerable success in their advance, virtually clearing France of German troops by the end of August, and entering Belgium.

liberating the Belgian capital and Antwerp respectively. The Guards entered Brussels on the evening of 3 September to great jubilation, while 11th Armoured received a similar welcome in Antwerp.

Le Havre

The battle for Le Havre, undertaken by the British I Corps, was a far more difficult prospect than the advances undertaken by XII and XXX Corps. The port was well defended, and the commander, Colonel Eberhard Wildermuth, was faced with a dilemma. He was anxious to avoid heavy casualties, but could not simply surrender because of the inevitable consequences this would have for his family. As a result, the city had to be taken by force. RAF Bomber Command bombed the port for 10 consecutive days, and naval gunfire was added to the maelstrom of the preparatory bombardment. The infantry of the 49th and 51st Divisions carried out offensive patrolling as they moved into place for the attack, which was launched at dusk on 10 September.

The preliminary bombardment of Le Havre was immense, and rivalled the massive preparatory fire directed against German positions by the Red Army in the East. Bombers dropped 5080 tonnes (5000 tons) of bombs onto the port, and as the last one left the area, the artillery opened fire. Armour moved forward, closely followed by the infantry, and the British fought their way into the city. Despite the bombardment, it took all night and most of the following day before the outer defences were captured, and then another 24 hours passed before British troops entered the city centre, where Colonel Wildermuth was captured. Le Havre was in British hands, but at the cost of many more lives than would have been necessary had Hitler not given such stringent orders backed up by the threat of dire consequences for officers' families if they capitulated, and considerable damage to the port facilities, which meant that it took several weeks before Le Havre could be brought into use to aid the Allied advance.

Overall, the last two weeks of August 1944 saw the British and Americans covering up to 500 miles, taking thousands of Germans prisoner as they went. However, the logistics system supporting the advance was becoming increasingly strained as the Allies moved on. The situation was not helped by the fact that there was rampant inefficiency and corruption amongst the logistics organization under General J.C.H. Lee. An unpopular, flamboyant man (critics said his initials stood for 'Jesus Christ Himself'), Lee oversaw an organization that was drastically overstaffed, and which encompassed the brilliant creation of the 'Red Ball Express' to keep troops supplied, to wild profligacy in the form of Lee diverting resources to move his staff into opulent headquarters in Paris (in the form of no fewer than 290 hotels) when they were required at the front, and to straightforward black-marketeering, which is alleged to have encouraged around 10 per cent of Lee's command to desert and set up in business in Paris with their ill-gotten supplies. Coupled with this inefficiency, the Allies faced the simple problem that they needed to begin operating from ports closer to the front line, a difficult task given that some (such as Le Havre) needed weeks of repair, while Antwerp was not operational

Below: A dead German Waffen-SS soldier lies at the side of a track somewhere in France. By the end of August 1944, this scene had been repeated countless times throughout France, with the Germans sustaining thousands of casualties as they were pushed back towards Germany.

even after its capture, since the Germans controlled the approaches. This all meant that the Allies would not be able to sustain thrusts across a broad front, and resources would have to be carefully husbanded. This meant that trying to satisfy the demands of Patton and Montgomery would be a particularly difficult task for Eisenhower. Both his subordinates wished to be at the head of the Allied advance, and neither took kindly to the idea that they might have to take second place to the other as a result of supply problems.

Operation Market Garden

Montgomery wished to use 21st Army Group as the main offensive force, and developed a daring plan which, if it worked, would place his men across the River Rhine and in a position to sweep towards Berlin, possibly before the year was over.

Montgomery's plan contrasted dramatically with the more cautious approach he usually adopted for offensives, and when he proposed it to Eisenhower, the Supreme Commander was almost mesmerized by the audacity of the proposition before him.

The plan was to land some 30,000 British and American airborne troops at key river bridges while General Sir Brian Horrocks' XXX Corps drove north through Holland along the 60-mile-long corridor created by the landing. Montgomery suggested that such an operation could cause the Germans to collapse, shattering their will to continue fighting. Even if it did not, he contended, the Allies would still benefit since they would have gained a bridgehead across the Rhine. The major German defensive position on the West Wall (or Siegfried Line) would be outflanked by the move. The furthest bridge to be seized would be that at Arnhem, which the British 1st Airborne Division was to hold until relieved by XXX Corps. The plan was codenamed Market Garden with 'Market' covering the airborne component and 'Garden' the ground element. Eisenhower's amazement at Montgomery's suggestion did not prevent him from seeing the logic that lay behind it. He agreed to the plan, with the date of the operation being set for 17 September 1944.

While the plan was recognized as being particularly bold, it was not without difficulties. One of the key problems was that the Allied First Airborne Army was bedevilled by the poor relationship between its commander, General Lewis Brereton, and his deputy, Lieutenant-General Sir Frederick 'Boy' Browning. Browning had been involved with airborne operations since he had overseen the creation of the Parachute Regiment in 1940, and had harboured hopes that he would be given command of the Airborne Army. However, Brereton had been given the position, much to Browning's irritation. Brereton was an officer in the US Army Air Force, specializing in transport aircraft; since the bulk of the air transport strength available to the Allies was American, his appointment was not unreasonable.

Regrettably, Browning and Brereton disliked each other intensely, and the two barely spoke to one another. This culminated in the utter farce that ensued when it transpired that the two men had planned two completely different operations for the airborne troops on 6 September. Both had to be cancelled when Browning refused to cancel his plan, and threatened to resign if Brereton overruled him. Relations between the two could not have been worse, and to compound matters, their breakdown in relations occurred at a time when strong, unified leadership was required, given that the bulk of their staff was inexperienced and needed clear guidance. Of equal concern was the problem of aircraft availability. Although the USAAF and RAF had the largest air

transport fleet ever assembled, this was still not enough to transport more than a third of the army at a time, making additional air drops essential. The problem here lay in the danger that one element of the Airborne Army could land, vastly outnumbered, but be left cut off if the second and/or third part of the army could not be dropped as the result of bad weather obscuring the landing zone. On the positive side, the men were highly trained and amongst the most determined and professional on the Allied side. The forces included Lieutenant-General Matthew Ridgeway's XVIII Airborne Corps, consisting of the American 82nd and 101st Airborne Divisions, and the British 1st Airborne Division, supported by a brigade of Polish paratroopers.

The plans for Market Garden were complete by 15 September, and envisaged the seizure of bridges at Eindhoven, Nijmegen and Arnhem. Browning passed the now immortal comment 'I think we may be going a bridge too far', but it was too late to modify the plan. The precursor to the airborne assault came in the form of a heavy bombardment of German fighter airfields in Holland, beginning in the early hours of 16 September with an attack by RAF Bomber Command, and then a 1000-aircraft raid by

Above: Men of the 82nd Airborne Division aboard a C-47 transport aircraft as they await take-off as part of Operation Market Garden. The 82nd Airborne was assigned the task of seizing the bridge at Nijmegen, which was seized after some sharp fighting.

Right: The airlift in support of Operation Market Garden was enormous in its scale. When the operation began on 17 September, a stream of aircraft and gliders left England, carrying some 20,000 men and their equipment. By 14:00, the first phase of the airlift was complete, and 20,000 troops had been landed successfully, and were heading for their objectives.

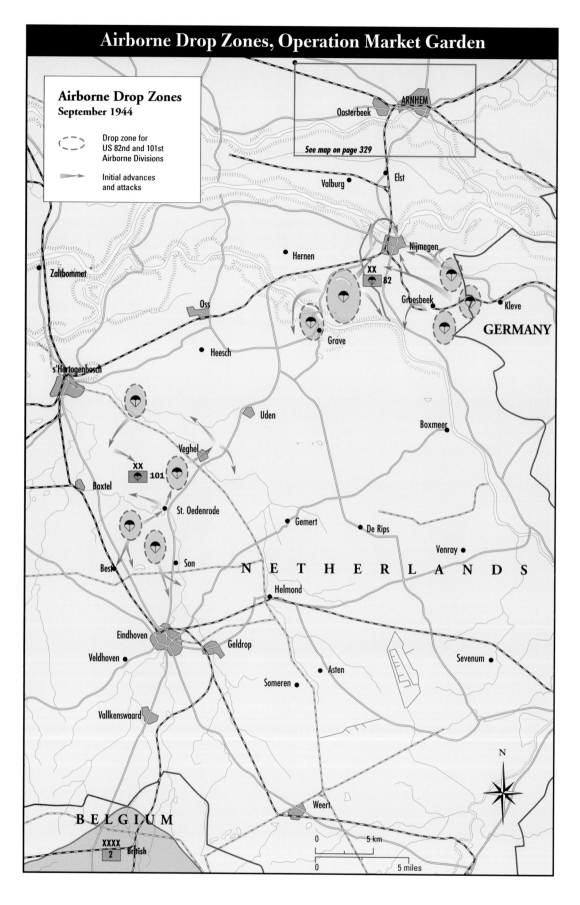

Airborne Drop Zones, Operation Market Garden

Airborne Drop Zones
September 1944

Drop zone for US 82nd and 101st Airborne Divisions

Initial advances and attacks

See map on page 329

American bombers which was targeted against known anti-aircraft positions that could interfere with the transport aircraft.

On 17 September, no fewer than airbases in England were alive to the sound of the massed transport fleet taking off to carry the airborne component into battle. The

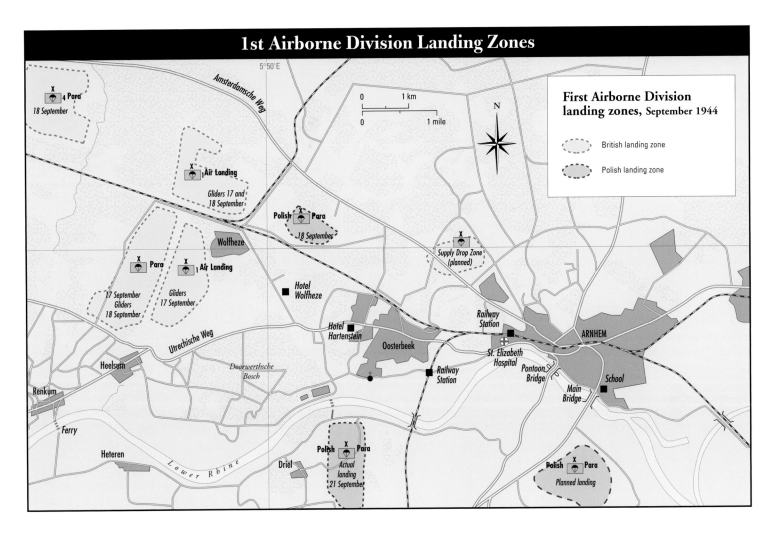

1st Airborne Division Landing Zones

First Airborne Division landing zones, September 1944

- British landing zone
- Polish landing zone

transports roared across southern England, bringing considerable excitement on the ground below as onlookers gaped in astonishment at the sheer scale of the airlift. A stream of aircraft and gliders carrying some 20,000 men and their equipment to Holland passed over them, with each aircraft heading on one of two routes – the northern route carried the 82nd Airborne and British 1st Airborne Divisions to their objectives at Nijmegen and Arnhem, while the southern track was made up of the aircraft carrying the US 101st Airborne. The southern stream suffered some losses from German flak, but reached the drop zone, where 7000 men were dropped. By 14:00, the first phase of the airlift was complete, and all 20,000 troops had been landed successfully.

The airborne troops enjoyed initial success, taking most of their objectives with ease (although 101st Airborne suffered the mortification of seeing one of the bridges they were meant to capture being destroyed as they approached it). The 82nd and 101st Airborne seized their objectives, and were ready to receive XXX Corps some time before that formation was able to break through increasingly stiff German defences.

The British troops ran into more difficulties than their American counterparts. German forces around Arnhem proved to be stronger than predicted. Worse still, as the 1st Airborne Division landed, Field Marshal Walther Model had broken off from his lunch to report the landings to Hitler. II SS Panzer Corps was instantly alerted for action, while 9th SS Panzer Division was immediately sent to Arnhem, and 10th SS Panzer Division told to make all haste towards Nijmegen.

Once the Americans succeeded in capturing the bridges at Eindhoven, they had to wait for XXX Corps to arrive. XXX Corps' tanks had to move along a single-track road,

Above: The landings by 1st Airborne Division were complicated by the fact that they occurred some distance away from Arnhem, presenting the division with the need to move swiftly into the town to secure the bridge. While this was achieved, problems with resupply meant that the division's position was tenuous, and made worse by the fact that the 9th SS Panzer Division was nearby and able to rush to the scene to engage them.

Above: Two German prisoners prepare firewood, under the watchful eye of one of their captors. The German in the camouflage suit is a Waffen-SS *trooper.*

which meant that even a small German force could block their path and disrupt the timing of the operation. Inevitably, they ran into German opposition. German anti-tank guns had inflicted some damage upon the lead elements of the advance before they were dealt with by air strikes and artillery fire. This skirmish delayed XXX Corps, a portent of things to come. Once past this obstacle, XXX Corps then ran into more German opposition, which again took time to overcome. By the afternoon of 19 September, XXX Corps had reached Nijmegen, and crossed the River Wahl. This left them only 10 miles south of Arnhem, the final objective – but German resistance was such that the advance ground to a complete halt, leaving 1st Airborne Division cut off.

1st Airborne had been fighting in and around Arnhem for three days, and things had not gone well. The bridge in the town was meant to be captured by a surprise attack by armed jeeps, but the gliders carrying these had failed to arrive intact. Although the 2nd Battalion of the 1st Parachute Brigade reached the northern end of the bridge, the reinforcements they anticipated coming to join them did not arrive. One of the reasons for this lay in the fact that Major-General Roy Urquhart, the commander of 1st Airborne Division, became detached from his headquarters and spent 36 hours hiding from German patrols until he was able to make his way back. In his absence, his subordinates disagreed over what course of action to take, and devoted their attention to securing high ground outside the town instead of sending reinforcements to the bridge. As a result, 2nd Battalion was completely isolated, and after beating off one attack, was subjected to a massive assault designed to literally blast them from their positions. An epic stand resulted, but the paratroopers' task was impossible, and the Germans retook the bridge on 21 September.

As the fighting in Arnhem continued, efforts to fly in supplies and reinforcements were made, but failed as a result of bad weather. XXX Corps battled on towards Arnhem, and finally broke through German resistance to reach the south side of the Rhine on 23 September. An attempt to cross the river failed, and Montgomery came to the conclusion that the airborne division had to be withdrawn, since there was no chance of success. Montgomery's plan had been predicated on the belief popular among the Allied high command that the German troops had lost their will to fight; Market Garden demonstrated that this was a fallacy. As a result, the remaining troops were evacuated from Arnhem across the river during the night of 25/26 September. Although Allied propaganda claims that the operation was 90 per cent successful were an exaggeration, the capture of the bridge over the Waal was to be of great utility in 1945 as a base from which to launch future operations.

Back to Attrition

With the failure at Arnhem it was clear the Germans were still a considerable way from being totally defeated in the West, even if their position was grave. The Germans might have been forced back onto their frontier, but they were falling back to prepared defensive positions that would be difficult to break through. In addition, the Germans had far shorter lines of communication than the Allies, who were beginning to notice the failings of their logistics organization. Until the supply situation improved, it was clear

'I would say the German as a military force on the Western front … is a whipped enemy.'

General Eisenhower, press conference, 28 March 1945

FIELD MARSHAL WALTHER MODEL

Walther Model was commissioned into the German Army in 1909. He served in staff positions during World War I, and remained in the Army after it was slashed in size after the Versailles treaties. Impressed with Hitler (as a politician, if not as a military commander), Model joined the Nazi Party, and remained loyal to Hitler for the rest of his life. He commanded IV Corps in Poland, the 3rd Panzer Division in France and then XXXI Panzer Corps in the early fighting in the USSR. Model was then given command of Ninth Army between 1942 and 1944, when he took over as commander of Army Group North in the Ukraine. He briefly commanded Army Group Centre from June 1944, before taking over Army Group B in August. Hitler had high regard for Model, and his constant use of him to deal with difficult situations, such as in Normandy and then at Arnhem, led to Model's nickname of 'the *Führer*'s Firefighter'.

Model realized that arguing with Hitler over some of his less sensible decisions never worked, and instead carried out the *Führer*'s instructions, but interpreting these orders in the loosest possible sense, which meant that he could go some way towards reconciling Hitler's ideas with reality. Model opposed the Ardennes offensive, but carried it out to the best of his ability, and commanded his army group until it was surrounded in the Ruhr pocket in April 1945. While he allowed his troops to surrender, Model decided that he would not, and he shot himself on 21 April 1945.

that the Allied advance would be slow, with the risk of increased attrition as the war dragged on. The question of how to improve the supply problem was of key concern to the Allies, and attention turned to Antwerp.

Although Antwerp was in Allied hands, it was of little use. The German Fifteenth Army controlled the entrance to the port, and their presence meant that the Allies would be unable to bring anything into Antwerp until they had dislodged the enemy from the banks of the Scheldt estuary. Quite understandably, Montgomery had given little priority to Antwerp while Market Garden was under way, and had left the task of clearing the estuary in the hands of the Canadian First Army. On 8 October, Admiral Sir Bertram Ramsay, commanding naval operations for Northwest Europe, reported to Eisenhower that the Scheldt would not be cleared until at least 1 November, since the Canadians had encountered stiff opposition and were now running short of supplies, particularly ammunition. The report alarmed Eisenhower, prompting him to order Montgomery to clear the Scheldt estuary with all haste. He made clear that unless Antwerp was brought into use, operations would come to a standstill. He concluded his signal to Montgomery by explaining that he considered Antwerp to be of the utmost importance to the Allied war effort. Unfortunately, Montgomery refused to accept that this task was anything more than an attempt to consign him to a quiet area, enabling the Americans to 'steal' the glory that was, in Montgomery's opinion, rightfully his. Being Montgomery, he could not keep these thoughts to himself, and added that the only reason that Arnhem had failed was because Eisenhower had an unsatisfactory campaign plan.

Eisenhower found it necessary to remind Montgomery as to who was in command of the Allied forces in Europe – whether or not Montgomery liked the fact, it was not him. To rein in Montgomery, Eisenhower explained that if he had no confidence in his handling of the matter, then they must 'refer the matter to higher authority' for arbitration. Montgomery knew all too well that such a course of action would be disastrous for him, since it was impossible to conceive of a situation where Roosevelt would side with Montgomery and remove Eisenhower. It was election year in the United States, and it would be politically impossible for an aspirant president, even one who had already served three terms in office, to side with a foreign general against an American hero. It was equally certain that Churchill would concur with Roosevelt, and despite his status, Montgomery would have to be sacrificed to protect the alliance. Montgomery carefully extricated himself from his apparently intractable position and issued orders that made clearing the Scheldt the main priority for his forces.

Clearing the Scheldt

Operations along the Scheldt were well under way even before Montgomery's about-turn. The Canadians, supported by the Polish Armoured Division, had removed the Germans from about 20 miles of the southern bank of the river, but this was still less than half the amount that needed to be cleared. The Germans, meanwhile, were fully aware of the significance of the Scheldt to the Allies, and maintained formidable defences in the mouth of the river, notably on Walcheren Island, where 12,000 men occupied well-fortified positions supported by heavy guns. The town of Flushing had been turned into a fortress, with individual houses converted into strongpoints.

The British and Canadian forces assaulted the enemy positions in terrible weather, which prevented air support from being called in to support the advance. Canadian 3rd Division fought its way along the Scheldt, employing amphibious armoured fighting

vehicles to convey them to their objective, until they finally captured the last strongpoint at Knocke-sur-Mer on 2 November. Canadian 2nd Division attacked along the Beveland peninsula on 24 October, while the British 52nd Division crossed the Scheldt with the aim of driving the Germans into the arms of the Canadians. By the end of October, the Germans had been pushed back onto Walcheren Island, which now had to be taken.

The plan for the operation addressed the formidable defences by taking the view that the best way of dealing with the island was to flood it by breaching the Westkapelle dyke. On 3, 7, 11 and 17 October, Mosquito and Lancaster bombers from the RAF carried out heavy raids on the dyke.

By the time the bombers had finished, most of the island was underwater, with the exception of the coastal dunes, and Middleberg and Flushing. Two more days of bombing and naval gunfire softened the defences of the remaining areas, and on 1 November, British commandos went ashore at Flushing and Westkapelle. A Canadian

Above: American M24 Chaffee tanks prepare to move out for another day's work. The M24 was designed to fulfil the light tank role, replacing the M3/M5 series. It was well armed, mounting a 75mm gun, and fast. The vehicle entered service in late 1944, and remained in American service after the war.

333

attack across the causeway was beaten back, and over the course of the next 48 hours there was fierce fighting, the advantage swinging back and forth between the warring sides. The commandos had a slightly easier task as a consequence of the flooding – a series of small islands created by the inundation stood in their way, and they took them one at a time. Flushing was far more difficult, but after yet more intense fighting, the Germans were induced to surrender on 4 November. That day, the Royal Navy began sweeping the Scheldt of mines, marking the start of a three-week-long operation. On 28 November, the first convoy of ships arrived safely, and by early December, the port was fully operational. This meant that Allied logistics were greatly improved. From a position of having far too little port capacity for months, they now had a surplus, which meant that forthcoming battles would be much easier to sustain.

American Advances

While the British cleared the Scheldt, the American First Army assaulted Aachen on 12 September. Bitter fighting ensued, and the defenders determined to follow Hitler's orders to fight to the last man. Six days of intensive street fighting saw the German perimeter pushed back into the city by 22 October, until the advance left the Germans in possession of just a four-storey air raid shelter. After 12 hours of artillery bombardment, the now rather battered and deafened Germans surrendered. The battle for Aachen was particularly bloody, but was totally surpassed by the sanguinary affair that followed in the Hürtgen Forest.

The Hürtgen Forest stretched over an area of 12 miles, intersected by elements of the West Wall. A series of American assaults between September and November cost them 33,000 casualties. Finally, on 8 December 1944, the Americans reached the banks of the River Roer; while First Army had fought its way through the Hürtgen Forest, Patton had led Third Army against Metz, which surrendered on 21 November. By the start of December, Third Army stood overlooking the West Wall – it had suffered 55,182 casualties in the process. As December began, the Allied armies appeared to have lost momentum following the bitter fighting of the previous two months. The attritional nature of the struggle concerned the Allies, particularly Montgomery, who was aware of the situation regarding the number of British reserves that could be called upon. He sought to persuade Eisenhower that finding some means of forcing the Germans into mobile warfare again was essential. As Eisenhower pondered the problem, the solution was provided by Hitler, in the form of a massive offensive in the Ardennes.

The Battle of the Bulge

Hitler's response to Allied success in the early summer of 1944 was to begin planning for a huge counter-offensive that would regain the initiative on the Western Front. Hitler decided that the target of his offensive should be Antwerp. There were many sound reasons for this, not least its importance to the Allies' logistics. A drive on the city would also have the major benefit of splitting the British and Canadian armies from the Americans, and they could then be destroyed. There were major difficulties in achieving the goal of Antwerp, but Hitler chose to ignore them.

The shortest distance to Antwerp was along the boundary between the American and British forces north of Aachen, but the terrain around the city made a quick advance impossible. Bisected by rivers and canals, the terrain presented too many obstacles to the tanks that were to drive through the Allied positions and bring victory. This forced the

Ardennes upon Hitler, but since this had been the scene of his success in 1940, this was not a concern to the *Führer*. Although the terrain was restrictive for manoeuvring forces, the campaign against France had proved that armour could move through the area. Other characteristics of the Ardennes commended the area. The forests in the German Eifel region would provide a useful means of disguising the build-up of an attacking force from aerial reconnaissance, and the distance to Antwerp was little more than 100 miles. Also, if the attack was successful, it would cut off the British and Canadians and trap the American armies around Aachen too. Hitler concluded that he could obtain a victory so decisive that the Anglo-American forces would be forced to sue for peace. The offensive would trap over half of the Allied forces, eliminate the threat to the Ruhr and its industry,

Below: An SS NCO signals to his men to advance during the Battle of the Bulge. This is a propaganda shot taken alongside a burning American column from which the survivors had been removed before the photographer arrived.

and allow Hitler to turn his attention to the Eastern Front by withdrawing troops from the West. All of this, Hitler decided, could be achieved within a week.

There remained one major problem with this plan, which was evident to almost everyone in the German high command (when they were let in on the secret) – it took absolutely no account of reality.

Hitler simply refused to accept that the situation was very different from 1940. Germany did not have air superiority and the proposed timing for the offensive sought to enlist that most unpredictable ally (unless one is Russian), namely the weather. The forces needed for the offensive would have to be created, and this would require removing troops and tanks from the Eastern Front, where they were desperately needed. Hitler intended to make the task for his troops slightly easier by using English-speaking commandos dressed in American uniform to spread confusion in rear areas by misdirecting traffic, spreading rumours and carrying out acts of sabotage, and by using an airborne assault to support the attack. Even these ideas failed to appreciate reality – the German parachute force had not conducted a combat drop since 1941, and many of the men now assigned to the formation did not even know how to use a parachute. The sacrifice of

Opposite: The German offensive in the Ardennes was designed to change the strategic situation on the Western Front. Hitler planned to seize the port of Antwerp, driving a wedge between the British and American armies and using the advantage gained to negotiate a separate peace with the Western powers. The plan was hopelessly optimistic, but the initial stages went well, with the Germans driving the Americans back and besieging Bastogne. By Christmas 1944, it was clear that the Germans were not going to achieve their objectives, and a series of Allied counter-attacks were under way.

Right, inset: From 23 December 1944, an Allied counter-attack in the Ardennes drove the Germans back, until by the end of January, their defeat was confirmed. The Germans lost over 120,000 men and 600 armoured vehicles in the offensive, weakening the forces available to defend against the crossing of the Rhine, and placing them in a far less favourable position than Hitler had intended.

transport crews on the Eastern Front meant that most of the pilots for the aircraft that would carry the paratroopers to their destination had never dropped paratroopers before, and to complete the farce, they were not allowed to carry out sufficient training to at least try to prevent the drop from turning into a disaster.

The idea of using undercover commandos was flawed as well, since there were too few English-speaking men prepared to volunteer for the mysterious mission offered them; and the majority of those who could speak the language fluently had an English accent rather than the required American one. Finally, there was not enough captured American equipment available to enable them to maintain their cover story.

When they learned of his plan, Hitler's generals were astounded at the fact that the goal set for them was virtually impossible. Outnumbered, short of fuel, men, transport, tanks and equipment, the idea seemed preposterous, but all attempts to tell Hitler fell on deaf ears. The only thing that suggested that the offensive would have any chance of success was the one obvious advantage the Germans had – surprise.

The attack started on 16 December 1944, and although the Americans were driven back, the pace of advance was nowhere near swift enough to allow for the goal of Antwerp to be achieved, a fact that was clear almost as early as the end of the third day. While the Germans inflicted serious reverses on the Americans in a number of places, dogged defence meant that the situation was kept under reasonable control, even if the response at SHAEF verged on panic at times. The Germans were delayed at St Vith and a host of other places, and found that Bastogne was far from easy to take. The 101st Airborne Division held out in the town, despite being totally surrounded – a German offer of surrender was presented to the temporary commander of the division, Brigadier-General Anthony McAuliffe, who responded with a pithy 'Nuts!' and left his staff officers to explain the sentiment behind it to the confused German officers who had been sent to parley.

After the shock of the first few days of the attack, Eisenhower ordered a counter-attack. The Germans were first slowed down even more, and then driven back in the face of a determined thrust by Patton. Bastogne was kept supplied from the air when the weather permitted, until it was relieved on 26 December, marking a turning point in the campaign. Although fighting continued until January 1945, and included another German offensive against American troops in Alsace, the Battle of the Bulge had been won by the New Year. Twenty-six American divisions were now in the Ardennes, and set about destroying the remaining German forces.

Exactly six weeks after the offensive began, the Americans were back in the positions they had occupied at the start, leaving the Germans facing the fact that they had suffered heavy casualties and

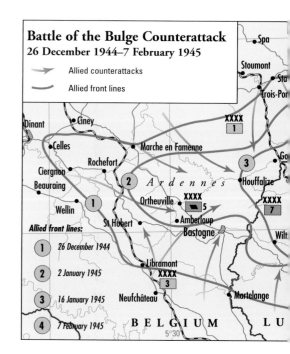

gained no ground for little in return other than the psychological effect caused by the attack. With the end of the battle, optimism was returning quickly, and the Allies looked forward to making the final push against the Germans in the spring of 1945, aiming to drive into the heart of Germany itself.

The Ardennes Offensive

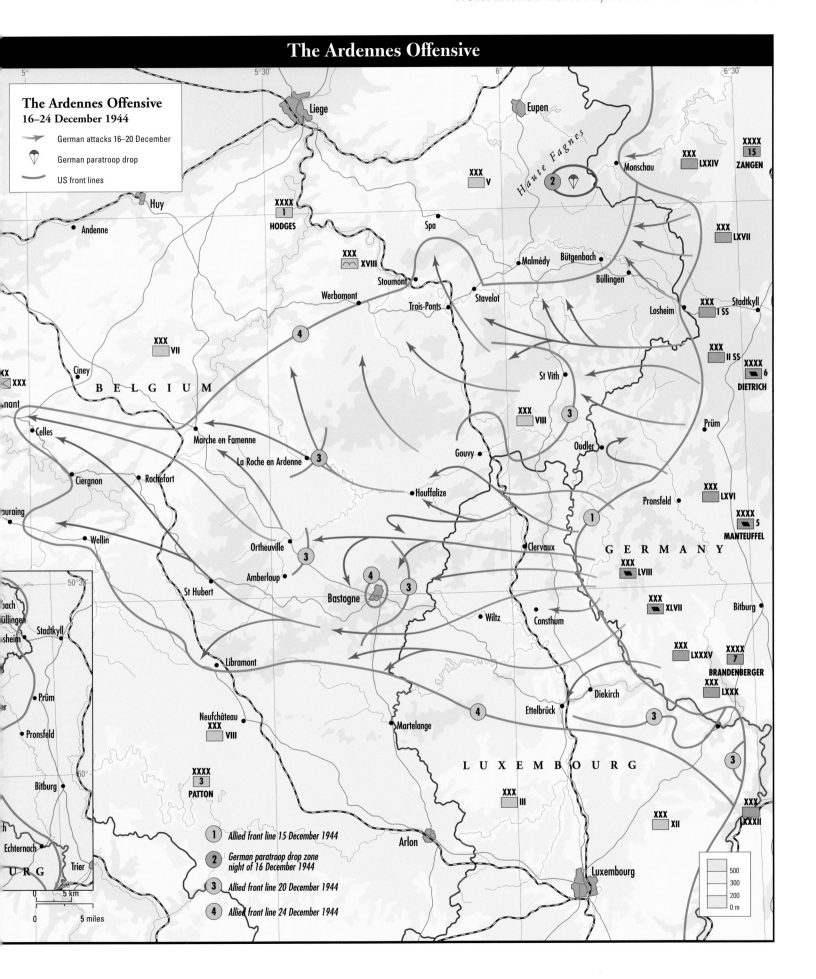

The Ardennes Offensive
16–24 December 1944

German attacks 16–20 December

German paratroop drop

US front lines

1   Allied front line 15 December 1944

2   German paratroop drop zone
night of 16 December 1944

3   Allied front line 20 December 1944

4   Allied front line 24 December 1944

HODGES — XXXX 1
V — XXX
ZANGEN — XXXX 15
LXXIV — XXX
LXVII — XXX
XVIII — XXX
I SS — XXX
II SS — XXX
DIETRICH — XXXX 6
VII — XXX
VIII — XXX
LXVI — XXX
MANTEUFFEL — XXXX 5
LVIII — XXX
XLVII — XXX
LXXXV — XXX
BRANDENBERGER — XXXX 7
LXXX — XXX
VIII — XXX
PATTON — XXXX 3
III — XXX
XII — XXX
XXXII — XXX

BELGIUM
GERMANY
LUXEMBOURG

Liege
Eupen
Monschau
Huy
Andenne
Spa
Malmédy
Bütgenbach
Büllingen
Losheim
Stadtkyll
Stoumont
Werbomont
Trois-Ponts
Stavelot
St Vith
Prüm
Ciney
Celles
Marche en Famenne
La Roche en Ardenne
Gouvy
Oudler
Pronsfeld
Ciergnon
Rockefort
Houffalize
Clervaux
Wellin
Ortheuville
Amberloup
St Hubert
Bastogne
Wiltz
Consthum
Bitburg
Libramont
Diekirch
Neufchâteau
Ettelbrück
Martelange
Arlon
Luxembourg
Haute Fagnes
Dinant

Stadtkyll
Prüm
Pronsfeld
Bitburg
Echternach
Trier
Büllingen

500
300
200
0 m

5 km
5 miles

Red Storm, 1944–45

German expectations that the 1943 offensives would end in December as a result of fatigue amongst Soviet forces were to be rudely shattered, since the Soviets had no intention of stopping – they in fact intended to begin the reconquest of western Ukraine before the year was out.

As a result, early on the morning of 24 December, 1st Ukrainian Front launched a massive preparatory bombardment against Army Group South's positions to the west of Kiev. Once this had finished, the assault divisions were thrown into battle, and made particularly short work of their opposition. As the day drew to a close, the Russians had advanced to a depth of 20 miles, and the Germans were in complete disarray. For once, though, luck was on their side, for it began to rain on Christmas Day. The rain was heavy and prolonged, and the downpour turned the countryside into a quagmire, through which movement was either difficult or, in places, impossible.

Despite this, the advance continued, albeit at a slower pace. The Germans were forced back, with the rail link between Army Group Centre and Army Group South being cut by Soviet troops on 5 January 1944. As a result of the offensive, a hole 150 miles wide and 50 miles deep was punched into the German front before the attack began to lose momentum. This was a temporary respite for the Germans, however, since 2nd Ukrainian Front launched an offensive of its own, which reached the outskirts of Kirovograd. After two weeks' preparation, both 1st and 2nd Ukrainian Fronts attacked, trapping 50,000 Germans in the Korsun-Shevchenkovsky salient.

Following on from previous orders given to troops trapped in near hopeless situations, Hitler refused to allow any effort to break out, ordering a counter-offensive. This was initially successful, but this time the weather worked against the Germans. Temperatures were unseasonably warm, and the thawing snow and ice turned the ground into a muddy, impassable mess – German armour was literally bogged down.

Orders permitting a retreat from the Korsun-Shevchenkovsky pocket were at last given, but although the withdrawal went well at the beginning, once the Russians realized what was happening, they intervened with some well-directed artillery fire. The withdrawal collapsed into a rout as command and control disappeared as officers were killed, wounded or otherwise separated from their men. Thousands of soldiers were

Opposite: Sitting in his foxhole, an SS soldier waits for the inevitable arrival of the Red Army. He is armed with the standard German service rifle, the Kar 98 bolt-action rifle.

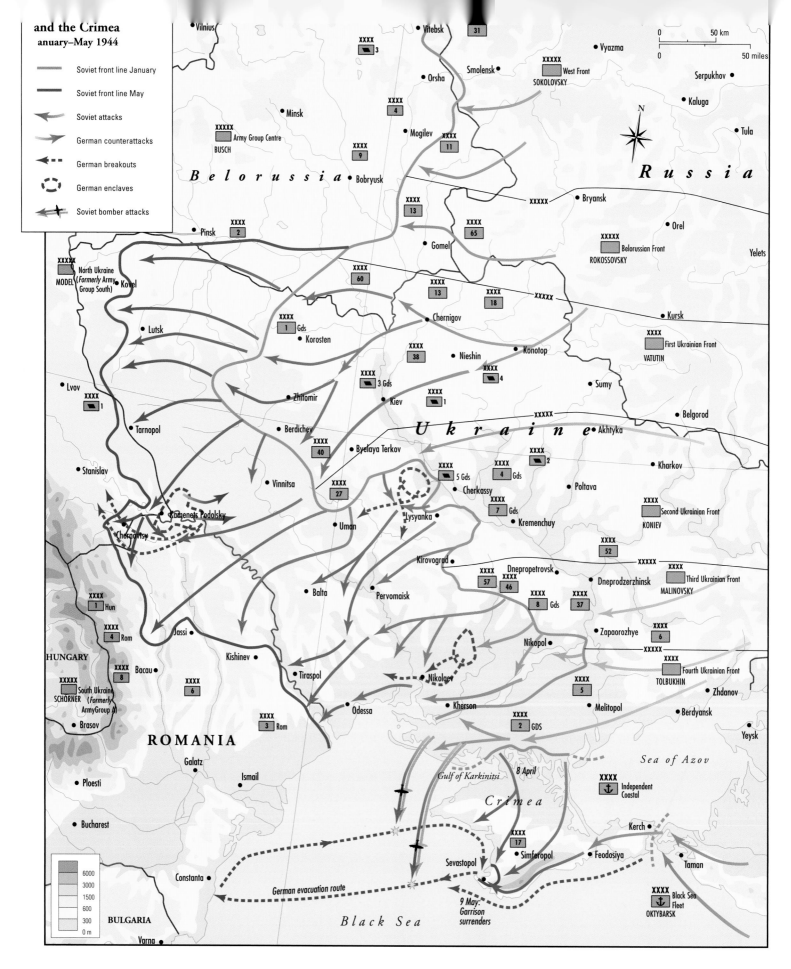

and the Crimea
anuary–May 1944

Soviet front line January

Soviet front line May

Soviet attacks

German counterattacks

German breakouts

German enclaves

Soviet bomber attacks

Vilnius

Vitebsk

31

Vyazma

Serpukhov

XXXX 3

Smolensk

Orsha

SOKOLOVSKY **West Front**

Tula

Minsk

Mogilev

Kaluga

XXXX 4

XXXXX Army Group Centre
BUSCH

XXXX 11

XXXX 9

Bobryusk

B e l o r u s s i a

R u s s i a

XXXX 13

Bryansk

Orel

Pinsk

XXXX 2

Gomel

XXXX 65

XXXXX Belorussian Front
ROKOSSOVSKY

Yelets

XXXXX North Ukraine
MODEL (*Formerly Army Group South*)

Kovel

XXXX 60

XXXX 13

Chernigov

XXXX 18

Kursk

Lutsk

XXXX 1 Gds

Korosten

XXXX 38

Nieshin

Konotop

XXXX 4

XXXX First Ukrainian Front
VATUTIN

Lvov

XXXX 1

Zhitomir

XXXX 3 Gds

Kiev

XXXX 1

Sumy

Belgorod

Tarnopol

Berdichev

Byelaya Terkov

U k r a i n e Akhtyka

XXXX 40

XXXX 5 Gds

XXXX 4 Gds

XXXX 2

Kharkov

Stanislav

Vinnitsa

XXXX 27

Lysyanka

Cherkassy

XXXX 7 Gds

Poltava

XXXX Second Ukrainian Front
KONIEV

Kamenets Podolsky

Chernovtsy

Uman

Kirovograd

Dnepropetrovsk

XXXX 57

XXXX 46

XXXX 52

Dneprodzerzhinsk

XXXX Third Ukrainian Front
MALINOVSKY

XXXX 1 Hun

Balta

Pervomaisk

XXXX 8 Gds

XXXX 37

XXXX 6

XXXX 4 Rom

Jassi

Zapaorozhye

Nikopol

XXXX 5

HUNGARY

Kishinev

Tiraspol

Nikolaev

Kherson

Melitopol

Zhdanov

Berdyansk

XXXX 8

Bacau

XXXX 6

Odessa

XXXX 2 GDS

Yeysk

XXXXX South Ukraine
SCHORNER (*Formerly ArmyGroup A*)

Brasov

XXXX 3 Rom

ROMANIA

Galatz

Sea of Azov

8 April

XXXX Independent Coastal ⚓

Ploesti

Ismail

Gulf of Karkinitsi

C r i m e a

Kerch

Bucharest

XXXX 17

Simferopol

Feodosiya

Taman

Sevastopol

XXXX Black Sea Fleet ⚓
OKTYBARSK

Constanta

German evacuation route

9 May: Garrison surrenders

B l a c k S e a

BULGARIA

6000
3000
1500
600
300
0 m

Varna

0   50 km

0   50 miles

N

killed trying to cross the Gniloi Tikitsch river, which was in full spate as a result of the thaw. Despite this, some 30,000 German troops escaped out of the 50,000 trapped, but they were in little condition to be returned to the front line in the near future. Stalin's initial anger at the escape of so many Germans was alleviated when he noted the parallels with Alexander Nevsky's destruction of the Teutonic Knights in 1200.

Soviet momentum did not slacken, and on 4 March, a new attack forced the Germans back across the Dniestr. In the course of these operations, the last rail link connecting the German forces in Poland and those in the southern USSR was captured when Chernovsty fell into Russian hands. General Malinovsky's 3rd Ukrainian Front and General Tolbukhin's 4th Ukrainian Front then opened offensives of their own, each enjoying notable success. Malinovsky succeeded in recapturing Odessa, while Tolbukhin launched an attack from Sicash-Perekop. The Independent Primorsk Army joined in the assault from the Kerch peninsula, and left the German Seventeenth Army facing serious difficulties as it fought desperately to maintain its positions. This was a hopeless task. By 12 April, the Germans were withdrawing from the Crimean peninsula, with the Red Army in pursuit. Just four days later, the Germans had been driven back into Sevastopol, where they received strict instructions from Hitler that they were not to leave the Crimea.

Sevastopol was assaulted on 6 May. Although the Germans put up stiff resistance, it was abundantly clear that they would be unable to hold out. While it had taken the Germans no less than 250 days to take the city from the Russians, the Soviet high command made clear that it expected success rather more swiftly, and preferably in a matter of hours. Two days of bloody fighting marked the opening of the battle, but by noon on 7 May, the way into Sevastopol lay open. The Germans began to fall back towards the centre of the city, as Russian troops made probing attacks. By the evening of 9 May, Sevastopol was entirely in Soviet hands. Stalin demanded that the rest of the Crimea be cleared as soon as possible, and definitely within 24 hours, and his troops did not disappoint him. A massive Soviet assault forced the Germans back into the Kherson spit, a finger of land at the water's edge, from where they began an evacuation under heavy bombardment and air attack. The end followed swiftly, and by midday on 12 May, the remnants of the Seventeenth Army surrendered, some 25,000 men in all out of an army that had once been 110,000 strong.

Liberating Leningrad

While operations against the Crimea were under way, the Soviets set about dealing with the siege of Leningrad. The city had been besieged for nearly three years and raising the encirclement was a key goal for the Soviets. Although a corridor had been opened into the city in 1943, this was well within range of German artillery fire, and did not represent a permanent solution to Leningrad's suffering. In addition, Stalin was anxious to deal with the problem posed by the Finns, who were fighting as co-belligerents with the Germans, with the intention of overturning the peace treaty that had been signed after the bitter Winter War between the two nations. The early days of 1944 represented the ideal time for the Russians to focus on Leningrad, since the Germans were distracted by the disasters befalling them in the south, while Army Group North's attention was increasingly focused on the possibility of a Russian offensive in Belorussia.

As a result, General Govorov's Leningrad Front and General Meretskov's Volkhov Front were told to combine for offensive operations in the Novgorod-Luga sector,

Opposite: On 24 January 1944, the Soviets began their offensive to liberate the Ukraine, swiftly driving back the Germans. The speed of the advance left German forces trapped in the Korsun-Shevchenkovsky pocket, and their attempt to break-out was accompanied by massive casualties. The Crimea was little different. By 16 April 1944, German forces had been driven back to Sevastopol, which fell on 10 May. Under 40,000 of the 150,000 Germans originally holding the Crimea escaped.

Above: Russian troops in winter camouflage make their way past a Red Army light tank as they head towards German positions. 'General Winter' played a large part in saving the USSR in 1941, and winter conditions (snow, ice and the thaws that followed) played a major part in the fighting on the Eastern Front.

beginning on 14 January 1944. The attack was preceded by a raid by heavy bombers on German artillery at Bezzabotny overnight, then, at 09:35, an artillery bombardment against the German positions began. One hundred thousand shells were fired in a barrage lasting for an hour and five minutes. Second Shock Army moved forward as soon as the bombardment ended, gaining 3000 yards along a five-mile frontage, with some units reaching the German second line of defence.

Although the advance went reasonably well on the first day, it was hampered by mist, followed by the fall of snow in the Soviet Forty-Second Army's area. Forty-Second Army made progress, but this was slow. Govorov's chief of staff was sent to investigate, and found that the infantry were advancing without support from artillery or tanks, not least since the latter had become stuck in the snow. Nevertheless, the Russians continued to advance until by 19 January the Second Shock and Forty-Second Armies linked up near Ropsha. In the process of doing this, Russian troops captured the German heavy gun batteries that had been used to shell Leningrad, with over 100 of these weapons being taken.

The Germans managed to withdraw unmolested from around Mga on 20/21 January, much to Govorov's irritation, but it was quite clear that they would not be in a position where they could threaten Leningrad for much longer. By 20 January, the Soviet breakthrough had been completed, and the Russians moved into a pursuit phase, chasing the Germans as they pulled back. However, as at Mga, the pursuit was slow, not least because of tactical deficiencies on the part of formation commanders. Having been based in the Leningrad area for most of the war, these senior officers had not been exposed to the learning process that generals engaged in fighting elsewhere in the USSR had faced. As a result, the Leningrad operation was characterized by a penchant for using infantry for almost everything, while armoured and artillery units were left kicking their heels since they had no tasks assigned to them. By 23 January, Govorov could no longer stand the ineptitude being demonstrated, and issued orders making it clear that linear tactics were to be abandoned in favour of the use of firepower and manoeuvre. Commanders were to ensure that they conducted all-arms operations, employing the full weight of heavy weaponry available to them.

These instructions came a little too late, however, and the Germans were able to avoid encirclement. Nonetheless, Leningrad's encirclement was brought to an end on 26 January, when the Moscow–Leningrad railway line was cleared of all enemy troops and returned to Soviet control. The Germans continued fighting as they pulled back in good order as town after town fell to the Russians; once again, the slowness of the Soviet pursuit meant that the Germans were able to avoid disaster. However, despite this disappointment, the Russians had achieved their aim. By 30 January, German forces had been driven back between 50 and 60 miles. Operations continued into February, but shortages of ammunition for the artillery made the Russians' task rather more difficult than it might have been. While it was not until August that all German units were driven from the Leningrad region, the battle had been won by the end of January. The main objective, namely freeing the city, had been achieved, and most of the Leningrad and Kalinin districts had been cleared of German troops. Army Group North's hold on Russian territory was distinctly weaker than it had been, with many of its formations having taken a savage mauling.

Below: A long column of German prisoners is guarded by a young Soviet soldier armed with a PPSh sub-machine gun. German prisoners were subjected to a brutal and long captivity, with the last of the few survivors being released from Soviet camps in the mid-1950s.

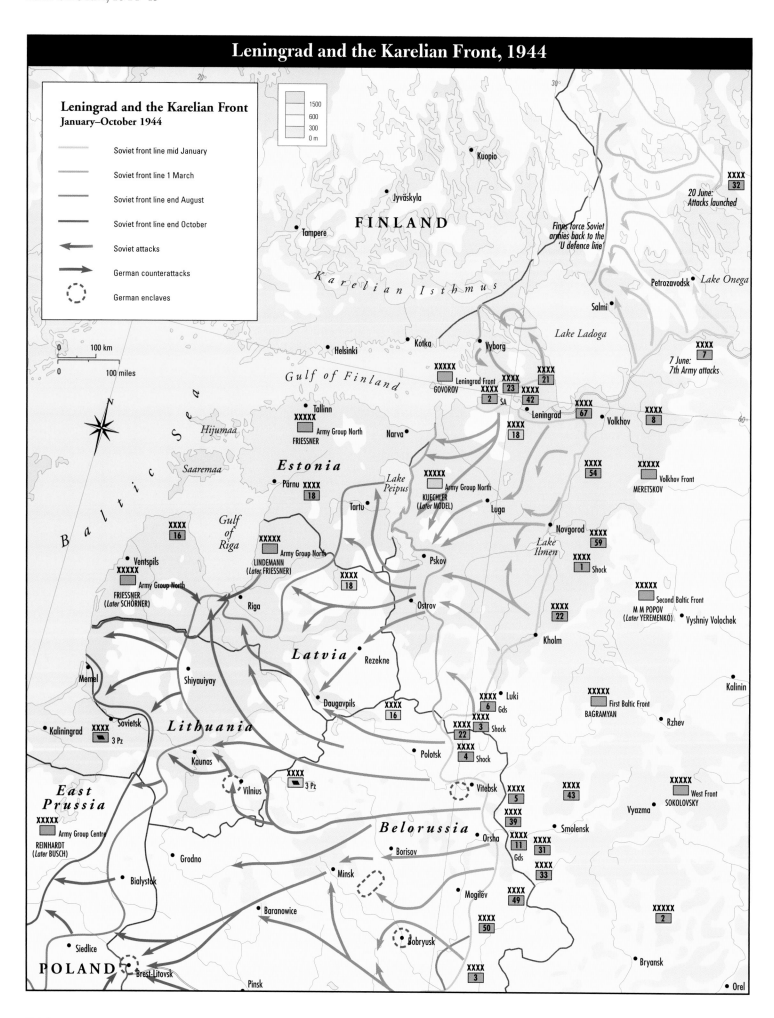

Leningrad and the Karelian Front, 1944

Leningrad and the Karelian Front
January–October 1944

Soviet front line mid January	
Soviet front line 1 March	
Soviet front line end August	
Soviet front line end October	
Soviet attacks	
German counterattacks	
German enclaves	

1500
600
300
0 m

0   100 km
0   100 miles

FINLAND

Kuopio

Jyväskyla

Tampere

XXXX 32
20 June:
Attacks launched

Finns force Soviet
armies back to the
'U defence line

Karelian Isthmus

Petrozavodsk • Lake Onega

Salmi

Lake Ladoga

XXXX 7
7 June:
7th Army attacks

Helsinki   Kotka   Vyborg

Gulf of Finland

XXXXX GOVOROV   Leningrad Front   XXXX 21
XXXX 2 SA   XXXX 23   XXXX 42
Leningrad   XXXX 67   XXXX 8
Volkhov

Tallinn

XXXXX FRIESSNER   Army Group North   Narva

XXXX 18

XXXX 54   XXXXX Volkhov Front   MERETSKOV

Estonia

Pärnu XXXX 18

Lake Peipus

Tartu

XXXXX KUECHLER (Later MODEL)   Army Group North

Luga

Hijumaa

Saaremaa

Baltic Sea

Gulf of Riga

XXXX 16

Ventspils
XXXXX FRIESSNER (Later SCHÖRNER)   Army Group North

XXXXX LINDEMANN (Later FRIESSNER)   Army Group North

Riga

XXXX 18

Pskov

Novgorod XXXX 59

Lake Ilmen

XXXX 1 Shock

Ostrov

XXXXX M M POPOV (Later YEREMENKO)   Second Baltic Front   • Vyshniy Volochek

XXXX 22

Kholm

Latvia   Rezekne

Memel   Shyauiyay

XXXX 16   Daugavpils

Kalinin

XXXXX First Baltic Front   BAGRAMYAN

• Rzhev

XXXX 6 Gds • Luki

XXXX 22   XXXX 3 Shock

XXXX 4 Shock

Kaliningrad • Sovietsk
XXXX 3 Pz

Lithuania   Kaunas

XXXX 3 Pz

Vilnius

East Prussia

XXXXX REINHARDT (Later BUSCH)   Army Group Centre

Polotsk

Vitebsk

XXXX 5

XXXX 43   XXXXX West Front SOKOLOVSKY

• Vyazma

XXXX 39

Belorussia   Orsha

XXXX 11 Gds   XXXX 31

• Smolensk

• Borisov

Grodno

Minsk

XXXX 33

• Mogilev

XXXX 49

XXXXX 2

Bialystok

Baranowice

XXXX 50   Bobryusk

Siedlce

• Bryansk

POLAND   Brest-Litovsk

Pinsk   XXXX 3

• Orel

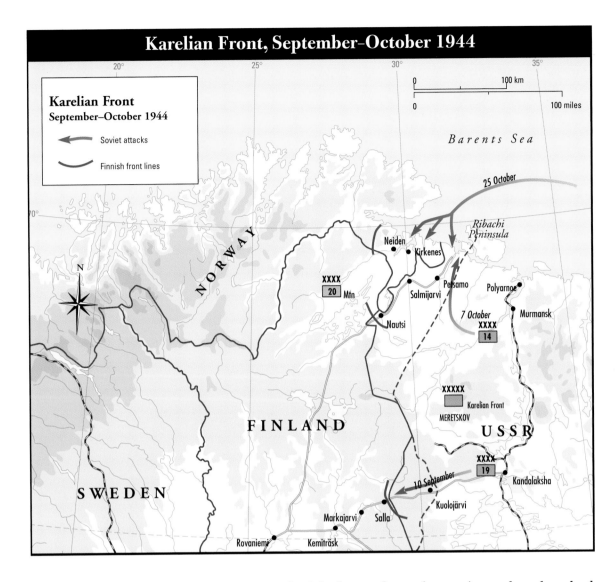

Karelian Front, September–October 1944

Karelian Front
September–October 1944

⟵ Soviet attacks

⟝ Finnish front lines

Barents Sea

Left: Operations in the Karelian Isthmus were intended to bring the conflict with Finland to an end; outnumbered by Soviet forces that were far more adept than those who had been routed in the earlier Winter War between the two countries, it came as no surprise that the Finns had to fall back as the Russians retook territory that had been theirs until 1941. An armistice soon followed, allowing the Russians to focus upon driving the Germans out of the USSR completely.

All that remained was to remove Finnish forces from the territory that they had occupied since 1941. The Finns could see that the success against Army Group North rendered their position increasingly difficult, and they began to attempt to make contact with the Soviet government through diplomatic contacts. As it was, General Meretskov's Volkhov Front was disbanded in February 1944 as the operations around Leningrad developed, and he was instead given command of the Karelian Front. On 10 June Meretskov launched the Svir-Petrozavodsk offensive, while the Leningrad Front attacked the Karelian Isthmus near Vyborg. Operations lasted until 9 August, when the Finns were driven back to the line of the 1939 Finnish-Soviet border; aware that there was nothing more that they could do, the Finns sought peace, an armistice being signed on 4 September.

Operation Bagration

Even as the Spring 1944 offensives drew to a close, the Soviet high command had begun planning for the next offensive. An extensive analysis of the possible options was undertaken. An operation in the Balkans was considered, but swiftly rejected on the grounds that such an attack would overextend supply lines across difficult terrain, with possibly dangerous consequences. Other options were debated, until it was agreed that the best course of action would be an attack against Army Group Centre's positions in Belorussia, with the initial aim of recapturing Minsk. The offensive, codenamed

Opposite: On 14 January 1944, an offensive was launched to lift the siege of Leningrad. While the conduct of operations was not as skilful as seen in the offensives in the Ukraine and Crimea as a result of Soviet commanders in the area being unfamiliar with the latest tactical methods, the siege was lifted by the end of the month, although the last German units were not ejected from the Leningrad region until the summer of 1944.

Above: The corpses of three German soldiers lie in the gutter, while soldiers and civilians walk by without giving them a second glance. By the later stages of the war, the civilian population in Russia and Germany had come to regard death and destruction as being largely unremarkable, and three dead soldiers lying in the gutter was certainly not something particularly shocking.

Operation Bagration after a famed Russian commander of the nineteenth century, aimed to encircle the German army groups in the Minsk–Vitebsk–Rogachev triangle, and to completely destroy them.

The Soviets enjoyed overwhelming air superiority, which meant that their troops were able to operate with little threat of interference from the Luftwaffe. They also held a considerable advantage in manpower, for despite the massive losses sustained in the war so far, the Soviets had demonstrated an unerring ability to draw upon the population of the USSR to provide more men for the front line, a feat that the Germans were simply unable to match. The Russians had 19 all-arms and two tank armies totalling 1.4 million men, supported by 5200 tanks and assault guns and 31,000 artillery pieces and mortars. The Germans had 1.2 million men, but while their manpower was nearly equal to that of the Soviets, they had just 9500 artillery pieces, and around 900 tanks and assault guns.

The goal of destroying Army Group Centre was agreed at a conference on 22/23 May 1944, and to achieve this a breakthrough in six sectors was envisaged, with the three Belorussian fronts aiming for the first objective, Minsk.

The Germans gained some intimation of the forthcoming offensive as a result of signals intelligence that revealed that the Soviets had sent instructions to partisan groups that they should destroy as much of the German logistic system as possible in the area behind the battlefront, while air attacks on airfields and railway lines suggested that the Russians were on the verge of launching an assault.

Operation Bagration began on 23 June 1944, and within three days the 1st Belorussian Front had broken into the German positions around Bobruysk, while 3rd Belorussian Front had punched its way into Army Group Centre's defences between

Vitebsk and Orsha. The Russians drove forward remorselessly, encircling first German LIII Corps, then the German Fourth Army. In each case, it was clear that a timely withdrawal could save the German formations, but when permission to withdraw was sought, Hitler refused. He remained stubborn in the belief that defending to the last round was in some way preferable to safely evacuating the bulk of his forces so that they could be used again.

On other occasions, the *Führer*'s approval for a retreat only came when it was far too late to achieve anything. The Germans faced a series of disasters as a result. First, IX Corps was destroyed at Vitebsk, which it was only allowed to abandon long after the time for doing this had passed. Then 70,000 men of Ninth Army were trapped in the Bobruysk pocket. On 29 June the city was stormed and the remainder of the German forces there were wiped out. Their commander had been sacked two days earlier, and had been ordered to report to Germany. While this ensured that he was not captured, it meant that his men were left generally leaderless, and chaos ensued in the final stages of the battle.

This was not all. A Soviet breakthrough at Orsha left the German Fourth Army in a completely untenable position. This was obvious, yet once again Hitler issued strict orders that the army was forbidden to withdraw and should fight to the death. General Tippelskirch found this too much to bear and disobeyed his orders and withdrew.

Below: German troops prepare to leave their trench for an attack against nearby Red Army positions. The soldier in the background is carrying a rifle with bayonet fixed, suggesting that he is expecting to be involved in close-quarter fighting at some point. He also has a grenade at the ready.

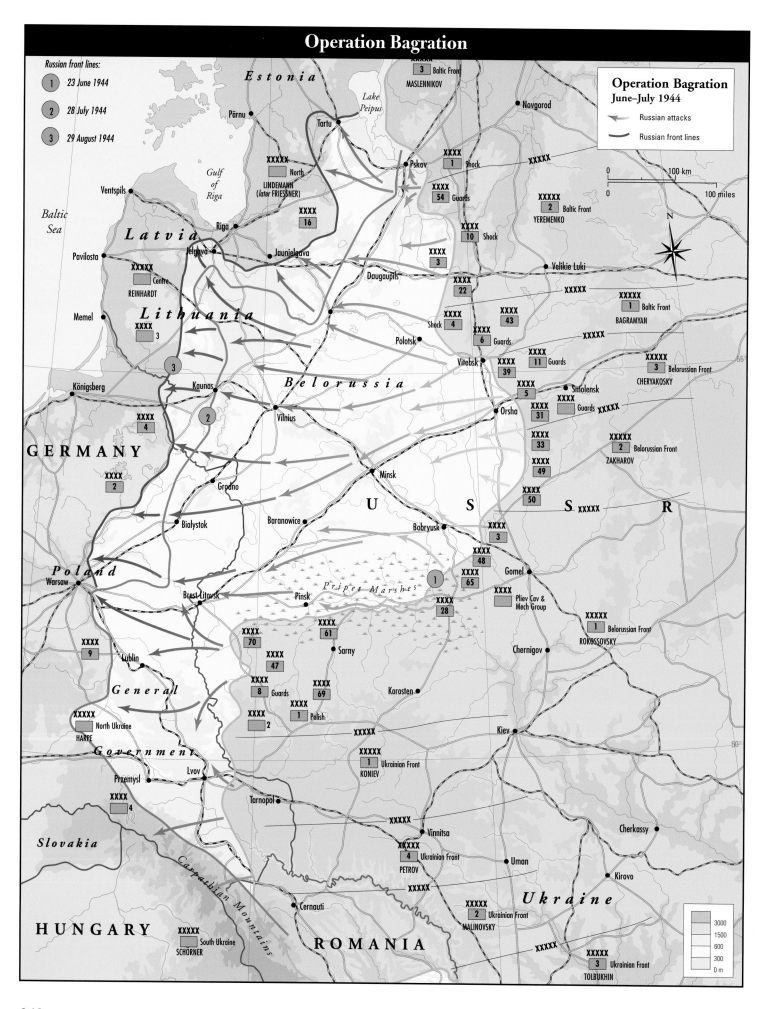

Operation Bagration

Russian front lines:

1 — 23 June 1944

2 — 28 July 1944

3 — 29 August 1944

Operation Bagration
June–July 1944

Russian attacks
Russian front lines

Tippelskirch began a trend amongst German generals, by carefully fabricating situation reports, which, when examined closely, justified his actions to the high command. He completed the deception by forging sets of orders, one set of which was sent to Hitler to show that his orders were being followed to the letter, while the real orders given to his troops outlined the way in which they were going to pull back. Despite this subterfuge, by 30 June the bulk of Tippelskirch's forces were trapped to the east of the River Berezina, where they were killed or captured *en masse.*

It was clear that Army Group Centre would be destroyed without rapid withdrawals, but Hitler's only response seemed to be ludicrous orders preventing timely retreats, and to sack Field Marshal Busch as commander of the army group, even though it is hard to see exactly what more Busch could have done in the circumstances.

Army Group North endured an equally torrid time as the Soviets advanced. The Soviets succeeded in trapping the German forces around Minsk by 3 July, and set about destroying them. The city itself fell on 4 July, and some 43,000 Germans were killed in fierce fighting that followed over the next week as they tried to extricate themselves from a desperate situation. Having taken Minsk, the Russians pushed on into Lithuania, heading for Vilnius. They arrived there on 8 July, and encircled the city, although about half the garrison was able to escape before it fell five days later. Second Belorussian Front pushed on to within 50 miles of East Prussia, while 1st Belorussian punched its way into Poland and crossed the Vistula. Finally, after 68 days, Operation Bagration ended on 29

Above: A graphic piece of Soviet propaganda shows Hitler being crushed by the pincers of the Red Army. By 1944, this was an extremely accurate description of the German position in the East, yet Hitler seemed unable to see that he was facing disaster.

Map, page 348:
Operation Bagration begin shortly after the Allied invasion of Normandy, with the deliberate aim of stretching the Germans to breaking point. On 23 June 1944, the offensive began, with four fronts attacking the Germans in the central sector of the Russian front. By the end of August, Soviet forces were in the Baltic States, Poland, and on the borders of Romania. Operation Bagration marked the heaviest German defeat of the war. Nearly half a million men had been lost, and it would not be long before the Red Army entered Germany itself.

August. Soviet forces had advanced between 340 and 375 miles along a 700-mile frontage, inflicting massive and near irreparable damage on Army Group Centre, and battering the other German formations that stood against the advance. The offensive placed the Soviets in an ideal position to advance on towards Germany itself.

The Advance to the Oder

The German position in the East became increasingly awkward, since from June 1944, Allied armies had been in France. After some hard fighting in June, July and early August, German resistance seemed to crumble momentarily, and the Allies were able to drive into the Low Countries. By September, they were in close proximity to the River Rhine, with the obvious implication that Germany would be invaded in the not too distant future. This meant that the situation everywhere was becoming dangerous for the Germans, but Hitler refused to see this. After surviving an assassination attempt on 20 July, the *Führer* had become convinced that some form of supernatural providence was protecting him; he also became even less trusting of his generals after a number of senior officers (including Rommel) were implicated in the plot.

As a result, by late 1944, Hitler's attention had turned from the Eastern Front to the West. He aimed to launch a daring (but over-optimistic) offensive in the Ardennes region, seeking to recreate the success of 1940. Hitler aimed to split the British and American forces from one another, and, by taking the port of Antwerp, place himself in a favourable position from which peace could be negotiated. This completely failed to appreciate the resolution of the Western Allies, but Hitler could not be dissuaded. Despite firm protestations from his generals, he refused to accept their observations that removing troops from the East to support the Ardennes operation left Germany vulnerable to another Soviet attack. Hitler dismissed these concerns with the assertion that the Soviets were not in a position to begin another offensive as they had been fighting

---

STURMOVIK

The most prolifically-produced aircraft of World War II was not a fighter or heavy bomber, but a robust and rather crude ground-attack aircraft, the Il-2 'Sturmovik' (armoured assault aircraft). The first aircraft were single-seaters, armed with a mix of cannon, machine guns, bombs and rockets, but they proved to be disappointing. Modifications were made, adding a second crew member with a machine gun to provide rear defence, while the wing-mounted 20mm (0.78in) cannons were replaced with high-velocity 23mm (0.9in) cannon instead. The new Sturmoviks began to enter service in 1942, and were a revelation. Their heavy armour meant that they were able to sustain a considerable battering from ground fire with little ill effect, and their success led to massive production output. Constant development saw even heavier cannon being added to later aircraft, along with more bombs or rockets. The Germans had little answer to the depredations of the Sturmoviks, and the aircraft proved extremely popular with both its crews and the ground forces that it supported. When production ended shortly after the war, no fewer than 36,183 Il-2s had been produced, more than any other aircraft before or since.

Left: Armourers load bombs onto a Red Air Force seaplane. In a practice common to air forces the world over, the bombs have been marked with a variety of pithy messages for the enemy, although these would not, of course, be seen unless the weapons failed to explode.

constantly for four months. In fact, the Ardennes offensive worked in favour of the Russians, just as the German generals feared. As they had pointed out, committing troops to operations in the West meant that they were not available to act as a reserve against a Russian attack. To deal with the developing crisis in Hungary, Hitler had been forced to denude the Vistula of forces to send them into the fray against the Russians there. This simply assisted the Soviets, who had, in fact, started planning for their 1945 offensives in October 1944, at about the time that Hitler had thought that all they would

Right: By the end of August 1944 as Operation Bagration came to an end, Soviet forces were in the Baltic States, Poland, and on the borders of Romania. 1st Belorussian Front punched its way into Poland and crossed the Vistula, leaving the Germans facing the clear threat of further advances through Poland. Bagration ended to allow the Soviets to regroup, thus giving the Germans the opportunity to crush the Warsaw Rising.

Opposite: The Polish Home Army's efforts to liberate Warsaw were ultimately thwarted by the lack of support provided from nearby Russian forces. Stalin's determination to ensure that the exiled government could not return to power meant that he was quite content to leave the Poles to their fate as the Germans sought to suppress the rising. When the fighting ended on 2 October, at least 75 per cent (perhaps over 90 per cent) of the city's buildings had been destroyed, while estimates of casualties range from between 150,000 and 200,000 Poles killed, along with some 17,000 Germans.

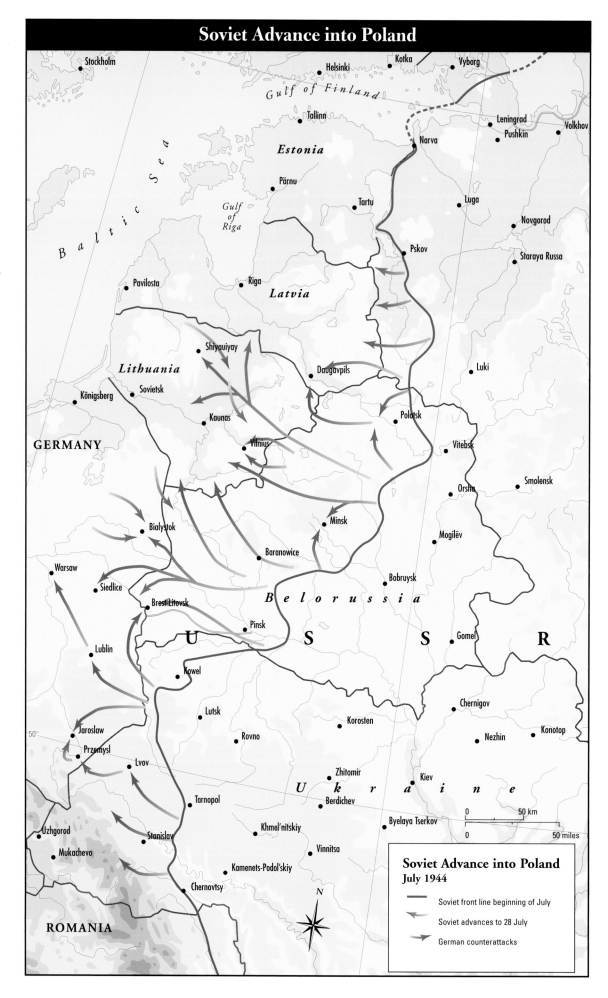

Soviet Advance into Poland

Soviet Advance into Poland
July 1944

⸻ Soviet front line beginning of July

← Soviet advances to 28 July

→ German counterattacks

The Warsaw Rising

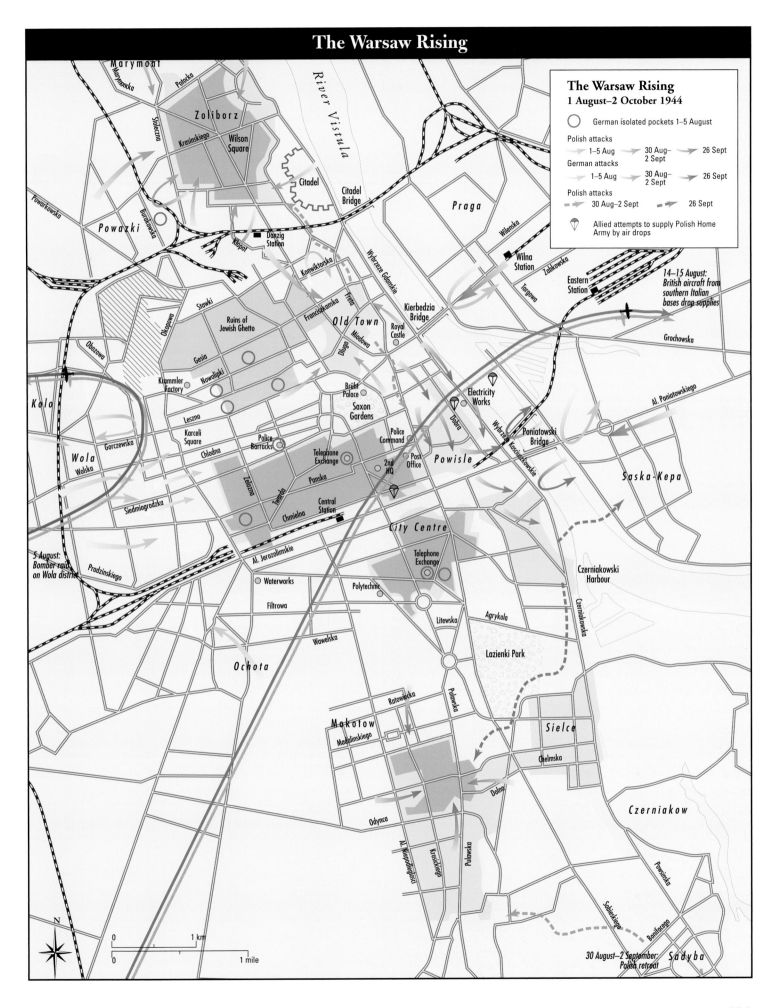

The Warsaw Rising
1 August–2 October 1944

- ◯ German isolated pockets 1–5 August
- Polish attacks
  - 1–5 Aug
  - 30 Aug–2 Sept
  - 26 Sept
- German attacks
  - 1–5 Aug
  - 30 Aug–2 Sept
  - 26 Sept
- Polish attacks
  - 30 Aug–2 Sept
  - 26 Sept
- Allied attempts to supply Polish Home Army by air drops

Marymont
Marzzonka
Potocka
Słoweczna
Zoliborz
Krasińskiego
Wilson Square
Powązki
Powarkowska
Burakowska
Kłopot
Citadel
Citadel Bridge
River Vistula
Praga
Wilenska
Wilna Station
Zabkowska
Targowa
Eastern Station

14–15 August:
British aircraft from
southern Italian
bases drop supplies

Grochowska

Konwiktorska
Danzig Station
Wybrzeże Gdańskie
Franciszkanska
Old Town
Freta
Młodowa
Długa
Kierbedzia Bridge
Royal Castle

Stawki
Okopowa
Ruins of
Jewish Ghetto
Gesia
Nowolipki
Krammler Factory
Kolo
Obozowa
Leszno
Karceli Square
Chłodna
Police Barracks
Wola
Gorczewska
Wolska
Żelazna
Twarda
Panska
Siedmiogrodzka
Chmielna
Central Station
Brühl Palace
Saxon Gardens
Telephone Exchange
2nd HQ
Police Command
Post Office
Powisle
Electricity Works
Dobra
Wybrzeże Kościuszkowskie
Poniatowski Bridge
Al. Poniatowskiego
Saska-Kepa

Al. Jerozolimskie
City Centre
Telephone Exchange
Waterworks
Polytechnic
Czerniakowski Harbour

5 August:
Bomber raid
on Wola district
Pradzinskiego
Filtrowa
Wawelska
Litewska
Agrykola
Czerniakowska

Ochota

Lazienki Park

Ratowiecka
Pulawska
Mokotow
Madalinskiego
Sielce
Chelmska

Odynca
Al. Niepodległości
Krosickiego
Pulawska
Dolna
Dolna
Czerniakow

Powsinska
Sobieskiego
Bonifarego

N

0   1 km
0   1 mile

30 August–2 September:
Polish retreat
Sadyba

Above: A weary German soldier, armed with an StG 44 assault rifle, trudges westwards at some point during the fighting in 1944. Although the Germans were able to introduce new automatic rifles that provided troops with a significant increase in firepower, there were never enough to go around.

be looking to do would be to remain on the defensive for some months while they recovered from the losses they had sustained.

The Offensive

By early January, 2.2 million Russian troops had been assembled opposite the River Vistula, and contrary to Hitler's expectations were in a position to attack. In response to a request from Roosevelt and Churchill, Stalin brought the start date of the offensive forward eight days to 12 January 1945, so that his operations would assist with the final stages of what had now become known as the Battle of the Bulge as the British and Americans sought to defeat the Germans in the Ardennes. The offensive began at 04:30 in a blizzard, with a massive bombardment against German positions. German Fourth Panzer Army and its flank protection, Seventeenth Army, were pounded for 30 minutes, before the bombardment eased and Russian troops went forward. They penetrated the German lines to a depth of up to 2 miles in places before they were halted.

At 10:00, another massive bombardment, lasting for an hour and three-quarters, was laid down upon the German lines. Fourth Panzer Army's headquarters was blown to oblivion in the process, and the formation lost all ability to fight, collapsing into confusion as the Russians attacked. Some Germans remained in their trenches, literally unable to move, their will shattered by the massive bombardment. Others simply turned and ran in the face of the enemy attack. As a blizzard developed, the main bodies of the attacking Soviet formation drove forward, sweeping all before them. When Koniev received reports that his tanks had destroyed the 16th Panzer Division in its assembly area, he decided that it would be appropriate to commit his exploitation forces, a decision reinforced by more reports of a general German collapse.

The exploitation troops swiftly broke through the German lines, and by nightfall on 12 January 1945 had reached a depth of 14 miles along a 25-mile front. The next day, over 2000 Russian tanks charged across the icy countryside, cutting the lines of communication between Warsaw and Kraków. The Germans were forced to withdraw from Warsaw, leaving Kraków and Silesia as the next targets for the Russians.

Further north, Marshal Zhukhov had sent his troops into action on 14 January against the German Ninth Army. After making impressive initial gains, Zhukhov then sent his

First and Second Guards Tank Armies into the fray, punching their way into the centre of Ninth Army. The weight of assault was such that Ninth Army began to collapse, allowing Second Guards Tank Army to sweep to the northwest, to threaten Warsaw. On the night of 16 January, it became abundantly clear to the German high command that to remain in Warsaw would be suicidal; as a consequence orders were given that XLVI Panzer Corps should retire from the city. These instructions were given without reference to Hitler, who was apoplectic when he discovered that Warsaw had been given up without the fight to the death that he customarily demanded. Rather than deal with the immediate difficulties facing him, Hitler spent some time dismissing generals and imposing a rigid command structure upon them – every commander from divisional level upwards was instructed that they were to obtain approval for every move they made, on pain of death. This neatly undercut the ability of commanders to respond to events in a flexible and timely fashion just at the time when having the ability to do this was becoming of critical importance. While this reorganization was under way, Zhukhov sent the First Polish Army, a formation under his command, to retake Warsaw.

Kraków and Silesia

On 17 January, a new directive was sent to Marshal Koniev's 1st Ukrainian Front, ordering it to take Kraków and Silesia, as a precursor for an advance towards the German city of Breslau. Fifty-Ninth and Sixtieth Armies were employed for these tasks, with proceedings beginning with an advance on Kraków, Fifty-Ninth Army assaulting from the north and west, while Sixtieth Army came in from the east. The Germans, appreciating the weight of forces ranged against them, withdrew to avoid being encircled, and left the Soviets with the simple task of entering the city.

Below: An ISU-152 assault gun ploughs its way through a cornfield in the Ukraine. The relaxed attitude of the men on the top of the assault gun suggests that they are probably being given a familiarization ride, and are well away from the front line. The ISU-152's 152mm gun proved an extremely useful weapon in clearing German strongpoints, particularly in urban fighting.

Right: As the Russians advanced through the Baltic States, they moved towards Königsberg, which they besieged after fierce fighting on the way to the city between 13 and 28 March 1945, at the end of which the German Fourth Army had all but ceased to exist. The German commander in Königsberg, General Otto Lasch, did his best to establish defensive lines, using the old nineteenth-century fortifications in the city as the basis of his positions but they were little match for the Soviet bombardment. The Germans were pushed back inexorably, and Lasch surrendered on 10 April 1945.

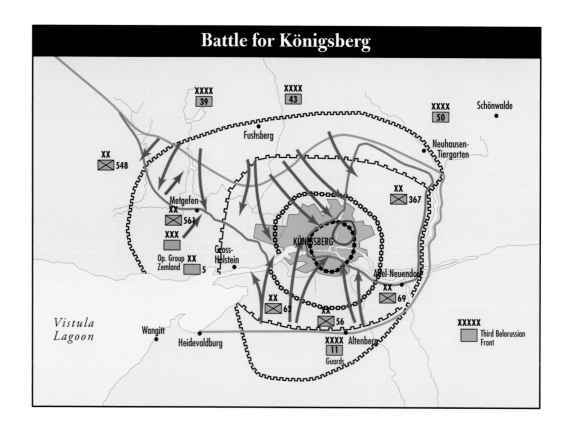

Silesia was a more difficult proposition, since it was heavily industrialized. As had been the case at Stalingrad, the nature of such an area, with large factories and urban areas, offered good defensive opportunities, but this time to the Germans. Painfully aware of this fact, Koniev decided that a slightly more innovative approach was required. He sent Third Guards Tank Army forward, and it crossed the German border on 20 January. It approached the River Oder, but when it reached the banks of the river, Koniev ordered it to turn through 90 degrees and drive along the right bank rather than cross. This technically awkward manoeuvre was conducted with aplomb, and succeeded in cracking the German defences. With Third Guards Tank Army approaching from the west, and the Fifty-Ninth and Sixtieth Armies coming from the east, it became obvious that encirclement was imminent. The decision was made for a retreat, and the Germans fell back towards the Carpathian mountains, leaving Silesia to the Russians.

Reaching the Oder

Zhukhov now issued orders for 1st Belorussian Front to drive on Poznan, the last major Polish city before the German border and the River Oder. As had been the case in Silesia, the decision to avoid urban areas was taken, and the Russians pursued the Germans across central Poland at speed. They then manoeuvred round the south side of Poznan itself on 26 January, a move that trapped 60,000 Germans there. Zhukhov then drove forward to the Oder, which Second Guards Tank Army and the forward elements of Fifth Shock Army reached on the last day of January. Units of Fifth Shock Army crossed the river and took the town of Kienitz in what was to be the last act of the offensive, which was halted on Stalin's orders on 2 February.

Stalin's decision was based on two practical reasons, both of which were eminently sensible. First, a thaw had set in, making it impossible to cross rivers until the water in them had gone down, something that would only happen in the spring. Hitler took the thaw as a sign of divine providence, and cheerfully predicted that his fortunes would

Advance to the Oder

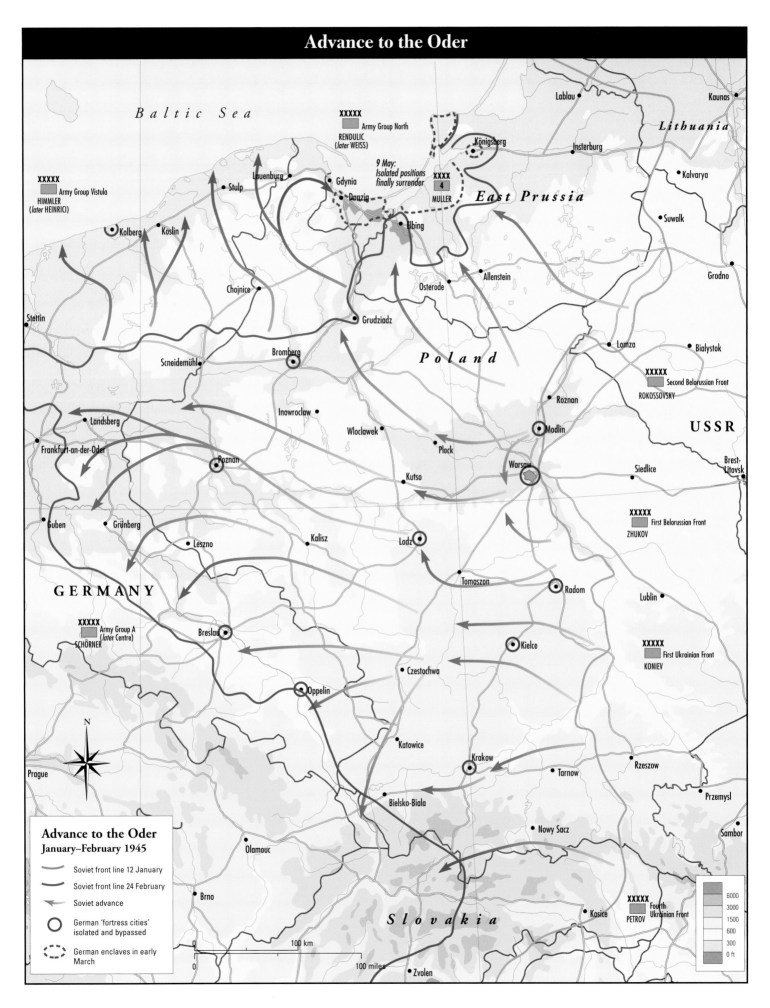

Baltic Sea

Lablau
Kaunas

Lithuania

XXXXX
Army Group North
RENDULIC
(*later* WEISS)

Königsberg
Insterburg

9 May:
Isolated positions
finally surrender

XXXXX
Army Group Vistula
HIMMLER
(*later* HEINRICI)

Lauenburg
Stulp
Gdynia
Danzig
Elbing

XXXX
4
MULLER

East Prussia

Kalvarya

Suwalk

Kolberg
Koslin

Chojnice

Grodno

Osterode
Allenstein

Stettin

Grudziadz

Poland

Scneidemühl
Bromberg

Inowroclaw

Lomza
Bialystok

XXXXX
Second Belorussian Front
ROKOSSOVSKY

Landsberg

Wloclawek
Roznan

USSR

Frankfurt-an-der-Oder

Poznan

Plock
Modlin

Brest-
Litovsk

Kutso
Warsaw

Siedlice

Guben
Grünberg
Leszno
Kalisz
Lodz

XXXXX
First Belorussian Front
ZHUKOV

GERMANY

Tomaszon
Radom
Lublin

XXXXX
Army Group A
(*later* Centre)
SCHÖRNER

Breslau

Kielce

XXXXX
First Ukrainian Front
KONIEV

Oppelin

Czestochwa

Katowice

Krakow
Tarnow
Rzeszow

N

Bielsko-Biala
Przemysl

Prague
Nowy Sacz
Sambor

Advance to the Oder
January–February 1945

——— Soviet front line 12 January

——— Soviet front line 24 February

◀—— Soviet advance

◯ German 'fortress cities'
isolated and bypassed

⬭ German enclaves in early
March

Olamouc

Brno

Slovakia

Kosice

XXXXX
Fourth
Ukrainian Front
PETROV

0   100 km

0   100 miles

Zvolen

6000
3000
1500
600
300
0 ft

Map, page 357: The Vistula–Oder operation began on 12 January 1945. German forces crumbled in the face of a massive artillery bombardment, and withdrew from Warsaw as their position collapsed. Kraków and Silesia soon followed, and by the end of the month, the Russians were on the banks of the Oder. The advance was hugely successful, gaining over 300 miles in two weeks, and destroying Army Group Centre in the process.

soon change. Yet again, Hitler's tenuous grasp on the reality of the situation confronting him was evident – the prospect of the Germans recovering sufficiently to throw the Russians back was now non-existent. Stalin's second reason for calling a halt – again rooted in a pragmatism his opponent lacked – lay in his appreciation that his troops would need to have time to prepare for the assault against the final prize, namely Berlin itself. Unlike previous sanguinary operations, the Vistula–Oder offensive had been completed for what were relatively light casualties on the Eastern Front; 15,000 Soviet troops had been killed and four times that number wounded, but Army Group Centre had been annihilated – more importantly, Soviet forces were now within 50 miles of Berlin. The operations also saw the removal of the Germans from the Baltic States, for although they could have been left in place to wither on the vine, to have ignored them would have been dangerous.

The Baltic

The reason for this concern lay in the fact that the Germans still controlled the Baltic Sea, which allowed troops in the Baltic States to be resupplied quite easily. The possibility remained that a well-equipped force could be used to drive out from the Baltic into the Russian flank as the advance across the Oder was under way. Before any attack on Berlin could be undertaken, it was quite evident that the north flank of the advance needed to be cleared. Although the German bridgeheads at Memel and Courland were already in danger of being cut off, the Soviet high command could not take the chance.

On 13 January 1945, 3rd Belorussian Front began an attack towards Königsberg. The offensive did not go smoothly, since the Germans put up stiff resistance, leaving the attack in danger of stalling. Marshal Chernyakovsky redeployed his forces for another attempt, and broke through the German lines on 20 January, heading for Königsberg. Within a week, Russian forces had nearly surrounded the city. Their tanks almost made it into Königsberg, but the arrival of six German assault guns saved the position for the Germans, and the Soviet armour was driven back. Their chance to take the city in a swift attack gone, the Russians completed the encirclement of Königsberg on 29/30 January, and laid siege to the conurbation.

The German commander in Königsberg, General Otto Lasch, did his best to establish defensive lines, using the old nineteenth-century fortifications in the city as the basis of his positions. The outer line was based upon 12 massive forts built between 1874 and 1882, while the inner line relied upon a line of interior forts of similar vintage. Although well built, they were little match for the Soviet bombardment, and the city simply could not be held – relief was needed, and by the middle of February it was on its way. The siege was lifted on 19 February when the German 5th Panzer and 1st Infantry Divisions broke through Russian lines, joining with elements of XXVIII Corps attacking out of Samland. The result of this attack was the creation of a narrow corridor from the city to Pillau, which could be used for the evacuation of civilians. A lull in the fighting then followed, not least because Chernyakovsky was killed on the day that the siege was lifted, robbing the Russians of a commander for a short time. Chernyakovsky's replacement, General Vasilevsky, arrived with instructions to incorporate 1st Baltic Front into his new command. Installing himself in command and making the necessary arrangements to coordinate the forces now assigned to him took Vasilevsky a little time, but he was soon ready to resume the attack. General Lasch had used the lull in the fighting profitably, in an attempt to enhance the defences along city's line of fortifications but, as Lasch always knew, this was not going to be enough to hold the Soviets off. Lasch made clear to Hitler that he thought that an evacuation should begin, and was permitted to begin a limited evacuation of the city. Before this could be completed, the Soviets resumed their assault on 2 April. Eleventh Guards Army led the way, and by 6 April they had broken through the German lines. Two days later, they linked up with Forty-Third Army, cutting the last link between Königsberg and the rest of East Prussia. Lasch knew that the position was untenable, and surrendered on 10 April.

West Prussia

The final area of concern for the Russians lay in West Prussia, which also needed to be cleared to ensure that troops could not be employed in a flank attack on advancing Russian troops. Although 2nd Belorussian Front had made some progress in the area, the thaw had turned the ground into an impassable swamp, forcing Marshal Rokossovsky to call off the attack on 19 February 1945. The Soviets could not allow the Germans to remain in West Prussia, in a position to interfere with the advance on Berlin, so it was necessary for the offensive to resume. At the start of March 1945, 1st and 2nd Belorussian Fronts attacked again. The attack cut the railway to the east of Koeslin, denying communications to German Second Army, and then pushed onwards to Danzig and Gdynia, the main supply bases for Königsberg and Courland, a factor that made the defence of both areas even more difficult, and which contributed to the events in the Baltic States described above. The Soviets advanced inexorably, and by the middle of March, the Germans were reduced to holding small enclaves in West Prussia. By 18 March, Kolberg fell, followed 10 days later by Gdynia and then, on 30 March, Danzig.

At the end of March 1945, therefore, the Russians had placed themselves in position for the final push on Berlin, in the knowledge that although Berlin would be their prize, the Germans would face not only the might of the Red Army, but that of the Anglo-American forces now moving to the west of the German capital.

Below: T-34/85 tanks in woodland near Berlin wait to begin their advance. The T-34/85 was heavier and slower than earlier models of the tank, but its 85mm gun made it a match for almost all German armoured vehicles.

The End of the Reich

By early 1945, the Third Reich was in a desperate state. The Ardennes offensive had failed to achieve the goals set for it by Hitler, and the Allies had resumed their approach to Germany itself. On the Eastern Front, the Red Army was sweeping all before it, and the best that German forces appeared capable of doing was to delay the advances rather than halt them.

In Italy, the German position was slightly better, but within a matter of weeks, the Allies had renewed their offensive and it was clear that it would be only a matter of time before the German position there gave way. The situation in the Balkans had collapsed, and German troops had been forced out of Greece, Yugoslavia, Hungary and Romania. The war at sea was lost, and although the Luftwaffe was still able to fly in defence of the Reich, Allied bomber formations could attack anywhere in Germany at will, bombing round the clock and supported by large fighter escorts in the daylight hours that prevented a meaningful defence against air attack. Despite all of this, Hitler remained optimistic to the last. Only when the battle reached the last remaining part of the Third Reich, its capital Berlin, did the *Führer* finally accept that his dream of a great Nazi Germany that would last for 1000 years was over. Before this situation was reached, however, there was still a great deal of fighting to be done.

The War in the West

After the shock caused by the Ardennes offensive had begun to wear off, the Allies made plans for crossing the Rhine and entering Germany itself. The Rhine provided a natural defensive feature for the Germans, and was bolstered by the West Wall, which had to be overcome before the advance into Germany could begin. To compound these challenges the appalling weather of early 1945 meant that much of the low-lying ground near the river was underwater, making forward movement utterly impractical. This situation did at least provide the Allies with time to refine their plans.

Eisenhower's scheme for crossing the Rhine involved two phases. In the first phase, Operation Veritable, Montgomery's 21st Army Group would clear the approaches to the Rhine opposite Wesel. XXX Corps was to advance from its positions in Nijmegen to the

Opposite: US and Soviet troops celebrate the link-up made between the two armies at Torgau on 25 April 1945. Relations between the two sides were soon to deteriorate, and for the next 45 years, the former allies would face each other in a tense stand-off in Germany.

Above: American anti-aircraft guns watch over the bridge at Remagen, the first Rhine crossing taken by the Allies. The weapons are quadruple Browning 0.5-inch machine guns, mounted on the rear of an M3 halftrack.

Reichswald. This was to be followed by Operation Grenade, in which Lieutenant-General William H. Simpson's US Ninth Army would push through Mönchengladbach and link up with the rest of Montgomery's forces. They would then pause to consolidate prior to the next phase of the operation. Once this was completed, 21st Army Group would then prepare to cross the Rhine, with the aim of outflanking the Ruhr from the north. Once this was completed, the army group would drive onto the North German plain. The plain offered excellent terrain for armour, and if the preceding operations succeeded, Montgomery would then be in a position to move on towards Berlin.

In the American sector, to Montgomery's south, General Bradley's 12th Army Group would carry out Operation Lumberjack. This would begin with an advance to clear the

approaches to the Rhine between Cologne and Koblenz. Patton's Third Army would head for Mainz and Mannheim, where it would link up with the US forces advancing from the Saarland as part of 6th Army Group's Operation Undertone. When all these aspects of the plan were complete, bridgeheads over the Rhine would be established.

Eisenhower's intention was that these bridgeheads would divert German attention away from Montgomery's attacks, but this was not at all popular with Bradley and Patton. They argued that American forces should play a much larger role, and that they felt that Eisenhower's plan as it stood was not acceptable. It may have been the case that had Montgomery not so irritated the American commanders with such consistency since 1942, the complaints from Patton and Bradley would not have been so uncompromising,

*Opposite: Eisenhower's
plan for crossing the
Rhine involved two
phases of operations.
The first would see
Montgomery's 21st Army
Group clearing the
approaches to the Rhine
opposite Wesel, leaving
him in a position to move
on towards Berlin.
Bradley's 12th Army
Group would advance to
the south of Montgomery,
clearing the approaches
to the Rhine between
Cologne and Koblenz.
Patton's Third Army
would swing towards
Mainz and Mannheim,
linking up with the US
forces advancing from the
Saarland. Once this was
achieved, bridgeheads
across the Rhine would
be established.*

but as it was, Eisenhower could simply not ignore the strength of feeling. There would be no alteration to the first part of the plan, but Eisenhower decided that he would revisit his notions of allowing Montgomery to make the main Allied thrust once across the Rhine when the goals of the first phase had been achieved.

All of these plans were contingent on breaching the West Wall and traversing the difficult ground in front of the River Ruhr, which the Germans could flood if they wished by opening the dams. The possibility of movement being denied by flooding meant that the coordination of the four operations could not be guaranteed.

Operations Veritable and Grenade

In keeping with his reputation, Montgomery's plans for Veritable and Grenade were drawn up in a thorough and methodical fashion, with almost every detail seemingly covered in the process. This was entirely appropriate for the circumstances, since the obstacles to success were formidable. The defences opposite the British were well prepared, and manned by 12,000 men. The defenders enjoyed the benefit of being on high ground, while the attackers would be forced by the waterlogged conditions in much of the region to use a series of narrow roads through the Reichswald, densely forested and difficult to fight through if properly defended.

At 05:00 on 8 February, First Canadian Army made the opening moves in Operation Veritable. A two-and-a-half hour bombardment opened proceedings. When it stopped, the Germans returned fire, and the British guns resumed the barrage, this time against the enemy positions, raining down high explosives for another three hours. Once this massive opening bombardment was over, the infantry at last moved forward.

The sodden ground made their advance difficult, and the troops were forced to advance with little in the way of artillery or air support. The advance was far slower than expected, and it took until the last week of February until all objectives were obtained, instead of the three or four days originally planned for. The Germans had also taken the opportunity to destroy all the bridges over the Rhine, and open the gates to the Ruhr dam. This prevented the launch of Operation Grenade until the waters had subsided. The operation had to be postponed until 23 February, but when the advance started Ninth Army found that the opposition was relatively weak. A link with Anglo-Canadian forces was made at Geldorn on 3 March, leaving the approaches to the Rhine from Nijmegen and Düsseldorf clear of German forces. Montgomery could now turn his attention to crossing the Rhine, which he planned to do on 23 and 24 March.

As the Germans had destroyed the bridges over the Rhine, 21st Army Group faced the problem that it would have to negotiate the Rhine via an assault crossing, rather than using bridges.

THE BUFFALO LVT

One of the key tools for crossing the Rhine was the LVT (Landing Vehicle Tracked), essentially a tracked armoured box that could 'swim' to the shore and then drive out of the water and serve as an armoured personnel carrier and supply vehicle. The LVT was known as the Buffalo in British service, and these were used with great success to cross the Rhine. The Buffaloes had a crew of three, and could carry a section of seven men.

The vehicles were equipped with a variety of weapons, and many of the Buffaloes used for the Rhine crossing were fitted with 20mm cannon in addition to their more usual machine guns, with the aim of suppressing German positions on the opposite bank should the need arise.

The American Sector

While Montgomery's troops were encountering difficulties in their operations, Bradley's attack went far more smoothly. The Germans had been forced to redeploy a significant number of units to defend against Montgomery's attack, which made the opening stages of the American advance a simpler proposition than they might have been (although to interpret this as meaning that the American advance was ludicrously easy would be grossly inaccurate). Cologne fell into American hands during the course of 6 March, German resistance being destroyed by all-arms operations. Other elements of First Army headed for Bonn, while the 9th Armoured Division made the link with Patton's forces at Sinzig. Late on 6 March, the division reached Meckenheim. To protect the division as it moved down the Ahr river valley, Combat Command B was instructed to close the Rhine at Remagen. To the astonishment of the first Americans to reach Remagen, the bridge across the Rhine was still intact.

The Americans crossed the bridge and reached the east bank of the Rhine at 16:00 on 7 March. News of the crossing spread quickly, and Eisenhower ordered that the success should be exploited immediately, even though sending forces over the Rhine at Remagen would demand that the plan for operations be recast. In fact, Eisenhower did not switch the weight of the Allied attack away from Montgomery as a result of the capture of the bridge, since the terrain around Remagen meant that the opportunities for a breakthrough would be limited. Patton's Third Army completed its part in Operation Lumberjack by ensuring that the Rhine was

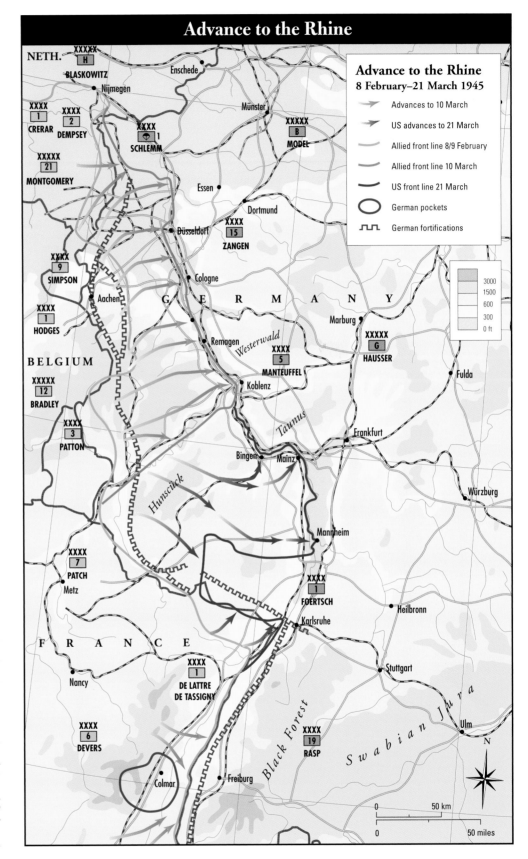

Advance to the Rhine

Advance to the Rhine
8 February–21 March 1945

- → Advances to 10 March
- → US advances to 21 March
- Allied front line 8/9 February
- Allied front line 10 March
- US front line 21 March
- ◯ German pockets
- ⊓⊔ German fortifications

3000
1500
600
300
0 ft

Above: An American soldier guards members of the Hitler Youth who surrendered near Martinzelli. While the Western Allies tended to treat the Hitler Youth as children fighting because they had no choice or were misguided rather than because they were ardent Nazis, the Soviets made no such distinctions, and treated Hitler Youth members as ruthlessly as adult soldiers.

secured as far as Koblenz, but Patton was not finished. The success of First Army at Remagen irritated Patton, and he ordered that his men should cross the river by boat on 22 March. The 11th Infantry Regiment completed the task, allowing Patton to issue a barbed press release proclaiming his success and attempting to belittle Montgomery by noting that the Americans had not required aerial bombardment, artillery, the use of smoke or airborne attacks but failing to mention that the reason for this was because the opposition at the crossing point – Nierstein – had been negligible.

The British Cross the Rhine

Montgomery ignored Patton's remarks, and continued to put the finishing touches to his plan to cross the Rhine, Operation Plunder. The assault was to take place on the night of 23/24 March, preceded by a massive preparatory bombardment, to which air attacks would be added. Montgomery's caution was justified, since the Germans were expecting the attack to be launched by 21st Army Group, and a set-piece attack was the only option open to Montgomery, rather than the opportunistic use of infantry in boats that Patton had been able to exploit.

A dense smokescreen was put across the river, and at 18:00 on 23 March, over 5000 guns bombarded the opposite bank of the Rhine and beyond. The assault troops moved down to the river bank and boarded the variety of landing craft and amphibious assault vehicles that would take them across, joined by the famed Sherman DD (Duplex Drive) swimming tanks that had gained their reputation 'swimming' ashore on D-Day.

The sheer weight of fire and preponderance of numbers Montgomery had so carefully built up in preparation for the crossing told. The British gained a foothold, and waited for a pre-arranged bomber attack on Wesel before they moved forward into the town. Over 200 bombers attacked at 22:30, and the raid completed the town's destruction. Then 1st Commando Brigade moved into Wesel and brought the town under control after a sharp fight. By dawn on 24 March, it was clear that the crossings had been a major success, with five bridgeheads being established.

The momentum of the attack was then maintained by Operation Varsity, a large airborne assault by US 17th and British 6th Airborne Divisions. The airborne troops were to consolidate the ground already taken, enabling the depth of the bridgehead to be increased swiftly. The operation was launched in daylight to take advantage of air supremacy, and unlike the drop at Arnhem, all the troops were to be landed in one lift. They were also scheduled to be landed almost on top of their objectives and within range of friendly artillery (again unlike Market Garden). The landings started at 10:00 on 24 March, but there were problems. Some of the paratroops were dropped in the wrong place, and gliders were released at the wrong time. This meant that the Germans were able to inflict casualties on the airborne troops and their aircraft, with over 100 gliders and aeroplanes being destroyed. Despite the casualties, the paratroops took their objectives, and the operation was a considerable success. The village of Hamminkeln was taken along with the three bridges over the River Issel. By the end of the day, 21st Army Group had secured its position on the other side of the Rhine, and the stage was now set for the break-out.

The Final Stages in the West

At this point, Eisenhower changed his strategy, partly in light of the concerns expressed by Bradley and Patton, but also because of the changed strategic situation which meant that Berlin was no longer the goal for the Western Allies. As Montgomery started planning his advance across the North German plain towards the capital, Eisenhower changed the focus of operations towards 12th Army Group, which would attack around the Elbe and Mulde rivers, with the aim of cutting the German Army in two before linking with the Red Army. Twenty-first Army Group would move towards the Baltic coast with the aim of reaching it before the Russians, clearing Holland, seizing the north German ports and cutting off Denmark as they went. To the south of 12th Army Group, the US Sixth Army was to drive into Austria and defeat German forces remaining there.

In accordance with the new plan, the British Second Army broke out of its bridgehead on 28 March, crossed the Weser River and, despite some spirited German resistance around Hanover, gained 200 miles in three weeks. By 18 April on 21st Army Group's front, I Corps had reached the Zuider Zee, XII Corps was well on the way to Hamburg, XXX Corps had reached Bremen and VIII Corps had taken Lüneburg and was closing in on the Elbe river. Meanwhile, 12th Army Group encircled the Ruhr, and began mopping up the German forces there. US Ninth and First Armies met at Lippstadt on 1 April, and by 12 April the Americans were in Essen, the Germans totally unable to counter the advance.

German troops were now surrendering in large numbers to the extent that the Allies were having serious difficulties in processing them all. Organized resistance in the West had collapsed totally in the American sector, and the British began to encounter the same phenomenon.

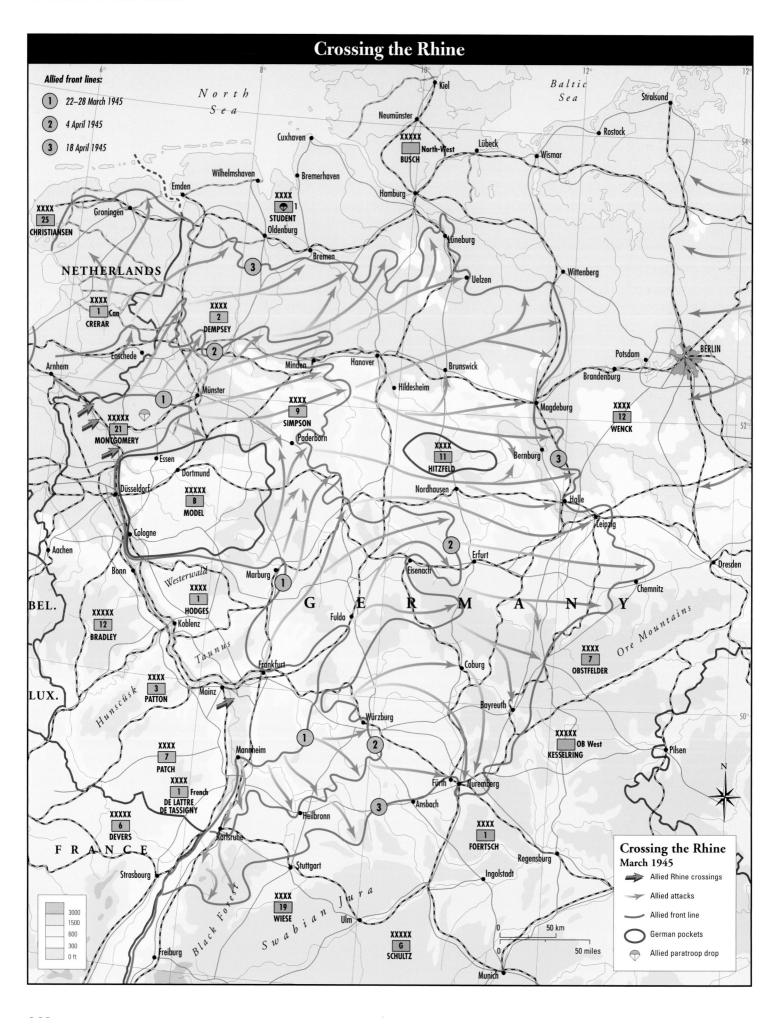

Crossing the Rhine

Allied front lines:

1 22–28 March 1945

2 4 April 1945

3 18 April 1945

North Sea

Baltic Sea

Kiel
Neumünster
Stralsund
Rostock
Cuxhaven
Wilhelmshaven
Bremerhaven
Lübeck
Wismar
XXXXX North-West BUSCH
Emden
Hamburg
STUDENT
Oldenburg
Lüneburg
XXXX 25 CHRISTIANSEN
Groningen
Bremen
Uelzen
Wittenberg
NETHERLANDS
Enschede
Minden
Hanover
Brunswick
Potsdam
BERLIN
XXXX 1 Can CRERAR
XXXX 2 DEMPSEY
Hildesheim
Brandenburg
Arnhem
Münster
XXXX 9 SIMPSON
Magdeburg
XXXX 12 WENCK
XXXXX 21 MONTGOMERY
Paderborn
Essen
XXXX 11 HITZFELD
Bernburg
Dortmund
Düsseldorf
XXXXX B MODEL
Nordhausen
Halle
Aachen
Cologne
Leipzig
Bonn
Westerwald
Marburg
Dresden
XXXX 1 HODGES
Chemnitz
Koblenz
Eisenach
Erfurt
BEL.
GERMANY
XXXXX 12 BRADLEY
Fulda
Taunus
Coburg
XXXX 7 OBSTFELDER
LUX.
Hunsück
Ore Mountains
XXXX 3 PATTON
Mainz
Frankfurt
Bayreuth
Würzburg
XXXXX OB West KESSELRING
Pilsen
XXXX 7 PATCH
Mannheim
Fürth
Nuremberg
XXXX 1 French DE LATTRE DE TASSIGNY
Ansbach
XXXXX 6 DEVERS
Heilbronn
XXXX 1 FOERTSCH
Karlsruhe
Regensburg
FRANCE
Stuttgart
Ingolstadt
Strasbourg
Black Forest
XXXX 19 WIESE
Swabian Jura
Ulm
Freiburg
XXXXX G SCHULTZ
Munich

Scale: 3000 / 1500 / 600 / 300 / 0 ft

N

Crossing the Rhine
March 1945

➤ Allied Rhine crossings

→ Allied attacks

— Allied front line

◯ German pockets

Allied paratroop drop

0   50 km
0   50 miles

Twenty-first Army Group moved into the Netherlands and on towards the Baltic coast, meeting little in the way of organized opposition as it went. By 18 April 1945, the army group was on the outskirts of Bremen, and closing in on Hamburg. To their south, the only serious opposition came from the Germans defending against US Seventh and French First Armies around Würzburg and Karlsruhe respectively; even this was not enough to seriously delay the advance. By 18 April, the Western Front did not have far to advance before the final defeat of Germany would be achieved. Attention now turned to the East, where the Russians had closed in on Berlin.

The Russian Advance to Berlin

By March 1945, it was quite clear that the advancing Red Army would shortly be turning Berlin into a battleground. Hitler issued orders for the defence of the capital, but these were characterized by a great deal of ideological rhetoric and exhortations to the German people, and lacking in the precise details of what exactly was required to defend the city. To make matters worse, Hitler's overwhelming confidence that everything would eventually turn in Germany's favour meant that efforts to turn Berlin into a fortress had not been fully implemented, since the pressure to do this had been lacking. One of the key features of the battle for Berlin was that the solid defensive positions that might have been expected were notable by their absence in many parts of the city.

Despite these problems, a plan for defending Berlin was completed by the second week of April, but the reality of the German situation was clear. No matter where the German high command looked, its units were short of ammunition. The artillery units were the most seriously affected by this situation. Movement was hampered by a shortage of fuel, which in turn meant that the mobility offered by German armour was lacking, since the tanks could not move. Supplies could not be transported because there were no vehicles to move them; and the *Luftwaffe* was all but gone, grounded by lack of gasoline for its remaining aircraft. Finally, while the Berlin garrison was a million strong, a figure that encouraged Hitler, many of the soldiers defending the city were boys beneath military age, or men who had been too old or unfit to serve with the Army before. Many lacked anything other than rudimentary training, with only those who had fought between 1914 and 1918 having experienced anything like a proper programme of instruction. All, though, were determined to defend against the Russians, the stories of the treatment meted out to German civilians by Soviet troops in areas already under their control being prominent in their thinking.

Hitler had moved to the fortified bunker underneath the Chancellery building, continuing to make over-optimistic plans to throw the Russians back. His spirits rose greatly on 12 April when news arrived that President Roosevelt had died. Ever one to see omens in events, Hitler took this as a positive sign, excitedly suggesting that this was the opportunity that he had been waiting for. He might negotiate a favourable armistice now that one of the leading proponents of unconditional surrender was dead. Over the next two days, Hitler began to think that success could still be achieved when news came that German troops had inflicted a serious reverse upon American bridgeheads over the River Elbe.

This was all illusory – neither the death of their president nor a tactical setback were going to dissuade the Americans from prosecuting the war to a finish. It was most improbable that Roosevelt would have appointed a vice-president who did not agree with the policy of forcing total surrender, while neither Stalin nor Churchill were likely

Opposite: Although the capture of the bridge at Remagen provided the first crossing point, the first concerted effort to move across the river began on 22 March, when troops from Patton's army crossed the river at Nierstein and Oppenheim. Operation Plunder, Montgomery's plan for the British crossing of the Rhine, began on 23 March, and was a notable success. By 25 March, 21st Army Group had gained a firm base on the east bank of the Rhine, consolidating the position three days later. With both British and Americans across the Rhine, attention turned to the final phases of the war.

Above: A Soviet 152mm howitzer crew prepare to engage targets near the Reichstag in late April 1945. The Soviets made considerable use of their artillery to blast the Germans out of their positions, firing over open sights at targets only a few hundred yards away; the effect of the shells was devastating.

to suddenly change their position either. More importantly, speculating on gaining a peace settlement in the West ignored the fact that the Soviet armies were very near to beginning their attack, which would hardly help negotiations even if the Western Allies intended to assist Hitler in realizing his flight of fancy. The Soviets had carried out a massive build-up since February, undertaking the largest and most complex redeployment of forces in history so that they were in the most favourable position to assault the enemy capital. Over 2.5 million men, 6000 tanks and armoured fighting vehicles and 45,000 guns and rocket launchers, along with supplies ranging from food to artillery shells, were moved into place by mid-April.

On 16 April, the attack on Berlin began. The Soviet plan was brutally simple – a number of attacks along a wide front would be launched, with the intention of encircling the German forces before destroying them. Zhukhov's 1st Belorussian Front would attack from its positions near Küstrin on the west bank of the Oder, and head direct for Berlin. Koniev would use his 1st Ukranian Front to cross the Neisse and would then attack the southwest of the enemy capital. Rokossovsky and 2nd Belorussian Front, meanwhile, would attack in the area around Stettin to ensure that Third Panzer Army could not be used to reinforce the beleaguered German defenders in Berlin. This plan irritated Koniev considerably. His rivalry with Zhukhov was intense, and he was extremely jealous that he would not have the opportunity to take Berlin, even if it seemed obvious that the task should fall to Stalin's nominated deputy commander. This apparently trivial case of ego was to be of some importance in the battle that followed, but was exploited to telling effect by Stalin as he urged his subordinates on towards the capture of the enemy capital.

At 03:00 on 16 April, Zhukhov's forces attacked, aiming to take the Seelow Heights. An enormous bombardment put down one million shells on the German positions, and was accompanied by a heavy bombing raid. In the Vistula–Oder operation, such massive firepower had subdued the enemy to the point of near passivity, but this was not the case now, since many of the Germans were fighting to protect their homes and families in the face of an enemy whose reputation for treating civilians in a proper fashion was not high. Zhukhov's forces did not break through that day, but Koniev enjoyed some success. After a second day of fighting in which Koniev made more gains, Stalin told Zhukhov that he

Map, page 372: Although Berlin was the main objective of the Soviet operation, consideration had to be given to defeating all of Germany, which meant linking with the Western Allies. The British and Americans drove towards the River Elbe, while the Russians carried out several manoeuvres to encircle Berlin and move beyond it to join their allies. Caught between the two sides, the German Army stood little chance. The first meeting of American and Russian troops occurred at Torgau on the Elbe, and it was not long before only small pockets of enemy resistance remained.

Left: A Soviet soldier equipped with a PPSh 43 sub-machine gun makes his way forward, demonstrating for the camera the way in which he would move in an urban area.

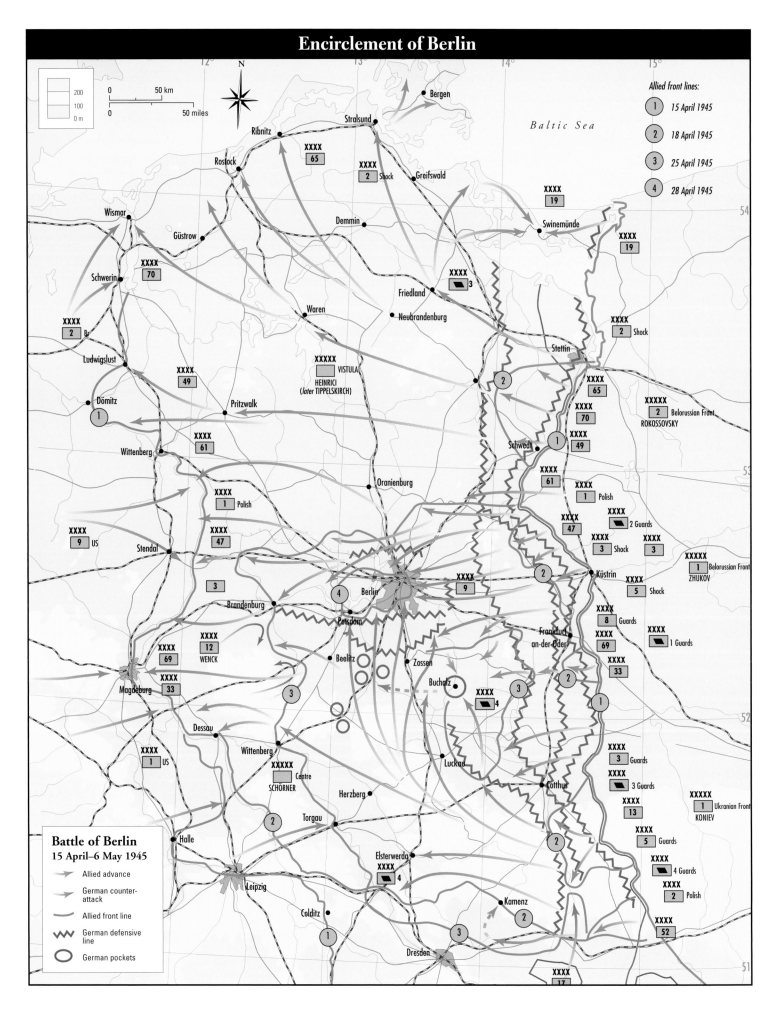

Encirclement of Berlin

Allied front lines:

1 *15 April 1945*
2 *18 April 1945*
3 *25 April 1945*
4 *28 April 1945*

Baltic Sea

Bergen

Stralsund

Ribnitz

Rostock

XXXX 65

Greifswald

XXXX 2 Shock

XXXX 19

Swinemünde

XXXX 19

Wismar

Güstrow

Demmin

Schwerin

XXXX 70

Waren

Friedland

XXXX 3

Neubrandenburg

Stettin

XXXX 2 B...

Ludwigslust

Dömitz 1

XXXX 49

XXXXX VISTULA HEINRICI (*later* TIPPELSKIRCH)

Pritzwalk

XXXX 2 Shock

XXXX 65

XXXXX 2 Belorussian Front ROKOSSOVSKY

XXXX 70

Schwedt 1

XXXX 49

Wittenberg

XXXX 61

XXXX 61

XXXX 1 Polish

Oranienburg

XXXX 1 Polish

XXXX 47

XXXX 2 Guards

XXXX 3 Shock

XXXX 3

XXXX 9 US

Stendal

XXXX 47

XXXX 2

Küstrin

XXXXX 1 Belorussian Front ZHUKOV

3

Berlin 4

XXXX 9

XXXX 5 Shock

Brandenburg

XXXX 8 Guards

Potsdam

Frankfurt an-der-Oder

XXXX 1 Guards

XXXX 12 WENCK

XXXX 69

Beelitz

Zossen

2

XXXX 69

XXXX 33

XXXX 33

Magdeburg

3

Buchalz

XXXX 4

3

2

Dessau

XXXX 1 US

Wittenberg

XXXXX Centre SCHÖRNER

Luckau

XXXX 3 Guards

XXXX 3 Guards

Herzberg

Cottbus

XXXXX 1 Ukranian Front KONIEV

XXXX 13

Torgau

2

XXXX 5 Guards

Halle

2

Elsterwerda

XXXX 4 Guards

XXXX 4

XXXX 2 Polish

Colditz

Kamenz

2

1

3

XXXX 52

Dresden

XXXX 17

Battle of Berlin
15 April–6 May 1945

→ Allied advance
→ German counter-attack
— Allied front line
〜 German defensive line
◯ German pockets

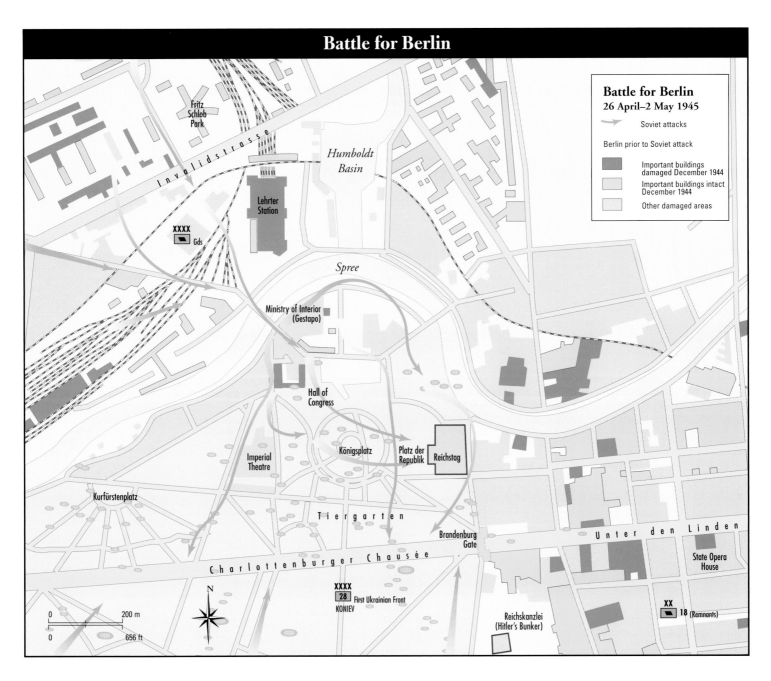

Battle for Berlin

Battle for Berlin
26 April–2 May 1945

→ Soviet attacks

Berlin prior to Soviet attack

Important buildings
damaged December 1944

Important buildings intact
December 1944

Other damaged areas

Fritz
Schlob
Park

Invalidstrasse

*Humboldt
Basin*

Lehrter
Station

XXXX
Gds

Spree

Ministry of Interior
(Gestapo)

Hall of
Congress

Imperial
Theatre

Königsplatz

Platz der
Republik   Reichstag

Kurfürstenplatz

Tiergarten

Brandenburg
Gate

Unter den Linden

Charlottenburger Chausée

State Opera
House

N

0   200 m

0   656 ft

XXXX
28   First Ukrainian Front
KONIEV

Reichskanzlei
(Hitler's Bunker)

XX
18 (Remnants)

might allow 1st Ukrainian Front to seize Berlin if he could not capture the Seelow Heights.

This threat energized Zhukhov, who could not bear the thought of being denied the final victory. He set about encouraging, cajoling and threatening his subordinates, making clear to some of them that failure would result in them being stripped of their rank and privileges and sent to join the first wave of the next Soviet assault. Although little progress was made on 18 April, the pressure on the German lines began to tell, and Zhukhov broke through the next day, without having to demote any of his generals.

On 21 April, Zhukhov's Third and Fifth Shock Armies entered the suburbs of Berlin, and then advanced towards the centre. Koniev's troops reached the Tetlow canal by the end of 22 April, and began to push towards Zhukhov's forces. On 24 April, 1st Ukrainian and 1st Belorussian Fronts met on the River Havel, encircling Berlin in the process. The Russians now began a methodical, street-by-street battle, using tanks and artillery to blast through German positions. The Germans were pushed ever further back, their defensive position contracting almost hourly.

Above: After holding Russian forces outside Berlin for some days, the weight of attack told against the Germans. Gaps started to appear in their lines on 18 April, and the next day, a breakthrough was made. The upper floors of the Reichstag were taken on 30 April, but fighting in the cellars continued until, on 2 May, the garrison surrendered.

Above: German prisoners are marched down an autobahn near Giesen, as American tanks roll past them on their way to the front. By late April 1945, German units were surrendering en masse to the British and Americans, aware that the war was all but over, and that there was little point in fighting on.

By 27 April the Germans were left in a small corridor about 10 miles long and no more than three miles wide. The defensive perimeter was fractured on 28 April, and the last pockets of resistance were reduced to fighting isolated skirmishes with the Russians, still fighting with a determination that belied the hopelessness of their position. Two days later, Hitler committed suicide. The Reichstag itself was taken the same day, although some Germans remained in the cellars, continuing to fight. Finally, on 2 May the Berlin garrison surrendered, although mopping-up operations continued for a few more days. The final acts could now take place.

While the Russians had fought their way into Berlin, fighting around the city continued. On the Western Front, the final phase of the Allied advance continued to be met by a rapid collapse of German resistance. In 21st Army Group's area, Bremen was taken on 27 April, while Lübeck and Hamburg fell on 2 May. On 19 April, 12th Army Group captured Halle and Leipzig, and Dessau three days later. Finally, on 24 April, US First Army reached its stop line on the River Mulde. The Soviet forces not engaged in Berlin had driven on towards their advancing allies in the West, and on 25 April, made the first link-up on the Elbe.

US Third Army crossed the Danube on the same day, and moved on to take Regensburg. Patton then headed into Austria, taking Linz on 5 May. To his right, US

Seventh Army had taken Nuremberg on 20 April after a five-day battle, and then crossed the Danube along with French First Army. This finally destroyed resistance from Army Group G, and left the way open for the French to move towards the Swiss border. Hitler's suicide was now known about, and it was obvious that the end was near. By 4 May, almost all German resistance had ceased. At Montgomery's headquarters on Lüneburg Heath, the Germans surrendered all their forces in Holland, Denmark and North Germany; the next day, emissaries arrived at Eisenhower's headquarters and after some attempts to delay the process, signed on 7 May at 02:40. Eisenhower signalled London and Washington just a moment later:

'The mission of this Allied Force was fulfilled at 02:41 local time, May 7, 1945. Eisenhower.'

This was not quite true. Eisenhower and some of his deputies still had one more task to fulfil. At a ceremony in the Soviet sector of Berlin, representatives of the victorious Allies sat and signed the final act of surrender early in the morning of 8 May.

The war in Europe was over. Hitler's Reich, meant to last 1000 years, but managing just over 12, had finally fallen.

Left: Field Marshal Montgomery looks on as the German forces in Holland, Denmark and North Germany are surrendered to him at Lüneburg Heath on 4 May 1945. This was the first of three major surrender ceremonies – on 7 May, the Germans surrendered to Eisenhower, and the next day the final surrender to all three major Allies was signed.

Symbol Guide

Army Group		Army Division		Regiment	
Army		Airborne		Company	
Corps		Armoured Division		Platoon	

Artillery		Antitank		Mechanized Infantry	
Engineer		Communication		Naval	

Bibliography

Atkinson, Rick. *An Army at Dawn: The War in North Africa 1942–43*. London: Little, Brown, 2003.

Beevor, Anthony. *Stalingrad*. London: Viking, 1998.

Bessonov, Evgeni. *Tank Rider: into the Reich with the Red Army*. London: Greenhill Books, 2003.

Bishop, Chris. *Encyclopedia of Weapons of WWII*. New York: Metro Books, 1998.

_____. *SS Hell on the Western Front*. St. Paul, Minn: Motorbooks International, 2003.

Black, Jeremy. *World War Two: a Military History*. London: Routledge, 2003.

Blumenson, Martin. *Patton: the Man Behind the Legend*. London: Cape, 1986.

Churchill, Winston. *The Second World War*. London: Cassell, 1949.

Command Magazine. *Hitler's Army: The Evolution and Structure of German Forces, 1933–1945*. Cambridge, Massachussetts: DaCapo Press, 2000.

Deighton, Len. *Blitzkrieg*. London: Jonathan Cape, 1979.

Drury, Ian and Bishop, Chris. *Great Battles of the 20th Century*. London: Hamlyn, 1988.

Dunphie, Christopher. *The Pendulum of Battle: Operation Goodwood, July 1944*. Barnsley: Leo Cooper, 2004.

Eisenhower, Dwight D. *Crusade in Europe*. London: Heinemann, 1948.

Erickson, John. *The Road to Stalingrad*. London: Weidenfeldt & Nicholson, 1975.

_____. *The Road to Berlin.* London: Weidenfeld & Nicholson, 1983.

Erickson, John. *The Road to Stalingrad.* London: Weidenfeld & Nicholson, 1983.

Forty, George. *The Desert War.* Stroud: Sutton, 2002.

Graham, Dominick and Shelford Bidwell. *Tug of War: The Battle for Italy, 1943–1945.* New York: St Martins Press, 1986.

Guderian, Heinz. *Panzer Leader.* London: Arrow, 1990.

_____. *Achtung Panzer.* London: Arms and Armour Press, 1992.

Hough, Richard. *The Longest Battle: The War at Sea 1939–45.* London: Cassell, 2001.

Jordan, David. *Battle of the Bulge: the first 24 Hours.* London: Greenhill, 2003.

Jordan, David. *Wolfpack: the U-boat War and the Allied Counter-attack 1939–1945.* Staplehurst: Spellmount, 2002.

Keegan, John. *Six Armies in Normandy: From D-Day to the Liberation of Paris.* London: Penguin, 1983.

Liddell Hart, Basil. *The Second World War.* London: Cassell, 1970.

MacDonald, Charles. *The Battle of the Bulge.* London: Phoenix, 1998.

Macintyre, Donald. *The Battle of the Atlantic.* London: Pan Books, 1969.

Marix Evans, Martin. *The Fall of France.* Oxford: Osprey, 2000.

Mitcham, Samuel W. *Hitler's Field Marshals.* London: William Heinemann, 1988.

Montgomery of Alamein, Viscount. *Memoirs.* London: Companion Book Club, 1960.

Padfield, Peter. *War Beneath the Sea.* Hoboken, New Jersey: Wiley, 1998.

Parker, Matthew. *Monte Cassino.* London: Headline, 2003.

Pitt, Barrie. *The Crucible of War.* London: Cassell Military, 2001.

_____. *The Military History of World War II.* London: Temple Press/Aerospace, 1987.

Rommel, Erwin (ed. Liddell-Hart, Basil). *The Rommel Papers.* London: Collins, 1953.

Seaton, Albert. *The German Army 1933–1945.* New York: New American Library, 1982.

Shirer, William L. *The Rise and Fall of the Third Reich.* New York: Simon and Schuster, 1960.

Showell, Jak P. Mallman. *U-Boat Commanders and Crews 1935–1945.* Malmsbury: The Crowood Press, 1998.

Stilwell, Alexander (ed). *The Second World War: a World in Flames.* Oxford: Osprey, 2004.

Sweetman, John. *The Dambusters Raid.* London: Arms & Armour Press, 1990.

Trevor-Roper, Hugh (Ed). *Hitler's War Directives.* London: Sidgwick and Jackson, 1964.

Von Mellenthin, F.W. *Panzer Battles 1939–1945.* London: Cassell, 1955.

Webster, Sir Charles & Frankland Noble. *The Strategic Air Offensive Against Germany 1939–1945. Volume I: Preparation, parts 1, 2 and 3.* London: HMSO, 1961.

Weeks, Albert L. *Stalin's Other War: Soviet Grand Strategy, 1939–1941.* Lanham, MD: Rowman & Littlefield, 2002.

Index

INDEX

Picture Credits

All photographs courtesy of TRH Pictures, except:

Popperfoto: 24, 29, 36, 62, 88, 260

Ukrainian State Archive: 156–157, 164, 169, 172, 181, 245, 252, 342, 346, 351, 355, 359, 370, 371

Will Fowler: 161

U.S. National Archives: 197, 322, 333, 335